Toward Positive Youth Development

Toward Positive Youth Development: Transforming Schools and Community Programs

Editors

Marybeth Shinn
Hirokazu Yoshikawa

UNIVERSITY PRESS

2008

Oxford University Press, Inc., publishes works that further
Oxford University's objective of excellence
in research, scholarship, and education.

Oxford New York
Auckland Cape Town Dar es Salaam Hong Kong Karachi
Kuala Lumpur Madrid Melbourne Mexico City Nairobi
New Delhi Shanghai Taipei Toronto

With offices in
Argentina Austria Brazil Chile Czech Republic France Greece
Guatemala Hungary Italy Japan Poland Portugal Singapore
South Korea Switzerland Thailand Turkey Ukraine Vietnam

Published by Oxford University Press, Inc.
198 Madison Avenue, New York, New York 10016

www.oup.com

Library of Congress Cataloging-in-Publication Data

Toward positive youth development: transforming schools and
community programs / Marybeth Shinn and Hirokazu Yoshikawa, (editors).
p. cm.
Includes bibliographical references and index.
ISBN: 978-0-19-532789-2
1. Classroom environment—United States.   2. School environment—United States.
3. Youth development—United States.   4. Educational sociology—United States.
I. Shinn, Marybeth.   II. Yoshikawa, Hirokazu.
LC210.5.P69 2008
371.102′4—dc22
2007031282

9 8 7 6 5 4 3 2 1

Printed in the United States of America
on acid-free paper

For Adam, Aaron, Clare, Elea, Eliot, Ethan, Evan, Helen, Henry, Jesse, Jessica, Joe, Jonah, Grace, Kaja, Karin, Lorelei, Margalit, Melissa, Mikito, Monica, Nathan, Samuel, Tavi, Thomas, Tyler and all their contemporaries. May the settings they enter help them to thrive.

Acknowledgments

The volume grew out of an interdisciplinary conference sponsored by the W.T. Grant Foundation in association with its research priority for understanding and improving social settings, and cochaired by the two editors. The Foundation has taken on the goal of building capacity in the social sciences to conduct interventions at the level of social settings because of their potential for large preventive and promotive impacts. This volume is a result of one of their earliest capacity-building endeavors in this arena. We thank Robert Granger, Edward Seidman, and Vivian Tseng of the Foundation for their guidance and support throughout this process; Nicole Yohalem of the Forum for Youth Investment and Laura Zamborsky of New York University for helping to make the conference so successful; Stuart Freeman for artistic expertise and all other kinds of support; and the editors and reviewers of Oxford University Press for their very helpful comments.

Contents

Toward Positive Youth Development

Chapter 1
Introduction

MARYBETH SHINN AND HIROKAZU YOSHIKAWA

After decades of intervention and research to promote positive youth development, we know a lot about how to change youth behavior. However, we still know too little about how to change the settings of youths' daily lives in ways that matter for their development. Recently, policy makers, practitioners, and researchers have made major strides in identifying features of schools and community programs for youth that are associated with positive developmental outcomes. A National Research Council report (Eccles & Gootman, 2002) stated that community programs should provide safety, supportive relationships, appropriate structure, opportunities for belonging and skill building, positive social norms, and support for efficacy and mattering. However, the report said little about how to attain these goals. A second report (National Research Council, 2003) offered a bit more guidance for changing schools to foster student engagement and motivation to learn. One suggestion was restructuring large schools to create smaller learning communities that could foster more socially supportive relationships between teachers and students. However, this report suggests that such structural changes must be accompanied by others that seem harder to prescribe: for example, teachers and principals must promote an environment of trust and respect. The most prominent policy effort to change educational settings today, the No Child Left Behind Act (2002), requires schools to make adequate yearly progress in percentages of students achieving proficiency on tests, overall and in defined subgroups, but offers little guidance for how schools should attain these goals. A multitude of reports suggest how schools and youth programs in the United States should be improved, but few provide a clear theory of change to guide schools and other programs serving youth to reach their goals. The reports describe what is needed, but not how to get there.

There is also a large practice literature about how to improve schools and a smaller one on youth programs. Some of these efforts have been studied and linked to youth outcomes. Although hundreds of studies have shown how to assess characteristics of youth development, very few focus on assessing youth-serving settings. When we lack the ability to assess the aspects of settings that matter for youth, youth-serving organizations lack effective ways to set clear goals for improvement, to monitor and encourage quality, or to provide a data-driven basis for staff development.

Goals of the Book

This book focuses on how to improve social settings to promote positive youth development. It shifts the debate away from simply improving youth outcomes at the individual level to transforming the settings where youth live, learn, work, and play, as a route to individual change. We consider settings such as classrooms, schools, universities, out-of-school-time programs, community-based programs focused on health or youth empowerment, programs for supplementary education for immigrant youth, and youth organizing efforts. We also examine how broader contexts such as school districts, community coalitions, and networks of youth-serving organizations can guide and support, or hinder, change.

Instead of discussing how features of the immediate environment bring about better outcomes for youth, as the majority of youth development research does, we examine how to change or create settings to bring about these positive environmental features. And instead of discussing ways to measure characteristics of youth, the chapters describe ways of assessing social settings, and of using these assessments to promote change. We also focus on youth who are marginalized for reasons of race, ethnicity, immigration status, or sexual orientation, but again consider the role of settings—how can schools and youth organizations increase representation of these youth? How can they improve the quality of their experiences in these settings? We expect the varied approaches and examples in this book to stimulate researchers and practitioners to focus on changing settings as a means for changing youth, from elementary school through college.

Although the chapters differ somewhat in their emphases, all authors describe a theory for how to change settings to influence youth outcomes, with one or more exemplars of change efforts (Weiss, 1995). These theories describe the process of setting transformation and include definitions of setting features targeted for change and ways to measure these features. As we describe in more detail later in this introduction, we deem measurement of setting features to be critical to motivate, guide, and monitor change. Changing settings is complex, and unlikely to be accomplished by scholars from any one discipline. The authors of this book come from multiple disciplinary backgrounds—psychology, education, human development, sociology, anthropology, economics, law, public policy—and offer different sorts of evidence for the success of change efforts.

Organization of the Book

This book is divided into five sections. We begin with interventions focused on changing classrooms. Pianta and Allen (chapter 2) present a coaching program—MyTeachingPartner—to help teachers offer youths more instructional and emotional support and improve classroom management by changing their own behavior in ways that have been shown to promote youth development. Henry (chapter 3) discusses how to change classroom norms concerning aggression, by feeding back data on actual beliefs about aggression, which are typically less favorable than students imagine. Jones, Brown, and Aber (chapter 4) describe the Reading, Writing, Respect, and Resolution (4Rs) Program targeted at classroom instructional and climate features related to socioemotional development and conflict resolution.

The next five chapters focus on changing schools. The first four of them also suggest how to make schools and youth programs work for diverse youth, particularly those who often face social exclusion. Weinstein (chapter 5) describes a participatory process involving researchers, teachers, and administrators that serves to create a school or change existing ones so that they convey high expectations for all students. Pollock (chapter 6) discusses how educators often avoid talking about race or talk imprecisely, for example, lumping diverse groups together or ignoring their own contributions to racial disparities, and urges more precise "race talk" among educators. Maton, Hrabowski, Özdemir, and Wimms (chapter 7) describe a transformative institutional change process that created the Meyerhoff program to promote representation, retention, and achievement of minority students in the sciences at the University of Maryland, Baltimore County. Russell and McGuire (chapter 8) focus on creating school climates that are safe and welcoming for lesbian, gay, bisexual, and transgender (LGBT) students. Desimone (chapter 9) uses Porter's policy attributes theory (Porter, Floden, Freeman, Schmidt, & Schwille, 1988) to discuss factors affecting successful implementation of an entire class of change efforts, namely whole-school change or comprehensive school reform.

In the third section, our volume shifts away from schools to community organizations. Miller, Kobes, and Forney (chapter 10) describe multiple strategies of capacity building for community-based organizations, including small organizations that may lack staff, resources, and even clearly defined organizational structures. Smith and Akiva (chapter 11) use feedback of data about program quality to improve out-of-school-time programs, such as Boys and Girls Clubs, or after school programs. Speer (chapter 12) discusses how youth organizing following the People Improving Communities through Organizing (PICO) model empowers youths to change their schools and communities. Zhou (chapter 13) describes how Chinese schools forming an ethnic system of supplementary education have helped Chinese immigrant children to succeed in the American educational system and in society. The theme of making settings work for youth who are often subject to social exclusion continues in this section. Both community-based organizations discussed by Miller et al. (chapter 10) and community organizing efforts described by Speer (chapter 12) often serve low-income and disenfranchised communities, although they need not do so, and Zhou (chapter 13) describes settings created by an ethnic immigrant group to help their children achieve success.

The fourth set of chapters describes change in the larger structures within which schools and community organizations are embedded, such as school districts, communities, service systems, and jurisdictions. Kahlenberg (chapter 14) cites evidence for the importance of socioeconomic integration of schools for children's achievement and describes how districts have used a system of controlled choice to integrate schools, by making every school a magnet school. Socioeconomic integration, which makes schools work better for poor children without harming their middle-class peers, also contributes to racial integration. Datnow (chapter 15) describes the interplay among federal, state, district, and school-level policies and personnel in "co-constructing" school reform, using the example of Data-Driven Decision Making. Fagan, Hawkins, and Catalano (chapter 16) illustrate the Communities That Care program, in which community coalitions collect data on risk and protective factors experienced by students in the community, set priorities for change, and select evidence-based prevention programs to reduce risk or increase protective factors. McLaughlin and O'Brien-Strain (chapter 17) present the Youth Data Archive, which integrates data about both youth-serving systems in a particular community and youth themselves to inform evaluation, planning, and service delivery.

Of course, the interventions do not fit neatly into categories of classrooms, schools, community organizations, or larger structures. The interventions selected by community coalitions (Fagan et al., chapter 16) and youth organizers (Speer, chapter 12) often alter or take place in schools and community organizations. Desimone (chapter 9) and Russell and McGuire (chapter 8), respectively, show how whole-school interventions and school climates are influenced by policies at district or state levels. Jones et al. (chapter 4) train teachers and offer a curriculum to students to change classrooms, but also train other school personnel, creating change at the level of schools. Some of the interventions described for one sort of setting, such as Henry's intervention to change classroom norms regarding aggression (chapter 3), might work just as well in another, for example, an out-of-school-time program.

In addition, interventions that improve the overall pattern of interactions among youth and adults in schools and other settings may increase opportunities for youth who are socially excluded, even if they do not work explicitly toward this goal. For example, the 4Rs program, which helps students resolve conflicts, could reduce bullying and harassment of members of minority groups.

The final section of the book has two cross-cutting chapters. Martinez and Raudenbush (chapter 18) show that evaluations of setting-level change strategies depend centrally on the reliability of the setting-level measures that the other authors employ. Using the example of the Classroom Assessment Scoring System (CLASS) instrument (described by Pianta and Allen in chapter 2, and used by several other authors as well), it examines the sources of unreliability, and offers a strategy for determining how to maximize reliability wherever similar observational measures are employed. And Yoshikawa and Shinn (chapter 19) draw from the other chapters to discuss intervention themes at the level of particular organizations and at the broader levels of context and policies. We suggest that key intervention goals and strategies to change settings include fostering participatory approaches, enhancing capacity for use of setting-level data to shape programs, and increasing both the representation and the quality of developmental experience of youth from all backgrounds.

In the remainder of this introduction, we address two more themes that are central to this book: features of settings that provide potential targets and levers for social change, and the use of measurement to motivate and guide change efforts.

A Theory of Settings as a Guide to Change

Tseng and Seidman (2007) conceptualize social settings as dynamic systems characterized by three features: social processes or patterns of transaction between people or groups of people; human, economic, physical, and temporal resources; and the organization of resources (e.g., how students are grouped in classrooms). The change processes described in this book target one or more of these features of settings.

At the classroom level, interventions tend to target social processes directly. Both MyTeachingPartner (chapter 2) and the 4Rs (chapter 4) change teachers' interactions with students, whereas the 4Rs and Henry's intervention to change classroom norms regarding aggression (chapter 3) change patterns of interactions among students. Particular resources, such as the 4Rs curriculum, or MyTeachingPartner's video library of exemplary interactions may facilitate changes in social processes.

At the level of entire schools, interventions may influence social processes directly or indirectly, via changes in resources and their organization.

Pollock's effort to promote more precise talk about race (chapter 6) targets social processes of exclusion directly. Weinstein (chapter 5) works directly with school staff to alter their expectations of students, but also seeks to change the distribution of resources in a school, for example, by allowing self-selection into honors classes for students who want to do additional, more difficult work rather than barring admission to students deemed low achievers. Maton et al. (chapter 7) suggest considerable synergy among social processes and resources in the Meyerhoff program. For example, structured resources such as research experiences and study groups change patterns of interaction among faculty, graduate students, and undergraduates, as well as among undergraduates themselves. Greater representation of minority students in the sciences (a change in distribution of resources) also creates more supportive patterns of interaction. Russell and McGuire (chapter 8) suggest that resources such as gay-straight alliances in schools and antiharassment policies change social processes: they reduce harassment both directly and via changes in teachers' responses to harassment incidents. The whole-school reforms described by Desimone (chapter 9) typically involve resources, such as new curricula, and professional development, but are critically dependent on social processes as well to create teacher buy-in and commitment.

Collectively, the community interventions in the third section of the book influence all three features of settings, but different change efforts have different emphases. Miller et al. (chapter 10) describe multiple interventions to build capacity in community-based organizations. Some, like coaching, training, and technical assistance, increase resources of knowledge and skills. Others, like participatory team building and creating a learning community, focus more on social interactions. And still others, like organizational restructuring and resource reallocation, focus on the organization of resources. Smith and Akiva (chapter 11) attempt to change both interpersonal processes and access to resources such as opportunities for youth to participate in small groups or make choices based on interests. PICO organizing (Speer, chapter 12) begins with a focus on interpersonal processes, namely building relationships among youth in a community, and then moves to actions to resolve identified problems. These actions often serve to garner resources for youth in the community. PICO also attempts to allocate a specific resource—cultivation of leadership skills—broadly among many youth. The supplementary system of ethnic education described by Zhou (chapter 13) was organized not by outside change agents but by community members who felt existing educational resources for children in the community were inadequate, and so created new ones.

At the broader levels of districts and communities, interventions tend to emphasize resources and their allocation, but social processes are often important to the successful use of these resources. Kahlenberg (chapter 14) writes about mechanisms for changing the organization of resources, by providing all students the opportunity to attend a predominantly middle-class school. Datnow (chapter 15) focuses both on resources, including data management systems and time that allow schools to do Data-Driven Decision Making, and on social processes, by which people in schools and at higher policy levels co-construct school reform. The Communities That Care program (Fagan et al., chapter 16) provides communities with specific resources—an epidemiological survey of students' risk and protective factors, a facilitator, a menu of proven prevention programs, and a budget for purchasing them, but also creates new social processes within the community coalitions that decide how to use these resources. Finally, the Youth Data Archive (McLaughlin & O'Brien-Strain, chapter 17) provides archived data from many organizations and data analyses as resources to facilitate planning and evaluation by participating youth-serving agencies. The Archive also changes social processes as agency staff interact with researchers to ask new and more sophisticated questions of the data.

Setting-Level Measurement

As several of these examples suggest, data about settings form a key resource used by many of the change efforts. The ability to measure features of social settings is important in establishing goals to motivate change, and in guiding and monitoring change. We briefly discuss these two functions of setting-level measurement, and then turn in more detail to some of the challenges of measuring not individual characteristics, but the social settings that shape them.

Measurable Goals to Motivate Change

Policy makers understood the value of measurable goals in the No Child Left Behind Act. They mandated that schools make "adequate yearly progress" in percentage of students achieving proficiency in core subjects, overall and in subgroups defined by race and ethnicity, economic disadvantage, disability, and English proficiency. They assumed that simply setting goals would create momentum for change. There is much truth to this idea. Pianta and Allen (chapter 2) suggest that a measurable target "can focus and organize the activity of the system that is the focus of change." Some years ago, Davis and Salasin (1975) drew an analogy between phototropism, in which plants orient themselves and grow toward sources of light, and "target tropism," in which people orient themselves and strive toward goals. Even earlier, Lewin (1951) described change as a three-step process of unfreezing the status quo, creating change, and then refreezing the new state in order to sustain the improvements. In many of the change models in this book, data that suggest that the current situation is discrepant from ideals, or that problems are widely shared, can be useful in the unfreezing process. The image of refreezing may be less apt. In many of the change efforts in this volume, the goal is an ongoing cycle of assessment and action, leading to continuous improvement and adaptive responses to shifting challenges, rather than a static, frozen end state.

Wilson-Ahlstrom, Yohalem, and Pittman (2007) suggest that efforts to change settings vary in how prescriptive they are. Some of the efforts described in this book begin with clear a priori goals and a system to measure them. For example, Pianta and Allen (chapter 2) seek to help teachers increase particular social and instructional interactions that have been shown to predict growth in student performance. With the help of a consultant, teachers learn to score their own interactions with children, recorded on videotape, according to how well they embody the desired interactions using the well-validated CLASS assessment tool. They can also view video clips of interactions deemed exemplary according to the CLASS system from a video library. With coaching from the consultant, teachers strive to change their interactions to be more like the prototypes. Smith and Akiva (chapter 11) have similarly identified and validated dimensions of quality in out-of-school-time programs for youth, codified in the Youth Program Quality Assessment (YPQA). Outside observers or staff themselves can score their program on this instrument, and target change efforts to areas where their program falls short of ideals. Focusing on resources, rather than social processes, Kahlenberg (chapter 14) assesses socioeconomic integration according to the proportion of students in a school who are eligible for free or reduced-price lunches. The a priori goal is for every school in a system to have a majority of middle-class children and a minority of poor children, defined in this way.

In other cases, setting measurable goals is an aspect of the change process. For example, in the Communities That Care program (Fagan et al., chapter 16), researchers use a standardized survey administered in schools to determine the percentage of youths who report specific risk and protective factors. However, it is up to the community coalitions to decide whether or not the measured levels of risks such as substance abuse, thrill seeking, or access to weapons are a problem for their community, and to set priorities and specific percentage goals for change on selected dimensions to be assessed with a subsequent survey. In a more qualitative vein, Weinstein (chapter 5) starts with the a priori goal of helping teachers and administrators to set high expectations for all students, but school personnel work collaboratively with researchers to identify current practices that reflect low expectations in their school and ways to alter them. An example of a measurable goal is the elimination of high school classes that do not offer college preparatory credit. Similarly, in the PICO approach to youth organizing as described by Speer (chapter 12), goals emerge from the concerns of youth who take part in the organizing process.

Simply engaging in measurement can often provoke change, as in the self-reflection Pollock (chapter 6) stimulates about "race talk." At other times it is the feedback of information that motivates change. For example, Henry (chapter 3) suggests that because most children overestimate the extent to which classmates favor aggressive behavior, simply reporting on the true normative level of approval for aggressive behavior in a classroom may stimulate change. In other cases measurement is a more neutral basis for goal setting, as in data schools use in Data-Driven Decision Making (Datnow, chapter 15), the Communities That Care intervention (Fagan et al., chapter 16), and the Youth Data Archive (McLaughlin and O'Brien-Strain, chapter 17). Participants must interpret the data to decide on their priorities.

Goals may change over time. For example, Zhou (chapter 13) explains that the Chinese system of supplementary education initially served to teach immigrant children the Chinese language so that they could return to China or gain employment in Chinatowns. Later the goals evolved to giving children tools for success in the American educational system, as well as socializing them in Chinese culture.

Of course, an intervention designed for one purpose may have positive or negative spillover effects in other areas. For example, Allen, Kuperminc, Philliber, and Herre (1994) found that a program to get youth involved in meaningful volunteer work, where they had both positive relationships with adults and autonomy in carrying out activities, increased academic success and lowered teen pregnancy without targeting these outcomes. But diffuse interventions, designed to improve "quality" or make schools "better" without sufficiently specific goals, are unlikely to accomplish much of anything at all.

Measurement to Guide and Monitor Change

Just as good intentions are not enough to motivate change, discomfort with the status quo is not enough to guide it. Data can be used not only to set goals but also to monitor change efforts. Under No Child Left Behind, annual achievement tests are used to monitor whether schools are making adequate yearly progress. Several of the interventions in this book such as MyTeachingPartner (Pianta and Allen, chapter 2), the Youth Program Quality Intervention (Smith and Akiva, chapter 11), and Communities That Care (Fagan et al., chapter 16) use repeated cycles of assessment over time intervals as short as 2 weeks and as long as 2 years to monitor progress, and guide new change efforts. In Data-Driven Decision Making (Datnow, chapter 15) frequent assessments are used not just for a high-stakes evaluation of schools, but to set meaningful and challenging goals for students, plan classroom instruction, and identify teachers and students who need additional supports or alternative instructional strategies. In some schools assessments are shared with students, who monitor their own progress and that of their class. Weinstein (chapter 5) describes a more qualitative cycle of "inquiry, action, and evaluation" and PICO organizers (Speer, chapter 12) similarly build in cycles of action and evaluation.

Measurement can also monitor progress in less cyclical ways. Maton et al. (chapter 7) describe a diversity score card that colleges can use to monitor progress toward more inclusive processes. For example, African American students in the Meyerhoff program attain GPAs comparable with those of Caucasian and Asian students, and nearly 50% of entering students go on to Ph.D.s in the sciences. In the Communities That Care program (Fagan et al., chapter 16), coalition members monitor the fidelity with which chosen prevention programs are implemented to maximize the likelihood that they will have the desired effects. Similarly, Jones et al. (chapter 4) assess the number of lessons in the 4Rs curriculum that teachers actually teach to monitor fidelity to their intervention. Speer (chapter 12) uses measures of social networks to understand whether PICO organizing has had the desired effects of promoting linkages among youth in the community. Given the small size and limited resources of the community-based programs that Miller et al. (chapter 10) target for capacity building, the authors suggest that qualitative and ethnographic methods may be most appropriate for monitoring the success of change.

Issues in Measuring Settings

Psychologists and educators have a long history of measuring individuals; however, the science of measuring settings is still in its infancy. We hope this volume will help educators and policy makers select valid, reliable measures that accurately capture important features of settings. The controversy over measurement related to the No Child Left Behind Act illustrates some of the challenges. First, the meaning of both "adequate yearly progress" and "highly qualified teachers" required by the Act is determined by state standards. Some argue that states have an incentive to set low standards, so as to appear to be making progress. Indeed, reported progress by many states is at odds with reports of declines in reading achievement and low levels of mathematics proficiency in the National Assessment of Educational Progress (Grigg, Donahue, & Dion, 2007). Second, many educators criticize standardized tests as failing to capture all the skills that they strive to teach, and bemoan distortions in the curriculum when teachers teach to the tests. In measuring outcomes to guide change, it is crucial that researchers and practitioners measure what they really want to change, and not an imperfect proxy, which can displace the real goal. Both these concerns relate to the validity of the tests for their intended purposes of assessing students and schools. Other critics worry more about whether a single "high-stakes" test is sufficiently reliable to assess student progress.

Another question is even more salient from the perspective of this book. When is it appropriate to consider an aggregation of information about *individuals* (such as aggregate individual achievement scores) as a measure of the quality of a *setting*, such as a school? Shinn (1990) and Shinn and Rapkin (2000) discuss these issues in detail. Briefly, in the case of aggregate opinions, such as the school climate data, the proportion of overall variability in responses that is between settings rather than within settings is important, along with meaningful relationships between setting-level measures and other indicators that are plausibly predictors or outcomes of setting features. So, for example, Russell and McGuire (chapter 8) found meaningful variation between schools in perceived school safety for LGBT students and in anti-LGBT slurs. Because slurs were positively related to student reports of LGBT education and of knowing where to go for LGBT information, the authors conclude that education efforts may have been undertaken in response to safety problems in the schools.

Whether the information that is aggregated concerns perceptions or other individual characteristics such as achievement, it is important to disentangle the extent to which the characteristics arise from backgrounds that individuals bring to settings, from socialization that settings provide, and from interactions among individuals within settings. We have known from the time of the Coleman et al. (1966) report that students' socioeconomic background is highly related to their achievement (see Kahlenberg, chapter 14). Thus aggregate achievement may better reflect the mix of students who attend a school than the quality of instruction they receive. The school's contribution to student achievement might be measured better by tracking achievement trajectories of cohorts of students over time rather than measuring new cohorts of students each year, or by modeling how well the student body does compared with other students with similar class backgrounds. The composition of the student body is indeed an important characteristic of schools and a plausible target of intervention. Kahlenberg's central point in chapter 14 is that changing the mix of students in a school so that the majority are middle class can have strong positive effects on poor students' achievement without harming achievement for more advantaged students. But it is important to distinguish between improving aggregate performance by changing the proportion of students in a school who are middle class, and by increasing the performance of students who are already part of the student body.

When policy makers focus only on aggregate individual outcomes, such as achievement scores, and not on the features of settings that affect outcomes, they risk holding settings accountable for issues that are not under their control. Worse, they miss the opportunity to hold settings accountable for features that they do control and can change to improve outcomes for youth. Whereas poorly targeted measures are likely to lead to frustration, better targeted, valid, and reliable measures of malleable features of settings are important tools to produce desired outcomes.

The chapters in this book use a variety of ways to assess characteristics of settings and processes of change, carefully matched to their definitions of quality. Some rely on aggregating characteristics that youth bring to a setting, as in Kahlenberg's measure of the proportion of children eligible for free or reduced-price lunches (chapter 14). Others examine characteristics youth achieve there, as in Maton et al.'s diversity scorecard, which includes, in part, grade point averages, enrollment patterns, and graduation rates for college students from different ethnic groups, in addition to observational measures of intergroup interaction and survey measures of school climate (chapter 7). Datnow's ongoing measures of student achievement, which are the grist for Data-Driven Decision Making, are also of this type (chapter 15). Russell and McGuire survey adolescents' views about their environment, in particular, school climate and safety for LGBT students (chapter 8). And Fagan et al. use surveys of youth to assess multiple risk and protective factors, such as the proportion of youth in a community who report low commitment to school or friends who engage in problem behaviors (chapter 16).

A number of chapters use data from or about youth in more elaborate ways than simply counting or averaging. For example, one way in which Weinstein (chapter 5) assesses equality of teacher expectations for youth is via the discrepancy between students' report of how a teacher would deal with a hypothetical low- and high-achieving student. Henry (chapter 3) assesses classroom norms regarding aggression by examining the degree of approval students express for different behaviors (such as yelling at another student) that vary in levels of aggressiveness to create a profile of approval scores. He analyzes the features of this profile, called a return potential measure, to consider targets for change. In the youth organizing process described by Speer (chapter 12), network analysis assesses the extent to which youth are broadly connected to others in a setting rather than divided into cliques or interacting only indirectly via a few youth who broker connections with others. McLaughlin and O'Brien-Strain (chapter 17) track event histories of youths' involvement in multiple service systems across periods of months or years to evaluate each setting's contributions to children's behavior above and beyond the contributions of other settings in which children are engaged.

Still other authors assess settings on the basis of the adult leader's behavior. For example, Pianta and Allen (chapter 2) use the CLASS observational system to assess teacher's social and instructional interactions with youth with respect to motivational processes, organizational processes, and instructional supports. Jones, Brown, and Aber (chapter 4) also use the CLASS, and additionally ask teachers to report on their own ability to perceive, understand, regulate, and use their emotions and on their relationships with students. At a more qualitative level, Pollock (chapter 6) asks educators to assess the precision of their own discussions about race. To what extent are they talking about the needs of specific groups in ways that are too general or too specific? When analyzing causes of racial disparities, do they include the roles of all relevant actors, including themselves? Does talk about race reduce or increase access to educational opportunity for students of color?

A number of authors use direct measures of the setting-level processes or the organization of resources, rather than focusing on adult leaders or aggregating information about youth. Smith and Akiva (chapter 11) describe an observational system to assess multiple dimensions of quality in out-of-school-time programs such as the opportunities made available to youth (e.g., to set goals and make plans) and staff support for youth (e.g., in building new skills). Weinstein (chapter 5) uses qualitative interviews with teachers and administrators, analysis of narrative records from meetings, and analysis of policies, such as tracking or self-selection into honors classes, in addition to quantitative measures from students to assess the degree to which schools create high expectations for all students.

Finally, some authors use multiple methods to assess different aspects of implementation. Desimone (chapter 9) describes measures of implementation tuned to the policy attributes that her model suggests determine change. Each attribute requires different considerations. For example, in assessing power, that is, the rewards and sanctions associated with implementation, perceptions may be more important determinants of behavior than objective measures, because teachers are unlikely to respond to sanctions of which they are unaware. For professional development, objective measures, such as hours spent in training relevant to the reform model, may be more appropriate. Miller et al. (chapter 10) describe the particular challenges associated with assessing capacity building for small community-based organization that serve youth. For example, surveys may be of little use in an organization with only one or two staff. Qualitative methods such as case studies and town hall meetings, as well as observations and reviews of archival documents, will often be more appropriate.

Each method chosen for assessing settings has its own strengths and limitations. In the penultimate chapter, Martinez and Raudenbush discuss in detail the sources of unreliability in one sort of measure (direct observations of interpersonal processes in settings). These include disagreement among raters, temporal instability across successive rating periods, temporal instability across days, and interactions among these features. They describe a strategy for measuring the different sources of unreliability in a particular measurement context, in order to allocate raters and observation periods across setting in the most cost-effective ways. Consideration of unreliability in other approaches to measurement is critical to research to establish how well approaches to intervention work. For example, the proportion of variance in perceived social climate that can be attributed to schools, rather than to different views of individuals within the same school, is one measure of the school-level reliability of social climate (as Russell and McGuire discuss in chapter 8). Raudenbush and Sampson (1999) suggested that we need a new science of measuring social settings, an "ecometrics" parallel to the science of measuring persons, or psychometrics. The chapter by Martinez and Raudenbush is an important example, rendered in nontechnical language. Because of the central role of measurement in motivating and monitoring change, ecometrics is also critical to the science of promoting youth development by changing social settings.

Conclusion

Progress in transforming settings to improve youth development will require advances on three fronts: understanding features of settings that affect youth, understanding how to measure these features, and understanding how to create desired changes. The first front is most advanced (Eccles & Gootman, 2002; National Research Council, 2003; Tseng & Seidman, 2007). The current book seeks to advance the other two. The next 16 chapters offer theories of setting-level change; strategies for measuring theoretically meaningful features of settings to motivate, guide, and monitor change; and exemplars of change efforts. The last two chapters advance our understanding of how to measure settings in reliable ways, and offer an overarching theory of setting-level intervention. We hope that this book will stimulate researchers, policy makers, and practitioners to think more creatively and precisely about how to measure settings and how to change them to foster positive youth development.

Acknowledgment

We thank Edward Seidman, Vivan Tseng, and Nicole Yohalem for helpful comments on this chapter.

References

Allen, J. P., Kuperminc, G., Philliber, S., & Herre, K. (1994). Programmatic prevention of adolescent problem behaviors: The role of autonomy, relatedness, and volunteer service in the teen outreach program. *American Journal of Community Psychology, 22*(5), 617-638.

Coleman, J., Campbell, E., Hobson, C., McPartland, J., Mood, A., Weinfeld, F. D., et al. (1966). *Equality of educational opportunity.* Washington, DC: Department of Health, Education and Welfare.

Davis, H. R., & Salasin, S. E. (1975). The utilization of evaluation. In E. Struening & M. M. Guttentag (Eds.). *Handbook of evaluation research* (Vol. 1, pp. 621-666). Beverly Hills, CA: Sage.

Eccles, J., & Gootman, J. A. (Eds.). (2002). *Community programs to promote youth development.* Washington, DC: National Academy Press.

Grigg, W., Donahue, P. L., & Dion, G. (2007). *The Nation's Report Card: 12th grade reading and mathematics 2005*. Retrieved April 1, 2007, from http://nces.ed.gov/nationsreportcard/pubs/main2005/2007468.asp

Lewin (1951) *Field theory in social science.* New York: Harper & Row.

National Research Council. (2003). *Engaging schools: Fostering high school students' motivation to learn.* Washington, DC: National Academy Press.

No Child Left Behind Act of 2001, Pub. L. No. 107-110, 115 Stat. 1425 (2002).

Porter, A. C., Floden, R., Freeman, D., Schmidt, W., & Schwille, J. (1988). Content determinants in elementary school mathematics. In D. Grouws & T. Cooney (Eds.), *Perspectives on research on effective mathematics teaching* (pp. 96-113). Reston, VA: The National Council of Teachers of Mathematics.

Raudenbush, S. W., & Sampson, R. J. (1999). Ecometrics: Toward a science of assessing ecological settings with application to the systematic social observation of neighborhoods. *Sociological Methodology, 29,* 1-41.

Shinn, M. (1990). Mixing and matching: Levels of conceptualization, measurement, and statistical analysis in community research. In P. Tolan, C. Keys, F. Chertok, & L. Jason (Eds.). *Researching community psychology: Issues of theory and methods* (pp. 111-126). Washington, DC: American Psychological Association.

Shinn, M., & Rapkin, B. D. (2000). Cross-level analysis without cross-ups. In J. Rappaport & E. Seidman (Eds.), *Handbook of community psychology* (pp. 669-695). New York: Kluwer Academic/Plenum.

Tseng, V., & Seidman, E. (2007). A systems framework for understanding social settings. *American Journal of Community Psychology, 39,* 217-228.

Weiss, C. H. (1995). Nothing as practical as good theory. In J. P. Connell, A. C., Kubisch, L. Schorr, & C. H. Weiss (Eds.), *New approaches to evaluating community initiatives* (pp. 65-92). Washington, DC: The Aspen Institute.

Wilson-Ahlstrom, A., Yohalem, N., & Pittman, K. (2007, March). *Building quality improvement systems: Lessons from three emerging efforts in the youth-serving sector.* Washington, DC: The Forum for Youth Investment, Impact Strategies, Inc. Retrieved April 10, 2007, from http://www.forumfyi.org/Files//building_quality_full.pdf

PART I

CHANGING CLASSROOMS

Chapter 2

Building Capacity for Positive Youth Development in Secondary School Classrooms: Changing Teachers' Interactions With Students

ROBERT C. PIANTA AND JOSEPH P. ALLEN

I n schools, the classroom is the most proximal and powerful setting for influencing youth outcomes, and within classrooms, students' social and instructional interactions with teachers either produce or inhibit achievement and behavioral/emotional health to the extent that they engage and motivate youth. There is overwhelming evidence that the capacity of classrooms to function in this development-promoting role is low and at best extremely uneven, thus the need for theory and approaches for how to change (improve) the capacity of classrooms (e.g., social and instructional interactions between students and teachers) is considerable. Our central thesis is that motivation-producing interactions with teachers (how we are defining capacity for classroom settings) can be improved by an intervention that increases teachers' knowledge of adolescent development and provides them with ongoing, pragmatic support and feedback to apply that knowledge in classrooms on a daily basis.

Underperformance of the Classroom Setting as a Context for Youth Development

There is little question that academic achievement, personal well-being, and civic-related outcomes for adolescents are in dire need of improvement and enhancement (Carbonaro & Gamoran, 2002; National Center for Education

Statistics [NCES], 2003a). Students spend one-quarter of their waking hours in schools, most of it in classrooms, yet for all of the resources devoted to schooling, the capacity of secondary classrooms as settings for positive youth development is sorely lacking. Social and task-related disengagement and alienation reported by adolescents result from classroom experiences that are disconnected from youths' developmental needs (Crosnoe, 2000; Dornbusch, Glasgow, & Lin, 1996; Eccles, Lord, & Midgley, 1991). Youth describe school experiences as irrelevant and lacking appropriate and meaningful challenges. These patterns are exacerbated dramatically for youth attending schools in low-income communities, rural communities, large schools, and for those with histories of poor achievement or problem behavior (e.g., Crosnoe, 2001; Eccles, Lord, Roeser, Barber, & Jozefowicz, 1997).

Even more disconcerting is recent evidence from observational studies of large samples of fifth grade classrooms, that the nature and quality of the instructional and social supports actually offered to early adolescents in class-rooms is generally low, and even lower for the groups noted above (Pianta, Belsky, Houts, Morrison, & the NICHD ECCRN, 2007). Moreover, findings from studies of large and diverse samples of middle schools demonstrate quite clearly that competitive, standards-driven instruction in de-contextualized skills and knowledge contributes directly to this sense of alienation and dis-engagement (Eccles et al., 1997; Shouse, 1996). Engagement in school begins to decline early in adolescence and by entry into high school this decline is pronounced to the point where more than half of high school students from all types of schools report that they do not take their school or their stud-ies seriously (Marks, 2000; Steinberg, Brown, & Dornbusch, 1996). Further, adolescents bring their peers along with them: doing well in school switches from being a positively valued behavior among peers in childhood to a some-what negatively valued behavior by mid-adolescence. Yet, engagement and intrinsic motivation become pivotal in adolescence, as students at this age have not only the means to withdraw energy from educational pursuits but also the ability to drop out altogether (National Research Council [NRC], 2004).

With regard to achievement outcomes, there is recent evidence that middle and high school youth are underperforming and that performance gaps related to culture, race, and income are not closing despite years of rhetoric and attention (NCES, 2003b). For example, more than 5 years into educational reform under No Child Left Behind (NCLB), roughly 40% of poor or African American eighth graders in Virginia perform below standards for reading achievement and the corresponding rates of failure for youth in the District of Columbia are close to 80% (Aratani, 2006). These rates of failure in reading, a central focus of reform under NCLB emphasized in schools' attempts to meet state standards, reflect a fundamental misunderstanding of the mechanisms by which students are engaged by schooling and the need to reconceptualize and redesign how we support teachers. Consider a second outcome of reform, the dropout rate. Fewer than 60% of ninth graders in certain demographic groups (NCES, 2003b) actually graduate 4 years later. Yet for 10 years decreasing the dropout rate has been a singular focus of most secondary schools and the average *annual* dropout rate remains near 10% and ranges up to almost 30% for recently immigrated Latinos. These recent findings make strikingly clear that the high school classroom as a setting for youth development is fundamentally broken. Put another way, it does not appear to us that the central problem in school reform is curriculum, school/class size, or outcomes assessment, but rather how teachers are supported to implement instruction and form positive relationships with students that engage and motivate them to learn and develop personally.

Although there have been promising efforts to reform schools to improve such outcomes, most focus on the structural features of schools (e.g., "schools within a school" models; see Felner, Favazza, Shim, & Brand, 2001) and instructional content aspects of the educational process (e.g., mandating that teachers have content area degrees, see Whitehurst, 2002). On the other hand, youth report that they are more concerned with the actual experiences they have in classroom settings, which they find lacking in terms of meaningful challenges, supportive relationships, and competence-building experiences (Crosnoe, 2001; Csikszentmihalyi & Schneider, 2000; Marks, 2000; NRC, 2002; Roeser, Eccles, & Sameroff, 2000). Perhaps they are right and the capacity of schools to support youth development, particularly for "high risk" youth, depends on whether the relationships and interactions among students and teachers within a classroom offer a developmentally meaningful and challenging experience (NRC, 2002). Because these interactions embody the capacity of the classroom to promote positive development, our focus is on improving and changing these relationships and interactions through working with teachers. Thus, our theory and method of change is centered on teachers' relationships and interactions with students.

A Theory of Classroom Settings

Schools all fundamentally rise or fall on the success of what occurs within the classroom (e.g., Crosnoe, 2001; Nye, Kostantopolous, & Hedges, 2004; Resnick et al., 1997) Ironically, close observation of almost any secondary school in America reveals that adolescents—both at-risk and high functioning—often display remarkably high degrees of motivation and engagement within the school setting. Rarely, however, does this occur *within* the classroom. High school hallways and lunchrooms literally brim over with youthful energy, excitement, and enthusiasm. Intense interactions occur in sports and extracurricular activities, and interactions with peers dominate students' perception of the social ecology of school. It is only when these students enter their classroom that energy levels decline precipitously and it is rare that a given student will "connect" with a teacher or material in classroom or subject area in such a way that they perform at high levels of capacity or "flow" (Csikszentmihalyi, 2000). The classroom setting looks equally bleak from the perspective of teachers, who are also dropping out and becoming more disengaged. Fifteen percent of the entire teaching workforce turns over every year. Rates of teachers leaving the profession are increasing. And those who stay report a sense of malaise and frustration—they feel their job is getting harder and they have fewer tools with which to work and feel effective (Hart, Stroot, Yinger, & Smith, 2005).

A fundamental principle in addressing the chronically resource-starved classroom in the American high school is that modifying the classroom as a setting to engage teachers and youth more fully may be the single best way to unleash and expand the level of *human resources* (e.g., energy, effort, and enthusiasm) available to the educational process (Sarason, 1982). In the following sections, we discuss three features of classrooms likely to influence adolescents' levels of motivation—relational supports, competence supports, and relevance. We believe this theory of the classroom as a setting for youth development is a fundamental precursor to understanding our theory and approach to *changing* classroom settings. Readers will recognize applications and extensions of Vygotsky's ideas about the contextualized nature of learning and development and close, interdependent connection among relational supports, task-related challenges, and learning. Pianta (1999) has also discussed the connection between classroom contexts and learning in terms of the relational, structural, and motivational affordances available in classrooms. Central to each of these perspectives, and elaborated in the following sections with regard to adolescents, is an appreciation of learning as a contextualized process and the need, when talking about classroom contexts, to analyze that setting from a developmentally informed standpoint with regard to its value.

Relational Supports

As a behavior setting, the classroom runs on interactions between and among participants: the relationship between the student and the teacher and the relationships of students with one another. These relationships and their value emotionally, instrumentally, and psychologically to adolescents are fundamental supports to the value of their experience in the classroom setting for furthering development. It is not an overstatement to suggest that most adolescents *live* for their social relationships (Collins & Repinski, 1994). Yet, the qualities of these relationships are frequently afterthoughts in battles over curricula, testing, school structure, and funding. Positive relationships with adults are perhaps the single most important ingredient in promoting positive youth development. When teachers learn to make modest efforts to form a personal connection with their adolescent students—such that the students feel known—they can dramatically enhance student motivation in school and emotional functioning outside of school (Roeser, Eccles, & Sameroff, 1998; Skinner, Zimmer-Gembeck, & Connell, 1998). Adolescents report both that they would learn more if their teachers cared about them personally and that such personal connections are rare (Public Agenda, 1997). A close, supportive relationship with a teacher is a key feature distinguishing at-risk adolescents who succeed in school from those who do not (Resnick et al., 1997) and youths' sense of social connection within settings predict outcomes ranging from higher achievement scores to greater student engagement and more positive academic attitudes (Bryk & Driscoll, 1988; Bryk, Lee, & Holland, 1993; Connell & Wellborn, 1991; Crosnoe, Johnson, & Elder, 2004; Ryan & Deci, 2000; see also NRC, 2004, for extended review of other similar findings). Notably, even for relatively highly motivated late adolescents in college, recent experimental work has shown that a sense of isolation can significantly reduce energy for intellectual pursuits and that this reduction is powerful enough to temporarily depress results on IQ tests (Baumeister, Twenge, & Nuss, 2002), while increasing irrational and risk-taking behavior (Twenge, Catanese, & Baumeister, 2002).

Autonomy/Competence Supports

Teens are engaged by challenges that are within reach and that provide a sense of self-efficacy and control: experiences that offer challenges viewed as adult-like but for which appropriate scaffolding and support are provided (Bandura, Barbaranelli, Caprara, & Pastorelli, 1996; Eccles et al., 1993). Any setting that intends to advance development and learning outcomes for youth must carefully craft the nature of experience it provides to give adolescent participants a sense of control, autonomy, choice, and mastery. Absent these considerations, or in settings that rely on top-down approaches, classrooms for youth are doomed to be places lacking in engagement and motivation. One of the most tragically avoidable errors that some secondary school teachers make is to assume that youth strivings for autonomy and self-expression represent negative forces to be countered rather than positive energies to be harnessed. This basic misunderstanding of adolescent development (one often promoted in teacher education courses and reinforced by school policies) then takes form in highly controlling and punitive classroom and school settings and in instruction that is highly teacher-driven and discouraging of exploration and curiosity. Teachers also have many opportunities to provide adolescents with meaningful choices and autonomy in classrooms in ways that do not threaten teacher authority. They do not always recognize these opportunities or their importance in adolescent motivation. Supporting student autonomy does not mean giving up teacher control. On the contrary, autonomy can be supported by giving students choices of partners for group projects, types of projects to perform, and so forth (Allen, Kuperminc, Philliber, & Herre, 1994; Anderman & Midgley, 1998). The fundamental challenge to teachers in this regard is to understand adolescents' developmental push for autonomy so that they can then seek to guide and direct it. This mismatch of classroom and development, driven by profound misunderstanding of teens, results in schools narrowing, rather than expanding, the "space" in which zones of proximal development can be created for youth.

Relevance

Adolescents, like adults, deploy a considerable amount of effort in attempts to make meaning in their lives; for many, adolescence is a period in which this becomes a focus for the first time. This process ultimately leads to a bias in adolescents' evaluation of experience (particularly those experiences offered by adults) toward choices they view as relevant, or connected to their emerging views on what is meaningful and what is not. Too often, the high school curriculum and the rationales behind it are taken as a "given" without recognition that these rationales need to be made clear to each new cohort of students. Drawing even very distal connections between what occurs within high school and the larger "real-world" can alter student behavior. For example, involving students in significant, real-world, voluntary community service and then discussing it within the classroom in an ongoing way has been found to reduce failure rates by 50%, in randomly controlled trials, with similarly profound effects upon other behaviors in youths' lives as well (Allen, Philliber, Herrling, & Kuperminc, 1997). Centuries ago, late adolescents were commanding armies and running countries (Barzun, 2000). Today, an ever more competent generation of adolescents is confined to a classroom for hours a day with little vision of how what occurs within that classroom relates to the larger world. Consciously addressing the relevance of what occurs within the classroom to the students' future options in that larger world is critical to engaging otherwise restless young minds. On a smaller scale, teachers may increase the relevance of the classroom by making repeated, explicit ties between curricular material and real-world applications and engaging peer group processes in learning (given the intrinsic meaningfulness of peer interactions to youth). The key factor here is that the real-world connections must be made in ways that are meaningful *as perceived by the student*. Connecting school work to actual careers in meaningful ways can significantly enhance students' sense of the meaningfulness of what they are being taught, and hence of their motivation to learn it.

These ideas about the central role of interactions and relationships in determining the motivational value of experiences in classroom settings form the basis for our developmentally informed analysis of classroom effects on *student* outcomes. In our view, the capacity of classroom settings to engage

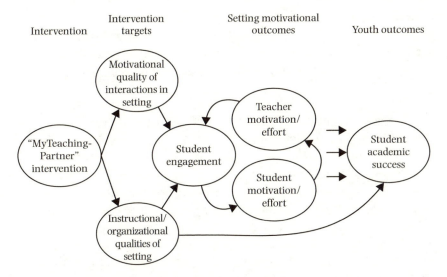

Figure 2.1. Conceptual Model of Classroom Settings.

and motivate youth is the core "criterion" by which they should be judged, and the features of relational supports, autonomy/competence supports, and relevance are how classrooms accomplish that goal. In Figure 2.1, we embed this larger construct of classroom supports for motivation/engagement (relational, autonomy, relevance) in the framework of an effort to modify the affordance value of classrooms for producing positive outcomes for youth.

In this model, we place motivational supports as central features of the classroom, along with instructional supports, in relation to producing cycles of student engagement, teacher efficacy, and student performance. We suggest that in the best classrooms, motivational and instructional supports operate in concert to initiate self-reinforcing linkages among engaged students, effective teachers, and growth in student performance. We also note that the model emphasizes relationships and interactions in the classroom as the media through which motivational and instructional supports are made available to students. In the next section, we present our conceptualization and technical approach to *setting-level change*, which by this definition of setting targets interactions and relationships between teachers and students as the focus of change.

Changing Interactions Between Teachers and Students in Classrooms

The question then is how to effectively, accountably, and systematically produce desired changes (improvements) in instructional interactions, motivation-producing interactions, and personal relationships that teachers have with youth in secondary classrooms. This is not a new challenge and educators have decades of experience in attempts to address it. We briefly summarize some of what is known about those attempts and then present our own approach to conceptualizing and implementing change.

Prior Efforts: The Shortcomings of Traditional Professional Development

Professional development for teachers has a long history of being fragmented and incoherent (Ball & Cohen, 1999); teachers pursue learning opportunities on their own (e.g., weekend workshops, MA courses), pick up advice within informal settings at school (e.g., in the lunchroom, at the copying machine), attend district-mandated workshops, and learn from daily experiences with children in the classroom (Wilson & Berne, 1999). Short-term direct trainings, often knowledge- or technique-based, are the most common form of in-service training with substantial variation in the mechanisms of delivery and intensity of the source and follow-up (Birman, Desimone, Porter, & Garet, 2000). These efforts to promote change fall short in a multitude of ways, not the least of which is their nearly complete lack of connection to a theory of classroom effects and change and their de-contextualized content: teachers are placed in a passive learner role; content is vague, irrelevant, or disconnected from teachers' actual experience in a classroom context; and there is limited follow-up (Sandholtz, 2002). Such longstanding criticisms are reflected in Borko's (2004) recent comment that "each year, schools, districts, and the federal government spend millions, if not billions, of dollars on in-service seminars and other forms of professional development that are fragmented, intellectually superficial, and do not take into account what we know about how teachers learn" (p. 3).

Education theorists have begun to generate lists of key characteristics of effective professional development for teachers, predominantly based on literature concerning adult learning (Abdal-Haqq, 1995; Darling-Hammond & McLaughlin, 1995; Putnam & Barko, 2000; Richardson & Anders, 2005). These visions conceptualize professional development as learning that is active, collaborative, and embedded within a classroom context (Darling-Hammond & McLaughlin, 1995; Lieberman, 1995). NCLB legislation describes high-quality professional development for teachers as intensive, sustained, and classroom focused. Increasingly, mentoring and consultation are viewed as models for addressing some of the shortcomings of typical professional development for teachers, particularly in relation to providing more individualized and contextualized support (Ingersoll & Kralik, 2004; Pianta, 2005). For example, novice teachers are often provided with mentoring support, wherein an experienced teacher becomes an agent of change through support and guidance of less experienced colleagues (Fideler & Haselkorn, 1999). However, although mentoring does address the need for individualized and contextualized support, recent studies have shown that such supports are rarely, if ever, tied to a validated metric for evaluating classroom practice, nor have the active components and consequent effects of mentoring been specified theoretically or empirically (see Pianta, 2005).

Putting "Development" Back Into Professional Development

Classrooms are complicated social systems involving materials and physical arrangements, management of time, and interactions between and among students and teachers. As we have discussed earlier, our analysis of classrooms suggests that the active ingredients of the classroom as a setting for positive youth development are interactions, particularly those with a teacher but clearly involving peers as well. Importantly, classroom settings are designed to be intentional; by this we mean that the experiences offered in these settings are, by design, intended to produce learning. Increasingly, learning outcomes are highly specified and so classroom experiences are more and more directed toward producing such ends. Thus, teachers' instructional, social, and relational interactions with students, and the strategies they use to manage time and arrangements in the classroom, are intended to be active levers for developmental change. In our view, increasing the capacity of the classroom to produce such change involves strategies to alter these interactions through working with the teacher.

Our approach to changing teacher-child interactions is modeled on systems theory conceptualizations of developmental change (see Sameroff & Emde, 1989) in which forces internal and external to systems exert pressures that force adaptation of some sort: reorganization, differentiation, and integration (Pianta, 1999). In terms of teachers' interactions with children, Pianta (1999) has described a systems model of student-teacher relationships with components that include teacher's knowledge and beliefs, social and instructional interactions, and external forces such as school discipline policy or climate, teachers' own developmental histories, as well as features of the student. Importantly, these form a system of connected components that has consequences for students' learning, motivation, and engagement (see Pianta, La Paro, Payne, Cox, & Bradley, 2002, for a comprehensive review of this work). Ultimately, if the goal is to create and sustain change in the mechanisms by which classrooms enhance youth development (i.e., social and instructional interactions with teachers) a theory and method for change must focus on interactions as well as knowledge, beliefs, and emotional experiences of teachers.

We posit four levers producing developmental change for teacher-student interactions: (a) teachers' knowledge and cognitions related to their interactions with students, (b) availability of ongoing relational supports for teachers themselves, (c) teachers' regular exposure to individualized feedback about their actual interactions with students, and (d) a standard and valid "target" around which to focus efforts to change interactions. Intervention packages that activate these levers in a coordinated way are most likely to induce and maintain change, given the systemic nature of teacher-student interactions in classrooms. In the following section, we describe the theoretical and technical features of MyTeachingPartner (MTP), an innovative professional development approach that by design incorporates these four levers for changing teacher-student interactions and relationships. MTP utilizes a collaborative consultation process and web-based resources to provide ongoing, classroom-focused in-service training across a distance.

MyTeachingPartner

MTP is an ongoing, systematic professional development program for teachers, one feature of which centers on a supportive consultation relationship, which is sustained via web-based interactions (Pianta, 2006a). This consultation emphasizes teachers' implementation of curriculum and how teachers form effective relationships with students. The web-based consultation revolves around observation-based reflection and feedback that is enacted through a regular cycle of interactions between a teacher and consultant. Every 2 weeks, teachers videotape their practices in the classroom and share this footage with consultants. Together, they then use the Classroom Assessment Scoring System (CLASS; Pianta, La Paro, & Hamre, 2006) as a common lens with which to observe and reflect upon aspects of teaching and teacher-child interactions that have known links to children's skill development and start by choosing a dimension of the CLASS that will serve as the basis for consultation and feedback. Another key feature of MTP professional development is continuous, on-demand access to a dynamic, interactive website (www.myteachingpartner.net). This website provides diverse teaching resources, including video examples of teachers implementing evidence-based activities, lesson plans and materials, and video clips that exemplify high-quality interactions with preschool children.

The intervention integrates information-based training delivered through workshops together with *personalized* review of classroom observations using a carefully designed web- and video-conference assessment and feedback process. MTP consultants provide *direct*, *individualized*, *regular*, and *systematic* feedback to teachers based on validated, observational assessment of the classroom environment. The MTP consultancy process functions by increasing teachers' knowledge and skills to observe the qualities of their interactions with students and the contingencies involved, and their awareness of the meanings of these interactions in terms of their contributions to motivational, relational, and competence-enhancing processes. The process also encourages reflection on the teachers' own personal motivations and tendencies in these interactions and their impact on interactive behaviors in an effort to internalize change and sustain it. Three key features of the MTP approach are important for addressing "capacity" problems in secondary classroom settings: (a) a personally, supportive, nonsupervisory relationship with a "consultant"; (b) regular, individualized feedback on teachers' own classroom interactions; and (c) a standard, validated approach to identifying, describing, and measuring classroom interactions.

A supportive relationship is key for inducing change through trust and a willingness to risk new approaches to interaction and beliefs. In a current evaluation of MTP (Pianta, 2006a) it is clear that teachers' emotional connection to their consultant is the basis for much of their engagement in the other aspects of the intervention, such as reviewing tapes and receiving feedback. Joint review of videotaped classroom interactions and individualized feedback provided to the teacher focus the teachers' attention on interactions, elicits beliefs, and transmits new knowledge in ways that reshape the teachers' views of self and their interactions and provides new models for interaction. Video-conference-based interactive dialogue regarding classroom interactions between teachers and consultants reinforces, extends, and personalizes feedback and is yet another setting in which information and support can be exchanged and linked to teachers' actual classroom experience. Over the course of an academic year the "consultancy cycle" serves as an iterative, highly personalized process of teacher feedback and development that repeats 12-15 times. Collectively, these social, informational, and relational linkages between teacher and consultant create a set of "pressures" that promote developmental change in the teachers' classroom interactions with students. The cycle is intended to produce a stream of communication between consultant and teacher based on observation of that teacher's interactions with students in the classroom and a process of joint reflection on strategies to improve those interactions, using a standardized, validated classroom observation procedure as the focus and metric for teachers' interactions with students.

Teachers have many opportunities over the academic year to receive feedback and support from the consultant and to offer their insight and feedback in return. Because of the extended nature of contact between consultants and teachers, consultants must recognize that the consultancy relationship builds over time, in terms of the capacity to give and receive feedback, particularly feedback that can be interpreted as critical. For this reason, consultants must attend, in the initial stages, to the need to build a relationship with the teacher and focus initially on support, slowly transitioning to more challenging aspects as there is evidence the relationship with the teacher can tolerate such challenges. One teacher describes her experience of the consultation process in the following text, in ways that illuminate the various components of this intervention.

I have been teaching for 27 years and have never had a more involved and personal type of professional development. Naturally I don't *see* [italics added] my consultant on a regular basis, but our I-chats have created a most wonderful bond. Through our tapes, she has also been able to learn about my students, and know them quite well. It's such a joy to be able to share moments in the classroom "across the miles." The best part is that we are able to think and work on possible strategies and solutions together, and she's never even stepped foot in my classroom. What could be better?

Measurement of Setting-Level Processes— A Lever and a Target for Change

Central to any intentional effort to induce or direct developmental change is a target or desired outcome that can focus and organize the activity of the system that is the focus of change (in this case teacher-student classroom interactions). In fact, Pianta (2005) has argued that validated, objective, standardized observational assessment of classroom interactions is the foundation for establishing teacher professional development supports aimed at improving classroom effects. Thus, a key feature of the MTP approach is that the feedback and support provided to teachers during the ongoing consultation process is directly tied to validated, standardized observational systems shown to assess aspects of teachers' social and instructional interactions that predict growth in student performance. This system is known as the CLASS (Pianta et al., 2006). The vocabulary we use to describe these interactions is based on CLASS-Secondary, an upward extension of the CLASS (Pianta et al., 2006). The CLASS dimensions are based on developmental theory and research suggesting that interactions between students and adults are the primary mechanism of student development and learning (Greenberg, Domitrovich, & Bumbarger, 2001; Hamre & Pianta, 2005; Morrison & Connor, 2002; Pianta, 2006b; Rutter & Maughan, 2002). The CLASS dimensions are based on the *interactions* of teachers and students in the classroom; scoring for any dimension is not determined by the presence of materials, the physical environment or safety, or the adoption of a specific curriculum. The CLASS assesses the quality of teachers' social and instructional interactions with students as well as the intentionality and productivity evident in classroom settings. This distinction between *observed interactions* and physical materials or reported use of curriculum is important, because in most school settings, materials and curricula are usually prevalent and fairly well organized. In the CLASS, the focus is on what teachers *do* with the materials they have and on the *interactions* they have with students.

The dimensions of interaction assessed by the CLASS elementary version predict growth in literacy and math as well as reduced teacher-child conflict and problem behavior from pre-K through fifth grade (Hamre & Pianta, 2005; Howes et al., in press; NICHD ECCRN, 2004; Pianta et al., 2007). The CLASS, originally designed for elementary settings, has been recently redesigned and adapted for secondary settings, and is now being used in K-12 teacher quality assessments in Ohio, and in research on teacher education programs conducted as part of the Carnegie Corporation's Teachers for a New Era initiative (Hart et al., 2005). MTP consultants rely on the dimensions of interaction presented as observational rating scales in the CLASS and the detailed descriptions of scale points on those dimensions that are provided in the CLASS manual when they provide feedback to teachers. The CLASS is one of the most current and widely used standardized assessments of social and instructional interactions in classrooms (Hart et al., 2005; McCaslin, Burross, & Good, 2005; NICHD ECCRN, 2002, 2005).

The CLASS-Secondary version, or CLASS-S, is explicitly designed to capture precisely those aspects of classroom interactions that we hypothesize in preceding text to be resources for adolescent engagement and motivation. As such, it builds on and incorporates all of the strengths of the CLASS system at elementary levels, while adding specific dimensions conceptualized and operationalized to maximize adolescent engagement. The CLASS-S scales are organized into three overarching dimensions, similar to those reported in factor analyses of the elementary version: Motivational Processes (e.g., Sensitivity, Relational Supports, Autonomy Supports), Organizational Processes (e.g., Effective Behavior Management, Instructional Learning Formats), and Instructional Supports (Content Knowledge, Quality of Feedback, Cognition Supports).

Figure 2.2 provides an overview of these domains and the dimensions within each domain that are measured by the middle/secondary version of the CLASS. This organizational structure for classroom interactions has been

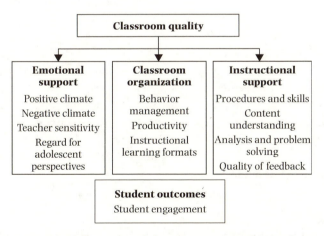

Figure 2.2. Overview of Domains and the Dimensions Within Each Domain Measured by the Middle/Secondary Version of the CLASS.

validated in over 3,000 classrooms from preschool to fifth grade (Hamre, Pianta, Mashburn, & Downer, 2006). As the middle/secondary version is entering its pilot phase, similar data will be collected to confirm or validate this structure for grades 6-12 classrooms.

Summary and Conclusions

Although classrooms are complex social systems and student-teacher relationships and interactions are also complex, multicomponent systems, we posit that the nature and quality of social and instructional interactions between teachers and children can be changed by providing teachers knowledge about developmental processes relevant for classroom interactions and personalized feedback/support about their interactive behaviors and cues. For work with teachers of younger children, MTP support positively influenced teachers' interactions in classrooms, which in turn were related to improved achievement (Pianta et al., 2006), results consistent with related literature suggesting that observation of teacher-child interaction, knowledge about development in language and literacy, and effective implementation of instruction contributes to higher ratings of observed sensitivity, language stimulation, and implementation in quasi-experiments (Cassidy, Buell, Pugh-Hoese, & Russell, 1995; Howes, Galinsky, & Kontos, 1998; Rhodes & Hennessy, 2000). It is this link between direct and individualized support for teachers, improvements in the classroom setting, and better child outcomes that we posit as a model for improving capacity in secondary classrooms.

A theory of classroom settings must be premised on an understanding of the developmental significance of those settings' influence on youth and the mechanisms of these effects. Once that knowledge base is established, then theory can move to how those mechanisms (in this case, the capacity of classrooms settings as reflected in student-teacher interactions) themselves can be changed. In this chapter, we focused on the theoretical and empirical links between classroom interactions and motivational and achievement outcomes and we presented an approach to intervention designed to increase the quality of such interactions and, in turn, increase student engagement and motivation, and ultimately achievement. Recognizing general principles of development in complex systems, a theory of the classroom as a setting for youth development and a theory of change specific to this social setting are the ultimate goals of this work.

References

Abdal-Haqq, I. (1995). *Making time for teacher professional development* (Digest 95-4). Washington, DC: ERIC Clearinghouse on Teaching and Teacher Education.

Allen, J. P., Kuperminc, G., Philliber, S., & Herre, K. (1994). Programmatic prevention of adolescent problem behaviors: The role of autonomy, relatedness, and volunteer service in the teen outreach program. *American Journal of Community Psychology, 22*(5), 617-638.

Allen, J. P., Philliber, S., Herrling, S., & Kuperminc, G. P. (1997). Preventing teen pregnancy and academic failure: Experimental evaluation of a developmentally based approach. *Child Development, 68*(4), 729-742.

Anderman, L. H., & Midgley, C. (1998). Motivation and middle school students. *ERIC Digest*, EDO-PS-98-5.

Aratani, L. (2006, July 13). Upper grades, lower reading skills. *The Washington Post*, B1.

Ball, D. L., & Cohen, D. K. (1999). Developing practice, developing practitioners: Toward a practice-based theory of professional education. In L. Darling-Hammond & G. Sykes (Eds.), *Teaching as the learning profession: Handbook of policy and practice* (pp. 3-32). San Francisco: Jossey-Bass.

Bandura, A., Barbaranelli, C., Caprara, G. V., & Pastorelli, C. (1996). Multifaceted impact of self-efficacy beliefs on academic functioning. *Child Development, 67*(3), 1206-1222.

Barzun, J. (2000). *From dawn to decadence: 500 years of western cultural life 1500 to the present*. London: Harper Collins.

Baumeister, R. F., Twenge, J. M., & Nuss, C. K. (2002). Effects of social exclusion on cognitive processes: Anticipated aloneness reduces intelligent thought. *Journal of Personality and Social Psychology, 82*, 817-827.

Birman, B. F., Desimone, L., Porter, A. C., & Garet, M. S. (2000). Designing professional development that works. *Educational Leadership, 57*(8), 1-8.

Borko, H. (2004). Professional development and teacher learning: Mapping the terrain. *Educational Researcher, 33*(8), 3-15.

Bryk, A. S., & Driscoll, M. (1988). *The high school as a community: Contextual influences and consequences for teachers*. Madison, WI: University of Wisconsin, National Center on Effective Secondary Schools.

Bryk, A. S., Lee, V. E., & Holland, P. B. (1993). *Catholic schools and the common good*. Cambridge, MA: Harvard University Press.

Carbonaro, W. J., & Gamoran, A. (2002). The production of achievement inequality in high school English. *American Educational Research Journal, 39*, 801-827.

Cassidy, D. J., Buell, M. J., Pugh-Hoese, S., & Russell, S. (1995). The effect of education on child care teachers' beliefs and classroom quality: Year one evaluation of the TEACH Early Childhood Associate Degree Scholarship Program. *Early Childhood Research Quarterly, 10*, 171-183.

Collins, W. A., & Repinski, D. J. (1994). Relationships during adolescence: Continuity and change in interpersonal perspective. In R. Montemayor, G. Adams, & T. P. Gullotta (Eds.), *Personal relationships during adolescence* (pp. 7-36). San Francisco: Sage Publications.

Connell, J. P., & Wellborn, J. G. (1991). Competence, autonomy, and relatedness: A motivational analysis of self-system processes. In M. Gunnar & L. A. Sroufe (Eds.), *Self processes in development: Minnesota symposium on child psychology* (Vol. 23, pp. 43-77). Hillsdale, NJ: Erlbaum.

Crosnoe, R. (2000). Friendships in childhood and adolescence: The life course and new directions. *Social Psychology Quarterly, 63,* 377-391.

Crosnoe, R. (2001). Academic orientation and parental involvement in education during high school. *Sociology of Education, 74,* 210-230.

Crosnoe, R., Johnson, M. K., & Elder, G. H., Jr. (2004). Intergenerational bonding in school: The behavioral and contextual correlates of student-teacher relationships. *Sociology of Education, 77*(1), 60-81.

Csikszentmihalyi, M. (2000). *Beyond boredom and anxiety: Experiencing flow in work and play.* San Francisco: Jossey-Bass, Inc.

Csikszentmihalyi, M., & Schneider, B. (2000). *Becoming adult: How teenagers prepare for the world of work.* New York: Basic Books.

Darling-Hammond, L., & McLaughlin, M. W. (1995). Policies that support professional development in an era of reform. *Phi Delta Kappan, 76*(8), 597-604.

Dornbusch, S. M., Glasgow, K. L., & Lin, I.-C. (1996). The social structure of schooling. *Annual Review of Psychology, 47,* 401-429.

Eccles, J. S., Lord, S., & Midgley, C. (1991, August). What are we doing to early adolescents? The impacts of educational contexts on early adolescents. *American Educational Journal,* 521-542.

Eccles, J. S., Lord, S. E., Roeser, R. W., Barber, B. L., & Jozefowicz, D. M. H. (1997). The association of school transitions in early adolescence with developmental trajectories during high school. In J. Schulenberg, J. L. Maggs, & K. Hurrelmann (Eds.), *Health risks and developmental transitions during adolescence* (pp. 283-321). New York: Cambridge.

Eccles, J. S., Midgley, C., Wigfield, A., Buchanan, C. M., Reuman, D., Flanagan, C.,et al. (1993). Development during adolescence: The impact of stage-environment fit on young adolescents' experiences in schools and in families. *American Psychologist, 48*(2), 90-101.

Felner, R., Favazza, A., Shim, M., & Brand, S. (2001). Whole school improvement and restructuring as prevention and promotion: Lessons from project STEP and the project on high performance learning communities. *Journal of School Psychology, 39,* 177-202.

Fideler, E., & Haselkorn, D. (1999). *Learning the ropes: Urban teacher induction programs and practices in the United States.* Belmont, MA: Recruiting New Teachers.

Greenberg, M. T., Domitrovich, C., & Bumbarger, B. (2001). The prevention of mental disorders in school-aged children: Current state of the field [Special issue]. *Prevention and Treatment, 4*(1), 1-62.

Hamre, B. K., & Pianta, R. C. (2005). Can instructional and emotional support in the first grade classroom make a difference for children at risk of school failure? *Child Development, 76*(5), 949-967.

Hamre, B. K., Pianta, R. C., Mashburn, A. J., & Downer, J. T. (2006). Building and validating a theoretical model of classroom effects in over 4000 early childhood and elementary classrooms. Manuscript in preparation.

Hart, P., Stroot, S., Yinger, R., & Smith, S. (2005). *Meeting the teacher education accountability challenge: A focus on novice and experienced teacher studies.* Mount Vernon, OH: Teacher Quality Partnership.

Howes, C., Burchinal, M., Pianta, R., Bryant, D., Early, D., Clifford, R., et al. (in press). Ready to learn? children's pre-academic achievement in pre-kindergarten programs. *Early Childhood Research Quarterly.*

Howes, C., Galinsky, E., & Kontos, S. (1998). Child care caregiver sensitivity and attachment. *Social Development, 4,* 44-61.

Ingersoll, R., & Kralik, J. M. (2004). *The impact of mentoring on teacher retention: What the research says.* Denver: Education Commission of the States.

Lieberman, A. (1995). Practices that support teacher development. *Phi Delta Kappan, 76*(8), 591-596.

Marks, H. M. (2000). Student engagement in instructional activity: Patterns in the elementary, middle, and high school years. *American Educational Research Journal, 37*(1), 153-184.

McCaslin, M., Burross, H. L., & Good, T. L. (2005, January 2). Change and conti-nuity in student achievement from grades 3 to 5: A policy dilemma. *Education Policy Analysis Archives, 13*(1). Retrieved February 2, 2006, from http://epaa. asu.edu/epaa/v13n1/

Morrison, F. J., & Connor, C. M. (2002). Understanding schooling effects on early literacy: A working research strategy. *Journal of School Psychology, 40*(6), 493-500.

National Center for Education Statistics. (2003a). *Overview and inventory of state education reforms: 1990-2000.* Washington, DC: U.S. Department of Education, Institute of Education Sciences.

National Center for Education Statistics. (2003b). *The condition of education 2003.* Washington, DC: U.S. Department of Education, Institute of Education Sciences.

National Research Council (NRC). (2002). *Achieving high educational standards for all.* Washington, DC: National Academy Press.

National Research Council. (2004). *Engaging schools: Fostering high school students' motivation to learn.* Washington, DC: National Academy Press.

NICHD Early Child Care Research Network (ECCRN). (2002). The relation of global first-grade classroom environment to structural classroom features and teacher and student behaviors. *The Elementary School Journal, 102*(5), 367-387.

NICHD Early Child Care Research Network. (2004). Social functioning in first grade: Associations with earlier home and child care predictors and with current classroom experiences. *Child Development, 75,* 1639-1662.

NICHD Early Child Care Research Network. (2005). A day in third grade: A large-scale study of classroom quality and teacher and student behavior. *The Elementary School Journal, 105,* 305-323.

Nye, B., Konstantopoulos, S., & Hedges, L. (2004). How large are teacher effects? *Educational Evaluation and Policy Analysis, 26,* 237-257.

Pianta, R. C. (1999). *Enhancing relationships between children and teachers.* Washington, DC: American Psychological Association.

Pianta, R. C. (2005). Standardized observation and professional development: A focus on individualized implementation and practices. In M. Zaslow & I. Martinez-Beck (Eds.), *Critical issues in early childhood professional develop-ment* (pp. 231-254). Baltimore: Paul H. Brookes Publishing.

Pianta, R. C. (2006a). *Professional development interventions to support effective teaching*. Manuscript in preparation, University of Virginia, Charlottesville.

Pianta, R. (2006b). Schools, schooling, and developmental psychopathology. In D. Cicchetti & D. Cohen (Eds.), *Developmental psychopathology: Vol. 1. Theory and method* (pp. 494-529). Hoboken, NJ: John Wiley & Sons, Inc.

Pianta, R. C., Belsky, J., Houts, R., Morrison, F., & the NICHD Early Child Care Research Network. (2007). Opportunities to learn in America's classrooms. *Science, 315*, 1795-1796.

Pianta, R. C., La Paro, K. M., & Hamre, B. K. (2006). *Classroom Assessment Scoring System [CLASS]*. Unpublished measure, University of Virginia, Charlottesville.

Pianta, R. C., La Paro, K. M., Payne, C., Cox, M., & Bradley, R. (2002). The relation of kindergarten classroom environment to teacher, family, and school characteristics and child outcomes. *Elementary School Journal, 102*(3), 225-238.

Public Agenda. (1997). *Getting by: What American teenagers really think about their schools*. New York: Author.

Putnam, R., & Borko, H. (2000). What do new views of knowledge and thinking have to say about research on teacher learning? *Educational Researcher, 21*(1), 4-15.

Resnick, M. D., Bearman, P. S., Blum, R. W., Bauman, K., Harris, K. M., Jones, J., et al. (1997). Protecting adolescents from harm: Findings from the National Longitudinal Study of Adolescent Health. *Journal of the American Medical Association, 278*, 823-832.

Rhodes, S., & Hennessy, E. (2000). The effects of specialized training on caregivers and children in early-years settings: An evaluation of the foundation course in playgroup practice. *Early Childhood Research Quarterly, 15*, 559-576.

Richardson, V., & Anders, P. L. (2005). Professional preparation and development of teachers in literacy instruction for urban settings. In J. Flood & P. L. Anders (Eds.), *Literacy development of students in urban schools: Research and policy* (pp. 205-230). Newark, DE: International Reading Association.

Roeser, R. W., Eccles, J. S., & Sameroff, A. J. (1998). Academic and emotional functioning in early adolescence: Longitudinal relations, patterns, and prediction by experience in middle school. *Development & Psychopathology, 10*(2), 321-352.

Roeser, R. W., & Eccles, J. S., & Sameroff, A. J. (2000). School as a context of early adolescents' academic and social-emotional development: A summary of research findings. *The Elementary School Journal, 100*, 443-471.

Rutter, M., & Maughan, B. (2002). School effectiveness findings: 1979-2002. *Journal of School Psychology, 40*, 451-475.

Ryan, R. M., & Deci, E. L. (2000). Self-determination theory and the facilitation of intrinsic motivation, social development, and well-being. *American Psychologist, 55*(1), 68-78.

Sameroff, A. J., & Emde, R. N. (1989). *Relationship disturbances in early childhood: A developmental approach*. New York: Basic.

Sandholtz, J. H. (2002). Inservice training or professional development: Contrasting opportunities in a school/university partnership. *Teaching and Teacher Education, 18*(7), 815-830.

Sarason, S. B. (1982). *The culture of the school and the problem of change* (2nd ed.). Boston: Allyn and Bacon.

Shouse, R. C. (1996). Academic press and sense of community: Conflict, congruence, and implications for student achievement. *Social Psychology of Education, 1*(1), 47-68.

Skinner, E. A., Zimmer-Gembeck, M. J., & Connell, J. P. (1998). Individual differences and the development of perceived control. *Monographs of the Society for Research in Child Development, 63*(2-3).

Steinberg, L., Brown, B. B., & Dornbusch, S. M. (1996). *Beyond the classroom: Why school reform has failed and what parents need to do.* New York: Simon & Schuster.

Twenge, J. M., Catanese, K. R., & Baumeister, R. F. (2002). Social exclusion causes self-defeating behavior. *Journal of Personality and Social Psychology, 83*(3), 606-615.

Whitehurst, G. J. (2002). *Research on teacher preparation and professional development.* White House Conference on Preparing Tomorrow's Teachers, Washington, DC. Retrieved September 23, 2006, from www.ed.gov/adminis/tchrqual/learn/preparingteachersconference/whithurst.html

Wilson, S. M., & Berne, J. (1999). Teacher learning and the acquisition of professional knowledge: An examination of research on contemporary professional development. In A. Iran-Nejad & P. D. Pearson (Eds.), *Review of research in education* (pp. 173-209). Washington, DC: American Educational Research Association.

Chapter 3

Changing Classroom Social Settings Through Attention to Norms

DAVID B. HENRY

The school classroom is a social context that influences child development and offers opportunities for intervention (Bronfenbrenner, 1979; Tolan & Guerra, 1994). Even though classrooms are temporary behavior settings, children spend a greater proportion of their waking hours in classrooms than in any other proximal social setting. They are the context within which many preventive interventions are delivered. Less attention has been paid to changing setting characteristics of classrooms than has been paid to schools, although research in the past 25 years has shown that classroom characteristics can have substantial effects on child behavior.

Characteristics of classrooms as settings have been found to relate to friendship formation (Buysse, Goldman, & Skinner, 2002), self-regulation and control (Albion, 1983), aggression (Henry et al., 2000), and overall adjustment (Pianta, Steinberg, & Rollins, 1995). Classrooms vary substantially in setting characteristics such as norms (Henry, 2000; Henry, Cartland, Ruch-Ross, & Monahan, 2004), teacher direction, structure (Pianta, La Paro, Payne, Cox, & Bradley, 2002), and instructional and emotional climate (Jones, Brown, & Aber, this volume, chapter 4). Classroom setting characteristics are potentially important targets for intervention because classrooms are accessible for intervention, because they vary in setting-level characteristics, and because of their importance to youth development.

Social settings are held together by feedback circuits that link individual responses to environmental stimuli and environmental change to individual behavior (Barker, 1968, pp. 138-139). Individuals sense the condition of the setting, test their perceptions against mental representations of the setting's program, and act to change the setting or maintain the setting's current activity, if appropriate. Through the constant operation of these feedback circuits, settings maintain dynamic homeostasis, that is, they maintain consistency in their programs despite constant change in setting participants and their behavior.

Improving classrooms as social settings is possible through understanding and changing these feedback circuits. Barker (1968, pp. 167-185) identified four types of feedback circuits operating in behavior settings such as classrooms. *Program circuits* consist of the schedule of class activities. They reside primarily in the teacher(s), but students, once classroom programs have been established, will also carry the classroom's program. A substitute teacher who deviates from the normal class routine is likely to be admonished that, "Mr. _____ doesn't do it that way!" *Goal circuits* link the setting's program with the goals, aims, and needs of the individual students. Through them, students reap the rewards of participation in the classroom. *Veto circuits* remove students whose behavior consistently threatens the setting's program, and *deviation-countering circuits* regulate less serious disruptive behavior through the teacher's behavior management activities and student norms.

Injunctive norms, or standards of appropriate behavior, are part of each of these circuits. Norms define behavior that supports the classroom program, and discourage behavior that disrupts or is inappropriate to the classroom program. Normative influence is a dynamic process through which individuals receive feedback from the setting (and give feedback to others in the setting) regarding appropriate behavior. Such feedback may occur in multiple ways. Physical space in the classroom may be structured to direct student attention to the teacher and discourage disruptive behavior. There may be codified standards for behavior, made salient by lists of classroom rules or other visual devices. Students may provide indications that they approve of or disapprove of certain behaviors. In the absence of such injunctions, students will infer the appropriate behavior from the typical behavior of classmates. Cialdini and colleagues (Cialdini, Kallgren, & Reno, 1991; Cialdini, Reno, & Kallgren, 1990) drew a distinction between such "descriptive norms" and "injunctive norms" that define appropriate behavior.

As an example of the operation of feedback circuits in a classroom setting, consider a teacher who uses a variant of the Good Behavior Game (Embry, 2002). This teacher draws five hash marks on the board and tells the students, "I will erase one mark each time one of you disrupts the class. If there are any marks left at the end of the day, we will have an extra 15 minutes of free play." Shortly thereafter, a student throws a paper wad at another student. Without saying a word, the teacher erases a mark. The same student, a few minutes later, starts making faces at another student. The teacher removes another mark. This time, however, three other students, almost simultaneously, tell the offender to "Stop it!" After two more incidents in which students provide feedback to other students, the rest of the day passes without further disruption. One mark is left at the end of the day, and the class receives the reward.

When classroom feedback circuits are functioning well, normative influence processes keep disruptive behavior to a minimum and promote the classroom program. There are, however, several ways in which classroom feedback circuits may not function properly. There may be insufficient clarity about the classroom program. There may be insufficient opportunities for students to reap the rewards of participating in the classroom program. Teachers may not provide sufficient positive and negative behavioral feedback to students. Finally, student-to-student feedback circuits may be weak or may actually encourage behavior that runs counter to the classroom program. Much advice is available to teachers on making the classroom program more clearly evident or more rewarding for students. There are several empirically validated systems that assist teachers in improving the behavioral feedback they provide to students. This chapter introduces a method for measuring and intervening with the norms that exist among students and are enforced through student-to-student feedback circuits. The following details a theory of change, a method for measuring classroom norms, and an intervention model, each with reference to current and past literature.

A Theory of Change for Classrooms as Social Settings

Nearly a century ago, Thomas (1917) noted the resistance of norms to change: "Human behavior norms are not only very arbitrary, but also are so highly emotionalized that they claim to be absolutely right and final and subject to no change and no investigation." In the midst of constant activity, norms help settings maintain a steady state, and resist change. Understanding how norms maintain a steady state in the midst of the constant activity of social settings provides a clue to how norms and settings may be changed. As is the case with other systems such as families (Bowen, 1978, p. 260) and organizations (Katz & Kahn, 1978, pp. 675-679), change requires understanding and altering the feedback circuits of the setting (Barker, 1968, p. 163).

Classroom social settings may be changed by providing feedback that either establishes injunctive norms where they are lacking or makes existing injunctive norms salient. Injunctive norms in settings promote behavior change because people define their ideal selves, at least partly, by the groups with which they identify (Tajfel, 1978; Tajfel & Turner, 1979). Discrepancy between one's own behavior and the injunctive norms of such reference groups is anxiety-provoking, leading people to adjust their behavior to be consistent with the perceived norms.

The term, "feedback," as it is used here, refers both to efforts to establish injunctive norms for behavior in classrooms and to normative feedback used to make injunctive norms salient. Because norms, like other aspects of a social setting, are dynamic in nature, these two approaches to change are interrelated. The establishment of injunctive norms will change the typical behavior (descriptive norms) of the classroom. When the descriptive norms change, the legitimacy of the injunctive norms is strengthened.

Measurement of norms is an important component of normative feedback interventions. Descriptive norms may be measured with assessments of the target behavior (cf., Henry et al., 2000), but measures of injunctive norms must assess desirable behavior. Two other aspects of norms are also important to assess. These are norm salience and the discrepancy between actual and perceived injunctive norms. Measures of norm salience can assist in structuring normative feedback interventions, and measures of discrepancy provide guidance for choosing specific behaviors to target.

Katz and Kahn (1978, p. 386) offered three necessary criteria for inferring the existence of a system injunctive norm.

1. There must be beliefs about appropriate and required behavior for group members as group members.
2. There must be objective or statistical commonality of such beliefs.
3. There must be an awareness by individuals that there is group support for a given belief.

Each of these aspects provides an opportunity for establishing or changing norms. Students and teachers are instrumental in establishing norms for behavior, and both are important in the effects of norms on behavior (Henry et al., 2000), but because student actions tend toward reinforcing existing norms, teachers are most likely to be agents of change in, and establishment of, norms.

Teachers may establish injunctive norms by making explicit their expectations for behavior early in the life of the classroom as setting. Norms for behavior are established very early in the life of any group (cf., Yalom, 1995, p. 111), particularly in unfamiliar anxiety-provoking situations (Schachter, 1959). Because classrooms as social settings come into existence at the beginning of the school year, it is likely that norms for behavior are established very quickly, perhaps within the first few hours of the classroom's existence.

Teachers may increase objective commonality of norms by providing regular behavioral feedback to students. VanAcker, Grant, and Henry (1996) found that teachers seldom provide behavioral feedback, and most behavioral feedback takes the form of reprimand. Students express group support for a norm by overt and covert indications of approval or disapproval for certain behaviors. In one classroom, a child who hits another is rewarded by the laughter of other students. In another, the same action is met by icy stares or a chorus of reprimand from other students.

Classroom social settings also may be improved if injunctive norms are made salient to individuals. Individuals tend to overestimate group normative support for risk behaviors. In the literature, this tendency has been attributed to "pluralistic ignorance" (Cohen & Shotland, 1996) or "self-serving bias" (Harrison & Shaffer, 1994). Efforts to change college drinking norms have found that overestimation of norms is related to drinking behavior, particularly among high risk drinkers, and overestimation appears in a variety of contexts (Neighbors, Oster-Aaland, Bergstrom & Lewis, 2006). In a recent study, Henry, Meyer, Schoeny, Martin, and The Multisite Violence Prevention Project (2006) found a similar effect for sixth graders on aggression. Students in 12 urban schools consistently overestimated peer support for aggression, and underestimated peer support for nonviolent problem solving. Incorrect estimation of norms for aggression involved both overestimation of approval of aggression and underestimation of disapproval of aggression. The opposite effect was seen for norms regarding nonviolent problem solving; youth overestimated disapproval and underestimated approval.

All aspects of incorrect estimation provide opportunities for intervention through normative feedback. Efforts to change other risk behaviors such as binge drinking, gambling, and condom use among college students have employed poster campaigns, brochures, and personal computer-delivered feedback. The following describes a hypothetical normative intervention model for classrooms. In the classroom setting, the teacher is best equipped to deliver normative feedback interventions. Preparation and delivery of such interventions would involve five steps as follows:

1. In consultation with the teacher, choose behavioral dimensions to assess and target (e.g., class disruption, responses to teacher requests, assignment completion). Identify specific behaviors that lie on each dimension and occur with sufficient frequency in the classroom to make them important intervention targets. Identify contrasting behaviors so that each dimension includes positive alternatives to negative behaviors and vice versa.

2. Assess actual and perceived injunctive norms for specific behaviors on the dimension. Construct assessments to include the full range of positive and negative behaviors on each target dimension.

3. Use the results of the assessment to identify specific behaviors for intervention. Choose behaviors about which there is substantial classroom-level discrepancy between individual normative beliefs and perceived classroom norms. Examine variance of approval among students in the classroom. Ideal intervention targets will be behaviors about which there is high variance in individual normative beliefs.

4. Choose whether to focus the intervention on approval or disapproval of the behaviors. Henry et al. (2006) found that incorrect estimation of norms involved both processes. We describe in the following section a method for measuring the manner in which the class characteristically sanctions a potential target behavior. If the classroom characteristically sanctions behavior through disapproval, focus initially on student approval of contrasting behaviors.

5. Create a format or follow an existing format for delivering feedback. An example of such a format might be a regular class discussion called, "What you think." Based on the steps above, the teacher would begin by giving class-wide normative feedback by saying, "When we asked you what you thought other students would think about a student who hit another student who hadn't done anything first, ## out of ## of you said you thought other students would like it. But when we asked you what you really thought, you said. ..." Opportunity for class discussion included in such sessions would increase the salience of injunctive norms. Additionally, personal normative feedback could be provided to each student with a simple age-appropriate handout comparing the student's responses with class averages.

This intervention model needs to be refined through future research. The devices to facilitate assessment and intervention creation and delivery are being planned. Such devices include software to create assessments that can be entered via hand, scannable form, or computerized administration. This software would score the measures, calculate all characteristics of norms and discrepancy information for the class, and output this information in a form that is useful in the teacher's creation of feedback and in providing personalized normative feedback to students.

This intervention model depends upon a method for measurement that can assess features of classroom injunctive norms in a manner appropriate for developing interventions, and assess the discrepancy between individual normative beliefs and perceived classroom norms. The next section describes this measurement strategy in detail.

Measuring Classroom Norms

Setting norms are often assessed by taking the mean of individual beliefs or behaviors (Allison et al., 1999; Henry et al., 2000). However, this approach carries a fundamental limitation of estimating features of settings (such as normative processes) from the average of individual measures (Shinn, 1990). Such an approach does not organize individual data to represent the processes by which a social setting regulates behavior. The return potential model overcomes many of these limitations.

The return potential model offers a method for measuring norms grounded in longstanding definitions of injunctive norms as the potential approval or disapproval for a range of behaviors (e.g., March, 1954). Based on March's (1954) definition of norms as distributions of approval or disapproval for a range of behaviors, Jackson (1966) developed a method for measuring the association between behavior and approval in a social setting. This model can be used to quantify actual injunctive norms (based on what setting participants think) as well as perceived norms (based on what participants believe others think) in social settings.

Among the aspects of norms that can be measured are the distribution of approval and disapproval for different levels of behavior, the optimal level of behavior in a setting, the degree to which there is agreement among participants as to the norm, the potential loss or gain in approval likely to follow a change in behavior, and whether the setting enforces norms primarily through approval or disapproval.

Figure 3.1 presents this model as it applies to aggression, and indicates various measures that can be derived.

Two orthogonal dimensions form the basis of the model: one for the average degree of approval across all students in the classroom (shown on the y-axis), and the other for the degree of behavior (shown on the x-axis). In Figure 3.1, each bar represents an item measuring a different aggressive behavior.

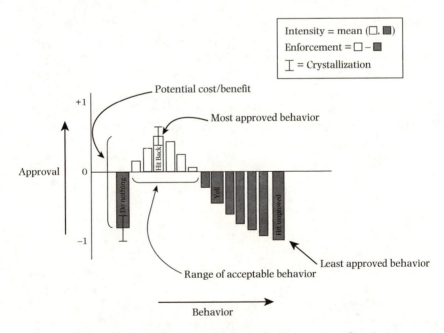

Figure 3.1. Theoretical Return Potential Curve for Aggression, Showing Derivation of Measures.

Developing a return potential measure is aided by expressing the behavior along a single dimension from the least to the greatest degrees. The model assumes that any relation between the degree of approval and the degree of behavior is due to the norm; thus, expressing the behavior along a dimension must be done independently of measures of approval.

Some behaviors lend themselves to being expressed on a dimension. For example, Hammitt and Rutlin (1995) assessed approval for increasing numbers of encounters with others in wilderness areas. Similarly, Sasaki (1979) assessed approval for different numbers of days absent among workers in Japanese factories. Other studies have relied on the wording of questions to express a degree of behavior that is not directly quantified. In studying norms for authoritarianism in organizations, Jackson (1966) constructed 59 situations, each of which had six possible responses, ranging from democratic to authoritarian leadership. Using a similar measure to study cross-cultural variation in norms for leadership behavior, Torres (1999) used expert judges to position leadership behaviors along a single dimension.

Organizing behaviors along a dimension may be difficult if discrete behaviors are believed to vary on more than one underlying or latent dimensions. This is the case with aggression, for which the underlying aggressiveness of an action may vary substantially with context, the age of the participants, intonation, and other variables. For example, threatening someone may represent greater underlying aggression than yelling among adolescents, but the reverse may be true among first graders. In such cases, it may be possible to use expert judges, as did Torres (1999) and Henry et al. (2004), to locate different behaviors along a single dimension. Yet, even if behaviors cannot be reliably located on a dimension, most aspects of the return potential model can be reliably and usefully calculated.

The second element of a return potential measure is a way to measure the approval and disapproval of each behavior on the dimension. Jackson (1966) used a 9-point semantic differential scale for rating approval, whereas others (Santee & Jackson, 1977; Torres, 1999) have used 21-point scales. Likert-type scales with large numbers of anchors may not be as understandable to younger children as they are to adults. For this reason, Henry et al. (2004) used a 3-point scale, anchored by "would like it," wouldn't care," and "would not like it," with young children.

If the behavior and approval dimensions are incorporated in a single measure, several aspects of the norms of each classroom setting can be calculated. These are shown in Figure 3.1. The most- and least-approved behaviors are the behaviors associated with the greatest and least approval in the setting. If the behavior can be reliably organized along a single dimension, the meaning of these terms can be quantified. When the behaviors under study are difficult to place on a single dimension, identifying the specific behavior that has the greatest or least approval in the setting may still be useful in planning intervention.

The range of acceptable behavior describes the specificity of the norm. A wide range of acceptable behavior would indicate toleration for considerable variance in behaviors, whereas a narrow range of acceptable behavior would indicate little tolerance for variation from a specific behavioral pattern. Because aggression is a behavior with low acceptance in most classrooms and schools, the range of acceptable behavior for aggression may be zero in many classrooms and schools. When it is difficult to organize the behaviors on a single dimension, the range of acceptable behavior may be expressed as a count of the number of discrete behaviors receiving approval in the setting.

Intensity is an index of how strongly individuals in a social system feel about the norm, and thus the strength of the norm. It is independent of the positive or negative valence of normative expectations. By this definition, strong positive and negative norms might have equal intensity. Intensity is calculated by taking the mean, within individuals, of the absolute values of the approval and disapproval values for all behaviors, and then taking the mean of the resulting values across all class members. Henry et al. (2004) found that greater intensity was associated with lower aggression in 158 classrooms in urban, rural, and suburban schools. The ability to express behaviors on a single dimension does not affect the calculation of intensity.

Enforcement combines two elements of intensity to express whether a social setting generally enforces norms through approval or disapproval. It is the difference between positive and negative intensity. A positive value indicates that the setting enforces norms primarily through approval, and a negative value indicates that a setting enforces norms primarily through disapproval. Henry et al. (2004) found that classrooms enforce norms for aggression primarily through disapproval. Like intensity itself, the calculation and utility of the potential return difference are not affected by whether the behavior can be expressed on a single dimension.

The potential cost or benefit of behavior change is the distance between the greatest and least degrees of approval over all behaviors being studied. Children in classrooms with a high potential cost/benefit would experience a noticeable decrease in approval from their classmates if they violated the norm, whereas children in classrooms with a small potential cost/benefit might not notice any decrease in their classmates' approval if they violated a norm. Henry et al. (2004) found that greater potential cost/benefit was associated with lower aggression, and Henry (2007) found that greater potential cost/benefit was associated with decreasing aggression over time.

Crystallization assesses the degree of consensus about a norm. It is shown in Figure 3.1 by the error bars on two of the bars representing behaviors. However, it is calculated using the average variance around all of the behaviors on the dimension. Greater crystallization (lower variance) was associated with lower aggression in the Henry et al. (2004) cross-sectional study and with longitudinal reductions in aggression in the Henry et al. (2006)

study. Calculation of crystallization is not affected by the ability to express the behavior along a single dimension.

Research thus far permits some hypotheses about the uses of this measurement strategy for normative feedback interventions. First of all, assessment of classroom norms should contain desirable as well as undesirable behaviors, and should query the individual's normative beliefs and beliefs about the norms of classmates. These things were done in the Multisite Violence Prevention Project, and they produced evidence that middle-school students overestimate peer approval of aggression and underestimate peer approval of positive problem-solving strategies (Henry et al., 2006). Second, several return potential characteristics can provide guidance for creating normative feedback interventions. Enforcement can guide the type of feedback that is delivered. If classrooms enforce norms with disapproval to a greater extent than approval, feedback might begin by stressing the degree of approval for desirable behaviors rather than the degree of disapproval for undesirable behavior. As was noted earlier, incorrect estimation of norms for aggression involves overestimation of approval and underestimation of disapproval; thus, intervention around either would be possible. Research will be needed to determine the effects of approval versus disapproval feedback under different conditions of enforcement. The potential cost/benefit provides an index of the possible success of normative feedback. The degree of approval found for each behavior can help diagnose the normative climate of settings for planning normative feedback. Behaviors that are, or are close to, the most- or least-approved behaviors may not be desirable targets for feedback interventions. Rather, beginning with behaviors about which there is some ambiguity in the classroom may increase the likelihood of support for behavior change. Along this line, the degree of variance among individuals in approval of specific behaviors can also help assess the likelihood that normative feedback will effect change. Behaviors with high variance among individuals may be most apt to respond to normative feedback or to attempts at the establishment of norms because there is little commonality of belief about appropriate behavior. Low variance of normative beliefs is the characteristic of setting norms that has led investigators for nearly a century to note their resistance to change (Roethlisberger & Dickson, 1939; Rohrer, Baron, Hoffman, & Swander, 1954; Thomas, 1917).

Finally, the discrepancy between individual and perceived classroom injunctive norms can provide guidance as to the most appropriate content for feedback sessions. An initial hypothesis is that behaviors about which there is greater discrepancy between aggregated individual normative beliefs (actual norms) and aggregated perceptions of classroom norms would be the most fruitful targets for intervention. This follows from the notion that motivation for change in normative feedback interventions stems from discrepancy between real and ideal selves, and as ideal selves derive from reference groups, discrepancy between perceived classroom norms and individual normative beliefs should motivate change through intervention.

When applied to aggression, the return potential method of measuring norms has limitations and countervailing advantages compared to other methods, such as taking the mean of normative beliefs items (cf., Henry et al., 2000). Among the possible limitations of the return potential method is social desirability bias. Aggression is generally negatively sanctioned in society and in schools, and children may respond to questions about approval in ways they believe to be socially desirable. Henry et al. (2006) tested the social desirability hypothesis by comparing the discrepancy between individual and perceived norms for behaviors with different levels of provocation. They found that, although the discrepancy was reduced in more socially desirable behaviors (such as retaliation for equal provocation), it was still sizeable. From the standpoint of intervention, social desirability bias might even tend to work in favor of intervention effectiveness, as it would tend to exaggerate the discrepancy between individual beliefs and perceived peer norms.

A second possible limitation to the return potential method is the difficulty of expressing aggressive behaviors along a single dimension, relative to other behaviors, such as tardiness or absenteeism. As has been seen, even if behaviors cannot be reliably expressed on a single dimension, return potential characteristics can be useful.

Exemplars of Normative Feedback Interventions

Research on normative feedback interventions provides evidence for their effectiveness in changing a variety of behaviors. Research also identifies some important strengths and limitations that should be considered when adapting these interventions for use in school classrooms. The vast majority of normative feedback studies have been conducted with participants of at least college age. Many studies have combined normative feedback with other interventions, and some have compared the effects of normative feedback to these interventions or as an adjunct to other interventions.

Borsari and Carey (2000), for example, tested a brief intervention combining information with feedback on personal drinking and perceived drinking norms on a sample of students who had exhibited high-risk drinking in preceding weeks. They found positive effects of the intervention on alcohol consumption and binge drinking as well as on mediating variables such as perceived drinking norms and perceived effects of drinking. Other studies have compared the effects of other interventions with those of normative feedback (e.g., Neal & Carey, 2004). Larimer et al. (2001) randomly assigned fraternity houses to receive either a didactic presentation regarding alcohol use, or the same didactic presentation plus a normative feedback intervention using college-wide and house drinking norms. They found that the intervention with normative feedback was associated with significant reduction in alcohol consumption compared to the didactic presentation condition alone.

Two studies used other methods for presentation of the intervention. Collins, Carey, and Sliwinski (2002) mailed personalized normative feedback to high-risk college drinkers. At 6 weeks post-intervention, they found significant differences in measures of discrepancy and alcohol consumption, but these differences did not maintain until the 6-month follow-up assessment. Another randomized trial (Neighbors, Larimer, & Lewis, 2004) evaluated a computer-delivered personalized normative feedback intervention with heavy-drinking students. The treatment involved receiving information, via computer, on their own drinking behavior, their perceptions of typical student drinking, and actual typical student drinking. Those assigned to the intervention showed decreases in a composite index of alcohol consumption at both 3- and 6-month intervals.

Cunningham, Wild, Bondy, and Lin (2001) demonstrated the utility of normative feedback in a community setting. Six thousand households in a Toronto neighborhood received, by mail, an intervention pamphlet encouraging the reader to record his/her own drinking for a week, and providing charts for comparing the reader's drinking patterns with gender-specific national norms. Comparison with randomly assigned control households showed intervention-related reductions in alcohol consumption among high-risk drinkers and elevations in consumption among low-risk drinkers.

Normative feedback interventions have been applied to other behaviors and in other settings. Takushi et al. (2004) piloted an application of a normative feedback intervention to college student gambling, finding a reduction in gambling, and a reduction in gambling with alcohol consumption. Chernoff and Davison (2005) found that men randomly assigned to receive normative feedback on sexual behavior increased condom use and women decreased the number of sexual partners, relative to controls.

Other studies have applied normative feedback to desirable or neutral behaviors. Schultz (1999) assigned 605 single-family households to five interventions to increase participation in curbside recycling, and then observed recycling over a period of 4 weeks. The two conditions that added personal and neighborhood normative feedback to pleas and information showed significant increases in participation, but interventions involving pleas and information alone did not differ from controls.

Gaudine and Saks (2001) tested the effects of normative feedback on employee absenteeism with a sample of Canadian hospital workers. Feedback on individual absenteeism and descriptive norms of absenteeism was given in the form of letters that presented the information and reminded employees that the hospital did not wish employees to attend when ill. They found that absenteeism was reduced significantly in the experimental group and was not reduced in the control group. The effects were stronger among those with high levels of absenteeism than among those with average or below average absenteeism.

The effects of normative feedback interventions for college student drinking compare very favorably to those of other interventions for alcohol and general substance use. In a meta-analysis of 47 high-quality evaluations of substance use prevention programs classified as involving comprehensive life skills training (e.g., Botvin, Baker, Botvin, Filazzola, & Millman, 1984; Botvin, Baker, Dusenbury, Tortu, & Botvin, 1990), Tobler et al. (1999) found a mean effect size of -0.17 (99% CI $= -0.22$ to -0.07), indicating a significant reduction in substance use. This same meta-analysis, considering 23 high-quality evaluations of alcohol prevention programs that involved interaction with participants, found a mean effect size of -0.14 (99% CI $= -0.20$ to -0.08), indicating reduction in consumption of alcohol.

Determining the effect sizes of six studies of normative feedback interventions for alcohol use allowed comparison with the effects of the other types of interventions represented in the Tobler et al. (1999) meta-analysis. Studies were considered if they were published since 2000, reported effects on alcohol consumption (no studies reported normative feedback intervention for other drug use), as opposed to beliefs about alcohol, intentions, or indices of alcohol problems. Meta-analytic combination of the effect sizes for measures of alcohol consumption using a random effects model returned a mean effect size of -0.18 (99% CI $= -0.33$ to -0.03), indicating, overall, a significant average reduction in alcohol consumption. As is noted above, some effect sizes represent effects of normative feedback in excess of, or combined with, those of other interventions. This meta-analytic combination of published studies probably overestimates the actual effect size that would be found if unpublished "file drawer" studies were included. Nevertheless, it suggests a consistent pattern of effects in a desirable direction for these interventions.

Would such effects be found if normative feedback interventions were implemented with children and youth? Would they be as effective for positive behaviors as they are for risk behaviors? This research has revealed some important boundary conditions and issues to consider in translating such interventions for use with behaviors such as aggression in school classrooms. The first is that normative feedback interventions tend to be more effective with persons already displaying risk behavior than in preventing the emergence of risk (Grabosky, 1996; Lintonen & Konu, 2004). This is true in the case of normative feedback interventions for risk behaviors, but it is not known if such mixed effects would be obtained for other behaviors. Schultz's (1999) recycling intervention did not find that the intervention decreased recycling significantly among those who were high recyclers at baseline.

Second, normative feedback interventions may be more successful if the reference group is geographically and demographically close to the individual (Cunningham et al., 2001; Lewis & Neighbors, 2004). For example, Thombs,

Ray-Tomasek, Osborn, and Olds (2005) found, in a study of college student drinking, that distal "typical student" norms had no relation to drinking behavior, but close friend norms were strong predictors. There is some evidence that same-sex norms have stronger effects than opposite-sex norms (Korcuska & Thombs, 2003) but Thombs et al. (2005) found that opposite-sex norms predicted drinking behavior beyond that predicted by same-sex norms. Classroom norms are likely to have stronger effects than school norms or national norms, and delivery of feedback by same-sex classmates or teachers may be more effective than feedback delivered by administrators, counselors, or outside interventionists.

Third, the decay in effects found in some of the studies reviewed (e.g., Collins et al., 2002) suggests that, to be effective over the long term, normative feedback should be delivered on more than a single occasion. The relative ease of construction and implementation, the potential for integration with the classroom setting program, and the potential cost-effectiveness of these interventions make it possible to implement them on more than a "one shot" basis. Research will be necessary to determine the optimal interval between feedback sessions, and whether regular or random spacing is best.

Conclusions and Future Directions

Normative feedback interventions may be useful for a variety of desirable and undesirable behaviors. Basically, any behavior about which students are likely to have opinions is a candidate for this type of intervention. This chapter has argued that the idea of norms is shorthand for a dynamic process, which can be changed through measurement and feedback. It has offered a method for measuring injunctive norms, and a model for intervention. It has provided examples of normative feedback interventions and assessed the effects of existing normative feedback studies in comparison to other types of interventions. Finally, it has drawn cautions and guidelines for adapting normative feedback interventions to classrooms and with children from previous research.

Current research on normative influences in aggression suggests that aggressive behavior is one potentially fruitful target of normative feedback interventions. By extension from aggression, behaviors that are disruptive but not aggressive such as interrupting others or outbursts in class can also be used to form these types of interventions. Other potential targets are positive behaviors related to academic achievement such as responding to teacher requests, completing assignments, and helping others. Research on normative feedback interventions suggests their utility with desirable as well as undesirable behaviors.

Research also suggests that normative feedback interventions may be effective if implemented as an adjunct to social cognitive or other types of interventions. In the case of aggression, such interventions teach children techniques for dealing with potentially violent situations, but do not necessarily increase motivation for using such techniques. Normative feedback interventions aim specifically at changing motivation, as they target discrepancies that induce behavioral change. The scope and importance of the problem of youth violence in this society makes it important to investigate the potential of these methods.

At this juncture, the notion that normative feedback interventions can be adapted for children to address problems such as aggression and disinvestment in education awaits confirmation through randomized trials. Methods for practical application of these interventions in classrooms need to be developed and tested. Future research can also refine the measures and methods of administration, the ways in which such interventions are derived from measures, and the frequency of intervention delivery. Research thus far into normative influences among school children and effectiveness of normative feedback interventions among adults suggests the promise of this approach, and the desirability of further investigation.

References

Albion, F. M. (1983). A methodological analysis of self-control in applied settings. *Behavioral Disorders, 8,* 87-102.

Allison, K. W., Crawford, I., Leone, P. E., Trickett, E., Perez-Febles, A., Burton, L. M., et al. (1999). Adolescent substance use: Preliminary examinations of school and neighborhood context. *American Journal of Community Psychology, 27,* 111-140.

Barker, R. G. (1968). *Ecological psychology: Concepts and methods for studying the environment of human behavior.* Stanford, CA: Stanford University Press.

Borsari, B., & Carey, K. B. (2000). Effects of a brief motivational intervention with college student drinkers. *Journal of Consulting and Clinical Psychology, 68,* 728-733.

Botvin, G., Baker, E., Botvin, E., Filazzola, A., & Millman, M. (1984). Prevention of alcohol misuse through the development of personal and social competence: A pilot study. *Journal of Studies on Alcohol, 45,* 550-552.

Botvin, G., Baker, E., Dusenbury, L., Tortu, S., & Botvin, E. (1990). Preventing adolescent drug abuse through a multimodal cognitive-behavioral approach: Results of a 3-year study. *Journal of Consulting and Clinical Psychology, 58,* 437-446.

Bowen, M. (1978). *Family therapy in clinical practice.* Northvale, NJ: Jason Aronson.

Bronfenbrenner, U. (1979). Contexts of child rearing: Problems and prospects. *American Psychologist, 34,* 844-850.

Buysse, V., Goldman, B. D., & Skinner, M. L. (2002). Setting effects on friendship formation among young children with and without disabilities. *Exceptional Children, 68,* 503-517.

Chernoff, R. A., & Davison, G. C. (2005). An evaluation of a brief HIV/AIDS prevention intervention for college students using normative feedback and goal setting. *AIDS Education and Prevention, 17,* 91-104.

Cialdini, R. B., Kallgren, C. A., & Reno, R. R. (1991). A focus theory of normative conduct. *Advances in Experimental Social Psychology, 24*, 201-234.

Cialdini, R. B., Reno, R. R., & Kallgren, C. A. (1990). A focus theory of normative conduct: Recycling the concept of norms to reduce littering in public places. *Journal of Personality and Social Psychology, 58*, 1015-1026.

Cohen, L. L., & Shotland, R. L. (1996). Timing of first sexual intercourse in a relationship: Expectations, experiences, and perceptions of others. *Journal of Sex Research, 33*, 291-299.

Collins, S. E., Carey, K. B., & Sliwinski, M. J. (2002). Mailed personalized normative feedback as a brief intervention for at-risk college drinkers. *Journal of Studies on Alcohol, 63*, 559-567.

Cunningham, J. T., Wild, T. C., Bondy, S. J., & Lin, E. (2001). Impact of normative feedback on problem drinkers: A small area population study. *Journal of Studies on Alcohol, 62*, 228-233.

Embry, D. D. (2002). The good behavior game: A best practice candidate as a universal behavioral vaccine. *Clinical Child and Family Psychology Review, 5*, 273-297.

Gaudine, A. P., & Saks, A. M. (2001). Effects of an absenteeism feedback intervention on employee absence behavior. *Journal of Organizational Behavior, 22*, 15-29.

Grabosky, P. N. (1996). Unintended consequences of crime prevention. In Homel & Clarke (Eds.), *Crime prevention studies* (Vol. 5). New York: Criminal Justice Press.

Hammitt, W. E., & Rutlin, W. M. (1995). Use encounter standards and curves for achieved privacy in wilderness. *Leisure Sciences, 17*, 245-262.

Harrison, D., & Shaffer, M. (1994). Comparative examinations of self-reports and perceived absenteeism norms: Wading through Lake Wobegon. *Journal of Applied Psychology, 79*, 240-251.

Henry, D., Cartland, J., Ruch-Ross, H., & Monahan, K. (2004). A return potential model of setting norms for aggression. *American Journal of Community Psychology, 33*, 131-149.

Henry, D., Guerra, N. G., Huesmann, L. R., Tolan, P. H., VanAcker, R., & Eron, L. D. (2000). Normative influences on aggression in urban elementary school classrooms. *American Journal of Community Psychology, 28*, 59-81.

Henry, D., Meyer, A., Schoeny, M. E., Martin, N., & The Multisite Violence Prevention Project. (2006). *Pluralistic ignorance of school norms for aggression and non-violent alternatives to aggression.* Paper presented at the Annual Meeting of the Society for Prevention Research, San Antonio, TX.

Henry, D. B. (2007, June 10). *Changing classroom social settings through attention to norms (Symposium S-11462: "Transforming Settings: Toward Positive Youth Development").* Paper presented at the Bienniel Meeting of the Society for Community Research and Action, Pasadena, CA.

Jackson, J. (1966). A conceptual and measurement model for norms and roles. *Pacific Sociological Review, 9*, 35-47.

Jones, S. M., Brown, J. L., & Aber, J. L. (this volume). Classroom settings as targets of intervention research.

Katz, R., & Kahn, D. (1978). *The social psychology of organizations.* New York: Wiley.

Korcuska, J. L., & Thombs, D. L. (2003). Gender role conflict and sex-specific drinking norms: Relationships to alcohol use in undergraduate women and men. *Journal of College Student Development, 44*, 204-216.

Larimer, M. E., Turner, A. P., Anderson, B. K., Fader, J. S., Kilmer, J. R., Palmer, R. S., et al. (2001). Evaluating a brief intervention with fraternities. *Journal of Studies on Alcohol, 62*, 370-380.

Lewis, M. A., & Neighbors, C. (2004). Gender-specific misperceptions of college student drinking norms. *Psychology of Addictive Behaviors, 18*, 334-339.

Lintonen, T. P., & Konu, A. I. (2004). The misperceived social norm of drunkenness among early adolescents in Finland. *Health Education Research, 19*, 64-70.

March, J. G. (1954). Group norms and the active minority. *American Sociological Review, 19*, 733-741.

Neal, D. J., & Carey, K. B. (2004). Developing discrepancy within self-regulation theory: Use of personalized normative feedback and personal strivings with heavy-drinking college students. *Addictive Behaviors, 29*, 281-297.

Neighbors, C., Larimer, M. E., & Lewis, M. A. (2004). Targeting misperceptions of descriptive drinking norms: Efficacy of a computer-delivered personalized normative feedback intervention. *Journal of Consulting and Clinical Psychology, 72*, 434-447.

Neighbors, C., Oster-Aaland, L., Bergstrom, R., & Lewis, M. A. (2006). Event- and context-specific normative misperceptions and high-risk drinking: 21st birthday celebrations and football tailgating. *Journal of Studies on Alcohol, 67*, 282-289.

Pianta, R. C., La Paro, K. M., Payne, C., Cox, M. J., & Bradley, R. (2002). The relation of kindergarten classroom environment to teacher, family, and school characteristics and child outcomes. *Elementary School Journal, 102*, 225-238.

Pianta, R. C., Steinberg, M. S., & Rollins, K. B. (1995). The first two years of school: Teacher-child relationships and deflections in children's classroom adjustment. *Development and Psychopathology, 7*, 295-312.

Roethlisberger, F. J., & Dickson, W. J. (1939). *Management and the worker.* Cambridge, MA: Harvard University Press.

Rohrer, J. H., Baron, S. H., Hoffman, E. L., & Swander, D. V. (1954). The stability of autokinetic judgment. *Journal of Abnormal and Social Psychology, 49*, 495-497.

Santee, R. T., & Jackson, J. (1977). Cultural values as a source of normative sanctions. *Pacific Sociological Review, 20*, 439-454.

Sasaki, K. (1979). Present status of research on group norms in Japan. *American Journal of Community Psychology, 7*, 147-158.

Schachter, S. (1959). *The psychology of affiliation.* Stanford, CA: Stanford University Press.

Schultz, P. W. (1999). Changing behavior with normative feedback interventions: A field experiment on curbside recycling. *Basic and Applied Social Psychology, 2*, 25-36.

Shinn, M. (1990). Mixing and matching: Levels of conceptualization, measurement, and statistical analysis in community psychology. In P. H. Tolan, C. B. Keys, F. Chertok, & L. Jason (Eds.), *Researching community psychology: Issues of theory and methods* (pp. 111-126). Washington, DC: American Psychological Association.

Tajfel, H. (Ed.). (1978). *Differentiation between social groups: Studies in the social psychology of intergroup relations*. London: Academic Press.

Tajfel, H., & Turner, J. C. (1979). An integrative theory of intergroup conflict. In W. G. Austin & S. Worchel (Eds.), *The social psychology of intergroup relations* (pp. 33-47). Monterey, CA: Brooks/Cole Publishing Company.

Takushi, R. Y., Neighbors, C., Larimer, M. E., Lostutter, T. W., Cronce, J. M., & Marlatt, G. A. (2004). Indicated prevention of problem gambling among college students. *Journal of Gambling Studies, 20*, 83-93.

Thomas, W. (1917). The persistence of primary-group norms in present-day society and their influence in our educational system. In H. S. Jennings, J. B. Watson, A. Meyer, & W. Thomas (Eds.), *Suggestions of modern science concerning education* (pp. 157-197). New York: MacMillan Co.

Thombs, D. L., Ray-Tomasek, J., Osborn, C. J., & Olds, R. S. (2005). The role of sex-specific normative beliefs in undergraduate alcohol use. *American Journal of Health Behavior, 29*, 342-351.

Tobler, N. S., Roona, M. R., Ochshorn, P., Marshall, D. G., Streke, A. V., & Stackpole, K. M. (1999). School-based adolescent drug prevention programs: 1998 Meta-analysis. *The Journal of Primary Prevention, 20*, 275-335.

Tolan, P. H., & Guerra, N. G. (1994). Prevention of delinquency: Current status and issues. *Applied & Preventive Psychology, 3*, 251-273.

Torres, C. V. (1999). *Leadership style norms among Americans and Brazilians: Assessing differences using Jackson's Return Potential Model*. Doctoral dissertation, California School of Professional Psychology, San Diego, CA.

VanAcker, R., Grant, S. G., & Henry, D. (1996). Teacher and student behavior as a function of risk for aggression. *Education and Treatment of Children, 19*, 316-334.

Yalom, I. D. (1995). *The theory and practice of group psychotherapy* (4th ed.). New York: Harper Collins.

Chapter 4

Classroom Settings as Targets of Intervention and Research

STEPHANIE M. JONES, JOSHUA L. BROWN, AND J. LAWRENCE ABER

This chapter focuses on the classroom context as a primary setting for positive youth development. We describe a school-wide intervention in social-emotional learning and literacy development whose theory of change begins with the professional development of teachers to strengthen their ability to create classroom communities characterized by mutual respect among and between students and teachers and active problem-solving skills. The chapter begins with a discussion of the theory of change of two theoretically and practically linked programs, the Resolving Conflict Creatively Program (RCCP) and its most recent incarnation in the New York City (NYC) public school system, the Reading, Writing, Respect, and Resolution (4Rs) Program. We follow this discussion with a description of our theory of the classroom setting as a dynamic system of interconnected elements related to positive youth development. We then describe how the theory of change of the RCCP and 4Rs Program targets the primary domains in our conceptualization of the classroom system. Finally, we provide an illustration from our current research of how we have operationalized and measured one or two features of each domain of our model of the classroom system.

Theory of Setting-Level Change: Classroom Settings as a Target of RCCP and 4Rs

The RCCP and 4Rs Program, both developed by the Morningside Center for Teaching Social Responsibility (formerly named Educators for Social Responsibility Metropolitan Area), are fundamentally similar in their focus on conflict resolution and intergroup understanding. Both programs aim to promote caring classroom communities marked by consistent and positive rules and norms, a safe and secure environment for diversity, and respect for student ideas and autonomy. Specific goals include fostering warm and supportive classroom environments that promote the positive growth of both teachers and students, providing teachers with effective tools for managing classroom environments and their own experiences of stress in the classroom, building positive teacher-student relationships, and helping students develop key conflict resolution and social-emotional learning concepts and skills.

Both programs have two primary components: (a) a comprehensive lesson-based curriculum in conflict resolution and social-emotional learning and (b) training and ongoing coaching of teachers to support them in teaching the curriculum. The program's theory of change emphasizes the role of introducing teachers to a set of social-emotional learning skills and concepts and then supporting them in the use of these skills and concepts in their everyday interactions in the school with each other, with school administrators, and with the children in their classrooms. To support their focus on teachers and classrooms as levers for change in schools, training is also provided to school administrators and other school staff in the same concepts and in how to support the integration of the program into the daily life of the school.

The intensive professional development activities provided to teachers to support their use of the curriculum consist of 5 days of training in conjunction with ongoing classroom coaching by trained program staff developers. Teacher training emphasizes both individual and collective learning and support for sustained program implementation. Thus, teachers are trained in large groups and in individual sessions; they receive individually tailored ongoing support but also work in within- and cross-grade groups to coordinate and align curriculum implementation, share experiences and complementary activities, and plan as a cohesive unit. The introductory training is designed (a) to introduce the teachers to the curricular units and the specific lessons and activities tied to each unit, (b) to give them an opportunity to practice conflict resolution skills at the adult level through role play and experiential learning, and (c) to inspire them to employ the ideas and skills embodied in the curriculum in their own lives both professionally and personally.

Ongoing classroom coaching encompasses modeling of class lessons and workshops led by program staff developers, co-planning and teaching of lessons by the teacher and staff developer, and finally, lesson observations and feedback. In addition, staff developers convene regular conferences with teachers either in a one-on-one format or with a group of teachers from one or multiple grades.

At its core, the programs' theory of change is that teachers who more deeply assimilate, find utility in, and become skilled at teaching and practicing the concepts of the RCCP and 4Rs Program in their own lives and in the classroom will provide greater social-emotional learning opportunities and supports to their classroom and to the school community. The alignment of teachers' own values, beliefs, and perceptions of ability with the underlying pedagogy of a particular intervention is critical to their ability to understand, accept, and implement the intervention, and to the effectiveness of the intervention itself (Conduct Problems Prevention Research Group, 1999; Fullan & Stiegelbauer, 1991; Hauer, 2003; Kmitta, Brown, Chappell, Spiegler, & Wiley, 2000). In other words, when teachers buy in to, believe, and practice the principles and implementation strategies of the program, they establish a set of expectations and norms for behaviors in their classrooms, and children begin to use those skills and behaviors. For example, a teacher who practices the basics of good listening skills (e.g., direct eye contact, paraphrasing, acknowledging comprehension) in his or her interactions with other adults and students, and who is able to teach these skills and provide real-life, real-time examples of how they are effective, increases the chances that students will employ them in their own interactions. But it is not merely the practice of good listening skills by the teacher or any given student that is important; it is how the use of these skills reflects a set of transactional social processes enabling teachers and students to develop closer, more intimate relationships (Tseng & Seidman, 2007). Increases in the quality of the relationships among teachers and students in turn facilitates future positive communications by fostering a more responsive classroom overall. What this example illustrates about the RCCP and 4Rs programs' theory of setting-level change is that teachers are employed as a gateway to changing broad characteristics of classrooms including relationships and climate, as well as to the development of individual children.

Although highly similar in their approach to training teachers in practicing and teaching conflict resolution skills, the RCCP and 4Rs Program have some differences. Indeed, the 4Rs Program was developed 5 years ago by our program partners, Morningside Center, in direct response to several national and local policy shifts. From a national perspective, the 4Rs evolved in response to the tension between the movement to reform education between standards-based accountability with its focus on academic achievement on the one hand (e.g., the policy and practice zeitgeist promoted by the No Child Left Behind Act of 2001) and social and character development with its focus on social-emotional competence and prosocial and negative attitudes and behaviors on the other (e.g., the growing recognition of social-emotional skills as critical to school success; CASEL, 2003). From a local perspective 4Rs evolved in response to the dramatic reorganization of schools and districts in NYC and the new requirement that schools adopt a balanced literacy approach to reading. By integrating the conflict resolution lessons into a balanced literacy curriculum, Morningside Center made it possible for schools to adopt the program into an increasingly tightly scheduled school day by embedding it in the new regularly scheduled balanced literacy block.

To summarize, the 4Rs program and RCCP both aim to teach the same conflict resolution skills. However, under the framework of building a caring community in their classrooms via social-emotional learning, the 4Rs Program embeds the core lessons of the curriculum within a comprehensive literacy-based approach that uses high-quality children's stories to reinforce prosocial values and ideas. At the level of the teacher and classroom, 4Rs professional development helps teachers work with universal themes of conflict, feelings, relationships, and community encountered in children's literature adding social and emotional meaning and depth to rigorous literacy instruction and providing a pedagogical link between the teaching of conflict resolution and the teaching of fundamental academic skills. Integrating these two domains strengthens their linkages in the classroom and promotes their mutual influence on successful youth development (Hinshaw, 1992). At the individual level, the literacy focus in the 4Rs fosters students' enjoyment of reading and writing, enables students to experience reading and writing's relevance for their lives, helps students meet the rigorous new learning standards for language arts and applied learning, and helps students and teachers develop "habits of mind" for thinking about literature and life.

Both the RCCP and 4Rs Program have been subject to rigorous evaluation, the former using a quasi-experimental design to assess features primarily at the child level and neglecting teacher- or classroom-level features as specific targets of intervention, and the latter using an experimental design to assess changes in setting-level features, more appropriately reflecting the program's theory of change. We briefly describe the evaluation of the RCCP first, motivating a discussion of a theory of settings we developed and are currently testing in our evaluation of the 4Rs Program.

The Evaluation of RCCP (Aber, Brown, & Jones, 2003; Aber, Jones, Brown, Chaudry, & Samples, 1998)

A defining characteristic of ESR Metro's approach to implementing social-emotional learning programs in schools is to begin by recruiting and training a few highly motivated volunteer teachers and to slowly recruit and train more teachers over a period of several years until the school is completely "saturated" with the program. Thus, in this implementation model, while teachers "select" into the intervention (some as early "volunteers," some as later "draftees," some not at all), children do not. For these reasons, we employed a quasi-experimental evaluation design to reflect the typical evolution of the program within a school and to maximize external validity for a test of the program as implemented on children's development. In other words, in collaboration with our program partners, we decided to evaluate the program as it existed and operated in the real world of the NYC public school system.

Four schools were identified and recruited in each of four districts in NYC to participate in the evaluation. Each group of schools represented a different stage of program evolution. Teachers were expected to vary in their level of interest and enthusiasm in participating in and implementing RCCP. We examined the unique and combined effects of (a) teacher training and ongoing coaching and (b) classroom instruction in the curriculum on children's trajectories of social-emotional skills and behaviors. We found that, in general, children showed increases from ages 6 to 12 (over the elementary school years) in the skills and behaviors thought to underlie later aggression and violence. In addition, after accounting for the amount of teacher training and coaching provided by program staff, children whose teachers taught a high number of lessons in the curriculum showed significantly slower rates of growth in social-cognitive processes thought to underlie aggressive and violent behavior, for example, hostile attribution biases; behavioral symptomatology, for example, depressive symptoms; and teacher perceptions of child behavior, for example, aggressive behavior. In contrast, children whose teachers received relatively higher amounts of training and coaching in the curriculum but taught a low number of lessons demonstrated significantly faster rates of growth in the outcome domains listed above. The two different patterns of implementation of RCCP, while not hypothesized, are consistent with the voluminous intervention literature on fidelity of treatment and variation in program implementation (Murnane & Nelson, 2005; Shadish, Cook, & Leviton, 1991). Despite very similar training, there were important differences among teachers in how they implemented RCCP in their classrooms and these differences had implications for how well children did.

The most important limitation of this evaluation, and in our opinion, its most valuable theoretical insight, derived from the use of a quasi-experimental design. Because teachers volunteered for RCCP and independently decided how many lessons to teach, it was not clear whether the observed effects on children's developmental trajectories were due to the lessons themselves, to unobserved characteristics of classrooms and teachers, or to some combination of the two (Adalbjarnardottir, 1994; Adalbjarnardottir & Selman, 1997; Clayton et al., 2001; Thornton et al., 2000). Candidate-unobserved characteristics of the teachers and classrooms that emerged both from discussions of the findings with our partners at Morningside Center and from a deeper review of the literature include dimensions such as teacher's own social-emotional development, past experience, levels of program buy-in, and the overall climate of the classroom. In the next section, we present a general theoretical framework for the role of teachers, and in particular, the classroom settings they create and maintain, as important targets and mediators of school-based preventive interventions addressing children's social and emotional development. This model evolved directly out of our findings from the evaluation of the RCCP.

A Theoretical Framework for Classroom Settings as Targets of Intervention Research

Developmental contextual models view development as taking place in a nested and interactive set of contexts ranging from the most immediate microcontexts to the more distal meso- and exo-contexts. Within each context, individual experience and behavior is dynamically mediated by numerous proximal processes (Bronfenbrenner & Morris, 1998; Sameroff, 1995). In the microcontext (e.g., family, classroom, or school), among the most salient proximal processes are important relationships (Pianta, 1999). Children experience classrooms through their relationships with their teacher and with their peers, and together, children and teachers each contribute to a dynamic and enduring set of interactions characterized by regular and consistent patterns (Kontos & Wilcox-Herzog, 1997; Meehan, Hughes, & Cavell, 2003; Meyer, Wardrop, Hastings, & Linn, 1993; Pianta, 1999; Pianta & Stuhlman, 2004). This set of relationships in aggregate comprises features of the culture and climate of the classroom environment for all children. Teacher-student relationships are a joint function of child characteristics, both individually and on average across the classroom (e.g., social-cognitive attributions and problem-solving style), and teacher characteristics (e.g., professional experience in the classroom, experiences of stress and burnout, and belief systems), and each of these contribute to the emotional and instructional climate of the classroom. In turn, this classroom system contributes to the development of children's social and academic competencies in school. To illustrate this system we employ the active listening example again. The primary operative components of the classroom system include (a) a teacher who buys in to, practices, and teaches the basics of good listening skills; (b) a classroom of children who on average are motivated and engaged in practicing these same skills; (c) a level of interaction between teachers and students that builds from (a) and (b) to create closer, more intimate relationships; and (d) a more emotionally supportive and responsive classroom overall. One can see how the functioning of the system and the relationships between the components can shift by altering any one of the primary components. For example, a small group of highly disruptive and disengaged students might both shift the attentional balance of the teacher away from instructional activities and reduce the emotional resources that support relationships with other children in the classroom, resulting in a less emotionally and instructionally supportive classroom overall. Said another way, we theorize that the primary components operate interactively to achieve various forms of dynamic balance. Consequently, in order to develop and maintain high quality, positive relationships between teachers and students in the context of a highly disruptive classroom, teachers need better management skills, a core set of effective strategies to draw upon, and a deeper well of internal emotional resources and external supports in the school. The RCCP and 4Rs Program directly target, through intensive initial training and ongoing follow-up coaching and support, the development of these pedagogical and emotional resources among teachers.

Thus, in our theory of classroom settings (see Figure 4.1), we hypothesize four domains that together constitute the culture and climate of the classroom system: (a) Teacher Affective and Pedagogical Processes and Practices refers to characteristics of teachers including domains such as skills and beliefs in social-emotional learning, their job-related stress and burnout, and their classroom management practices; (b) Child Behavioral Dispositions and Normative Beliefs refers to classroom average levels of children's social-cognitive skills such as beliefs about the acceptability of aggression, their attributional styles and response strategies, and their levels of motivation and engagement; (c) Teacher-Student Relationships refers to the quality of the teacher-child relationship as perceived by teachers and students; and (d) Classroom Emotional and Instructional Climate refers to dimensions of the emotional and instructional character of the classroom as a whole measured using independent observations of the interactions of teachers and children in the classroom.

Literature on Model Features

An extensive literature supports this theory of classroom setting-level features, although it is not without challenges. Much of the research on the

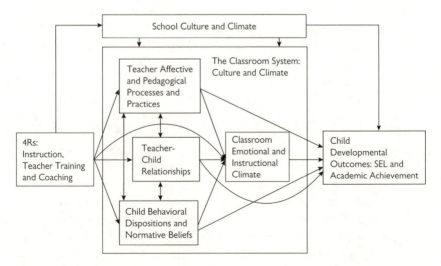

Figure 4.1. Heuristic Model of the Impact of the 4Rs Program on Classroom and School Settings.

relations among setting-level features is correlational in nature. Frequently, setting-level constructs are measured and used at levels lower than that of the setting (i.e., using children's individual-level perceptions of school or class-room climate to represent the whole-school or classroom climate). Moreover, in cases in which measures are gathered and used at different levels (i.e., setting-level school observations and individual child-level outcomes), analyses are sometimes conducted at the lowest level resulting in overestimates of impacts. Nonetheless this body of research represents a great deal of promise in identifying important features of settings to subject to a rigorous experimental test.

Teacher Affective and Pedagogical Processes and Practices

There is an important set of related skills, processes, and practices that have been underinvestigated in research examining the effects of social-emotional learning and literacy development programs. Dimensions identified in the literature that are primarily affective and belief processes include teachers' perceptions of their role in attending to students' social-emotional needs (Daniels & Shumow, 2003; Ryan, Gheen, & Midgley, 1998), their interest and ability in forming close relationships with their students (Hamre & Pianta, 2001; Ladd & Burgess, 1999; Pianta, Steinberg, & Rollins, 1995), and their experience of stress associated with individual student behavior and feelings of job-burnout overall (Abidin & Robinson, 2002; Barbaresi & Olson, 1998; Emmer & Stough, 2001; Gold, 1984; Greene, Beszterczey, Katzenstein, Park, & Goring, 2002; Maslach, Jackson, & Schwab, 1996; Yoon, 2002). Pedagogical processes and practices include such constructs as classroom management styles and strategies (Webster-Stratton, Reid, & Hammond, 2001; Wentzel, 2002) and skill in promoting reading comprehension, word analysis, and writing skills (Rowan, Correnti, & Miller, 2002). Together this set of related dimensions have direct implications for the type of classroom-setting teachers create for children and for the effectiveness of classroom- and school-based interventions with children.

Child Behavioral Dispositions and Normative Beliefs

A core set of social-cognitive skills has been shown to place children at-risk for future aggressive and violent behavior (Coie & Dodge, 1998; Dodge, Pettit, Bates, & Valente, 1995; Dodge, Pettit, McClaskey, & Brown, 1986; Schultz & Selman, 2002; Selman, Beardslee, Schultz, Krupa, & Podoresky, 1986). For example, children with deficits in social information-processing skills may misinterpret or fail to recognize friendly overtures from teachers or peers, and to respond more aggressively to situations of interpersonal conflict, leading them to miss key opportunities for prosocial engagement and learning activities and to disengage from the classroom (Hawkins, Guo, Hill, Battin-Pearson, & Abbott, 2001). Interventions intended to promote positive social-cognitive skills in individual children may prove less effective when children are in classrooms in which aggressive and disengaged behavior is considered acceptable (Aber et al., 1998; Henry, this volume, chapter 3).

Teacher-Child Relationships

Research has shown that elementary school teachers play a critical role in shaping children's academic and social-emotional developmental pathways (Baydar, Brooks-Gunn, & Furstenburg, 1993; Birch & Ladd, 1998; Coie & Bagwell, 1999; Entwisle & Alexander, 1999; Hamre & Pianta, 2001; Pianta & McCoy, 1997; Ryan, Gheen, & Midgley, 1998; Stevenson & Newman, 1996; Wentzel, 2002). In particular, the quality of teacher-child relationships is a key feature of classroom settings that contributes both to classroom climate and student outcomes (Pianta & Allen, this volume, chapter 2; Pianta, Steinberg, & Rollins, 1995; Mantzicopoulos, 2005). Teacher-child relationships also have favorable effects on children's relationships and interactions with peers in the classroom. Children who have positive relationships with teachers tend to be more accepted by their peers (Ladd, Birch, & Buhs, 1999) and to be well-liked and considered socially competent by the other students in the classroom (Hughes, Cavell, & Willson, 2001). Close and connected relationships with the teacher are the primary proximal processes through which the classroom optimizes children's academic and emotional functioning and, because of their central importance, they are a key target for intervention (Bronfenbrenner & Ceci, 1994; Pianta & Allen, this volume, chapter 2; Webster-Stratton et al., 2001).

Classroom Emotional and Instructional Climate

An abundance of research suggests that classroom climate influences children's social-emotional and academic outcomes. Positive classroom climate has been associated with greater self-esteem, perceived cognitive competence, internal locus of control, mastery motivation (Ryan & Grolnick, 1986), school satisfaction (Baker, 1999), academic performance, and less acting-out behavior (Toro, 1985), while poorer classroom environments have been associated with poor peer relations, poor academic focus, and higher levels of aggression (Maslach et al., 1996). This research has also identified teacher-child relationships as an essential process feature that contributes to classroom quality (NICHD ECCRN, 2003; Pianta, LaParo, Payne, Cox, & Bradley, 2002). However, a limitation of this research is that it often utilizes measures such as checklists and analyses based on composite scores so that classroom processes are not adequately captured. Improvements in such measures include observational tools such as the Classroom Observational System (NICHD ECCRN, 2002) and the Classroom Assessment Scoring System (CLASS) (Pianta, La Paro, & Hamre, 2005). Using such observational methods, research has found evidence that emotional and instructional aspects of classroom processes are critical factors in early schooling. For example, Hamre and Pianta (2005) found that children identified as at-risk and placed in first-grade classrooms with high instructional and emotional support had achievement scores similar to those of first-grade students considered low risk, while at-risk students in classrooms with lower levels of support had lower achievement scores. Increased classroom quality in kindergarten has also been associated with reduced problem behaviors in whole class settings and increased social conversation and cooperation between students in small-group settings (Rimm-Kaufman, La Paro, Downer, & Pianta, 2005). This research highlights the potential of emotional and instructional climate for promoting children's healthy social-emotional development and academic success as well as the power of independent observational methods to capture these critical features of the classroom.

The Impact of Interventions on Classroom Settings

Although only a few experimental and quasi-experimental studies have examined the effect of interventions on classroom and school settings, there is research suggesting that aspects of the classroom and school environment are malleable. For example, the Fast Track prevention program, a social competence intervention delivered by first-grade teachers, produced significant positive effects on observer ratings of four classroom atmosphere scales: expressing feelings appropriately, following rules, staying focused and on task, and level of interest and enthusiasm (CPPRG, 1999). The Child Development Project, a comprehensive elementary school intervention, found that sense of community (students' perceptions of the classroom and school environment as supportive, caring, and welcoming of student participation) was higher for students in intervention than comparison schools (Battistich, Schaps, Watson, & Solomon, 1996). The Good Behavior Game, a classroom-based behavior management strategy, reduced the aggressive behavior of highly aggressive boys by reducing high levels of aggression in the classroom (Kellam, Ling, Merisca, Brown, & Ialongo, 1998). The Comer School Development Program has been associated with changes in school social and academic climate (Cook, Murphey, & Hunt, 2000), and other programs that specifically targeted changes in the classroom setting have also shown positive effects on classroom climate in elementary schools (Fraser & O'Brien, 1985; Hertz-Lazarowitz & Od-Cohen, 1992).

Linking the Theory of Classroom-Setting Change to the Theory of Developmentally Salient Classroom-Setting Features

To illustrate the ways in which the actual practice of the RCCP and 4Rs Program targets the primary domains of our conceptual model, we provide in this section examples of concrete intervention activities that are expected to affect the four theoretical domains hypothesized to represent the classroom setting.

We focus on the teacher training and professional development component of the programs, which target teacher's beliefs and actions as the primary lever for effecting change in the classroom as a whole. It is through the initial training and ongoing support that teachers are introduced to and become skilled at using the curriculum in their classrooms. We begin by describing a set of workshops focused on issues of handling anger and conflict that occur over the first 3 days of training. During the first day teachers reflect on and report "things that kids do that trigger your anger," and "things that you do to cool yourself down when you are angry." Teachers then work in pairs to discuss and identify positive strategies for handling angry and disruptive children in the classroom. This emotional self-reflection exercise is followed on the second day of training with a workshop on aggressive, submissive, and assertive forms of communication. On the third day of training these emotional competence and classroom management activities are elaborated in a workshop on conflict in relationships. Specifically, teachers reflect on their own history of exposure to and responses to interpersonal conflict and identify ways they would like to change how they respond to conflict. This activity is followed again by a workshop on positive strategies and communications for effectively managing and resolving conflicts and developing these skills in children.

The sequence of workshops abstracted here alternates activities focused on teacher's own emotional abilities and beliefs with those designed to provide teachers with actual strategies they can use in the classroom and lessons they deliver to students. This sequencing makes explicit for teachers the links between their own experiences and beliefs and their actions in the classroom with the goal of changing not just *what* teachers do but their *belief* in the value of what they are learning and doing. As we describe above, over the course of the intervention, changes in teacher beliefs and practices are expected to both foster and be fostered by parallel changes in student's behavior and their experience of being valued and supported by the teacher, thereby cultivating a set of closer relationships between teachers and students and a more emotionally and instructionally supportive classroom. (Changes in students and teachers are also expected to result from exposure to the curriculum *delivered* by the teacher in the classroom.) While some teacher training occurs before the beginning of the school year, training activities are ongoing, and teachers receive direct, in-classroom support and assistance from program staff developers throughout the school year, making changes in the teacher, changes in the students, and changes in the quality and character of the relationships parallel and mutually reinforcing over time.

Example Measures of Classroom Settings

We are currently conducting a school-randomized experimental study of the 4Rs Program in which we are following over 900 children from grade 3 to grade 5, across six waves of intensive data collection, and between 80 and 240 classrooms over 1-3 years. We have partially embedded in the "child-level" study a "setting-level" study that focuses specifically on classrooms and other school microcontexts as both targets and outcomes of 4Rs intervention, and tests the hypothesized model of a dynamic classroom system presented in Figure 4.1.[1]

Together, these two studies assess the impact of the intervention on the characteristics of teachers' own development, and classroom and school contexts, as well as youth developmental outcomes.

Our setting-level study employs a variety of measures of each domain of the classroom system. While these measures are all intended to describe features of classrooms and schools, they are assessed at different levels of the ecological hierarchy, and as such, some require averaging across the students in the classroom and some do not. Because our study is longitudinal, we will be able to distinguish features of classroom and school settings that are purely compositional (e.g., those that represent features we do not expect to change as a result of the intervention such as the proportion of low-income students in the classroom) from those that are dynamic and changing in response to the intervention (Shinn, 1990). A strength of our approach is that we measure each setting-level domain from a variety of perspectives and operationalize many constructs in multiple ways. We present examples next.

Teacher Affective and Pedagogical Processes and Practices

As described in our brief review of the literature relevant to this domain, one central construct is teacher's emotional competence. Teachers' perception of their own ability to perceive, understand, regulate, and use emotions is assessed using the 23-item Perceived Emotional Intelligence Scale (Brackett & Mayer, 2003). This measure assesses several key aspects of emotional ability including the ability to perceive the emotions of others ("By looking at people's facial expressions, I recognize the emotions they are experiencing"), access and understand one's own emotions ("I have a rich vocabulary to describe my emotions"), regulate one's emotions ("When I'm in a bad mood, it takes me a long time to get over it"), and employ one's emotions to effectively manage social situations ("When someone I know is in a bad mood, I can help the person calm down and feel better quickly"). Respondents indicate for each item how accurately or inaccurately the item describes them. Responses are indicated on a 5-point Likert scale ranging from *Very Inaccurate* (1) to *Very Accurate* (5). Total and subscale scores for the teacher are computed by averaging across items. This assessment of teachers' emotional ability is a marker of the classroom setting because all children in the classroom are exposed to any affective and/or pedagogical manifestations of the teacher's emotional competence (although exposure will vary with student attendance). As outlined in our model, we expect the 4Rs Program to influence such teacher-level phenomena and to explain the influence of the 4Rs Program on independent measurements of the overall culture and climate of the classroom, and ultimately, on children's developmental outcomes.

At the school level, total and subscale scores can be operationalized in several ways: as an average across teachers in the school, as the degree of variation between teachers in their ratings across the school or within and between grades, and as the degree of saturation of high scores (e.g., how many teachers in the school score very high compared to how many score very low; Shinn, 1990). These different characterizations of the school and classroom settings provide a varied and more holistic picture of the school environment, one that would be missed by relying on any single method alone.

Teacher-Child Relationships

An example construct in this domain is teachers' perceptions of the quality of their relationship with each student in their class. This is measured using the Student-Teacher Relationship Scale (STRS) (Pianta, 2001) that includes 20-items assessing three dimensions including: (a) Closeness (e.g., "I share an affectionate, warm relationship with this child"), (b) Conflict (e.g., "This child and I always seem to be struggling with each other"), and (c) Dependency (e.g., "This child reacts strongly to separation from me"). Together these subscales can be used to form a total score reflecting overall positive relationship from the teacher's perspective (+Closeness, −Conflict, −Dependency; Pianta, Steinberg, & Rollins, 1995). Subscale and total scale scores are calculated as the average score across relevant items. As in the Teacher Affective and Pedagogical Process and Practices domain, this set of constructs can be computed as a classroom average, as the degree of variation within and between classrooms, and as the degree of saturation of high- and/or low-quality relationships. In addition, in this domain we also included a measure of the quality of teacher-child relationships from the child's perspective. Trust in

Teachers and Teacher Support for Learning is measured using an adapted version of the Identity Safe Classrooms measure (Steele, 2005). Children rate each of 13 items including "I can talk to my teacher if I have a problem," My teacher at this school really cares about me," and "My teacher thinks I'm a good student." In this domain, therefore, it is possible to assess the degree to which children and teachers match or are mismatched in their reports of their relationship and then to consider the extent of match/mismatch as a classroom aggregate of the forms already described.

Child Behavioral Dispositions and Normative Beliefs

One indicator in this domain, children's normative beliefs about the acceptability of aggressive behavior, is assessed using the Normative Beliefs About Aggression Scale (Huesmann & Guerra, 1997). Children respond to the acceptability of aggressive responses in each of 20 items such as "It is wrong to hit other people" and "It is OK to push or shove other people around if you're mad." In this case, child-level total scores can be averaged within a classroom (excepting the reporter) to represent classroom level "injunctive norms," which refer to a classroom-level measure of how people are expected to behave (Henry, this volume, chapter 3). As with school-level aggregates of teacher stress and burnout, this construct can be also operationalized in a number of additional and important ways (e.g., as variability or degree of saturation of high scores). Again, as outlined in our model, we expect such classroom-level phenomena, which in this case are based on child reports, to causally influence the overall culture and climate of the classroom, measured independently, and to mediate the influence of intervention on climate, and ultimately, on children's developmental outcomes.

Classroom Emotional and Instructional Climate

Our final domain, the emotional and instructional climate of classrooms is assessed using CLASS (Pianta et al., 2005), an observational instrument developed to assess classroom quality in preschool through fifth grade classrooms. The CLASS scales are based on interactions among teachers and children in the classroom, assessing the quality of teachers' social and instructional interactions with children, social interactions among the children, and the productivity evident in classroom settings. Because it relies on observer ratings, this measure offers an opportunity to offset bias associated with teacher and child reports of similar features of classroom settings. Moreover, independent ratings such as these can be used in conjunction with other perspectives to illustrate the degree of agreement/disagreement across reporters, which is itself an important setting-level indicator. This measure is described in detail in Pianta and Allen (this volume, chapter 2) and therefore will not be described further.

As described earlier, we selected conceptually meaningful and thematically linked constructs to represent the four domains of the classroom system. One goal of our work is to better understand the structure and organization of the variables indexing our conceptual domains and the degree to which they together represent a unified classroom system. To date there has not been a careful empirical examination of a conceptual system such as that hypothesized here. Thus, we will examine the interrelationships among the key constructs sampled to represent each domain as well as if and how they function as coherent domains and together as part of a dynamic classroom system.

Summary and Conclusions

In this chapter, we presented two thematically parallel programs that aim to promote caring classroom communities and positive youth development through the professional development of teachers and the implementation of a social-emotional learning curriculum. The core theory of setting-level, in this case, classroom-level, change is that by introducing teachers to a set of social-emotional learning skills and concepts and then supporting them in the use of these skills and concepts in their everyday interactions, teachers will provide greater social-emotional learning opportunities and supports in their classrooms and to their school community. In this theory it is not just the basic use of social-emotional skills and concepts that is important; it is the resulting set of transactional social processes that result from their use that promotes a more positive and effective classroom climate, and ultimately, positive youth development. The place-randomized, experimental study of the impact of the 4Rs Program on a dynamic model of classroom-setting features will allow us to empirically test this theory of setting-level change, adding to the growing body of research on settings as targets of interventions designed to promote positive youth development.

Note

1. These studies are supported by the Institute of Education Sciences, the Centers for Disease Control and Prevention, and the William T. Grant Foundation.

References

Aber, J. L., Brown, J. L., & Jones, S. M. (2003). Developmental trajectories toward violence in middle childhood: Course, demographic differences, and response to school-based intervention. *Developmental Psychology, 39*(2), 324-348.

Aber, J. L., Jones, S. M., Brown, J. L., Chaudry, N., & Samples, F. (1998). Resolving conflict creatively: Evaluating the developmental effects of a school-based violence prevention program in neighborhood and classroom context. *Development and Psychopathology, 10*(2), 187-213.

Abidin, R. R., & Robinson, L. L. (2002). Stress, biases, or professionalism: What drives teachers' referral judgments of students with challenging behaviors? *Journal of Emotional and Behavioral Disorders, 10*(4), 204-212.

Adalbjarnardottir, S. (1994). Understanding children and ourselves: Teachers' reflections on social development in the classroom. *Teaching and Teacher Education, 10*(4), 409-421.

Baker, J. A. (1999). Teacher-student interaction in urban at-risk classrooms: Differential behavior, relationship quality, and student satisfaction with school. *The Elementary School Journal, 100*(1), 57-70.

Barbaresi, W. J., & Olson, R. D. (1998). An ADHD educational intervention for elementary school teachers: A pilot study. *Developmental and Behavioral Pediatrics, 19*(2), 94-100.

Battistich, V., Schaps, E., Watson, M., & Solomon, D. (1996). Prevention effects of the child development project: Early findings from an Ongoing Multisite Demonstration Trial. *Journal of Adolescent Research, 11*, 12-35.

Baydar, N., Brooks-Gunn, J., & Furstenburg, F. (1993). Early warning signs of functional illiteracy: Predictors in childhood and adolescence. *Child Development, 64*, 815-829.

Birch, S. H., & Ladd, G. W. (1998). Children's interpersonal behaviors and the teacher-child relationship. *Developmental Psychology, 34*, 934-946.

Brackett, M. A., & Mayer, J. D. (2003). Convergent, discriminant, and incremental validity of competing measures of emotional intelligence. *Personality and Social Psychology Bulletin, 29*(9), 1147-1158.

Bronfenbrenner, U., & Ceci, S. J. (1994). Nature-nurture reconceptualized in developmental perspective: A bioecological model. *Psychologocal Review, 101*(4), 568-586.

Bronfenbrenner, U., & Morris, P. (1998). The ecology of developmental process. *The Handbook of Child Psychology, 1*, 993-1029.

CASEL. (2003). *Safe and sound: An education Leader's guide to evidence-based social and emotional learning (SEL) Programs* (Collaborative for Academic, Social, and Emotional Learning). Retrieved February 16, 2007, from http://www.casel.org/

Clayton, C. J., Ballif-Spanvill, B., & Honsaker, M. D. (2001). Preventing violence and teaching peace: A review of promising and effective antiviolence, conflict resolution, and peace programs for elementary school children. *Applied and Preventive Psychology, 10*, 1-35.

Coie, J., & Bagwell, C. (1999). School-based social predictors of serious adolescent psychopathology and dysfunction: Implications for prevention. In D. Cicchetti & S. Toth (Eds.), *Developmental approaches to prevention and intervention* (Vol. 9, pp. 25-55). Rochester, NY: The University of Rochester Press.

Coie, J. D., & Dodge, K. A. (1998). Aggression and antisocial behavior. In N. Eisenberg (Ed.), *Handbook of child psychology: Social, emotional, and personality development* (5th ed., Vol. 3, pp. 779-862). New York: John Wiley & Sons.

Conduct Problems Prevention Research Group (CPPRG). (1999). Initial impact of the fast track prevention trial for conduct problems: II. Classroom effects. *Journal of Consulting and Clinical Psychology, 67,* 648-657.

Cook, T. D., Murphy, R. F., & Hunt, D. H. (2000). Comer's school development program in Chicago: A theory-based evaluation. *American Educational Research Journal, 37*(2), 535-597.

Daniels, D. H., & Shumow, L. (2003). Child development and classroom teaching: A review of the literature and implications for educating teachers. *Journal of Applied Developmental Psychology, 23*(5), 495-526.

Dodge, K. A., Pettit, G. S., Bates, J. E., & Valente, E. (1995). Social information-processing patterns partially mediate the effect of early physical abuse on later conduct problems. *Journal of Abnormal Psychology, 104*(4), 632-643.

Dodge, K. A., Pettit, G. S., McClaskey, C. L., & Brown, M. (1986). Social competence in children. *Monographs of the Society for Research in Child Development, 51*(2, Serial No. 213).

Emmer, E. T., & Stough, L. M. (2001). Classroom management: A critical part of educational psychology, with implications for teacher education. *Educational Psychologist, 36*(2), 103-112.

Entwisle, D., & Alexander, K. (1999). Early schooling and social stratification. In R. Pianta & M. Cox (Eds.), *The transition to kindergarten: Research, policy, and practice* (pp. 13-38). Baltimore: Paul H. Brookes.

Fraser, B. J., & O'Brien, P. (1985). Student and teacher perceptions of the environment of elementary school classrooms. *The Elementary School Journal, 85*(5), 566-580.

Fullan, M., & Stiegelbauer, S. (1991). *The new meaning of educational change.* New York: Teachers College Press.

Gold, Y. (1984). Factorial validity of the Maslach Burnout inventory in a sample of California elementary and junior high school classroom teachers. *Educational and Psychological Measurement, 44,* 1009-1016.

Greene, R. W., Beszterczey, S. K., Katzenstein, T., Park, K., & Goring, J. (2002). Are students with ADHD more stressful to teach? Patterns of teacher stress in an elementary school sample. *Journal of Emotional and Behavioral Disorders, 10*(2), 79-89.

Hamre, B. K., & Pianta, R. C. (2001). Early teacher-child relationships and the trajectory of children's school outcomes through eighth grade. *Child Development, 72*(2), 625-638.

Hamre, B. K., & Pianta, R. C. (2005). Can instructional and emotional support in the first-grade classroom make a difference for children at risk of school failure? *Child Development, 76*(5), 949-967.

Hauer, J. (2003). Educating for character and teachers' moral vitality. *Journal of Research in Character Education, 1*(1), 31-42.

Hawkins, J. D., Guo, J., Hill, K. G., Battin-Pearson, S., & Abbott, R. D. (2001). Long-term effects of the seattle social development intervention on school bonding trajectories. *Applied Developmental Science, 5*(4), 225-236.

Henry, D. B. (this volume). Changing classroom social settings through attention to norms.

Hertz-Lazarowitz, R., & Od-Cohen, M. (1992). The school psychologist as a facilitator of a community-wide project to enhance positive learning climate in elementary schools. *Psyhcology in the Schools, 29*(4), 348-358.

Hinshaw, S. P. (1992). Externalizing behavior problems and academic underachievement in childhood and adolescence: Causal relationships and underlying mechanisms. *Psychological Bulletin, 111*(1), 127-155.

Huesmann, L. R., & Guerra, N. G. (1997). Children's normative beliefs about aggression and aggressive behaviors. *Journal of Personality and Social Psychology, 72*, 408-419.

Hughes, J. N., Cavell, T. A., & Willson, V. (2001). Further support for the developmental significance of the quality of the teacher-student relationship. *Journal of School Psychology, 39*(4), 289-301.

Kellam, S. G., Ling, X., Merisca, R., Brown, C. H., & Ialongo, N. (1998). The effect of the level of aggression in the first grade classroom on the course and malleability of aggressive behavior into middle school. *Development and Psychopathology, 10*(2), 165-186.

Kmitta, D., Brown, J. L., Chappell, C., Spiegler, J., & Wiley, P. (2000). Impact on educators: Conflict resolution education and the evidence regarding educators. In T. S. Jones & D. Kmitta (Eds.), *Does it work? The case for conflict resolution in our nation's schools* (pp. 39-60). Washington, DC: Conflict Resolution Education Network.

Kontos, S., & Wilcox-Herzog, A. (1997). Teachers' interactions with children: Why are they so important? *Young Children, 52*(2), 4-12.

Ladd, G. W., Birch, S. H., & Buhs, E. S. (1999). Children's social and scholastic lives in kindergarten: Related spheres of influence? *Child Development, 70*(6), 1373-1400.

Ladd, G. W., & Burgess, K. B. (1999). Charting the relationship trajectories of aggressive, withdrawn, and aggressive/withdrawn children during early grade school. *Child Development, 70*, 910-929.

Mantzicopoulos, P. (2005). Conflictual relationships between kindergarten children and their teachers: Associations with child and classroom context variables. *Journal of School Psychology, 43*(5), 425-442.

Maslach, C., Jackson, S. E., & Schwab, R. L. (1996). Maslach Burnout Inventory-Educators Survey (MBI-ES). In C. Maslach, S. E. Jackson, & M. P. Leiter, *MBI Manual* (3rd ed., pp. 27-32). Palto Alto, CA: Consulting Psychologists Press.

Meehan, B. T., Hughes, J. N., & Cavell, T. A. (2003). Teacher-student relationships as compensatory resources for aggressive children. *Child Development, 74*(4), 1145-1157.

Meyer, L. A., Wardrop, J. L., Hastings, C. N., & Linn, R. L. (1993). Effects of abilities and settings on kindergarteners' reading performance. *Journal of Educational Research, 86*, 142-160.

Murnane, R. J., & Nelson, R. R. (2005). *Improving the performance of the education sector: The valuable, challenging, and limited role of random assignment evaluations* (Working Paper 11846). Cambridge, MA: National Bureau of Economic Research. Retrieved February 16, 2007, from http://www.nber.org/papers/w11846

NICHD Early Child Care Research Network. (2002). The relation of global first-grade classroom environment to structural classroom features and teacher and student behaviors. *The Elementary School Journal, 102*(5), 367-387.

NICHD Early Child Care Research Network. (2003). Social functioning in first grade: Associations with earlier home and child care predictors and with current classroom experiences. *Child Development, 74*(6), 1639-1662.

Pianta, R. C. (1999). *Enhancing relationships between children and teachers.* Washington, DC: American Psychological Association.

Pianta, R. C. (2001). *Student-teacher relationship scale.* Odessa, FL: PAR, Inc.

Pianta, R. C., & Allen, J. P. (this volume). Building capacity for positive youth development in secondary school classrooms: Changing teachers' interactions with students.

Pianta, R. C., La Paro, K., & Hamre, B. K. (2005). *Classroom Assessment Scoring System (CLASS).* Unpublished measure, University of Virginia, Charlottesville, VA.

Pianta, R., La Paro, K., Payne, C., Cox, M., & Bradley, R. (2002). The relation of kindergarten classroom environment to teacher, family, and school characteristics and child outcomes. *The Elementary School Journal, 102*(3), 225-238.

Pianta, R. C., & McCoy, S. (1997). The first day of school: The predictive validity of early school screening. *Journal of Applied Developmental Psychology, 18*, 1-22.

Pianta, R. C., Steinberg, M. S., & Rollins, K. B. (1995). The first two years of school: Teacher-child relationships and deflections in children's classroom adjustment. *Development and Psychopathology, 7*, 295-312.

Pianta, R. C., & Stuhlman, M. (2004). Conceptualizing risk in relational terms: Associations among the quality of child-adult relationships prior to school entry and children's developmental outcomes in first grade. *Educational and Child Psychology, 21*, 32-45.

Rimm-Kaufman, S. E., La Paro, K. M., Downer, J. T., & Pianta, R. C. (2005). The contribution of classroom setting and quality of instruction to children's behavior in kindergarten classrooms. *Elementary School Journal, 105*(4), 377-394.

Rowan, B., Correnti, R., & Miller, R. J. (2002). *What large-scale survey research tells us about teacher effects on student achievement: Insights from the prospects study of elementary schools* (CPRE Research Report Series, RR051). Consortium for Policy Research in Education, University of Pennsylvania, Graduate School of Education, Philadelphia.

Ryan, A. M., Gheen, M. H., & Midgley, C. (1998). Why do some students avoid asking for help? An examination of the interplay among students' academic efficacy, teachers' social-emotional role, and the classroom goal structure. *Journal of Educational Psychology, 88*, 1-8.

Ryan, R. M., & Grolnick, W. S. (1986). Origins and pawns in the classroom: Self-report and projective assessments of individual differences in children's perceptions. *Journal of Personality and Social Psychology, 50*(3), 550-558.

Sameroff, A. J. (1995). General systems theories and psychopathology. In D. Cicchetti & D. Cohen (Eds.), *Developmental psychopathology* (Vol. 1, pp. 659-695). New York: Wiley.

Schultz, L. H., & Selman, R. L. (2002). *The relationship questionnaire: A method to assess social competence in children and adolescents from a developmental perspective.* Unpublished manuscript, Cambridge, MA.

Selman, R. L., Beardslee, W., Schultz, L. K., Krupa, M., & Podoresky, D. (1986). Assessing adolescent interpersonal negotiation strategies: Toward the integration of structural and functional models. *Developmental Psychology, 22,* 450-459.

Shadish, W. R., Cook, T. D., & Leviton, L. C. (Eds.) (1991). *Foundations of program evaluation: Theories of practice.* Newbury Park, CA: Sage Publications.

Shinn, M. (1990). Mixing and matching: Levels of conceptualization, measurement, and statistical analysis in community research. In P. Toal, C. Keys, F. Chertok, & L. Jason (Eds.), *Research in Community Psychology* (pp. 111-126). Washington, DC: American Psychological Association.

Steele, D. (2005). *Identity, safety and student achievement.* Unpublished manuscript, Stanford University, Stanford, CA.

Stevenson, H., & Newman, R. (1996). Long-term prediction of achievement and attitudes in mathematics and reading. *Child Development, 57,* 646-659.

Thornton, T. N., Craft, C. A., Dahlberg, L. L., Lynch, B. S., & Baer, K. (2000). *Best practices of youth violence prevention: A sourcebook for community action.* Atlanta, GA: Division of Violence Prevention, National Center for Injury Prevention and Control, Center for Disease Control and Prevention.

Toro, P. A. (1985). Social environmental predictors of children's adjustment in elementary school classrooms [Special issue: *Children's environments*]. *American Journal of Community Psychology, 13*(4), 353-364.

Tseng, V., & Seidman, E. (2007). A systems framework for understanding social settings. *American Journal of Community Psychology, 39,* 217-228.

Webster-Stratton, C., Reid, J. M., & Hammond, M. (2001). Preventing conduct problems, promoting social competence: A parent and teacher training partnership in head start. *Journal of Clinical Child Psychology, 30*(3), 283-302.

Wentzel, K. R. (2002). Are effective teachers like good parents? Teaching styles and student adjustment in early adolescence. *Child Development, 73*(41), 287-301.

Yoon, J. S. (2002). Teacher characteristics as predictors of teacher-student relationships: Stress, negative affect, and self-efficacy. *Social Behavior and Personality, 30*(5), 485-493.

PART II

CHANGING SCHOOLS

Chapter 5

Schools That Actualize High Expectations for All Youth: Theory for Setting Change and Setting Creation

RHONA S. WEINSTEIN

T he promotion of high expectations for all students has become the underpinning of the U.S. national agenda for educational reform. Under No Child Left Behind (NCLB) (2002), federal policy has targeted low academic expectations in schooling as the root cause of the achievement gap—a gap that disadvantages poor, ethnic, and linguistic minority and special needs children. This policy represents a societal-level expectancy intervention, by mandating higher educational standards (subject-matter competencies) and high-stakes accountability for the improved performance of each of these subgroups. In sharp contrast to the policy world, a highly contested research literature, with rare exceptions (see Good & Nichols, 2001; Weinstein, 2002; Weinstein & McKown, 1998), has concluded that educational expectancy effects are typically small and teacher expectations for students are largely accurate (Jussim & Harber, 2005). This assessment has constrained the development of empirically validated interventions.

Thus far, the results of the NCLB policy appear far from promising (Meier & Wood, 2004). This is not surprising, however, since both policy and research views about the workings of expectancy effects and the theory for setting change are extremely limited with regard to real world application. These views do not reflect an ecological theory of expectancy effects or expectancy change (Weinstein, 2002; Weinstein, Gregory, & Strambler, 2004). In such a theory, the power of self-fulfilling prophecies (whether negative or positive) is heavily context specific and multilayered. It is fueled by interactions between qualities of individuals and settings, nested relationships at multiple levels of educational systems, and accumulation over time—all of which can accentuate or lessen such effects. Accordingly, setting change or setting creation efforts must address both the local ecology and the multiple pathways by which expectancy effects can be expressed in order to change conditions for learning. Setting members need to understand these dynamics of self-fulfilling prophecies and to work collaboratively as well as continuously to strengthen policies, instructional practices, and services so that positive expectations are *fully* actualized in their setting.

Drawing upon ecological perspectives, this chapter articulates setting-level theory about the promotion of high expectations for diverse populations of students. First, classroom and school setting features are described and measurement issues identified. Second, a setting-level theory of expectancy change and/or creation is developed. These theoretical propositions are illustrated by four exemplars of expectancy interventions (within a tracked high school, a low-performing elementary school, a high expectation elementary school, and an "early college" secondary school for first in the family to attend college). Finally, conclusions about the literature and future directions are drawn.

School Setting Features That Actualize High Expectations

Setting Features

An extensive research literature has documented that the expectations of teachers are communicated in the differential treatment of students. Two primary pathways of influence have been articulated: first, differential opportunities to learn, and second, differential as well as limiting cognitive and affective messages about ability, of which students as young as first graders are acutely aware (Brophy & Good, 1974; Weinstein, Marshall, Sharp, & Botkin, 1987). Opportunity to learn directly impacts student achievement by shaping access, that is, widening or restricting curricular exposure, practice, and support. Awareness of inequity in expectations and treatment erodes children's motivation to learn, their self-concept of ability, and identification with schooling, which ultimately but indirectly (through self-processes) impacts achievement (Kuklinski & Weinstein, 2001; McKown & Weinstein, 2003; Steele & Aronson, 1995). Research has shown that the achievement gap (as well as self-perception gap) between groups of students is wider in high differential treatment classrooms where ability differences are made salient than in low differential treatment classrooms (Brattesani, Weinstein, & Marshall, 1984; Kuklinski & Weinstein, 2001). Similarly, experimental studies have shown that the achievement gap between stigmatized ethnic minority and majority elementary-aged students is wider under test conditions that prime for ability stereotypes (tests as diagnostic of ability) as compared to test conditions that stress the processes of learning (McKown & Weinstein, 2003).

While differential treatment that favors some students over others can be seen in teacher-student behavioral interactions, such treatment is given life systemically by instructional choices made at both the classroom and school level, thereby creating differing cultures of achievement. Observational study of classrooms that elementary school children identified on the Teacher Treatment Inventory (TTI) as higher or lower in degree of differential teacher treatment reveal six domains of expectancy expression (Marshall & Weinstein, 1988; Weinstein, 2002). These include the domains of curriculum, instructional grouping, evaluation, motivational strategies, student agency, and climate of relationships.

Elementary classrooms with high expectations are environments in which, first, all children receive challenging instruction with appropriate and nonstigmatized supports for diverse learning needs and for catch-up. Second, children are grouped in fluid ways for differentiated interventions without reducing access to high challenge instruction and without stigma. Third, the evaluation of learning rests upon the belief that ability is malleable (rather than innate), demonstrates expected proficiency standards, charts individual progress toward those standards, and reflects diverse competencies as well as modalities for the demonstration of achievement. Fourth, motivational strategies stress a learning (rather than a performance) orientation, intrinsic interest over extrinsic reinforcement, and the use of cooperation, effort, and strategy. Fifth, student agency is encouraged over teacher-directed learning through metacognitive learning strategies, self-evaluation, leadership, and the development of self-efficacy. Finally, relationships between teachers, students, and parents are positive, respectful (honoring cultural differences), trusting, and fair, resulting in inclusive community of learners. The aligned synergy between these dimensions of instruction can create classroom cultures that are perceived by students as *equitable* ("all children can learn") where all talent is developed or *differentiated* ["not much they (the low achievers) can do"] where those with greater talent are selected for different and better pathways. It is important to note that the differential treatment highlighted here is treatment that favors one group over another. Equity in opportunity may indeed require differentiated instructional approaches but not interventions that stigmatize and lessen access to challenge.

The evidence suggests that the same expectancy features apply in middle and high school environments, at classroom and school levels, as well as in the professional development environments for teachers and faculty, who are also learners (Weinstein, 2002). However, expectancy features play out differently in different contexts, both related to the variations in school organization from elementary to secondary levels and to characteristics of setting inhabitants. Thus, in high schools, differential treatment can occur between classrooms in the form of academic tracking as well as within classrooms. In districts where demographics and funding differs greatly between schools, differential treatment can be seen between schools in the existence of high or low expectation schools. Differential expectations can also be targeted toward different groups of students defined by ethnic membership, gender, language, social class, special need, or, simply, level in the achievement hierarchy.

Aggregate or within-setting achievement cultures (whether at the individual, group, classroom, or school level) can be fueled or undermined by qualities of the school, subject-matter departments, or district culture. Decisions about these dimensions of instruction may be out of the hands of individual teachers and instead rest at the school, department, or district level. One example lies in choices about the differential allocation of challenging curriculum (in ability-based reading groups, academic tracks, and grade retention practices). The aggregate characteristics of the student population (economically, ethnically, linguistically, and with regard to special needs) in a school and district may also support or make more difficult the creation of positive expectancy environments. For example, schools with a high proportion of poor and ethnic minority youth are more likely to have poorer facilities, less instructional materials, and less prepared teachers (Darling-Hammond, 2004). This may diminish the capacity to mount the needed educational supports for a more challenging curriculum. In addition, the design of the school environment also creates student learning opportunities as well as communicates messages about ability, along these same domains reflected in classroom life. The expectancy qualities of the school culture can further enrich student development and importantly, support, buffer, or reduce expectancy influences in the classroom. Thus, to promote high expectations for all students, the above-identified curricular/instructional, self, and relational elements must be aligned both in classrooms and at the school level to attain the strongest effects (see Desimone, this volume, chapter 9).

Measurement of Setting Features

It is important to measure these setting features not only to identify baseline conditions of the expectancy environment but also to assess how a setting has changed in response to intervention. By-products of setting-level interventions would include changes in the six expectancy features such as *increased equity* in the provision of challenging curricula, supports for learning (appropriate, nonstigmatized, and fluid), standards- and progress-based evaluations of learning that identify learning goals and convey a malleable ability, intrinsic and learning-focused motivational strategies, opportunities for self-regulated learning and leadership, and a climate of positive, inclusive, and fair relationships. Such changes would provide all students with the opportunity to learn, with the beliefs and strategies to empower their own education, and with a valued place in an inclusive and supportive community of learners—creating a culture of talent development for all.

When we began this research on educational expectancy effects, we first developed tools to capture children's perceptions of *differential* teacher expectations and *differential* teacher treatment, rather than of the climate on average. The identified expectancy features are subsumed under such an overall index of differential treatment. We found our measures of differential treatment to be reliable and highly predictive of the gap in student outcomes within classrooms.

With regard to assessing classroom differential treatment (whether equitable or differentiated in favoring the so-called academically able students), the TTI was designed for use at the elementary level and with children as young as first graders (Weinstein et al., 1987). This 30-item questionnaire asks students to *independently* rate on a 4-point scale the frequency of their teachers' interactions with a hypothetical high or low achiever in their own classroom. The items are organized into three subscales: negative feedback (e.g., "The teacher makes him/her feel bad when he/she does not have the right answer"), work/rule orientation (e.g., "The teacher asks other students to help him/her"), and high expectations (e.g., "The teacher calls on him/her to answer questions"). The difference score (by scale and summed across scales) in the perceived treatment of the hypothetical high and low achiever provides an *indirect* class-level index of differentiation. In classrooms with greater differential and privileging treatment, low achievers would receive more negative feedback and more structuring of their work as well as lower expectations than high achievers. In five separate studies, we have demonstrated consensus of perceptions within classrooms. A short form of eight of the most discriminating items is also available, and items as well as descriptions can be adapted to include gender comparisons or to refer to student's own treatment from the teacher.

Wentzel (2002), for example, has used four of these negative feedback items in a middle school population to assess children's perceptions of their own negative treatment from the teacher. Roeser, Eccles, and Sameroff (1998) have developed two 3-item Perceived Discrimination Scales for use in middle and high school settings that *directly* assesses student awareness of negative treatment due to race (e.g., "Teachers think you are less smart than you really are because of your race") or due to gender (e.g., "You are disciplined more harshly than kids of the opposite sex"). Midgley et al. (2002) have developed a 7-item Academic Expectations Scale to assess student perceptions of the degree of academic press or high expectations from the teacher (e.g., "This teacher accepts nothing less than my full effort").

Assessment can also move beyond the overall climate of equity or differentiation to provide evidence for the six setting-level expectancy features in classrooms or in schools. In our research, we combined TTI data, student and teacher interviews, and narrative records of classroom observations to identify these setting-level features in classrooms (see Marshall & Weinstein, 1988; Weinstein, 2002). The classroom observation measures developed by Pianta and colleagues (see Pianta & Allen, this volume, chapter 2), which span preschool through secondary school, could also provide ratings of teacher instructional and emotional support, which capture opportunity to learn and the climate of relationships in the classroom. For example, in the secondary instrument, ratings of instructional support focus on productive use of time, promotion of concept development, learning formats that foster engagement, and feedback that expands learning. Ratings of emotional support include positive emotional tone, expressed negativity, teacher responsiveness to student needs, regard for student perspectives, and redirection of misbehavior. While these ratings reflect teacher behavior toward the average child, this instrument could be adapted to focus specifically on teacher interactions with high versus low achievers or, alternatively, it can be inferred that ratings at the highest level reflect consistent teacher behavior across all students. Measures exist that capture teachers' and students' ability beliefs (Dweck, 2000) and learning goals (Midgley, 2002). Skinner and Belmont (1993) offer a 3-item Teacher Care Scale (e.g., "The teacher likes me") and Solomon et al. (1996) at the Developmental Studies Center have developed a reliable measure of elementary student perceptions of their classroom climate as a supportive community (e.g., "My class is like a family").

Thus, there are measures available that would enable assessment of *equity* in opportunity to learn, opportunity to develop motivation and self-efficacy as a learner, and opportunity to have trusting relationships in the classroom and school community. The complexity, however, lies in tailoring measurement to the organizational characteristics of schooling at each level (e.g., multiple teachers in secondary school) and to the cognitive developmental level of child reporters as well as in utilizing assessments at both classroom and school levels. Classroom student perception measures can be aggregated to the school level to indicate the percentage of classrooms with certain qualities. However, in these analyses, if differentiation is not directly assessed, it is important to look at both mean level and differential reporting (within classes, between classes, groups such as ethnic groups, and schools), as inequity is a key feature of expectancy effects. In such cases, an examination of mean effects alone can obscure patterns of underlying inequity. While students are excellent reporters and critical to any assessment, the assessment of policies, interviews with teachers and principal, and observations are also needed to capture the roots of differential opportunity.

Theory of Expectancy Change or Creation

Varied Theories of Action

Expectancy effects have been described as closed circles of influence, impenetrable and highly resistant to change. The sociologist Robert Merton (1948) wrote that "the prophet will cite the actual course of events as proof that he was right from the very beginning" (p. 195). This impenetrability is especially evident when beliefs about the other are *perceived* to be confirmed, even in the face of nonconfirmatory behavioral data. As noted earlier, some researchers have described teacher expectations as largely accurate, given strong correlations with student achievement. An alternative view suggests that all but high expectations are, by definition, inaccurate. Supporting this latter view are the assumptions that achievement scores reflect only what has been taught and taught well, that potential to learn is not measurable, that the goal of education is to foster growth, and that optimal learning conditions have yet to be provided to all with equity. This holds true especially for youth of poverty and color and for those who come to school perceived as different—whether due to preparedness, cultural practices, learning styles, or histories of not being taught and of school failure. These students develop strong defenses against failure, often expressed as disinterest, lack of effort, and defiance (Gregory & Weinstein, in press).

Despite a large research literature about educational expectancy effects, intervention research has been relatively rare. Experimental studies of expectancy effects are, in fact, expectancy change efforts that implant falsely positive expectations on unsuspecting teachers (Rosenthal & Jacobson, 1968). While such experimental manipulations of beliefs have raised student achievement or intelligence scores, they do so under certain conditions, for example, early in the school year when teachers have little prior knowledge of their students (Raudenbush, 1984). The manipulation of beliefs, alone, is likely not robust enough to persist in complex settings. This is shown by several field expectancy induction experiments in work organizations (Eden et al., 2000). Given these findings, it behooves us to turn to the naturally occurring expectations of teachers (how they are instilled, reinforced, or undermined in varied schooling contexts), to the actions that flow from teacher expectations (the enabling polices and practices that have their own reverberating and cumulative consequences), and to more complex interventions.

Beyond the induction of false beliefs, cognitive-behavioral interventions have sought to increase awareness by teachers of biased treatment (through the provision of feedback about observed teacher-student interactions) and to promote equalization of student treatment. These efforts are firmly in place in staff development programs across the country but the results for student achievement have been limited (Gottfredson, Marciniak, Birdseye, & Gottsfredson, 1995).

More promising, due to its systemic emphasis, is the status equalization intervention by Cohen and Lotan (1997). In this instructional strategy, teachers are trained to talk about multiple abilities, to assign competence to low-status children, and to implement complex and cooperative instructional activities that make use of a diversity of student abilities. With status-equalization instruction, low achieving students have been found to participate more often. Finally, interventions studies have also directly targeted student expectations or ability beliefs, with some success. These include providing falsely positive feedback about ability (Rappaport & Rappaport, 1975) or teaching students that ability is malleable and can be increased with effort and strategy use (Good, Aronson, & Inzlicht, 2003).

The NCLB policy also targets teacher beliefs (that all children can achieve grade-level proficiency). This belief induction is highly specified, ups the ante every year, and comes with sharp teeth. Here, high expectations mean reaching grade-level standards in reading, mathematics, and science and such mandated expectations serve as a goal to guide action. An increasing percentage of children from each underperforming subgroup must meet grade-level standards each year until all are grade-level proficient by 2014. Here, too, compliance is monitored through yearly, public assessments of whether the goal is reached, on single administration, multiple choice tests. Failure is met with high-stakes punitive sanctions (e.g., student retention, failure to graduate, school reconstitution or closure). While many have lauded NCLB's shift to proficiency standards and to the disaggregation of achievement results, there are a myriad of problems in conceptualization as well as operationalization (Meier & Wood, 2004). But relevant to its theory of action, NCLB targets only half the expectancy equation—beliefs without intervening policies and practices. Its relative lack of attention to input factors is problematic. The few features specified (qualified teachers, tutoring, research-based curricula and school improvement models, and parent options to change schools) do not directly impact the conditions for learning (the opportunity structures, beliefs, and relationships) that prove critical in actualizing high expectations for a diversity of students. Further, negative sanctions are not likely to shape positive beliefs or build staff capacity but, rather, may drive behavioral compliance at the lowest level.

An Ecological Theory of Action

The above theories of expectancy change draw heavily on behavioral or cognitive-behavioral principles and focus primarily on prophet beliefs, with limited or narrowed attention to the enabling conditions that flow from beliefs. Merton's classic article (1948) pointed us toward the institutional sustenance for such beliefs—a call that was largely ignored. An ecological theory (Weinstein, 2002) targets institutional sustenance but as reflected in multilayered contexts and shaped by both person and setting. Choices made about curricular allocation, instructional grouping, evaluation, motivational strategies, student agency, and relationships must *all* be targeted in order to create achievement cultures that reflect equity in treatment and talent development for all. A more comprehensive effort to promote and actualize high expectations must bring together the relevant players in sustained collaborative and systematic developmental work.

Thus, the primary intervention lever for setting change is a *collaborative participatory process or set of processes* that importantly (a) targets the relevant players especially principal and teachers; (b) is informed by research findings; (c) is sensitive to local conditions; (d) reflects a regularized and continuous cycle of inquiry, action, and evaluation; and (e) works toward a vision that is aligned across levels of the system. Why choose a research-guided participatory approach? This enables a deeper process of continuous rather than episodic change, responsive to changing student needs (Weick & Quinn, 1999). The bringing together of principal and teachers creates a public and school-wide professional learning community where staff take collective responsibility for student learning (Lee, 2001). These features of the participatory process enable the setting of clear and ecologically relevant goals to guide change efforts—goals that draw from research findings about positive expectancy practices but are responsive to the realities of the particular school setting. These features also promote a data-driven accountability for school-wide change—fueled by progress reports, data about student outcomes, and teacher as well as principal participation. They provide supports for individual as well as collective capacity building to mount changes or new efforts in instruction, services, and policy—such as shifts in conceptual understanding, continuing feedback, and modeled practices. The application of positive expectancy principles to the participatory process itself models for the adult learners the very same practices that will be implemented in school settings and builds motivation, buy-in, and sustainability as each member develops leadership in this deliberative and developmental process.

Expectancy change rests on the capacity to see youth in more favorable light as capable of learning despite differences in background, preparedness, or stance. And expectancy change rests upon increased individual and organizational capacity to challenge and support the talent development of a diversity of all students. The seeing of talent as well as the support of talent development for all students requires a school-wide as well as classroom-based achievement culture shift or culture creation. What needs to change is expectations about what is possible (of self, staff, administrators, parents, and students) and the development of skills to bring about deep and sustained learning within the entire school community. Thus, this work reflects a knowledge-attitude-behavior model of change (Weiss, 1997) but one occurring at individual as well as organizational levels, one involving policy, service, as well as behavioral change, and one actualized in nonlinear ways. Sometimes policy or behavior change drives change in attitude; other times, new understanding or attitude change shifts practice. The work is conceptual, capacity building, and systemic at multiple levels of the school ecology, with parallel processes. The overarching participatory process allows co-construction of informed but local solutions in raising expectations for youth (Datnow, Hubbard, & Mehan, 2002).

In what ways, then, is setting creation different from setting change in implementing a high expectation school climate? Briefly put, there are trade-offs in emphases targeted and constraints encountered. While the creation of new school settings enables increased freedom (e.g., in teacher selection, student recruitment, and policy development), new settings also come with tougher resource challenges (Sarason, 1998). This includes incorporating new staff and students each year, lower funding levels than existing public schools, and planning needs that span current as well as future years of build-up. The hiring of principal and teachers with talent-development views and skills is necessary but not sufficient, as every policy, program, and service must be developed or selected, as well as funded, in the design of a new school setting. Thus, this collaborative participatory process, driven by positive expectancy practices as well as the needs of the local ecology, is similarly useful in designing school and classroom environments that promote high expectations for all its students.

Exemplars of Setting-Level Expectancy Interventions

Detracking a High School (9-12)

This intervention research project (Weinstein, Soule, Collins, Cone, Mehlhorn, & Simontacchi, 1991; Weinstein, 2002; Weinstein, Madison, & Kuklinski, 1994) took place in an urban high school of 1,500 students, of which 68% were ethnic minorities. Entry was facilitated by a teacher who participated in the author's university seminar on expectancy change and arranged for a school-wide staff development workshop. Here, the participatory process was first replicated, in brief, in a 3-hour session. As a result of this session, as well as meetings with school and district administrators, we collaboratively developed a "school within a school" structural approach to work with all ninth graders who entered at the lowest level of achievement. Through the existing school-wide tracking system, these students were regularly shunted into remedial rather than college preparatory or honors classes. Given this curricular policy, students could, in effect, successfully complete all high school courses yet not be college eligible. This was a racially tinged reality about which neither students nor their families were fully aware. Thus, our collective goal was to change the low expectations held and to prepare these students for college entry. The small learning community model enabled an interdisciplinary team of teachers to be responsible for 60-100 students per year, with a common preparation period for joint planning and closer monitoring of student performance. But importantly, using the *participatory process lever* described earlier, this interdisciplinary team of teachers joined the principal, vice-principal, the discipline dean, and college advisor, along with university researchers, in a 2-hour weekly meeting to put the positive expectancy principles into practice.

This project continued for two school years, serving two cohorts of ninth grade students. The weekly meetings focused attention first on changing the instructional environment of these remedial classes (through more challenging and supportive instruction), and second on implementing policy changes to integrate these students into the college preparatory curriculum. Teachers supported each other in learning and applying new instructional strategies in their classes, reflecting the six dimensions of positive expectancy environments. Not surprisingly, these proved to be the same strategies they utilized in teaching honors and advanced placement classes. With collaboration within and across subject matter, they revitalized their teaching of these students. They introduced higher order inquiry and cooperative learning in their instruction, which allowed them to draw upon the diverse competencies of their students, thereby broadening notions about ability and increasing motivation and student agency. Work with the disciplinary dean and counselor enabled an examination of referrals, absences, and grades, which helped inform the development of specific supportive interventions for students who did not respond to instructional changes.

Key implementation findings at the setting level included improved instructional quality reflective of positive expectations (assessed by teacher ratings of classroom practices), more positive teacher attitudes toward these students and greater teacher self-efficacy (assessed by qualitative analysis of narrative records from weekly meetings), and three policy changes, institutionalized over successive project years. These included "retroactive" college preparatory credit for successful class completion in the first year, the dismantling of noncollege preparatory classes in English and History in the second year, and change in admission criteria for honors classes to include self-selection and a work contract, for the third year. Thus, these students were not longer segregated in low-track classes and were included in the mainstream of the school community.

An early outcome evaluation of the first year cohort was conducted at year end and at the 1-year follow-up, using an archival-cohort and mixed methods design. As compared to similar students from the previous two school years, the intervention students demonstrated higher grades in intervention classrooms and a higher rate of return (less attrition) to the school for the 10th grade year. Qualitative data indicated that students were aware of higher teacher expectations, perceived greater support, and participated more in the extracurricular life of the school, including leadership positions. However, 1 year later, grades on average were not higher nor absences lower, but it must be noted that these students, as compared to controls, were participating in more rigorous college preparatory classes. Challenges to this intervention included administrative change and conflicting mandates (two principals in 3 years, district takeover by the state), parent resistance to opening up honors classes, departmental resistance to heterogeneous mathematics classes, and variation in teacher capacity to implement these instructional features. Nonetheless, the policy changes persisted for many years and increased opportunities for students to become college eligible.

Turning Around a High-Poverty Low-Performing
Elementary School (K-5)

With increasing numbers of low-performing schools facing potential closure under NCLB, principals and districts have turned to an array of consultants and external resources. This case study draws from this author's experiences working with such schools. Called in as one of a number of consultants when a new principal was hired to turn around high-poverty low-performing elementary school, we found a school setting littered with garbage and graffiti and every system in disarray, including the front office. The school was inhabited by teachers in locked classrooms who rarely collaborated, over-run by students who roamed corridors and concrete outdoor spaces without constructive activities to engage them, and permeated with punishment. There was much student fighting with rampant office referrals, teacher demoralization, and a community perception that this was a school to be avoided. The 500 students, with equal African American and Latino representation, were all economically disadvantaged. The school's academic performance ranked at the lowest level of 1 (only 10% of its students met grade-level proficiency), as compared to all schools and to schools with similar demographics.

While the school was required to meet annual yearly progress targets for the state and accountability targets for NCLB, our shared goal was to reach higher—shifting a school culture of low expectations toward one of high academic achievement for all students. The dilemma was where to start and how to address so many things at the same time, as all features were interlocking aspects of the school culture. Using the collaborative participatory process as a lever, we developed three tiers of interwoven participatory processes to take place weekly: principal coaching, grade-level teacher meetings, and instructional leadership team meetings (which included teacher leaders from each grade and staff representatives from all the services provided). Early in this collaborative work, we diagnosed school needs as well as capacities, explored resource allocation and development, and identified key expectancy setting features to target. Staff communication emerged as a key issue that the regularized meeting structure immediately addressed. Student interns and graduate student researchers (as part of a community intervention specialty clinic) were utilized to extend school resources. The principal shifted focus from outside to inside the school and visited classrooms daily. And we targeted instructional improvement, access to differentiated interventions for students in need, and the development of an inclusive school community that was academically focused, respectful, and motivated, as aspects of the expectancy climate.

Early meetings served simply to make sure that each classroom had books, functioning windows, and clean floors. With the development of trust, access to data (about student performance, absences, and referrals), and increased knowledge about best expectancy practices, meetings became focused on building teacher and school capacity to better serve a diversity of student needs—that is, to provide more challenging instruction, with stronger and more positive supports. In one example, facilitated by our weekly meetings, a teacher shifted from punishing a student's acting out behavior to diagnosing the underlying reason (failure to secure a place in the newly added instrumental program due to scarcity of instruments) and ultimately to finding a positive solution (identifying funds so that all children who desired could play). This example reflects more motivating strategies (supporting intrinsic interest), broadened views of ability (developing musical talent), and relationship building (diagnosing student anger and defusing it). A second example involved the implementation of a school-wide academic challenge in which all children could participate and succeed. Coaches, in addition to teachers, were made available to ensure a broader set of supports for student learning. The reward given to the students who met the challenge was academically enriching (a science museum field trip), which could further motivate student interest. In its first year, 32% of the students met the challenge, to the surprise of many, but not this consultant.

The obstacles to this participatory change process proved enormous. These included clashes between consultant perspectives, conflicting and late district mandates, a press to prescribe teacher performance (through daily walk-throughs dubbed Open Court Police after the curricular program), the earmarking for intervention of only students at the cusp of scoring higher on tests, lack of support from families, and community violence. Yet, over a period of 2 years, gains were seen in student performance, moving the school from the bottom to among the top gainers in the district.

Creating a High Expectation and "Motivating" Elementary School (K-6)

This theory-based case study about the creation and nurturing of an innovative independent elementary school was collaboratively written by the principal and this researcher, who was also a parent and school board member (Butterworth & Weinstein, 1996; Weinstein, 2002). Using ecological principles, we documented features of school-level opportunities and beliefs that actualized high expectations for its diverse students. This small school (with a pseudonym of Landmark) enrolled 112 students, with one class per grade. Admission was nonselective (on a first-come, first-serve basis) except to ensure sibling priority and ethnic minority representation. Because of a scholarship support and an after-school program, minority representation was approximately 30% higher than that of the neighboring district.

The school's philosophy was described by its founder as offering a strong academic program with a warm, nurturing atmosphere. Continuing her predecessor's focus on a family school, the principal-author extended the use of specialist teachers and the wealth of programs aimed at developing multiple talents. The environment at Landmark School pressed students to engage in varied and increasingly challenging learning opportunities, which were scaffolded by multiple teachers and which resulted in products such as student performances that built a strong and inclusive community of learners. A school constitution (cowritten with students and honoring diverse abilities, equity of opportunity, and student voice), a reframing of time, (with Fridays devoted to interdisciplinary projects, field trips, and jobs such as a school-journal, school-bank, and school-store), and the creation of underpeopled activities (more roles than individuals to hold them, which demanded involvement; Barker, 1968) were among the ways that this school provided students with challenges both inside and outside the classroom. Specific policy decisions were made to support teacher preparedness to mount and continually improve this rigorous yet supportive program. These included intensive weekly staff meetings, use of part-time specialist teachers (in science, art, Spanish, physical education, and music) who enriched the curriculum but importantly afforded teachers generous planning and classroom visiting time to develop innovative curricula, the matching of teacher talents to offerings, and principal support, including the teaching of classes. These enabled collaborative participatory opportunities that built upon strengths to design, implement, and evaluate the positive expectancy features of the school.

Challenging curricula in the classroom were enhanced by school-wide activities that flexibly regrouped students and teachers by interest (promoting intrinsic motivation) and students by age (enabling modeling of older to younger students) and that showcased diverse abilities in learning and expression (broadening notions of ability). For example, aligned with texts and writing assignments, students produced plays, literary journals, and newspapers, with advanced students taking increasing responsibilities. Participation of students was maximized by rotating casts, multiple roles, and involvement at every grade level. Similar interwoven opportunities could be seen in social studies instruction and the school government. Given requirements of twice yearly elections, campaign managers for each candidate, multiple posts including class representatives, and presentations, fully 68% of the student body prepared and delivered speeches during each year and 100% voted. Thus, a challenging, varied, and supportive opportunity structure was available to the entire student body and created an inclusive community of learners.

What can be said about potential but untested links between this rich achievement culture and motivational outcomes? Teacher turnover was nil despite lower salaries than those of surrounding school districts. Family attendance ran at an unusual 100% because every student performed or shared work that brought pleasure to the audience. A long waiting list for a place at this school attested to its local reputation. Finally, an overrepresentation of the school's graduates on the city's youth council reflects the motivating force of the school government experience. Most strikingly, the absence of conflicting district, state, and federal mandates enabled breathing room for this school to determine priorities and plan creatively for its students.

Creating an "Early College" Secondary School (6-12)

This last example is drawn from a project currently underway in which the author is codirector for research and development in the creation of a new school. The University of California at Berkeley and Aspire Public Schools (a nonprofit Charter Management Organization) are collaborating in the development of CAL Prep (California Preparatory College Academy). This is a regional 6-12 charter school that targets students across districts who would be first in the family to attend college and that aims to have students earn 30-60 credits in college-level courses by the time they graduate. At this writing, the school is in its second year, with approximately 150 students in grades 6-8. The student population is two-third African American and one-third Latino, with 68% of the students on reduced or free lunch. With an additional grade level to be added each year, enrollment is expected to reach 420 students by 2010-2011. This project was funded initially by the Gates Foundation Early College Initiative through The Woodrow Wilson National Fellowship Foundation.

Here, high expectations move beyond "College for Certain®" to "Early College" and target a seamless transition to a successful college experience. The impetus for university involvement was multidetermined: to participate in strengthening the academic pipeline for underrepresented groups, to develop an urban field station (for educational innovation, research-driven practice and practice-driven research, and training), and to involve the university in rethinking its own teaching and interface with secondary schooling. In this policy context, where schools are closed and new schools are created yearly, involvement in new school development was viewed as a high intellectual challenge in which to invest.

This project reflects a number of intersectoral partnerships (see McLaughlin & O'Brien-Strain, this volume, chapter 17) that have framed how the participatory processes (and organizational structure) for planning, implementation, and scale-up were developed. First, the Chancellor appointed a university governing committee with a diverse membership (a vice-chancellor, dean, faculty, staff, graduate student, and community member, all in all representing eight disciplines). This committee meets monthly and has been involved in preplanning (e.g., development of a memorandum of understanding and selection of the principal) and implementation (with subcommittees in math/sciences, humanities, R & D, and fundraising). Second, there are weekly partnership meetings that include the university team on the ground (two faculty codirectors for R & D, two staff, and a graduate student researcher), a charter administrator, and the school principal. There are also meetings with school staff and with parents. This is where the vision of the school is co-constructed, implemented, and evaluated, with representation of the partner perspectives. Finally, there are meetings with other partnerships, such as the K-20 team (university, community college, school, and charter district), the 10 University of California campuses (all of whom are involved in K-12 outreach), and the national early college network of schools.

In our collaborative work, we are drawing upon research findings in the disciplines as well as positive expectancy principles. An important theme is to prepare students for independent and inquiry-oriented academic work (i.e., learning by design) where they are being challenged to think critically, to apply, and to test hypotheses. It is this learning orientation that will enable the large steps necessary from underpreparedness at entry to successful college-level scholarship. We are building an adult-rich environment, interface with the university (undergraduate tutors, faculty lectures, summer programs, and Saturday science camp), differentiated supports, and strong personal relationships with teachers and students (through small group advisories). One example of the application of positive expectancy principles can be seen in the required exhibitions each year where students present their learning in an applied project (oral histories for sixth graders, scale/measurement for hypothetical carpet-laying in each student's home for seventh graders, and construction of a Rube-Goldberg machine in the eighth grade). This authentic assessment provides high challenge and differentiated supports (coaching, second chance to pass), tests multiple abilities with clear proficiency standards, involves student choice (intrinsic motivation) and agency (peer as well as faculty grading), and builds an inclusive community (parents are invited). This is high challenge work for the collaborators as well, as we face a student population that has not been previously held to high standards and is far behind academically, a regional rather than local community base to support students, and a severely underresourced funding model endemic to the creation of charter schools.

Conclusion

In spite of multiple legal and legislative efforts to secure equality of educational opportunity for ethnic and linguistic minorities, poor children, and children with special needs, the institution of schooling has long operated as a sorting mechanism by identifying the so-called talented for differentiated and more prestigious pathways and the less talented for remedial instruction. Remedies have moved from mandating equity of access (such as in desegregated schools and mainstreamed classrooms) to equity of resources (such as in qualified teachers and instructional materials), and currently, to equity of outcomes (Weinstein et al., 2004). As noted earlier, the academic standards movement and NCLB have decreed that all children reach grade-level competencies, and further, that the gap in achievement between demographic groups must be erased. This societal expectancy intervention would be far more likely to succeed if it targeted the conditions for student learning that communicate and actualize equity in opportunity and outcome.

While schools cannot do it alone, given differences in life chances before the start of and during schooling (e.g., Rothstein, 2004), schools can, indeed, reach higher. The current political climate presses for simple interventions with easily measured outcomes, such as accountability on high-stakes tests. In contrast, an ecological understanding of expectancy effects calls for more complex setting-level interventions—sensitive to the local conditions, systemic features, and capacity building. One size will not fit all and there will be no quick fix to the problem of low and differentiated academic expectations. Instead, a long-term commitment will be required as will regularized participatory processes that develop awareness of expectation cues and enable sustained building of capacity at the classroom and school level to challenge, support, engage, and include all students.

Future directions include paying greater attention to what is meant by high expectations and hence, what kinds of instructional rigor, supports, timeline, and academic identity are needed to meet such expectations as well as to assess whether they are in fact achieved. Under NCLB, high expectations for all means the achievement of grade-level competencies in reading, math, and science on single administration multiple choice standardized tests. Charter schools target expectations of "College for Certain" for groups of poor and ethnic minority youngsters. The Early College High School Initiative has raised the ante further to include the successful completion of 2 years of college while in high school, aiming for a more positive college experience. Other efforts (see Maton, Hrabowski, Özdemir, & Wimms, this volume, chapter 7) address expectations for math and science in order to remedy the underrepresentation of women and ethnic minority scholars in the STEM (Science, Technology, Engineering, and Mathematics) career track. Expectations might also embrace the creation of lifelong learners and serious readers or competencies beyond subject matter to include social-emotional skills and civic engagement.

The important issues here are to go beyond legal mandates by tracking attainment as well as achievement, by following individual student growth trajectories rather than group means (which include different students each year), and by supporting expectations with the appropriate instructional strategies that address student need. Low academic expectations have to be countered by the acceleration of learning, as those far behind have to go faster, learn longer, and/or learn differently. Gutierrez (1996) has distinguished between subject-matter departments that are organized for the advancement of its students (meeting them where they are and moving them forward) and departments that place students in courses on the basis of past performance—akin to the distinction between talent development versus talent selection (Weinstein, 2002).

Ultimately, to support schools that develop the talent of all, policies will need to address conditions for learning, by supporting teachers and principals in school-based efforts to improve instruction and climate for a diversity of students. Needed are coherent incentives and sustained supports for creating enriched schooling environments for all children. Drawing from the expectancy research literature, children's perceptions of their classroom and school experiences should become one important cornerstone of assessing whether equity and excellence in education have indeed been achieved.

References

Barker, R. (1968). *Ecological psychology*. Stanford: Stanford University Press.

Brattesani, K., Weinstein, R. S., & Marshall, H. H. (1984). Student perceptions of differential treatment as moderators of teacher expectation effects. *Journal of Educational Psychology, 76,* 236-247.

Brophy, J. E., & Good, T. L. (1984). *Teacher-student relationships: Causes and consequences.* New York: Holt, Rinehart, and Winston.

Butterworth, B., & Weinstein, R. S. (1996). Enhancing motivational opportunity in elementary schooling: A case study of the ecology of principal leadership. *Elementary School Journal, 97,* 57-80.

Cohen, E., & Lotan, R. A. (Eds.). (1997). *Working for equity in heterogeneous classrooms: Sociological theory in practice.* New York: Teachers College Press.

Darling-Hammond, L. (2004). Inequality and the right to learn: Access to qualified teachers in California's public schools. *Teachers College Record, 106,* 1936-1966.

Datnow, A., Hubbard, L., & Mehan, H. (2002). *Extending educational reform: From one school to many.* London: Routledge Falmer Press.

Desimone, L. M. (this volume). Whole-school change.

Dweck, C. S. (2000). *Self-theories: Their role in motivation, personality, and development.* Philadelphia: Taylor & Francis.

Eden, D., Geller, D., Gewirtz, A., Gorden-Terner, R., Inbar, I., Leberman, M., et al. (2000). Implanting Pygmalion leadership style through workshop training: Seven field experiments. *Leadership Quarterly, 11*, 171-210.

Good, C., Aronson, J., & Inzlicht, M. (2003). Improving adolescents' standardized test performance: An intervention to reduce the effects of stereotype threat. *Applied Developmental Psychology, 24*, 645-662.

Good, T. L., & Nichols, S. L. (2001). Expectancy effects in the classroom: A special focus on improving the reading performance of minority students in first-grade classrooms. *Educational Psychologist, 36*, 113-126.

Gottfredson, D. C., Marciniak, E. M., Birdseye, A. T., & Gottsfredson, G. D. (1995). Increasing teacher expectations for student achievement. *Journal of Educational Research, 88*, 155-163.

Gregory, A., & Weinstein, R. S. (in press). The discipline gap and African Americans: Defiance or cooperation in the high school classroom. *Journal of School Psychology.*

Gutierrez, R. (1996). Practices, beliefs, and cultures of high school mathematics departments: Understanding their influences on student achievement. *Journal of Curriculum Studies, 28*, 495-530.

Jussim, L., & Harber, K. D. (2005). Teacher expectations and self-fulfilling prophecies: Knowns and unknowns, resolved and unresolved controversies. *Personality and Social Psychology Review, 9*, 131-155.

Kuklinski, M. R., & Weinstein, R. S. (2001). Classroom and developmental differences in a path model of teacher expectancy effects. *Child Development, 72*, 1554-1578.

Lee, V. E. (2001). *Restructuring high schools for equity and excellence: What works.* New York: Teachers College Press.

Marshall, H. H., & Weinstein, R. S. (1988). Beyond quantitative analysis: Recontextualization of classroom factors contributing to the communication of teacher expectations. In J. L Green & J. O. Harker (Eds.), *Multiple perspective analyses of classroom discourse* (pp. 249-279). Norwood, NJ: Ablex.

Maton, K. I., Hrabowski, F. A., Özdemir, M., & Wimms, H. (this volume). Enhancing representation, retention, and achievement of minority students in higher education: A social transformation theory of change.

McKown, C., & Weinstein, R. S. (2003). The development and consequences of stereotype consciousness in middle childhood. *Child Development, 74*, 498-515.

McLaughlin, M., & O'Brien-Strain, M. (this volume). The Youth Data Archive: Integrating data to assess social settings in a societal sector framework.

Meier, D., & Wood, G. (Eds.). (2004). *Many children left behind.* Boston, MA: Beacon Press.

Merton, R. K. (1948). The self-fulfilling prophecy. *Antioch Review, 8*, 193-210.

Midgley, C. (Ed.). (2002). *Goals, goal structures, and patterns of adaptive learning.* Mahwah, NJ: Lawrence Erlbaum Associates.

No Child Left Behind Act of 2001, Pub. L. No. 107-110, 115 Stat. 1425 (2002).

Pianta, R. C., & Allen, J. P. (this volume). Building capacity for positive youth development in secondary school classrooms: Changing teachers' interactions with students.

Rappaport, M. M., & Rappaport, H. (1975). The other half of the expectancy equation: Pygmalion. *Journal of Educational Psychology, 76,* 531-536.

Raudenbush, S. (1984). Magnitude of teacher expectancy effects on pupil IQ as a function of the credibility of expectancy induction: A synthesis of findings from eighteen experiments. *Journal of Educational Psychology, 76,* 85-97.

Roeser, R., Eccles, J., & Sameroff, A. (1998). Academic and emotional functioning in early adolescence: Longitudinal relations, patterns, and prediction by experience in middle school. *Development and Psychopathology, 10,* 321-352.

Rosenthal, R., & Jacobson, L. (1968). *Pygmalion in the classroom: Teacher expectation and pupils' intellectual development.* New York: Holt, Rinehart, and Winston.

Rothstein, R. (2004). Even the best schools can't close the achievement gap. *Poverty & Race Action Council, 13,* 1-10.

Sarason, S. B. (1998). *Charter schools: Another flawed educational reform?* New York: Teachers College Press.

Skinner, E., & Belmont, M. J. (1993) Motivation in the classroom: Reciprocal effects of teacher behavior and student engagement across the school year. *Journal of Educational Psychology, 85,* 571-581.

Solomon, D., Watson, M., Battistich, V., Schaps, E., & Delucchi, K. (1996). Creating classrooms that students experience as communities. *American Journal of Community Psychology, 24,* 719-748.

Steele, C. M., & Aronson, J. (1995). Stereotype threat and the intellectual test performance of African Americans. *Journal of Personality and Social Psychology, 69,* 797811.

Weick, K., & Quinn, R. (1999). Organizational change and development. *Annual Review of Psychology, 50,* 361-386.

Weinstein, R. S. (2002). *Reaching higher: The power of expectations in schooling.* Cambridge, MA: Harvard University Press.

Weinstein, R. S., Gregory, A., & Strambler, M. J. (2004). Intractable self-fulfilling prophecies: Fifty years after Brown v. Board of Education. *American Psychologist, 59,* 511-520.

Weinstein, R. S., Madison, S. M., & Kuklinski, M. R. (1995). Raising expectations in schooling: Obstacles and opportunities for change. *American Educational Research Journal, 32,* 121-159.

Weinstein, R. S., Marshall, H. H., Sharp, L., & Botkin, M. (1987). Pygmalion and the student: Age and classroom differences in children's awareness of teacher expectations. *Child Development, 58,* 1079-1093.

Weinstein, R. S., & McKown, C. (1998). Expectancy effects in context: Listening to the voices of children and teachers. In J. Brophy (Ed.) *Advances in research on teaching: Expectations in the classroom* (Vol. 7, pp. 215-242). Greenwich, CT: JAI.

Weinstein, R. S., Soule, C. R., Collins, F., Cone, J., Mehlhorn, M., & Simontacchi, K. (1991). Expectations and high school change: Teacher-researcher collaboration to prevent school failure. *American Journal of Community Psychology, 19,* 333-364.

Weiss, C. H. (1997). Theory-based evaluation: Past, present, and future. In D. J. Rog & D. Fournier (Eds.), *Evaluation: Perspectives on theory, practice, and methods: New directions for evaluation* (Vol. 76). San Francisco: Jossey-Bass.

Wentzel, K. R. (2002). Are effective teachers like good parents: Teaching styles and student adjustment in early adolescence. *Child Development, 73,* 287-301.

Chapter 6

An Intervention in Progress: Pursuing Precision in School Race Talk

MICA POLLOCK

T his chapter discusses an intervention in progress. What I am working to improve is not typically measured nor classically "measurable." Unlike other contributors to this book, I am not trying to make an explicitly quantifiable intervention, for example, to assist high school students to take fewer drugs. Rather, I am trying to assist educators to talk and think more precisely about the complex issues of race they face in their own institutions. This intervention attempts to counter a damaging habit I have studied: in educational settings (as elsewhere), we often talk about racial issues reductively, quickly, and with insufficient information. Equally destructive, we also often refuse to talk about racial issues at all (Pollock, 2004a).

In a 3-year ethnographic study of a school and district in California, reported in *Colormute: Race Talk Dilemmas in an American School* (Pollock, 2004a), I found that refusing to talk about race, which I call "colormuteness," can have harmful consequences in schools. For example, when educators just talk about "low achievers," racial achievement gaps often stay unaddressed. When educators just talk about "the kids getting suspended," racially disparate suspension patterns often continue unabated. Educators' lives are made far more difficult when solutions remain unexplored. Yet conversations about race often display confused, murky, and partially informed thinking about racial inequality and racial disparities in education. This imprecise talk too is very consequential: when educators talk imprecisely about how disparities might be dismantled, they pursue this goal imprecisely as well. For example, my research suggests that people who analyze black students' disproportionately low test scores as simply a result of "black culture" or analyze Latino dropout rates as a result solely of Latino parenting will be less likely to seek to improve their teaching of black or Latino students, or to improve the in-school experiences of such youth (see also Diamond, 2008; Louie, 2008). In my second ethnographic analysis of contemporary arguments over racial inequality in schools (Pollock, 2008a), I found once more that educators who were resistant to discussing the role their own behaviors played in student outcomes were less likely to set forth to improve students' in-school experiences.

For the past several years, I have been using my research on race talk to help both preservice and inservice educators (teachers, principals, and superintendents) analyze how they currently talk and do not talk about race issues in their schools and districts. We do what linguists call "metapragmatic" analysis: we talk about our own talking, and its consequences for students and school communities.

Educators in schools and districts talk about racial issues all the time, if often only in private. More privately, as I found in *Colormute*, they discuss how white teachers and students of color get along, which students get which opportunities, where various "racial groups" of students sit at lunch, and so forth. Particularly, in private, they discuss racial patterns in who is being suspended or put in Special Education, the purported "attitudes" of various "culture" groups toward schooling, and so on. Increasingly publicly in the era of No Child Left Behind, they discuss things like "achievement gaps": for example, how various racial and ethnic groups are achieving on tests and on school-based measures of achievement such as grades and graduation.

Why intervene into such race talk? Because the ways in which educators talk about race issues in their schooling settings have major implications for how they analyze and address core issues of racial inequality there. Talking is an action that both reflects people's thinking on social problems and produces (or does not produce) further action to address those problems. Many scholars have proved that through everyday talk in social settings, people inside schools make crucial decisions about whom to serve and how.[1] Other scholars who study social problem solving have demonstrated that if a community wants to improve its own circumstances, it has to *talk about* its own social problems and analyze both causes and solutions precisely. For example, Hart (1997) demonstrates that children trying to solve environmental problems must precisely analyze those problems' production; Fine, Roberts, and Torre (2004) show the same for youth in New York researching local and national racial "opportunity gaps." So do Carlson and Earls (2002) trying to work with youth to analyze and address community problems in the United States and internationally. Kegan and Lahey (2002) show the same for adult professionals busy trying to improve their own social settings: "how we talk affects the way we work." Problem analysis involves talking. When people work to solve dilemmas, tensions, and inequities in their own social settings, they must seek to discuss and analyze those issues *precisely and thoroughly*. Hence, I work with preservice and inservice educators to think through how they talk (and do not talk) precisely about racial issues in their institutions. I define precise race talk as talk that *thoroughly and clearly analyzes the various actors, actions, and processes involved in the issue under discussion.* In school settings, this includes talk that clearly discusses what specific subpopulations of students need from schools in order to succeed, talk that thoroughly and clearly analyzes the actors and acts that produce a racial disparity, and talk that clearly discusses which everyday acts by educators move students (particularly students of color) toward educational opportunity and which acts move them further away from it.

Theories of Measurement and Change

Many well-known professional developers trying to prepare educators to engage issues of diversity urge educators to talk more about race in order to strive for racial equality of opportunity and outcome (Singleton & Hays, 2008). I, too, urge educators to avoid colormuteness whenever refusing to talk about race will be harmful to students. Yet in my interventions to try to make race talk in education more precise, I am urging (as does Singleton) that educators talk not just *more* about race but also *more skillfully.*

Researchers examining educators' "race talk" often imply that they measure educators' comments about race as more or less "racist."[2] I instead "measure" race talk on a scale from reductive to thorough and from murky to clear. I measure precise race talk in contrast to race talk that is too vague or confused to afford thorough analysis of educational problems. In my professional development efforts with educators, I suggest three racial topics that educators[3] can typically discuss more precisely:

1. Educators can pursue more precise talk about *student subpopulations and their needs.*
2. Educators can pursue more precise talk about the *causes of racial disparities.*
3. Educators can pursue more precise talk about the everyday educator acts that actually assist students of color and those that actually harm them.

In describing typical talk about each topic below, I offer a set of questions and, in two cases, a graphic tool designed to get speakers to think metapragmatically about whether their own race talk is precise enough.[4]

Let me state clearly that my goal in this work is not to prompt paranoia or what critics call a "politically correct" institutional environment that actually keeps people from talking about race issues out of fear that they will sound "racist" (Ely, Meyerson, & Davidson, 2006). Rather, I urge that educators struggle toward precise analysis of shared social problems, through discussions that are inherently difficult. Thus far, I have not literally assessed "how well" educators have done in these conversations; rather, I have asked participants to attend to the snags and dilemmas encountered as they attempt to talk about racial issues. Most of all, I prompt educators to consider whether their *own* conversations are assisting them to serve their students' needs. This intervention assumes that educators are motivated generally to help children and that to some extent they will be motivated to make their discussions more precise once they recognize how imprecise talk makes it difficult to analyze and meet children's needs.

This theory of change also assumes that to some extent, educators are motivated to better serve their students of color, typically on the receiving end of racial disparities, and to close racial "achievement gaps." Some are motivated directly by desires to not be racist and to do a better job of educating youth from diverse backgrounds and some are motivated more indirectly by federal and state requirements to measure the achievement of racialized groups. Some just want to be more successful teachers and administrators. Most educators, like most Americans, subscribe generally to an ideology of equal opportunity (Hochschild & Herk, 1990). A subset of educators seem to lack motivation to offer students of color additional opportunities in specific circumstances; depending on how demands for opportunity proceed, educators can sometimes angrily denounce demands to assist students of color in particular ways (Pollock, 2008a). But educators often lack not motivation to serve students of color equitably, but a clear analysis of how to do so (Harding, 2006; Hollins & Guzman, 2005; Watson, 2007). One might argue that my tools for more successful "race talk" offer skills that are useful only to those motivated to talk more precisely or successfully. But some participants also become more motivated by the understandings that an analysis of their discourse produces. After seeing that insufficient explanations of achievement gaps lead to insufficient efforts to close those gaps, for example, educators have much more desire to pay attention to their race talk.

Three Arenas in Which Race Talk in Schools Must Typically Become More Precise in Order to Thoroughly Analyze Issues of Race and Racial Inequality

Educators Can Pursue More Precise Talk About Student Needs

Educators trying to describe the needs of students of color in school buildings often retreat to using general, race-loaded words like "urban," "inner city," "disadvantaged," or "at-risk" when analysis gets too controversial or too complex. Such aggregated words often serve to gloss over the actual needs of student populations and subpopulations. These words do often describe what Cicourel (1981) calls "macrostructures": "urban" students do often live in cities, after all. (Of course, the race-loaded, imprecise nature of the word "urban" is revealed when adults call suburban or even rural students of color "urban," especially if they wear attire associated with hip-hop culture.) General words like "urban" and the like do not actually describe what particular students actually need from social settings in order to succeed in them.

Talk that describes the needs of "all students" might be called "hyperaggregated." Such talk often dominates educator and policymaker discourse (in the district I studied in *Colormute*, "all students can learn" was a mantra repeated on mission statements and in administrator conversations). Talk of "all students" needs can also sometimes be accurate: all students do need attention, care, and support from their teachers. But often, as shown in my research (Pollock, 2004a), such hyperaggregated talk of student needs actually substitutes for any discussion of specific subpopulations' needs, as people talk only about "all students" rather than the needs of smaller groups of them.

Indeed, using such aggregated or hyperaggregated terms can actually prevent precise needs analysis. For example, general talk about "needy" students in school settings can supplant discussion of the needs of specific subpopulations, such as English language learners (see also Olsen, 1995). General aggregated talk about a district or school's population as "at-risk" or "disadvantaged" can also gloss over talk about the specific risks or disadvantages that some students experience in their actual lives. While a school community might quickly be described in the aggregate as "low income," for example, some students may actually be living in stable housing, while some may be living in foster care and some might actually be homeless. Some students will have employed parents or guardians and some will not. These differences will affect what assistance students need to succeed in school. Some talk of student needs will need to consider the needs of *individuals*, some of *subgroups*, and so on. Individuals always have individual needs, but subpopulations also sometimes have shared needs.

The answer in some cases is to talk about racial groups' needs. Some needs might be shared, on average, by members of a particular racialized group: on average, one school's Latino students might live in one area that lacks a community center open after school, while another school's black students on average might lack access to preschool. Similarly, some life experiences might be shared by a racial group at a school: a program for "Latinos" at one school might be useful to many of its Latino students if it affords them a safe space to analyze a shared experience of *being* "Latino" at the school, in the city, or in the United States (Gándara, 2008).

Yet other overarching claims about "Latino" needs might be too imprecise to serve a school's smaller subpopulations (Suarez-Orozco & Suarez-Orozco, 2001). A school's Salvadoran students, on average, might need particular psychological supports to weather families' experiences of political violence; Brazilian immigrants may require a particular set of language supports. Urban Chinese immigrant students' math preparation may far outweigh that of Hmong students coming from rural areas, making talk of "Asians" and their needs too imprecise (Wang & Wu, 1996). The particular needs and circumstances of recent Filipino immigrants in a school may never be discussed in a conversation about "Asians," or even a conversation about "Filipinos."

In order to serve student needs precisely, educators must describe and analyze student needs precisely. The educator thus needs to ask, repeatedly, *whether discussions are pinpointing in sufficient detail which students need what from the school.* One superintendent I met in a professional development setting spoke importantly of needing to provide a "smorgasboard" of programs designed to meet the various needs of various subpopulations *and* of the student population as a whole.

When discussing student needs, educators can draw a "number line" (that follows this paragraph) and ask the following questions about their ongoing conversation. Which needs are shared by subgroups, larger groups, or all our students? Where on this spectrum does our current talk about the needs of students fall? Are we describing student needs precisely enough?

Individual students ↔ subgroups ↔ larger groups ↔ all students

Educators Can Pursue More Precise Talk About the Causes of Racial Disparities

In school settings, educators routinely try to analyze the causes of the racial disparities and patterns they see around them. *Imprecise* race talk is talk that analyzes such causation only partially. For example, teachers I analyzed in *Colormute* often remarked privately that the student population wandering in the hallways during class was disproportionately black. They then explained this disparity only partially, in part by proposing assumptions as facts: they would explain that the pattern was caused by black students' "attitudes," or black parents' "values," or, less frequently, by the administrators or security guards who did not stop black students from wandering.

In this partial and imprecise analysis, speakers failed to pinpoint other acts and actors contributing to the pattern's production. They rarely noted that they themselves were often ejecting black students disproportionately from their classes into the hallways. They rarely asked whether black students might be disproportionately disengaged from particular teachers' classes and thus disproportionately wandering the halls. They also rarely noted that nonblack students tended to stay home from school altogether when they wanted to cut class. Black students seemed to stay in the school hallways when cutting class as a visible protest of their situation, suggesting that different groups of students might be disengaging in different manners. In discussing only partially what "caused" the hallways' demographics, educators missed a chance to fully understand and improve their own interactions with black students.

Any precise analysis of a racial disparity needs to go beyond quick statements about one isolated group of people producing the disparity and instead thoroughly analyze the *various* people and acts involved in producing the racial disparity. (Precise analysis also has to go beyond simply stating a disturbing pattern. The teacher simply remarking upon black students' overrepresentation in the hallways may well clue in her peers to notice the pattern, but she will not provide them with any tools for figuring out how to dismantle it.)

The same thing can be said about educators' analyses of "achievement gaps," which, like many public explanations,[5] often boil down the analysis to incredibly reductive causal statements. Educators are increasingly asked to explain racial achievement patterns publicly in the era of No Child Left Behind, since they now have to analyze the achievement data of racial and ethnic subgroups in their schools (see Losen, 2004). Such causal analysis can often become dangerously reductive. For example, a common too-quick explanation analyzed in research (Carter, 2005) is that black and Latino students simply refuse *to* achieve for fear of alienating their same-race peers. Such quick causal claims attributing achievement outcomes to peer interactions alone remove all sorts of contributing actors and actions from the analysis. Speakers fail to analyze, for example, educators' role in tracking many young black and Latino students to low "ability" groups (see Tyson, 2008), or even the role of educators' instruction (Ferguson, 2008; Rubin, 2008; Weinstein, this volume, chapter 5). They fail to analyze how parents may lack knowledge of available educational opportunities (Mickelson & Cousins, 2008). They fail to analyze the complex "outside" opportunity systems denying children of color key early opportunities to learn or to be healthy (Noguera, 2003; see Rothstein, 2004), and so forth.

Educators trying to analyze racial achievement patterns are analyzing one of the most complex social problems in the nation. They need to be very careful about too-quick or too-shallow causal analyses that only scratch the surface of the problem's complexity. The "achievement gap's" causation can never be boiled down to one set of actors' actions. When educators talk as though it can, this imprecise analysis actually can harm both young people of color and themselves, since actors and actions that could help close the "achievement gap" are left out of both analysis and interventions.

Another way that educators reduce the analysis of racial achievement patterns is by arguing quickly that the presumed "cultures" of particular racialized/ethnic/national-origin groups "cause" their achievement. Imprecise talk about "culture" often particularly implicates racial-ethnic group parents as somehow single-handedly responsible for student achievement. Such imprecise talk fails to analyze how parents, *in interaction with school people, neighborhood people, larger opportunity systems, and their children,* play *a role* in producing children's performance. For example, Louie (2004) shows that Chinese parents (routinely the subject of quick "cultural" statements about "valuing education") do not directly "cause" their children's achievement through "caring" about it. Rather, through a complex set of interactions with other parents, school enrollment systems, neighborhood services, educators, and their children, Chinese parents acquire and share knowledge about how to push their children through the school system toward college, and then push their children in ways received favorably by schools (see also Zhou, this volume, chapter 13). In imprecise "culture" talk, educators fail to analyze the many, many actors that influence how any young Chinese American person achieves, including the educators who presume Chinese American parents and students to be "model minorities" (Louie, 2004). No child lives in a "group" bubble only influenced by people just from her ethnic-racial "culture." Children are raised by home adults, but those adults interact with educators and administrators in schools; children interact not just with their guardians and peers, but also with teachers and principals and security guards and neighbors and the media.

Imprecise analysis of the causation of any racial pattern misses drawing players into the solution. Educators can talk more skillfully about racial disparities by investigating how various players might help dismantle the racial disparity under discussion. Whenever talking about racial disparities, educators can ask: Are we considering and including all the actors who contribute to producing these disparities? Do we really have evidence for the contributions we're naming? Who else needs to be pulled in to help dismantle these disparities?

The goal in such conversations is not to demonstrate which actors or acts contribute *more* but rather to fully analyze all of the acts that produce the disparity being considered. Educators must take great care to also include *their own acts* when analyzing the production of the disparity as the typical tendency is to delete oneself from the analysis (Diamond, 2008; Pollock, 2004a, 2008a). Further, to avoid an unproductive blame game, facilitators should explicitly point out that the goal is to analyze distributed responsibility for social problems (Stone et al., 2000). I have called this pursuing "an urgent language of communal responsibility" (Pollock, 2001).

Educators Can Pursue More Precise Talk
About the Everyday Educator Acts That
Actually Assist Students of Color and Those
That Actually Harm Them

This final issue is extremely important. Much scholarship proposing ways to assist students of color in schools never takes the time to guide educators through the details of such attempts at equitable practice. Instead, scholarship offers educators shorthand, vague, and imprecise strategies ("celebrate diversity," or don't be "colorblind") that never precisely pinpoint which specific acts are actually helpful and harmful to students of color in which situations and why.

Imprecise talk about helping students of color can actually backfire on equity efforts. For example, a teacher urged to use a film or book or poster about "other cultures" to "diversify" her curriculum can easily use such a text in ways that oversimplify, stereotype, or misportray the people portrayed (Abu El-Haj, 2008; Chadwick, 2008; Deyhle, 2008; McCarty, 2008; Sharma, 2008; Sleeter, 2008). Educators need to talk more precisely about which pedagogical strategies engage diversity thoroughly. Similarly, an educator urged vaguely to "connect to the community" can easily do so clumsily and promote more shallow visions of communities (such as a quick bus tour that rolls without stopping through a school's most impoverished enrollment area, a tactic I myself have experienced). Rather, educators need to talk far more precisely about how to forge deeper connections with actual community members (Moll, Amanti, Neff, & Gonzalez, 1992; Wyman & Kashatok, 2008).

One key confusion makes our talk about helping and harming students of color imprecise. Educators must both treat students of color as complex individuals rather than racial group members *and* recognize their real experiences as racial group members in order to assist them, understand their experiences, and treat them equitably. For example, a teacher must consider her black students' experiences *as black students* struggling, against stereotypes, to be seen as smart (Cohen, 2008; Perry, Steele, & Hilliard, 2003); at times, she must afford her Latino students the chance to analyze their experiences *as Latino students* trying to make it to college (Gándara, 2008). Yet she does them a disservice at many moments by overlooking their individuality, or distorting their actual experiences by seeing them through a false "racial" lens (D. Carter, 2008; Lucas, 2008).

Educators need to ask a more precise question: which everyday acts by educators move specific students of color toward educational opportunity and which acts move them further away from it? To answer this question regarding any given act (e.g., a method of teaching a particular text; a way of talking to students about racial stereotypes; or a particular disciplinary practice), educators can draw a simple number line (that follows this paragraph) and ask one another: Do we think this act is moving specific students of color closer to educational opportunity or farther away from it? Why? What is our evidence?

Less educational opportunity ↔ more educational opportunity

This issue is so complex that I produced an edited volume, *Everyday antiracism: Getting real about race in school* (2008b), in which I asked 65 experts in race and education studies to each discuss precisely one concrete, research-based practice that an educator could employ in her typical day to counteract racial inequality of opportunity and outcome. It took work for the authors, too, to discuss their recommendations precisely. We were motivated by the idea that precise suggestions would best assist educators to equalize opportunity.

Conclusion

The point of pursuing precision in school race talk is to prompt more precise analysis of what assisting students to enjoy equal opportunity actually entails. When we talk imprecisely about this goal, we pursue it imprecisely in school settings as well. For this reason, improving talk is far more than "just talking." Rather, it hones educators' analyses of how to improve their service to students.

Notes

1. See Erickson (2004) for a thorough discussion of such research, and Mehan (1996) for a great example of it. See Cicourel (1981) and Mehan (1996) for a discussion of how analytically to link everyday talk to the production of social organization inside social settings.

2. See the many research studies on teacher "racism" discussed in Hollins and Guzman (2005).

3. By "educators," I primarily refer in this chapter to adults who work in K-12 schools and their surrounding districts, although I have argued elsewhere that researchers can also pursue more precise talk about race issues in education if we want to promote precise problem analysis (Pollock, 2004b). So can university professors and those running teacher and administrator education programs.

4. These tools are also presented and discussed in Mica Pollock, Talking precisely about equal opportunity, *Everyday antiracism: Getting real about race in school*, Mica Pollock (Ed.). New York: The New Press (2008b).

5. Debates over the causation of racial disparities obviously characterize educational research as well. One might say that research is often a battle over which actors in complex systems actually produce racial disparities or play *more* of a role in producing those disparities. Still, researchers ourselves often make reductive, overarching claims about what "causes" disparities and various school

"problems," rather than offering more precise analyses of causation. For a telling example of how such quick explanatory statements can coexist amidst complex debates over causation, see Farkas (2003).

References

Abu El-Haj, T. (2008). Arab visibility and invisibility. In M. Pollock (Ed.), *Everyday antiracism: Getting real about race in school*. New York: The New Press.

Carlson, M., Felton, E., & Fonseca, C. (2002, Fall). Children and democracy [Electronic version]. *ReVista: Harvard Review of Latin America*. Retrieved December 13, 2006, from http://drclas.fas.harvard.edu/revista/articles/view/174

Carter, D. (2008). On spotlighting and ignoring racial group members in the classroom. In M. Pollock (Ed.), *Everyday antiracism: Getting real about race in school*. New York: The New Press.

Carter, P. (2005). *Keepin' it real: School success beyond black and white*. Oxford University Press.

Chadwick, J. (2008). Teaching racially sensitive literature. In M. Pollock (Ed.), *Everyday antiracism: Concrete ways to successfully navigate the relevance of race in school*. New York: The New Press.

Cicourel, A. V. (1981). Notes on the integration of micro and macro levels of analysis. In K. Knorr-Cetina & A. V. Cicourel (Eds.), *Advances in social theory and methodology: Toward an integration of micro- and macro-sociologies* (pp. 51-80). Boston: Routledge & Kegan Paul.

Cohen, G. L. (2008). Providing supportive feedback. In M. Pollock (Ed.), *Everyday antiracism: Getting real about race in school*. New York: The New Press.

Deyhle, D. (2008). What's on your classroom wall?: Problematic posters. In M. Pollock (Ed.), *Everyday antiracism: Concrete ways to successfully navigate the relevance of race in school*. New York: The New Press.

Diamond, J. B. (2008). Focusing on student learning. In M. Pollock (Ed.), *Everyday antiracism: Getting real about race in school*. New York: The New Press.

Ely, R. J., Meyerson, D. E., & Davidson, M. N. (2006, September 1). Rethinking political correctness. *Harvard Business Review*, 1-11.

Erickson, F. (2004). *Talk and social theory: Ecologies of speaking and listening in everyday life*. Cambridge, UK: Polity Press.

Farkas, G. (2003). Racial disparities and discrimination in education: What do we know, how do we know it, and what do we need to know? *Teachers College Record, 105*(6), 1119-1146.

Ferguson, R. F. (2008). Helping students of color meet high standards. In M. Pollock (Ed.), *Everyday antiracism: Getting real about race in school*. New York: The New Press.

Fine, M., Roberts, R. A., Torre, M. E., Bloom, J., Burns, A., Chajet, L., et al. (2004). *Echoes of Brown: Youth documenting and performing the legacy of Brown v. Board of Education*. New York: Teachers' College Press.

Gándara, P. (2008). Strengthening student identity in school programs. In M. Pollock (Ed.), *Everyday antiracism: Getting real about race in school*. New York: The New Press.

Harding, H. (2006). *"All their teachers are white": Portraits of "successful" white teachers in predominantly black classrooms*. Unpublished Ed.D. dissertation, Harvard Graduate School of Education, Cambridge.

Hart, R. (1997). *Children's participation: The theory and practice of involving young citizens in community development and environmental care*. London: Earthscan.

Hochschild, J. L., & Herk, M. (1990). "Yes, but….": Principles and caveats in American racial attitudes. In J. W. Chapman & A. Wertheimer (Eds.), *Majorities and minorities, Nomos 31* (Yearbook of the American Society for Political and Legal Philosophy, pp. 308-335). New York: New York University Press.

Hollins, E., & Guzman, M. T. (2005). Research on preparing teachers for diverse populations. In M. Cochran-Smith & K. M. Zeichner (Eds.), *Studying teacher education: The report of the AERA panel on research and teacher education* (pp. 477-548). Mahwah, New Jersey: Lawrence Erlbaum.

Kegan, R., & Lahey, L. L. (2002). *How the way we talk can change the way we work: Seven languages for transformation*. San Francisco: Jossey-Bass.

Losen, D. J. (2004). Challenging racial disparities: The promise and pitfalls of the No Child Left Behind Act's race-conscious accountability. *Howard Law Journal, 47*(2), 243-298.

Louie, V. S. (2004). *Compelled to excel: Immigration, education, and opportunity among Chinese Americans*. Stanford: Stanford University Press.

Louie, V. S. (2008). Moving beyond quick "cultural" explanations. In M. Pollock (Ed.), *Everyday antiracism: Getting real about race in school*. New York: The New Press.

Lucas, S. R. (2008). Constructing colorblind classrooms. In M. Pollock (Ed.), *Everyday antiracism: Getting real about race in school*. New York: The New Press.

McCarty, T. L. (2008) Evaluating images of groups in your curriculum. In M. Pollock (Ed.), *Everyday antiracism: Getting real about race in school*. New York: The New Press.

Mehan, H. (1996). Beneath the skin and between the ears: A case study in the politics of representation. In J. Lave & S. Chaiklin (Eds.), *Understanding practice: Perspectives on activity and context* (pp. 241-268). Cambridge, UK: Cambridge University Press.

Mickelson, R. A., & Cousins, L. L. (in press). Undermine racially stratified tracking through minority parent involvement. In M. Pollock (Ed.), *Everyday antiracism: Concrete ways to successfully navigate the relevance of race in school*. New York: The New Press.

Moll, L., Amanti, C., Neff, D., & Gonzalez, N. (1992). Funds of knowledge for teaching: Using a qualitative approach to connect homes and classrooms. *Theory into Practice, 31*(2), 132-141.

Noguera, P. (2003). *City schools and the American dream: Reclaiming the promise of public education*. New York: Teachers College Press.

Olsen, L. (1995). School restructuring and the needs of immigrant students. In R. G. Rumbaut & W. A. Cornelius (Eds.), *California's immigrant children: Theory, research, and implications for educational policy* (pp. 209-231). San Diego: Center for U.S.-Mexican Studies, University of California San Diego.

Perry, T., Steele, C., & Hilliard, A., III. (2003). *Young, gifted, and black: Promoting high achievement among African-American students.* Boston: Beacon Press.

Pollock, M. (2001). How the question we ask most about race in education is the very question we most suppress. *Educational Researcher, 30*(9), 2-12.

Pollock, M. (2004a). *Colormute: Race talk dilemmas in an American school.* Princeton, NJ: Princeton University Press.

Pollock, M. (2004b). Race wrestling: Struggling strategically with race in educational practice and research. *American Journal of Education, 111*(1), 25-67.

Pollock, M. (2008a). *Because of Race: How Americans debate harm and opportunity in our schools.* Princeton, NJ: Princeton University Press.

Pollock, M. (Ed.). (2008b). *Everyday antiracism: Getting real about race in school.* New York: The New Press.

Rothstein, R. (2004). *Class and schools: Using social, economic, and educational reform to close the black-white achievement gap.* New York, NY: Teachers College, Columbia University; Washington, DC: Economic Policy Institute.

Rubin, B. C. (2008). Grouping in detracked classrooms. In M. Pollock (Ed.), *Everyday antiracism: Getting real about race in school.* New York: The New Press.

Sharma, S. (2008). Teaching representations of cultural difference through film. In M. Pollock (Ed.), *Everyday antiracism: Getting real about race in school.* New York: The New Press.

Singleton, G. E., & Hays, C. (2008). Beginning courageous conversations about race. In M. Pollock (Ed.), *Everyday antiracism: Getting real about race in school.* New York: The New Press.

Sleeter, C. E. (2008). Involving students in selecting reading materials. In M. Pollock (Ed.), *Everyday antiracism: Getting real about race in school.* New York: The New Press.

Stone, D., Patton, B., & Heen, S. (2000). *Difficult conversations: How to discuss what matters most.* New York: Penguin Books.

Suarez-Orozco, C., & Suarez-Orozco, M. (2001). *Children of immigration.* Cambridge, MA: Harvard University Press.

Tyson, K. (2008). Providing equal access to "gifted" education. In M. Pollock (Ed.), *Everyday antiracism: Getting real about race in school.* New York: The New Press.

Wang, T. H., & Wu, F. H. (1996). Beyond the model minority myth. In G. E. Curry (Ed.), *The affirmative action debate* (pp. 191-207). Reading, MA: Addison-Wesley.

Watson, D. (2007). *Norming suburban: How teachers describe teaching in urban schools.* Unpublished Ed.D. dissertation, Harvard Graduate School of Education, Cambridge.

Weinstein, R. S. (this volume). Schools that actualize high expectations for all youth: Theory for setting change and setting creation.

Wyman, L., & Kashatok, G. (2008). Getting to know students' communities. In M. Pollock (Ed.), *Everyday antiracism: Getting real about race in school.* New York: The New Press.

Zhou, M. (this volume). The ethnic system of supplementary education: Non-profit and for-profit institutions in Los Angeles' Chinese immigrant community.

Chapter 7

Enhancing Representation, Retention, and Achievement of Minority Students in Higher Education: A Social Transformation Theory of Change

KENNETH I. MATON, FREEMAN A. HRABOWSKI,
METIN ÖZDEMIR, AND HARRIETTE WIMMS

I ncreasing diversity on campuses requires a multifaceted perspective. One key facet of campus diversity is equal representation of ethnic and racial groups (Milem, Chang, & Antonio, 2005; Smith, 1997). This is one of the most common elements of diversity initiatives that have emerged in reaction to the historical exclusion of ethnic and racial groups from many social and civic institutions. However, increased representation of minority students cannot solely achieve the goal of creating stable campus populations composed of diverse groups (Smith, 1997). Disparity in retention rates is another major obstacle to the success of diversity initiatives. Programs thus must also aim at increasing retention rates of underrepresented minorities by altering campus climate and providing substantive, ongoing support, both socially and academically. Yet another critical facet of diversity in higher education is increased academic excellence for underrepresented ethnic and racial groups. Academic performance at high levels is necessary to reduce the achievement gap and to ensure pursuit of graduate education and equitable representation of minorities in leadership positions in society. Increasing enrollment, as well as retention and graduation rates, and strengthening academic achievement represent multiple, interrelated priorities of diversity initiatives.

Multiple frameworks for understanding organizational change exist that can be applied to change in higher education. These include biological (natural), teleological (planned), political, life cycle, social cognition, and cultural frameworks (for a further exploration of these change models, see Kezar & Eckel, 2002). To date, within higher education, research and campus change efforts have focused primarily on the natural and planned models for exploring naturally occurring or strategic change initiatives, respectively (Kezar & Eckel, 2002). Even while models of planned change have been critiqued for failing to describe the interrelationships among change strategies and for viewing change as a linear process, others have praised the planned change framework for its usability (Rajagopalan & Spreitzer, 1996). Key strategies of planned change include strategic planning, assessment, incentives and rewards, stakeholder analysis and engagements, restructuring, and reengineering (Kezar & Eckel, 2002). Development of goals, implementation and evaluation of strategies, and modification based on evaluation and lessons learned are also important components of the planned change process (Kezar & Eckel, 2002).

A subset of theorists have made the case for the necessity of transformative change efforts if enduring progress is to be made in empowering marginalized populations in our society (Hurtado, Dey, Gurin, & Gurin, 2003; Milem & Hakuta, 2000). Maton (2000), for example, has argued that deeply embedded features of social environments influence critical risk and protective processes, nullify person-focused programs, make it difficult to sustain and disseminate promising approaches, and prevent the large-scale mobilization of resources necessary for making a substantial difference. Williams, Berger, and McClendon (2005) argue that a series of transformations is required in organizational culture and behavior if campus diversity initiatives are to make a difference; otherwise, possible benefits of such initiatives may fade very easily. Ibarra (2001) makes the case that only a fundamental change in the culture of higher education related to diversity will result in substantive advances for minority students.

We propose a theory of change that is based in part upon a highly successful diversity initiative at the University of Maryland, Baltimore County (UMBC). In the late 1980s, UMBC, a medium-sized research university, was troubled by yearly student sit-ins by African American students, who, along with African American faculty members, perceived the campus as "cold" toward minorities and "racist." African American students in difficult science majors routinely performed very poorly (e.g., prior to the initiation of the diversity initiative no African American student had received above a "C" in a core biology or chemistry course). Change efforts were initiated in the late 1980s to address the negative racial climate. These efforts were spearheaded by Freeman Hrabowski, who began working at UMBC in spring 1987 as vice-provost and since 1992 has been the university president. As part of his efforts to enhance and transform the campus, Dr. Hrabowski initiated data-based reviews of minority student achievement (pinpointing the special low performance in science), ongoing dialogue within the campus community on issues related to race, a strengths-based rather than deficits-based view of minority students, and efforts to enhance the quality of minority (and non-minority) students admitted to the campus and the numbers of minority (and female) faculty. Of particular note, in 1988, the Meyerhoff Scholars Program was founded—a multifaceted support program to enhance the achievement of African American students in the sciences.

The Meyerhoff Program has achieved dramatic success. Science GPAs have dramatically turned around: the African American Meyerhoff students now achieve science GPAs comparable to those of their Caucasian and Asian peers. As a result of their high achievement levels, and related factors (e.g., research experience), close to 50% of entering African American Meyerhoff students now attend Ph.D. Programs in the sciences, a level substantially higher than equally talented comparison samples (Maton, Hrabowski, & Schmitt, 2000). The university has become a major contributor of black undergraduates to science and engineering Ph.D. programs (Maton & Hrabowski, 2004), and the Meyerhoff Program is widely viewed as a national model (cf. BEST, 2004; Staples, 2006).

The success of the Meyerhoff Program and the larger diversity initiative within which it was embedded can be perceived in campus-wide data as well. Whereas there were only 11 African American graduates in natural science, technology, engineering, or mathematics (STEM) majors in 1990, 15 years later, in 2005, there were 73, an increase of 564% (32 of the graduates were Meyerhoff students). In contrast, during this same period, the number of European American STEM graduates only increased 18% (223-262). Whereas 11.1% of graduating African American students in 1990 were in STEM majors, 33.6% were so in 2005; during this same period, the increase among European American students was more modest, from 22.4% to 30.0%. In addition, there was a marked increase in GPAs from 2.7 to 3.2 among African American STEM graduates from 1990 to 2005; in contrast, the GPAs among European American STEM graduates increased only modestly, from 3.1 to 3.2, during this period. The dramatic improvement in the overall campus climate for diversity is reflected in the fact that in 2002 UMBC was named by Kaplan/Newsweek as a "hot campus" in the diversity arena.

The Meyerhoff Scholars Program

The Meyerhoff Scholars Program was developed in 1988 at UMBC, as a response to low levels of academic performance among well-qualified African American STEM majors. Baltimore philanthropists Robert and Jane Meyerhoff provided the program's initial funding. The program developers, led by UMBC's then vice-provost (and since 1992 UMBC's president), endeavored to create a comprehensive, multicomponent program that addressed the factors research suggested were associated with minority student success in difficult science majors. These factors include knowledge and skill development, academic and social integration, support and motivation, and advising and monitoring (Maton et al., 2000).

In 1996, the program was opened to non-African American students (with an interest in the advancement of minorities in STEM fields). Currently, between 50 and 65 Meyerhoff students are selected each year (depending upon funding availability); the majority are African American. The program is situated on a campus with a diverse student population (34% minority), with more than half of the undergraduates and 60% of the doctoral students pursuing STEM degrees.

The program incorporates 16 components briefly described below (cf. Maton & Hrabowski, 2004; for a more detailed description, see Gordon & Bridglall, 2004, 2005).

Financial Aid

The Meyerhoff Program provides students with a comprehensive academic funding package that generally includes tuition, books, and room and board. This support is contingent upon maintaining a B average in a STEM major.

Recruitment

The top 100-150 candidates and their families attend one of the two recruitment weekends on the campus.

Summer Bridge Program

Meyerhoff students attend a mandatory prefreshman orientation program that includes taking math, science, and Africana Studies courses. They also participate in STEM-related cocurricular activities and attend social and cultural events.

Study Groups

The program staff strongly and consistently encourage group study, as study groups are viewed as an important aspect of success in STEM majors.

Program Values

Program values include support for academic achievement, acquiring help from a variety of sources, peer support, high academic goals (with an emphasis on Ph.D. attainment and research careers), and giving back to the community.

Program Community

The Meyerhoff Program presents students with a family-like social and academic support system. All Meyerhoff freshmen live in the same residence hall and are required to live on campus during subsequent years.

Personal Advising and Counseling

Full-time advisors monitor and support Meyerhoff students on a regular basis. These staff members focus not only on academic performance and planning but also on any personal issues that students face.

Tutoring

The Meyerhoff Program staff strongly encourages students to tutor others and/or be tutored to maximize academic achievement (i.e., to get As in difficult courses).

Summer Research Internships

Each student participates in summer research internships at leading sites around the country as well as some international locations.

Research Experience During the Academic Year

A number of students also participate in a program that requires involvement in a faculty member's research lab during the student's junior and senior years.

Faculty Involvement

STEM department chairs and key faculty are involved in the recruitment and selection processes of the program. A number of faculty also provide research opportunities for students in their laboratories.

Administrative Involvement

The university supports the Meyerhoff Program at all levels, including ardent support from the president.

Mentors

Each student is matched with a mentor who works in a science profession.

Community Service

All students are encouraged to participate in community service activities, which frequently involve volunteer work with at-risk Baltimore youth.

Family Involvement

Parents participate in social events and are kept advised of their child's progress.

Process Evaluation Surveys and Interviews

Surveys and interviews have been administered periodically to students and faculty to assess their perspectives on the program. African American Meyerhoff students perceived significantly more support and less stress than academically comparable comparison students. Analysis of the process evaluation data, taken together, highlights five factors that appear especially important: Program Community, Financial Support, Program Staff, Research Internships and Mentors, and Campus Academic Environment (Maton et al., 2000).

A Social Transformation Theory of Change

Based in part on the Meyerhoff Program and the larger change effort on the UMBC campus, and in part on extant research and scholarship on diversity initiatives in higher education, we propose a social transformation theory of change to guide efforts to enhance representation, retention, and achievement of minority students in higher education. Central to the theory is the creation of empowering settings that focus on minority student achievement (Maton & Salem, 1995) as part of a larger, transformative institutional change process centered on inclusive excellence (Williams et al., 2005). The components of this theory are described here and illustrated in the case of the diversity initiative from the late 1980s to the present at UMBC.

Empowering Settings for Minority Student Achievement

The goal of enhancing access, representation, and achievement of minority students in higher education can usefully be viewed as an empowerment process. Empowerment is a "group based, group member-driven process, through which marginalized or oppressed individuals and groups gain greater control over their lives and achieve reduced societal marginalization" (Maton, 2008; Maton & Brodsky, 2005, p. 2). The creation of settings (e.g., classrooms, programs, and universities) that facilitate such a process appears especially likely to make substantive changes in minority student achievement on campuses, thereby reducing or eliminating the achievement discrepancies between minority and majority students. The Meyerhoff Program, developed to enhance minority student achievement in STEM majors, provides such an empowering setting.

Research on the Meyerhoff Program and two other empowering settings (a church and a mutual support organization) revealed four sets of organizational characteristics common to the three settings studied (Maton & Salem, 1995). These were (a) a group-based belief system that is growth-inspiring, strengths-based, and focuses beyond the self; (b) an opportunity role structure that is pervasive, highly accessible, and multifunctional; (c) a multifaceted support system that is encompassing, peer-based, and provides a sense of community; and (d) empowering leadership that is inspirational, talented, shared, and committed. Each of these characteristics is evident in the Meyerhoff Program.

First, the program has an inspiring belief system that encourages students to strive for the highest levels of academic achievement. The belief system is strengths-based, as all students are viewed as having the capability to succeed in STEM majors, given the resources provided. It also includes a focus beyond the self—outstanding academic success is viewed as important to students' intentions to "give back" to the black community by increasing the small number of African American STEM Ph.D.s and research physicians.

The program has a highly accessible and pervasive role opportunity structure, distributed across multiple program settings. All students have access to study groups composed of their Meyerhoff peers. Additional opportunities emphasized by the program are involvement in faculty research laboratories, summer internships, and community service. The role opportunity structure is also multifunctional, containing opportunities both for learning and for using skills. Opportunities for learning occur as a student in a course, counselee, advisee, mentee, undergraduate research team member, study group member, and new student in the program; contributory opportunities occur in the roles of tutor, study group member, veteran student in the program, and community outreach mentor. The range and diversity of program settings in which meaningful, learning roles can be developed helps the program to effectively influence and engage the full population of students, differing in strengths, interests, and personality. The varied settings also serve to reinforce and complement the learning and skill development provided in each one.

The Meyerhoff Program support system is an encompassing one, providing support in multiple domains (i.e., financial, academic, and emotional). The support is available through both formal (i.e., staff) and informal (i.e., coresidence in the freshman year dorm, Meyerhoff roommates over the years, or friends) channels. The support system is proactive as well as reactive, as staff systematically monitor student progress and personal development with support provided when problems begin to appear (e.g., a poor grade on a quiz; an emergent personal problem). The peer-based support component, in both small group (study groups) and dyadic (friendship) contexts, and the provision of positive, highly successful peer models appear especially important. Beyond support per se, students often report a strong sense of belonging and community.

Empowering leadership begins with the program founder who communicates an inspiring vision to students of outstanding success and, as a successful university president, serves as a dynamic role model. Key faculty, including the chair of the Biological Sciences Department and the campus' Howard Hughes Medical Institute (HHMI) investigator, have become part of the leadership team, along with the program's formal leadership. The broad program leadership is affirming of students and relates effectively to them. It is committed to the students and to the program and is highly skilled; as student needs are identified, resources are mobilized to meet the needs and increase the odds for success.

Taken together, the organizational characteristics contribute to student empowerment via intrapsychological, relational, and instrumental pathways. The intrapsychological pathway involves student incorporation of key program values and norms, including the importance of excelling in the sciences, redressing the shortage of African American science Ph.D.s, seeking help from a variety of sources to achieve As, drawing on peer support and peer study, and giving back to the community. Students thus are both inspired and challenged to meet the high academic expectations that surround them. The relational pathway includes the provision of high levels of support—academic, social, personal, and financial. These relational resources are critical given the high levels of expectation and challenges experienced in the program. Finally, the instrumental pathway involves learning strategic skills to achieve both short-term (college) and longer-term (graduate school) outstanding academic success. These strategic skills include getting to know professors and the best students in the class, seeking help, participation in study groups, getting tutoring to help achieve As, tutoring others, and working every summer in research laboratories (often of eminent scientists). Furthermore, the program provides meaningful roles for students to help others, including community service with inner city children and representing the program to the external world.

In summary, the organizational characteristics and associated mediating pathways have resulted in a vibrant setting effective in recruiting a critical mass of talented minority students over the past 16 years, and once on campus, empowering them to achieve at levels that were not seen on campus before the program's initiation. The development and success of the program, however, cannot be understood in isolation from the larger university context and change processes within which they are embedded, to which we now turn.

Larger Institutional Change Process

In reviewing the diversity initiatives literature in higher education, Williams et al. (2005) propose an Inclusive Excellence Change Model that simultaneously embraces the diversity of students and promotes academic excellence for all students. Inclusive excellence is achieved through fundamental modifications in the culture of the university, including its mission, vision, values, traditions, and norms. Multiple dimensions of organizational behavior need to be encompassed in the change initiative, including the systemic, structural, collegial, political, and symbolic. These authors suggest an "Inclusive Excellence Scorecard" as a quantitative assessment and monitoring tool to guide inclusive change initiatives. Finally, a strategic change strategy to ensure successful implementation and sustainability over time includes the components of senior leadership, developing an institutional vision and promoting buy-in, building capacities necessary for transformation and maintaining change, and leveraging resources in order to satisfy all parties in the organization (Williams et al., 2005). Although space does not permit a detailed review of these varied facets of the model, several are highlighted in the following sections, and illustrated through application to the diversity initiative at UMBC.

Multiple Dimensions of Organizational Behavior Change

Williams et al. (2005) emphasize the need for change in multiple dimensions of organizational behavior if a diversity initiative is to succeed. These include the bureaucratic/structural, collegial, and symbolic dimensions of a university (the political is not included here). Suggested changes in the bureaucratic/structural dimension include making inclusive excellence an institutional priority; clearly articulating goals, strategies, and values; coordinating goals across levels and units; and routinizing strategies and processes for inclusive excellence. The collegial dimension includes building coalitions across campus to support inclusive excellence, developing models of collegiality, creating forums for open communication, and engaging numerous parties in the change process. The symbolic dimension includes acknowledging and addressing any campus history of inequity, clearly identifying core values with respect to inclusive excellence, articulating new values through symbols, and recognizing how meaning is constructed at multiple levels. Each of these dimensions is reflected in the inclusive excellence change process that occurred at UMBC, as highlighted here (cf. Hrabowski, 1999).

In the late 1980s, the UMBC President's Council decided to undertake a major initiative focused on inclusive excellence. Science, engineering, and math department chairs; several interested faculty from these departments; and other administrators were brought together to develop a greater understanding of why students were not succeeding in the STEM disciplines—with the ultimate goal of improving their academic performance. When data on student performance were examined, it was revealed that the GPAs of black students were far below those of whites and Asians. Focus groups with students, faculty, and staff were held to develop further understanding of the problem, and based on what was learned, meetings were held with department chairs and faculty to develop strategies for giving more support to students. Solutions devised included encouraging group study, strengthening the tutorial centers, encouraging faculty to provide feedback to students earlier in the semester, raising admission standards, helping students understand how much time and effort are needed to succeed, and enhancing the freshman experience (e.g., improving orientation and communicating to freshmen what it takes to succeed). Within this broader context, a vision was generated to develop a more positive climate for students of color by creating a cadre of science and engineering African American students who would become leaders and role models for the country. Once foundation funding was obtained, the latter vision resulted in the creation of the Meyerhoff Scholars Program.

These initial aspects of the inclusive excellence change process at UMBC included various elements of change in the structural/bureaucratic, collegial, and symbolic dimensions of the organization. Most prominent within the bureaucratic/structural dimension, inclusive excellence was instituted as a campus priority. This key development was the linchpin for all that followed. Most prominent at the collegial level was building successful coalitions with key science department chairs and faculty. Without such coalitions, it is unlikely that institutional change would have followed. In terms of the symbolic dimension, most noteworthy was the highly visible effort to address a campus history of inequality. This enabled both the campus and the larger institutional environment (e.g., the University of Maryland system) to make sense of and rally behind the change process.

Over the years, the diversity initiative has been sustained, with additional steps taken to address equity, access, and campus climate. Of special note was the decision to select the founder of the Meyerhoff Program, an African American mathematician, to become president of UMBC (in 1992). Over the years he has been a visible, positive presence on the campus, relating effectively to all segments of the university community, and in so doing, directly contributing to a positive campus climate. Targeted university efforts to hire minority faculty in the sciences and engineering and to recruit increased numbers of minority graduate students represent further aspects of the institutional change effort. Building on the success of the Meyerhoff Program, additional programs, all funded by large federal grants, were initiated and continue to this day. For example, at the undergraduate level the MARC U*STAR program, directed by the Biology Department chair, was developed, focused on research involvement of a select group of minority undergraduates in faculty laboratories. At the graduate level, the graduate Meyerhoff Scholars Program, directed by a Howard Hughes Medical Investigator, was initiated, providing financial and programmatic support to graduate students of color in the sciences. Additional federally funded programs include Louis Stokes Alliance for Minority Participation (LS-AMP: undergraduate, cross-campus program to support minorities in the sciences), Alliances for Graduate Education in the Professoriate (AGEP: provides workshops and seminars to support graduate students of color) and ADVANCE (program focused on advancing careers of women faculty in STEM disciplines).

These continuing aspects of the inclusive excellence change process at UMBC again encompass multiple dimensions of organizational behavior. Most prominent at the bureaucratic/structural level is the routinization of efforts to enhance minority student success, reflected in both the institutionalization of the Meyerhoff Program and the periodical addition of new, related programs focused on minority student achievement. Most prominent at the collegial dimension is inclusion of numerous parties in change efforts, reflected, for example, in the Chair of the Biology Department and the HHMI senior chemistry professor becoming key members of the inclusive excellence leadership on campus. Finally, at the symbolic level, especially noteworthy is the articulation of new values through the selection and ongoing presence of an African American university president.

Transformation in Organizational Culture

Organizational culture includes multiple levels or layers and transformation in organizational culture (organizational learning) requires change in the deeply shared values, assumptions, norms, and beliefs of a campus (Williams et al., 2005). In the 1980s, the UMBC campus culture included a devaluing of minority students, especially in science disciplines, and low expectations for their performance. Inclusive excellence was not a priority. The institutional change process noted in the earlier section, along with the success of The Meyerhoff Program, contributed directly and importantly to changes in the university culture (Hrabowski, 1999; Maton et al., 2000). Faculty attitudes toward African American students among science faculty underwent a dramatic transformation as African American Meyerhoff students achieved at the highest levels in the most difficult science courses and in many cases became valued research team members in faculty laboratories. More generally, the presence of a critical mass of highly talented African American students on campus, the large amounts of external funding received (i.e., multiple, multimillion dollar training grants), and substantially enhanced regional and national recognition resulted in an altered campus culture, one that has deeply incorporated an awareness of and commitment to inclusive excellence.

Assessment and Evaluation

Williams et al. (2005) advocate use of an assessment tool, the diversity score-card, to enhance diversity initiates. This data-driven approach relies on the development of quantitative indicators to monitor progress and highlight areas in need of future work for each of four key diversity dimensions: access and equity, diversity in the formal and informal curriculum, campus climate, and student learning and development.

Indicators of access and equity, including number of students, GPA, and graduation status, disaggregated by ethnicity, can easily be obtained from university databases. Refined analysis of these institutional data can examine, as relevant, differences across types of majors, and, as relevant, for specific types of courses (e.g., "gateway" courses in STEM majors). Measures of equity and access on campus can be compared to population indices to obtain indices of proportional representation.

Diversity in the formal and informal curriculum can be assessed through analysis of requirements and enrollment patterns in formal courses and analysis of extant information about the informal diversity curriculum (e.g., workshops, programs in residence halls, etc.). The nature and extent of informal interactions with diverse peers can be assessed through observational and self-report methods. Measurement of campus climate related to diversity in most cases requires administration of self-report measures and special efforts to obtain representative samples to complete the measures. Qualitative measures based on observation, interviews, or analysis of archival data can complement self-report. Assessment of student learning and development specifically related to diversity and multiculturalism will require development of reliable and valid self-report measures (Garcia et al., 2001; Hurtado et al., 2003; Smith, Wolf, & Levitan, 1994).

More broadly, measurement of organizational characteristics of empowering settings, organizational behavior and culture, and strategic change processes are central to theory testing and theory-based evaluation (Garcia et al., 2001; Smith et al., 1994). To date, most research focused on the change process has been qualitative in nature, relying primarily on case study methodology (e.g., Kezar & Eckel, 2002). While relevant quantitative measures of organizational characteristics, campus climate, and access and equity exist for some characteristics of interest, still others will need to be developed (cf. Garcia et al., 2001).

The diversity initiative at UMBC, as noted above, has effectively used institutional data related to access and equity of student performance in the sciences to initiate and monitor diversity-related change. Furthermore, realizing the importance of process and outcome evaluation of the Meyerhoff Program, external funding has been regularly obtained to allow systematic, ongoing study of the program, incorporating quantitative and qualitative methods (Hrabowski & Maton, 1995; Maton et al., 2000; Maton & Hrabowski, 2004; Maton, Hrabowski, & Özdemir, 2007). The evaluation findings have proved critical in helping to establish the program as a national model (BEST, 2004), thus contributing to the positive institutional changes noted above.

Change Strategy: Implementation and Sustainability

The successful implementation and sustainability of the Meyerhoff Program has been due in part to the combination of four strategic change elements: senior leadership, vision and buy-in, capacity building, and leveraging resources (Williams et al., 2005). The program has been fully supported, from its inception through to the present, by all high-level university administrators (e.g., president, provost, and deans). The compelling institutional vision of talented African American students achieving outstanding success in the sciences and proceeding to prestigious Ph.D. and M.D./Ph.D. programs around the country is well-suited to UMBC. Specifically, the medium size of the university, its location in a geographic region with many high-achieving minority students (Washington and Baltimore suburbs), its mission including a focus on STEM fields within the state university system, and an institutional culture that emphasizes undergraduate student involvement in faculty research all contribute to the match of the program to the institution.

Buy-in from department chairs, faculty, and staff has been facilitated in part by the effective, empowering leadership style of the president and other senior administrators, and in part by the enhanced university resources and public status that followed implementation of the program and the subsequent success of its African American students. The program goal to enhance the number of African American scientists is well aligned with funding priorities of federal agencies (e.g., NIH and NSF), corporations, and private foundations. This has facilitated a leveraging of resources on campus and capacity building efforts in departments as well as in campus units that support the program (e.g., admissions, financial aid, and tutoring center).

Challenges

There have been various external and internal challenges that the program, and the university, have faced over the years. In terms of the external environment, in the mid-1990s there was a growing antiaffirmative action climate in the country and an appellate court decision supporting a landmark lawsuit challenging the University of Maryland, College Park's Banneker Scholarship program, a program targeted exclusively to minority students. This led to the strategic decision to open the Meyerhoff Program to students of all races, as long as the applicant could demonstrate an interest in the advancement of racial/ethnic minorities in STEM fields. Within the campus, from the start there was resistance to the program among some faculty and students, criticizing the channeling of resources to minority students in science, rather than to all students in science and/or to all disciplines. Strategically, the university has responded by engaging in dialogue about the issue and ensuring that various university resources are directed to the larger goal of inclusive excellence. For example, university monies have been earmarked since 1996 to support scholarships for nonminority students in the Meyerhoff Program, and general efforts have been made to effect curricular changes that would benefit all students (e.g., revamping the introductory biology and chemistry courses using "active pedagogy," "discovery learning," and "inquiry based" elements to make them more accessible and engaging to all students). Within the Meyerhoff Program, students experience high levels of monitoring and challenge by program staff (along with high levels of support), both in public and private contexts, and for a subset of students this is viewed as overly intrusive and negative. Finally, the students also have to contend with attitudes from students not in the program that they are "elitist" and receive preferential treatment; for the African Americans students, this can present special challenges in terms of their relationships with both African American and non-African American students on campus.

Discussion

The proposed social transformation theory simultaneously encompasses a focus on programmatic means to enhance minority student achievement—the development of empowering settings—and the larger institutional change process that is necessary to support such program development and bring about necessary change in the larger institutional environment. The proposed theory is based upon and illustrated through a successful diversity initiative at UMBC, ongoing since the late 1980s. The social transformation theory combines empowering settings theory (Maton, 2008; Maton & Salem, 1995) with extant knowledge about transforming campuses to support inclusive excellence (Williams et al., 2005).

The proposed theory is consistent with related literature on social transformation. Kezar and Eckel (2002), for example, based on a review of the literature and six case studies (none related to diversity) of institutional transformation in higher education, suggest an Institutional Transformation Process Model. The model delineates core and secondary strategies and overarching principles of comprehensive, enduring change within higher education. Many of these components match those proposed in earlier sections (e.g., senior administrative support, collaborative leadership, robust design of vision and mission, and staff development); other components, though not explicit, are implicit in the proposed theory (e.g., sense making, balance, momentum, and communication). Maton (2000) proposed a Social Transformation of Environments model that included four key processes: capacity building, group empowerment, relational community building, and culture challenge (Maton, 2000). Each focuses primarily on a particular dimension of the social environment—respectively, the instrumental, structural, relational, and cultural. These processes and dimensions are also each reflected, either explicitly or implicitly, in the proposed theory.

The consistency with extant literature notwithstanding, the proposed social transformation theory of change represents only a beginning effort to understand the conditions necessary to enhance diversity on college .campuses. One limitation of the theory is that it is not sufficiently developed to specify the necessary and sufficient conditions for change and accompanying mechanisms. Instead, the theory focuses on articulation of programmatic, organizational, and strategic components that are plausibly linked to transformative change. A program of research is necessary to test directly the proposed theory of change beyond the single case study presented. Such additional research will help to generate an understanding of what initial conditions, contextual factors, and combination of strategic elements must be present if a transformational institutional change process is to be initiated and effectively sustained. For example, what roles do the size of the campus, the campus culture, student academic and social backgrounds, educational mission, and geographical locale play in facilitating the initiation of effective diversity initiatives? How high up, how skilled, and how widespread must senior leadership support be to make a difference? When do focal problems in campus racial climate contribute to, and when do they impede, such efforts?

A major challenge facing theory development and theory refinement related to inclusive excellence is the reality that the relative importance of the strategies and processes linked to transformational change can be expected to vary depending on the unique characteristics, culture, and history of the college or university in which a diversity change process is initiated. Thus, an important primary goal of theory testing is to encompass ecological specificity so that the theory of transformational change includes tailoring to the local context. Additional challenges for theory development are the need to specify "bottom-up" as well as top-down transformational processes, to address the dynamic, ongoing development of transformative processes once initiated, and to encompass transformative processes in the larger culture of higher education and society more generally related to the goal of inclusive excellence (cf. Maton, 2000).

Research to test and refine the proposed model will ideally combine qualitative and quantitative research methods and, over time, encompass both multiple case study and large-scale sample designs. To date, initial research has relied primarily on case study designs. Adequate theory testing in quantitative studies will require measures that assess the key organizational variables and multilevel processes enumerated in the theory that successfully address the challenges involved in the development of valid measures of environments (cf. Shinn & Toohey, 2003) and that address multiple outcome domains both at the level of students and of the larger campus environment. Data obtained from such measures can indicate areas where improvement is needed on campuses and thus serve to motivate and inform the change process at the same time that they provide baseline, process, and outcome measures in theory testing and evaluations of diversity initiatives.

Enhancing the representation, retention, and achievement of minority students in higher education represents one of the pressing issues of our times. Many approaches are being taken by universities and programs to address the issue. Research is needed to help generate, test, and refine theories of change related to inclusive excellence, and to evaluate the outcomes of such efforts. Data-based theories of change that are ecological, multilevel, and that incorporate practical levers for campus change agents will contribute importantly to progress in this critical arena. It is hoped that the current effort will contribute to this process.

References

BEST (2004, February). *A bridge for all: Gateways of higher education into America's scientific and technological workforce*. Retrieved March 8, 2004, from http://www.bestworkforce.org/PDFdocs/BEST_High_Ed_Rep_48pg_02_25.pdf

Garcia, M., Hudgins, C., Musil, C. M., Nettles, M. T., Sedlacek, W. E., & Smith, D. G. (2001). *Assessing campus diversity initiatives: A guide for campus practitioners*. Washington, DC. Association of American Colleges and Universities.

Gordon, E. W., & Bridglall, B. L. (2004). *Creating excellence and increasing ethnic minority leadership in science, engineering, mathematics and technology: A study of the Meyerhoff Scholars program at the University of Maryland, Baltimore County*. Unpublished report: Authors.

Gordon, E. W., & Bridglall, B. L. (2005). Nurturing talent in gifted students of color. In R. J. Sternberg & J. Davidson (Eds.), *Conceptions of giftedness* (2nd ed., pp. 120-146). New York: Cambridge University Press.

Hrabowski F. A., III. (1999). Creating a climate for success. *The presidency: The magazine for higher education leaders*, Winter, 34-39.

Hrabowski, F. A., III. & Maton, K. I. (1995). Enhancing the success of African-American students in the sciences: Freshmen year outcomes. *School Science and Mathematics, 95,* 18-27.

Hurtado, S. E. L., Dey, P., Gurin, P., & Gurin, G. (2003). College environments, diversity, and student learning. In J. C. Smart (Ed.), *Higher education: Handbook of theory and research* (pp. 145-190). UK: Kluwer Academic Publications.

Ibarra, R. (2001). *Beyond affirmative action: Reframing the context of higher education.* Madison: University of Wisconsin Press.

Kezar, A., & Eckel, P. (2002). Examining the institutional transformation process: The importance of sensemaking, interrelated strategies, and balance. *Research in Higher Education, 43*(3), 295-358.

Maton, K. I. (2000). Making a difference: The social ecology of social transformation. *American Journal of Community Psychology, 28,* 25-57.

Maton, K. I. (2008). Empowering community settings: Agents of individual development, community betterment, and positive social change. *American Journal of Community Psychology (March issue).*

Maton, K. I., & Brodsky, A. E. (2005, June). *Empowering community settings: Theory, research and action.* Paper presented at the Festschrift Conference in Honor of Julian Rappaport, University of Illinois, Champaign-Urbana.

Maton, K. I., & Hrabowski, F. A., III. (2004). Increasing the number of African American Ph.D.s in the sciences and engineering: A strengths-based approach. *American Psychologist, 59,* 629-654.

Maton, K. I., Hrabowski, F. A., & Özdemir, M. (2007). Opening an African American STEM Program to talented students of all races: Evaluation of the Meyerhoff Scholars Program, 1991-2005. In G. Orfield, P. Marin, S. M. Flores, & L. M. Garces (Eds.), *Charting the future of college affirmative action: Legal victories, continuing attacks, and new research* (pp. 125-156). Los Angeles, CA: The Civil Rights Project at UCLA.

Maton, K. I., Hrabowski, F. A., III, & Schmitt, C. L. (2000). African-American college students excelling in the sciences: College and post-college outcomes in the Meyerhoff Scholars Program. *Journal of Research in Science Teaching, 37,* 629-654.

Maton, K. I., & Salem, D. (1995). Organizational characteristics of empowering community settings: A multiple case study approach. *American Journal of Community Psychology, 23,* 631-656.

Milem, J. F., Chang, M. J., & Antonio, A. L. (2005). *Making diversity work on campus: A research-based perspective.* Report commissioned by the Making Excellence Inclusive Initiative. Washington, DC: Association for American Colleges and Universities.

Milem, J. F., & Hakuta, K. (2000). The benefits of racial and ethnic diversity in higher education. In D. J. Wilds (Ed.), *Minorities in higher education: Seventeenth annual status report* (pp. 39-67). Washington, DC: American Council of Education.

Rajagopalan, N., & Spreitzer, G. M. (1996). Toward a theory of strategic change: A multi-lens perspective and integrated framework. *Academy of Management Review, 22,* 48-79.

Shinn, M., & Toohey, S. M. (2003). Community contexts of human welfare. *Annual Review of Psychology, 54,* 427-459.

Smith, D. G., Gerbick, G. L., Figueroa, A. F., Watkins, G. H., Levitan, T., Moore, L. C., et al. (1997). *Diversity works: The emerging picture of how students benefit.* Washington, DC: Association of American Colleges and Universities.

Smith, D. G., Wolf, L. E., & Levitan, T. (1994). Introduction to studying diversity: Lessons from the field. *New Directions for Institutional Research, 81,* 1-8.

Staples, B. (2006, May 25). Why American college students hate science. *New York Times.* Retrieved June 15, 2006, from http://www.nytimes.com

Williams, D., Berger, J., & McClendon, S. (2005). *Toward a model of inclusive excellence and change in post-secondary institutions.* Association of American Colleges and Universities. Retrieved March 15, 2006, from http://www.aacu. org/inclusive_excellence/documents/Williams_et_al.pdf

Chapter 8

The School Climate for Lesbian, Gay, Bisexual, and Transgender (LGBT) Students

STEPHEN T. RUSSELL AND JENIFER K. McGUIRE

T he school environment is one of the most important development contexts for children and adolescents, not only for the development of academic and occupational skills but also for the development of the personal and social skills that shape the first 20 years of life. In recent years, there has been growing attention to understanding and supporting positive *school climate*, the "values, cultures, safety practices, and organizational structures" that characterize a school and its daily life; school climate refers to the influence that the school and its culture have on students (McBrien & Brandt, 1997, p. 89). Safety at school is an obvious foundation of the school climate. Following a series of school shootings, significant attention to school safety in the United States has resulted in new federal, state, and local education laws and policies during the past decade. These policies, most clearly typified in the No Child Left Behind (NCLB) Act of 2001 (2002), focus on aggregated individual student achievement rather than on the climate of schools. Our goal is to demonstrate that a focus on school climate in addition to individual student behavior is crucial for understanding policy innovation as well as student well-being. We focus on the school experiences of lesbian, gay, bisexual, and transgender (LGBT) students, who are arguably among those who are least safe in contemporary schools (Human Rights Watch, 2001).

Like most contemporary school policy, research on school safety has typically focused on understanding individual-level factors that are associated with student well-being; this approach is limited. With emphasis at the individual level rather than at the institutional level (the structural level, including school climate), efforts to improve student experiences must necessarily focus on changing perceptions, behaviors, or experiences of individual students.

By focusing on the skills and resources, individual students need to equip themselves to feel safer; thus the responsibility for personal safety rests with the individual student. We inadvertently "blame the victims" of unsafe school climates. These person-centered strategies divert attention from the responsibility of schools as social institutions to ensure the safety of all students.

There are few scientific evaluations of school safety policies in the United States. In Western Europe and the United Kingdom, where systemic efforts to reduce school bullying have been in place for a decade or more, findings suggest that change can be best achieved with a holistic approach that includes policy, curriculum, and school climate changes along with individual work with bullies and victims (Eslea & Smith, 1998; Mellor, 1997). The studies converged in finding that changing the climate to one that does not tolerate bullying requires comprehensive effort and that it can take as long as two years to begin to see evidence of school climate change (Arora, 1994).

In this chapter, we draw from Rogers' (2003) theory of diffusion of innovation in describing planned, structural changes in school policies and cultures that create the possibility for positive change in school LGBT climates and for LGBT students. Following a brief introduction to diffusion of innovation, we highlight a small body of recent research that points to school-level predictors of student safety for LGBT students. We discuss strategies for measuring individual- and school-level safety and climate, and provide empirical illustrations of these points using two distinct data sources. This research provides evidence of the efficacy of specific strategies schools can take to promote positive school LGBT climates. We close with a discussion of contemporary policy innovations and advocacy efforts that are consistent with an emphasis on improving school climates.

Diffusion of Innovation and School Climates

Diffusion of innovation theories are based on communications theories and social cognitive perspectives that argue that individuals or groups become exposed to an idea, over time assimilate it into their identity or culture, and ultimately experience the idea as their own (Oldenburg, Hardcastle, & Kok, 1997; Rogers, 2003). The theory is useful for interpreting change in public sentiment and behavior over time because it conceptualizes a process (rather than the outcome) of change. In the field of public health, the perspective has been used to understand organizational adoption of best practices (Hubbard & Hayashi, 2003). This perspective has been used in the field of education primarily to describe the adoption of technology (e.g., Keller, 2005), as well as innovations in pedagogy; there are a small number of applications relevant to school health programs that target structural changes to promote student health behavior (e.g., Alter & Lohrmann, 2005).

Five stages define the diffusion process: development, dissemination, adoption, implementation, and maintenance of an innovation. Each of these stages is marked by distinct processes of change, which can inform expectations about the outcomes of an innovation. The diffusion process begins with a development period during which decisions are made about which activities will best meet needs, and production of those activities begins; the diffusion process is complete in the maintenance period, at which point an innovation becomes "owned' by the community adopting it. A change agent is an outside entity that supports movement of the innovation along the stages of diffusion. A change agent may advertise the intervention as a form of dissemination, may provide training or motivation to encourage new groups to adopt the intervention, or may engage in technical support during the implementation phase (Oldenburg et al., 1997; Rogers, 2003).

When applied to schools and school safety, multiple levels of education systems are relevant for understanding innovation diffusion. The historic focus at the individual level is, of course, relevant; improving students' daily experiences and interactions is the ultimate goal of school safety innovations. However, educational innovations may occur because of the development and dissemination of new practices and strategies from policy makers and administrators to schools, teachers, and classroom (top-down) or may have their origins in the classroom and be disseminated and adopted at the structural level over time (bottom-up). While some school innovations may begin with and be led by students such as high school gay-straight alliance (GSA) clubs or other student-led school groups that exist for the purpose of advocacy and education about LGBT issues in schools (Herdt, Russell, Sweat, & Marzullo, 2007), it is more likely that innovations will begin among teachers, administrators, or at the district or state policy levels. These may take the form of advocacy for teacher training and education, school policy change, or changes in state education and policy law. These multiple levels of education systems are relevant for each stage of diffusion.

LGBT Students, School Climates, and LGBT School Safety Innovations

Studies of LGBT youth show them to be at risk for some of the greatest difficulties experienced by adolescents. Several of those problems pertain directly to education and schooling, such as poor academic performance, negative school attitudes, or victimization at school (Human Rights Watch, 2001; Kosciw & Cullen, 2003; Russell, Seif, & Truong, 2001). In addition, recent research has begun to link the negative mental health and risk behaviors of LGBT youth to challenges that they face in school, including harassment and discrimination (e.g., Bontempo & D'Augelli, 2002; Rivers, 2001). These challenges impede not only the students' academic performance but also their general emotional and social development.

At the school level, homophobia has been directly implicated in hostile school climates (Human Rights Watch, 2001; Kimmel & Mahler, 2003). In many high schools, antigay slurs, graffiti, and verbal abuse permeate every-day relations among students. These activities function to litter the social landscape, where the negative comments and graffiti create a harsher, more rejecting environment for everyone. In a recent survey of over 900 junior high and high school students, 57% reported hearing homophobic remarks at school. Sixty-nine percent of LGBT youth in grades 7-12 reported feeling unsafe in their schools, and 31% reported that they missed at least 1 day of school in the past month because they felt unsafe (Kosciw & Cullen, 2003). Such harassment defines the school climate and affects the experiences of all students, even those to whom it is not personally directed. This pervasive homophobia in the school setting is often expressed not only by fellow stu-dents but also by teachers (Human Rights Watch, 2001). Such school-based harassment is a primary antecedent of many of the risks that characterize the lives of LGBT youth (Rivers, 2001).

Research on homophobia and bullying has historically focused on violence or harassment rather than student perceptions of safety. Yet the National Research Council has described a safe learning environment as a key com-ponent to positive youth development (Eccles & Gootman, 2002). Skiba et al. (2004) argue for the importance of feelings of safety as a malleable experience that can be influenced by a variety of personal and school-level characteris-tics. We extend our focus on school safety to include individual perceptions of school safety as well as the aggregated perceptions of safety by multiple students within their schools (see also Welsh, 2001). We suggest that in con-temporary schools, aggregated student perception of LGBT student safety is a marker of the adoption, implementation, and maintenance of LGBT school safety policies and practices. Our goal is to disentangle factors that may influ-ence individual safety perceptions from factors that contribute to safe school climates as indicated by student consensus.

In recent years, a number of studies have begun to identify institutional characteristics of schools that are associated with school safety for LGBT students (both perceptions of safety by LGBT and other students, as well as school safety experiences; e.g., Goodenow, Szalacha, & Westheimer, 2006; O'Shaughnessy Russell, Heck, Calhoun, & Laub, 2004). These studies have been important for identifying innovations that make a difference in indi-vidual student's feelings about and experiences at school. Broadly speaking, four setting-level strategies have been identified that represent innovations in addressing LGBT student and school safety climate: (a) adoption of school safety policies that explicitly include attention to sexual orientation and gender identity, (b) teacher intervention to stop harassment and negative comments, (c) availability of GSA clubs or similar student organizations, and (d) student access to LGBT-related information and resources, including attention to LGBT issues in the curricula (Goodenow et al., 2006; O'Shaughnessy et al., 2004; Szalacha, 2003).

Each of these strategies may be measured at the individual or school level. In studies of Massachusetts public school students, the presence of a GSA has been linked with student safety perceptions (Goodenow et al., 2006; Szalacha, 2003). Does it matter more that a school has a GSA or that a majority of the students at the school know that there is a GSA? The initial adoption of a GSA (e.g., having one listed as a club) and the dissemination of an existing GSA within a school (having a high proportion of students who know about the GSA) might independently contribute to the overall LGBT safety climate of the school. Both initial adoption and subsequent dissemination might be encouraged through network-based diffusion of innovation processes. Similarly, one study suggests that having a school nondiscrimination or anti-harassment policy while certainly an important precursor to diffusions of LGBT school safety innovations may not itself be linked to individual student safety; rather, student awareness of school safety policies appears to be more closely linked to student perceptions of safety (O'Shaughnessy et al., 2004). In sum, each of the four setting-level strategies (policy, GSA, teacher intervention, and providing LGBT information) can be measured at the level of the individual or at the level of the school either through information about school policies and practices or through aggregated reports by students. Further, each may be conceived in terms of adoption by the school or district, implementation at the school, dissemination and adoption within the school at the classroom level, and maintenance at any or all of these setting levels.

Development, dissemination, and adoption of policies are an important first step in school safety innovation. Inclusive antiharassment and nondiscrimination policies provide a foundation for each of the recent innovations relevant to LGBT school safety. That is, once policies have been developed, disseminated, and adopted at local, district, or state levels, it is easier to implement programs such as teacher trainings, student clubs, and innovations in the curriculum. Recent research suggests that inclusive school safety policies are a crucial starting point for promoting school safety. A study of public school students in California indicates that when schools have policies that explicitly prohibit harassment on the basis of actual or perceived sexual orientation and gender, students report fewer instances of harassment, stronger connections at school, and stronger feelings of safety (O'Shaughnessy et al., 2004). In fact, a Massachusetts study showed that antibullying policies are protective factors against suicide attempts among LGBT students (Goodenow et al., 2006).

The essential role that school personnel play in establishing a safe school climate is well documented. A recent national study indicates that teachers are fundamental to supportive school climates in which all youth can grow and learn; among 7th-12th graders, sexual minority youth with positive feelings about their teachers were significantly less likely than their peers to experience troubles getting along with other students, paying attention, and getting homework done (Russell et al., 2001). A second study is the first to document the importance of teachers' sensitivity to LGBT issues in the curriculum. It showed that in schools with gay-sensitive HIV instruction, gay students reported lower sexual health risks (Blake et al., 2001). Further, teacher intervention in harassment has been linked to school safety; a California study showed that students who reported that their teachers had stopped slurs and harassment were more likely to feel safe, less likely to be harassed, and more likely to describe their school as safe for LGBT or gender nonconforming students than those reporting no intervention (O'Shaughnessy et al., 2004). Yet many schools and school personnel have limited awareness of, or are not prepared or trained to understand and manage, issues of same-sex sexuality or identity. For example, many teachers have expressed willingness to create safer environments overall but are uncomfortable with specifically addressing LGBT issues in the classroom (Bliss & Harris, 1999). School personnel often do not take sexuality-motivated harassment or victimization seriously, even for students for whom harassment and victimization experiences are pervasive. Some express the belief that victims "cause" their own harassment, and thereby do not support victimized youth (Human Rights Watch, 2001).

A focus on the critical role of social supports suggests that when victimization takes place, students who lack social support from peers and adults are less able to cope with it. When students have GSAs at their school, they report less harassment and more safety (Goodenow et al., 2006; O'Shaughnessy et al., 2004; Szalacha, 2003). Further, when students know where to go at their school for information and support related to sexual orientation and gender identity, they report more feelings of safety and fewer instances of hearing slurs or negative comments about sexual orientation by other students (O'Shaughnessy et al., 2004).

Measurement of School Safety and Its Consequences: Empirical Illustrations

To make the case for the importance of school climate using empirical data, we use school-level data to illustrate the contributions of attention to the school setting for understanding school safety processes that largely have been studied at the person level to date. We begin with a brief examination of data from the National Longitudinal Study of Adolescent Health (the Add Health Study, details of which are available from the Carolina Population Center, 2003). The in-school sample included over 90,000 students in 80 high schools and

52 middle schools during the 1994-1995 school year; it represents almost complete population data on the enrolled students in the participating schools.

Students were asked how strongly they agreed or disagreed with the following statement: "I feel safe at my school." Because students are grouped within their schools, with this question one can examine differences both between students as well as between schools (evidenced by the average of students within a school) in school safety perceptions. Analyses of unconditional multilevel school effects models (Raudenbush & Bryk, 2002; estimated using SAS PROC MIXED: Singer, 1998) indicate that 8.1% of the total variance in this measure of school safety is at the level of the school. Thus, while the great majority of variability (over 90%) has to do with differences between individual students in this nationwide study, it is also the case that a significant proportion of the variability has to do with differences between schools. With these data, it is not possible to determine if further variance can be attributed at the classroom level, but such an idea is plausible given the known variability among teachers in creating a classroom environment free from harassment. On one hand this finding is intuitive; it is not a surprise that some schools are safer than others. Yet research and policy foci on individual student behavior have undermined serious attention to understanding the safety climate of schools.

The Add Health data provide this national estimate of variability in school safety climates but do not allow investigation of school strategies that might be correlates of school safety climate. To understand the ways that innovations in LGBT school climate may influence student experiences, we turn to a study of LGBT school safety innovations in California high schools. Beginning in 2001, the passage of Assembly Bill 537 in California (AB537, the California Student Safety and Violence Prevention Act of 2000) required local districts to implement nondiscrimination and antiharassment policies that include specific attention to actual or perceived sexual orientation and gender identity. While the original development and dissemination of this school safety policy innovation had origins in local community activism before 2000, its adoption happened at the state level, with the goal of subsequent policy change in local school districts. The study was initiated by the California Safe Schools Coalition (CSSC), the change agent, with the goal of understanding the efficacy of school safety strategies across the state, and providing detailed information for local schools for advocacy purposes. The larger goal of the CSSC has been to promote adoption, implementation, and maintenance of the state policy while monitoring LGBT student and school safety.

Data were collected by students from 17 public schools, yielding over 6,000 surveys. The students who collected the data were typically GSA student leaders or members, and were engaged in advocacy training led by a nonprofit youth organization (Gay-Straight Alliance Network) that included a focus on assessing their school climates.[1] At the school level, we were interested in the associations between school demographic characteristics and students' experiences or beliefs about safety and harassment of LGBT youth. In addition, beyond those characteristics, which are largely outside the control of school districts, we wanted to estimate the associations between school safety strategies and school safety climates.[2] The participating schools were legally responsible to have inclusive policies, and all had active high school GSA clubs. Thus, our attention is on two of the four LGBT school safety strategies identified in prior work: teacher intervention in harassment when it takes place and student access to LGBT-related information, resources, and curriculum.

Three items were used as indicators of the school climate for LGBT youth. Knowledge of physical harassment of LGBT students or teachers was asked with a single item (1 = yes). Students were asked to report how often they heard generalized antigay slurs (e.g., "that's so gay"; 1 = never; 5 = all the time). Students reported their perceptions of school safety for LGBT teachers and students (1 = not at all safe; 5 = very safe). The survey also included questions that assess LGBT school safety strategies, including "How often do you hear teachers or school staff stop others from making negative comments or using slurs based on sexual orientation?" (1 = never; 4 = often; a similar question was asked about other students), "If you wanted more information and support from your school about sexual orientation, gender identity, or LGBT issues would you know where to go?" (1 = yes), and "In your classes at school, have you ever learned about LGBT people, discussed LGBT history or current news events, or received information about sexual orientation and gender identity?" (1 = yes). Because of the believed importance of coming out to others as a strategy for creating LGBT-supportive social change (McGarry & Wasserman, 1998), we included two additional questions that tap the LGBT climate of a school: whether students reported knowing LGBT teachers or others students who were LGBT (1 = yes). Finally, school-level demographic characteristics were collected from public data published by the California Department of Education (CDE), including the percentage of students eligible for the free lunch program, the percentage of students whose families received public assistance (CalWorks), the student-teacher ratio, the average SAT score, the average class size, the school's total enrollment, and the percentage of teachers who were credentialed.

Following the same analytic strategy as described earlier for our analysis of data from the Add Health Study, we have shown in Table 8.1 that, as was true for school safety in the national study, the majority of the variance in all of the items is between students.

There are, however, significant differences between the 14 schools in measures of school safety strategies and student safety outcomes. We find relatively strong between-school variability in the systemic indicators of

Table 8.1. Variance Within and Between Schools in Student Perceptions of School Safety Climate

	Percentage of Variance	
	Within Schools	Between Schools
School Safety Climate		
When slurs are made, teachers step in	96.2	3.8*
Have had education about LGBT issues	92.9	7.1*
Know where to get info about LGBT issues	89.3	11.7*
School Safety Outcomes		
Heard LGBT slurs not directed at specific person	92.9	7.1*
School is safe for LGBT students and teachers	89.4	10.6*
Know of physical harassment of LGBT students	100.0	0.0 *n.s.*

Note. $*p < .05$; *n.s.*, $p > .05$.

school safety climate—having been exposed to education about LGBT issues (7.1%) and knowing where to get information about LGBT issues (11.7%). In contrast, individual student perceptions and experiences are most important for understanding teacher interventions in harassment that takes place at school. For the school safety outcomes, two showed significant variance between schools: over 7% of the variability in student reports of LGBT slurs is between schools, and over 10% of the variability in perceived school safety for LGBT students and teachers is between schools. There were no differences across schools in reports of physical harassment.

Table 8.2 presents results from multilevel regression analyses reports of perceived school safety for LGBT students and teachers, as well as student reports of hearing slurs (we exclude physical harassment from analyses because there is no significant variability between schools). We include (a) individual students' school safety experiences, (b) demographic characteristics of schools, and (c) aggregated student reports of school safety climate, modeling these variable groupings individually and then simultaneously.

In predicting perceived school safety for LGBT students and teachers, teacher intervention has a strong positive association; students report more safety for LGBT people when they experience teacher intervention. The only school-level demographic characteristic linked to school safety for LGBT students and teachers is SAT scores: students at schools with higher average SAT scores rate their schools as more safe for LGBT students and teachers. We note that SAT scores and several of the demographic characteristics of the school population (proportion of student on free lunch or public assistance and the student-teacher ratio) are strongly correlated, yet it is not socioeconomic characteristics of the school population as much as the achievement level of the school that is linked to school safety. It is not the case that economically disadvantaged schools are less safe for LGBT students and teachers. One

Table 8.2. Multilevel Regression for School Safety Outcomes. Column 1 Presents Effects for Separate Models for Each Grouping of Variables; Column 2 Presents Results of Models That Combine the Student and School Levels

School Safety Outcomes	School LGBT Safety		Slurs	
	1	2	1	2
Student School Safety Experiences				
Teachers step in	.11*	.10***	.03	
Students step in	−.01		.05$^+$	.06*
Student knows where to go for information	−.01		−.02*	−.03**
Student reports LGBT education	.01		−.01	
Student knows LGBT student	.01		−.02	
Student knows LGBT teacher	−.01		−.02$^+$	−.02*
School Demographic Characteristics				
% free lunch	.48		−3.06	
% CalWorks	−2.12		4.40	
Student-teacher ratio	.13		.08	
Average SAT	.01*	.01***	.00	
Average class size	.10		−.15	
Total enrollment	−.00		.00	
% credentialed teachers	−1.26		−2.86	
School-Level Safety Climate				
% teachers step in	−8.28		2.48$^+$	1.89$^+$
% students step in	−2.60		−.33	
% students know where to go for information	−.55		.69***	.63***
% reporting LGBT education	−1.09		.39$^+$	.42**
% who know LGBT student	−.22		−.68*	−.63*
% who know LGBT teacher	1.79		−.60$^+$	−.60*
N	3,774		3,691	

Note. $^+ p < .10$, $* p < .05$, $** p < .01$, $***p < .001$.

interpretation may be that high achieving schools are safer for LGBT youth; considered another way, it may be that schools that are safer support and enable high achievement. Our results are only correlational but improve on prior research by distinguishing school-level from individual-level predictors and outcomes.

Students who know where to go for information and support "about sexual orientation, gender identity, or LGBT issues" and who report that they know an LGBT teacher who has openly disclosed his or her LGBT status report hearing fewer LGBT-related slurs; these students attend schools in which LGBT school safety practices have been adopted and maintained. However, when students perceive that other students intervene in harassment they also report hearing more slurs. At the level of the school safety climate, students report more slurs in schools that are characterized by reports of more teacher interventions and in which more students know where to go for information and support, and report more learning about LGBT issues. These results are likely the product of changing school climates and the evolution of innovations in school safety strategies that vary across schools. The climate characteristics we measure here may actually be *consequences* of the outcomes we modeled here; that is, teachers and students may step in, students may seek information, and schools may respond with LGBT education in schools where homophobic slurs are common. In fact, participation in this study was initiated by students who actively chose to become involved in LGBT student safety efforts; for many of them, involvement in this survey was a proactive response to school safety problems at their schools. Finally, in environments where greater proportions of students know a student or teacher who is openly LGBT, students report hearing fewer negative slurs aimed at LGBT persons. It is difficult to untangle whether students and faculty feel safer to come out about their sexual orientation in environments where slurs are relatively less common or whether the existence of openly LGBT students and faculty members functions to suppress the frequency of slurs. In either scenario, when more students know of someone who is LGBT at their school, all students (even those who do not know an LGBT person) report fewer slurs.

Clearly, there are limitations to our study. We have the advantage of over 5,000 students from 14 schools, but a larger and more diverse group of schools might yield stronger results at the school level. The data for this project were collected by student school safety activists, many through their high school GSA clubs. We are thus limited to schools that have already adopted and are in the process of maintaining several of the key LGBT school safety climate innovations. At a minimum, the schools are characterized by a subgroup of students concerned about LGBT school safety. A truly random sample of schools would likely yield more variability across schools. In addition, the surveys were short, and limited in breadth. We have little information about the demographic characteristics of the individual students who participated in our study; we might, for example, expect that students who themselves identify as LGBT would be more aware of and sensitive to LGBT student safety (e.g., Russell, McGuire, Lee, Larriva, Laub, & California Safe Schools Coalition, in press).

The study was designed to understand individual- and school-level factors associated with individual student reports of school safety for LGBT students. This work responds to emerging attention to the importance of distinguishing between factors at the student and school levels, and the need for research to move beyond exclusive focus on students to understand the institutional characteristics that are associated with school safety. The results of our analyses reaffirm that individual student perceptions of the school safety climate are some of the most important correlates for each of school safety outcomes we examined here: students report that schools are safer for LGBT students and staff when teachers intervene with harassment. Individual experiences make a difference for predicting safety outcomes, and at the same time, some schools do a better job than others in promoting school safety. Our point is not simply that school-level differences matter above and beyond individual differences; our goal, in addition, has been to illustrate the importance of school-level strategies for promoting safe school climates and ultimately student safety and well-being.

Exemplars of Advocacy and Innovations to Improve School Safety Climates

On a systemic level, scholars and policy makers recently have begun to promote district monitoring of school violence (Astor & Benbenishty, 2006) as well as laws that address the response to bullying at the state level (Limber & Small, 2003). Clearly, federal and state laws have greater potential to influence the policies and behaviors of local districts than do recommendations or policies left to be determined at the local level. To date, at least fifteen states have adopted laws mandating antibullying policies and/or interventions. These laws vary considerably with regard to specific implementation requirements in the areas of school-wide programs, employee training, requirements to report, and immunity from civil action against the reporting party (Limber & Small, 2003). Most of these laws have been developed within a broader national "security" culture (especially post 9/11) and focus on external, "random" threats to student and school safety rather than on pervasive school cultural factors (including cultures of masculinity and homophobia) that may create, allow, or sustain harassment and violence (see Human Rights Watch, 2001; Kimmel & Mahler, 2003). Some but not all of them include LGBT-based harassment.

In spite of contemporary efforts to characterize school safety solely in terms of security, there is a 15-year history of statewide school safety efforts that focus on LGBT issues. Most of the advocacy around LGBT student and school safety has been in local communities; in a few places, these efforts have led to statewide initiatives, the activities and accomplishments of which are more visible and easier to study than local efforts. We focus on successful state-level initiatives because they have broader systemic policy influence; they represent the work of individual and collective change agents active in developing and disseminating LGBT school safety innovations.

In February 1992, Massachusetts Governor William Weld established the *Governor's Commission on Gay and Lesbian Youth* (Executive order 325; updated in 1998; abolished in 2006 by Governor Romney). Governor Weld's action stemmed from a campaign promise to an active and organized gay and lesbian community that had mobilized to address LGBT youth suicide after the publication of the 1989 Department of Health and Human Services Report of the Secretary's Task Force on Youth Suicide (Gibson, 1989). With the establishment of the Commission, Massachusetts became a leader in the development and dissemination of LGBT school safety strategies and policies; the Commission focused on the establishment of school antiharassment policies, school personnel training in violence and suicide prevention, school-based support groups for LGBT students, and school-based counseling for LGBT students (Perrotti & Westheimer, 2001). In many ways this Commission signaled the beginning of systemic (specifically state-level governmental) approaches to addressing the school safety needs of LGBT students. The next year, in 1993, the *Safe Schools Coalition of Washington* was founded. It had its origins in a series of hearings on the needs of LGBT youth sponsored by the Seattle Commission on Children and Youth in 1988. An advisory committee grew out of the 1988 hearings and engaged in the development and dissemination of safe schools policy and educational practice in the city and county. Within 5 years, the committee became a statewide coalition that continues to support and sustain safe schools innovations in that state (Washington Safe Schools Coalition, n.d.). It became the model for statewide efforts to link policy makers, educators, LGBT youth advocates, and youth to develop and disseminate LGBT school safety resources and best practices. In the late 1990s, LGBT youth and youth advocates in California pressed for the passage of the *California Student Safety and Violence Prevention Act of 2000* (AB537), which was signed into law in January 2001. AB537 was the outcome of several years of grassroots advocacy; it was also the beginning of efforts to develop and disseminate school safety policies and practices consistent with the new law. The CSSC was founded to support the implementation of AB537, including monitoring safety in California schools.

These statewide commissions and coalitions are the change agents for the diffusion of LGBT student and school safety innovations. The existence of these statewide systemic efforts was not by chance. Each was grounded in historically progressive political state climates and linked to preexisting organizations and resources that support or advocate for LGBT youth and adults. As change agents for LGBT school safety innovations, each positioned itself to become the opinion leader (Rogers, 2003) for LGBT school issues in the context of the broader LGBT social movement. Thus, in most parts of the United States, LGBT school safety innovation happens within local school districts, schools, or classrooms. These three states are among a small handful in which LGBT school safety advocates have leveraged community, political, and institutional resources for the development of system-level educational innovations.

The history of LGBT student and school safety advocacy in California is important not just because it led to the most inclusive antiharassment and nondiscrimination policy in the United States (it is distinct in its inclusion of protection based on actual or perceived sexual orientation, gender, and gender identity). Because of its breadth, AB537 has become the basis for policy advocacy by the CSSC for further educational policy innovation. In 2004, SB71, the *California Comprehensive Sexual Health Education Law*, was passed; the existence of AB537 and the advocacy of the CSSC ensured that this law would encourage students "to develop healthy attitudes concerning adolescent growth and development, body image, gender roles, sexual orientation, dating, marriage, and family." Two subsequent laws, both vetoed in 2006, were strongly linked to the research and advocacy efforts of the CSSC. AB606, the *Safe Place to Learn Act*, would have provided clarification and guidance to school districts and the Department of Education regarding the steps that should be taken to ensure compliance with AB537. It was based on recommendations from the CSSC's *Safe Place to Learn* Report (O'Shaughnessy et al., 2004). SB1437, the *Bias-Free Curriculum Act*, would have prohibited discrimination based on sexual orientation and gender identity in textbooks, classroom materials, and school-sponsored activities. Advocacy for this law was based on results from the *Safe Place to Learn* Report, which showed that students who reported learning about LGBT issues at school felt safer at school and that school climates are safer when LGBT issues are part of the curriculum (Russell, Kostroski, McGuire, Laub, & Manke, 2006).

In summary, systemic educational strategies and policies designed to improve school climates in the United States began in earnest during the past decade; there is a long way to go before LGBT school safety policy and program innovations are established and maintained across the country. This chapter described the potential contributions to be gained by investigating LGBT school safety climates at the school level in addition to efforts to understand individual student safety. Attention to the level of the school acknowledges that individual students and their safety and well-being are influenced by the school climate, in addition to their personal experiences and perceptions. We have highlighted state-level school safety initiatives that suggest the possibility for the continued dissemination of innovative school safety programs and policies that focus on both individual students and the climate of schools. Such examples are encouraging for efforts to create systemic school climate change as well as to promote the safety of all students.

Acknowledgments

This research was supported in part by the California Safe Schools Coalition with funding from the California Endowment and by a William T. Grant Foundation Scholar Award to the first author. The authors thank the Coalition Research and Evaluation Committee for access to data and thoughtful input, Carolyn Laub and the Gay-Straight Alliance Network for their role in collecting the data, and Sun-A Lee, Cesar Egurrola, Jacqueline Larriva, and Nicole Lehman for assistance with data management.

Notes

1. In order to achieve a sample that was representative of the larger school, each GSA club worked with their school administration to sample classes from the entire school. The numbers of study participants within each school ranged from 71 to 1,108. Because there was a large range of number of participants per school, number of students in each school and percentage of responding students per school were included as control variables in all analyses. Surveys were administered anonymously during school time with passive parental consent procedures. Participation was voluntary. There are no estimates of how many students per class may have refused to take the survey. We calculated participation rates for each school based on total school enrollment; the average participation rate was 30%. Students were roughly evenly distributed across the 9th-12th grades (27.8%, 23.8%, 28.2%, and 19.4%). Fifty-two percent identified as female, 46% were male, and 1.5% were transgender or questioning their gender identity. Only half of the schools asked students to identify their sexual orientation (42% of students). Among those, 89% were straight, 1.2% was gay or lesbian, 4.3% were bisexual, and 5.3% reported their sexual orientation as queer, questioning, or other.

2. Each of the 17 participating schools were allowed to tailor and alter the survey questions; yielding 11 schools (4,232 participants) that could be included in the current analyses.

References

Alter, R. J., & Lohrmann, D. K. (2005). Building support for coordinated school health programs. *The Health Educator, 37*, 4-7.

Arora, C. (1994). Is there any point in trying to reduce bullying in secondary schools? A two year follow-up of a whole-school anti-bullying policy in one school. *AEP (Association of Educational Psychologists) Journal, 10*, 155-162.

Astor, R. A., Benbenishty, R., et al. (2006). The social context of schools: Monitoring and mapping student victimization in schools. In M. Furlong & S. Jimmerson (Eds.), *Handbook of school violence and school safety: From research to practice* (pp. 221-233). Mahwah, NJ, Lawrence Erlbaum Associates Publishers.

Blake, S. M., Ledsky, R., Lehman, T., Goodenow, C., Sawyer, R., & Hack, T. (2001). Preventing sexual risk behaviors among gay, lesbian, and bisexual adolescents: The benefits of gay-sensitive HIV instruction in schools. *American Journal of Public Health, 91*, 940-946.

Bliss, G. K., & Harris, M. B. (1999). Teachers' views of students with gay or lesbian parents. *Journal of Gay, Lesbian, and Bisexual Identity, 4*, 149-171.

Bontempo, D. E., & D'Augelli, A. R. (2002). Effects of at-school victimization and sexual orientation on lesbian, gay, or bisexual youths' health risk behavior. *Journal of Adolescent Health, 30*, 364-374.

Burchill, S. A. L., & Stiles, W. B. (1988). Interactions of depressed college students with their roommates: Not necessarily negative. *Journal of Personality and Social Psychology, 55*, 410-419.

Carolina Population Center. (2003). Add Health: The National Longitudinal Study of Adolescent Health. Retrieved January 28, 2007, from http://www.cpc.unc.edu/projects/addhealth

Eccles, J., & Gootman, J. A. (2002). *Community programs to promote youth development.* Washington, DC: National Academy Press.

Eslea, M., & Smith, P. K. (1998). The long-term effectiveness of anti-bullying work in primary schools. *Educational Research, 40,* 203-218.

Gibson, P. (1989). *Gay male and lesbian youth suicide: Report of the Secretary's Task Force on Youth Suicide* (Vol. 3, pp. 110-142). Washington, DC: Department of Health and Human Services, DHHS Pub. No. (ADM) 89-1623.

Goodenow, C., Szalacha, L. A., & Westheimer, K. (2006). School support groups, other school factors, and the safety of sexual minority adolescents. *Psychology in the Schools, 43*(5), 573-589.

Herdt, G., Russell, S. T., Sweat, J., & Marzullo, M. (2007). Sexual inequality, youth empowerment, and the GSA: A community study in California. In N. Teunis & G. Herdt (Eds.), *Sexual Inequalities* (pp. 233-252). Berkeley: University of California Press.

Hubbard, S. M., & Hayashi, S. W. (2003). Use of diffusion of innovations theory to drive a federal agency's program evaluation. *Evaluation and Program Planning, 26,* 49-56.

Human Rights Watch. (2001). *Hatred in the hallways: Violence and discrimination against lesbian, gay, bisexual, and transgender students in U.S. schools.* New York: Human Rights Watch.

Keller, C. (2005). Virtual learning environments: Three implementation perspectives. *Learning, Media and Technology, 30,* 299-311.

Kimmel, M. S., & Mahler, M. (2003). Adolescent masculinity, homophobia, and violence: Random school shootings, 1982-2001. *American Behavioral Scientist, 46,* 1439-1458.

Kosciw, J., & Cullen, M. (2003). The GLSEN 2001 National School Climate Survey: The school-related experiences of our nation's lesbian, gay, bisexual, and transgender youth. New York: Office of Public Policy of the Gay, Lesbian, and Straight Education Network.

Limber, S. P., & Small, M. A. (2003). State laws and policies to address bullying in schools. *School Psychology Review, 32*(3), 445-455.

McBrien, J. L., & Brandt, R. S. (1997). *The language of learning: A guide to education terms.* Alexandria, VA: Association for Supervision and Curriculum Development.

McGarry, M., & Wasserman, F. (1998). *Becoming visible: An illustrated history of lesbian and gay life in twentieth-century America.* New York: Penguin Studio.

Mellor, A. (1997). Bullying: The Scottish experience. *Irish Journal of Psychology, 18,* 248-257.

No Child Left Behind Act of 2001 (2002). 115 U.S.C. Article 1425.

Oldenburg, B. F., Hardcastle, D., & Kok, G. (1997). Diffusion of health education and health promotion innovations. In K. Glanz, B. F. Lewis, & B. Rimer (Eds.), *Health behaviour and health education: Theory, research and practice* (2nd ed., pp. 270-286). San Francisco, CA: Jossey-Bass.

O'Shaughnessy, M., Russell, S. T., Heck, K., Calhoun, C., & Laub, C. (2004). *Safe place to learn: Consequences of harassment based on actual or perceived sexual orientation and gender non-conformity and steps for making schools safer.* San Francisco: California Safe Schools Coalition.

Perrotti, J., & Westheimer, K. (2001). *When the drama club is not enough.* Boston: Beacon.

Raudenbush, S. W., & Bryk, A. S. (2002). *Hierarchical linear models: Applications and data analysis methods* (2nd ed.). Thousand Oaks, CA: Sage.

Rivers, I. (2001). The bullying of sexual minorities at school: Its nature and long-term correlates. *Educational and Child Psychology, 18,* 32-46.

Rogers, E. M. (2003). *Diffusion of innovations* (5th ed.). New York: The Free Press.

Russell, S. T. (2003). Sexual minority youth and suicide risk. *American Behavioral Scientist, 46,* 1241-1257.

Russell, S. T., Kostroski, O., McGuire, J. K., Laub, C., & Manke, E. (2006). LGBT Issues in the Curriculum Promote School Safety. (California Safe Schools Coalition Research Brief No. 4). San Francisco: California Safe Schools Coalition.

Russell, S. T., McGuire, J. K., Lee, S.-A., Larriva, J. C., Laub, C., & California Safe Schools Coalition. (in press). Adolescent perceptions of school safety for students with lesbian, gay, bisexual, and transgender parents. *Journal of LGBT Youth.*

Russell, S. T., Seif, H. M., & Truong, N. L. (2001). School outcomes of sexual minority youth in the United States: Evidence from a National Study. *Journal of Adolescence, 24,* 111-127.

Singer, J. D. (1998). Using SAS PROC MIXED to fit multilevel models, hierarchical models, and individual growth models. *Journal of Educational and Behavioral Statistics, 24,* 323-55.

Skiba, R, Simmons, A. B., Peterson, R., McKelvey, J., Forde, S., & Gallini, S. (2004). Beyond guns, drugs, and gangs: The structure of student perceptions of school safety. *Journal of School Violence, 3,* 149-171.

Washington Safe Schools Coalition. (n.d.). *Our History.* Retrieved April 8, 2007, from http://www.safeschoolscoalition.org/about_us.html#OurHistory

Welsh, W. N. (2001). Effects of student and school factors on five measures of school disorder. *Justice Quarterly, 18,* 911-947.

Chapter 9
Whole-School Change

LAURA M. DESIMONE

Outside of the home environment, schools and classrooms are arguably the most influential social settings to which children and youth are exposed. Because of the importance of the school setting for child growth and development, efforts are constantly focused on improving schools and schooling. Decades of research has shown that school/classroom environmental, instructional, and social factors, such as a constructive school climate, a focus on academics, high expectations, and productive student-teacher relationships, are positively related to students' social and academic outcomes. The myriad of efforts to improve schools have alternatively and often simultaneously included adoption of new curricula, teacher and leader training, reorganization, and class size and school-scheduling adjustments (e.g., extended year). A recent effort that has garnered substantial attention is whole-school reform, which seeks to transform schools by changing multiple aspects of the school environment to create a productive learning environment for kids.

Whole-school change efforts, also called comprehensive schoolwide reform (CSR), are an outgrowth of the effective schools movement. While effective schools research identified specific characteristics associated with successful schools, it generally did not prescribe methods by which schools might become successful (Purkey & Smith, 1983). CSR attempts to address this weakness by providing designs for the creation of effective schools. There are a myriad of "packaged" CSR designs, developed by practitioners and researchers, from which schools can choose. Among the most popular are Accelerated Schools, America's Choice, the Coalition of Essential Schools, and Success for All (SFA; see Herman et al., 1999). Alternatively, schools might develop their own whole-school or comprehensive reform by taking different aspects of a packaged reform and creating their own locally adapted version.

A central impetus for the development of CSR designs was the failure of previous waves of school reform to foster improved student learning and development (Tyack & Cuban, 1995). In theory, CSR is designed to create and/or provide school structures, organizations, mechanisms, relationships, curricula, and opportunities for professional development that enable improvements not only to school system functioning but also to the one area of schooling that has proven most resistant to change: teaching practice. Improving on previous top-down and macrolevel approaches, most CSR models are designed to lead to direct improvements in the content and delivery of instruction (Slavin, 1983) that in turn will accelerate student learning.

Theoretical Framework: Factors Affecting Successful Implementation of Whole-School Change Efforts

For CSR, implementation refers to the extent to which a school is adhering to each aspect of the reform effort. Depending on the model, this may include management techniques, reorganization, parent involvement, teacher professional community (e.g., collaboration, professional development), and classroom instruction (e.g., instructional strategies, content covered, assessment methods). Each whole-school reform model places a different emphasis on this set of factors. Some models are subject specific and focus mainly on the content and delivery of instruction, while other models comprise multiple subjects and include aspects of school structure and organization. CSR implementation studies have found substantial variation in the level of consistency of implementation of CSR models, both within and between schools (Berends, 2000; Bodilly, 1998; Desimone, 2002a; Muncey & McQuillan, 1996). Applying to the context of whole-school reform, a theoretical framework that posits the central factors necessary for successful policy implementation facilitates a systematic analysis and explanation of implementation variation. In addition, it has the potential to propel our understanding of factors affecting the successful implementation of whole-school reform (Desimone, 2002a).

Policy Attributes Theory

The policy attributes theory is a powerful framework useful for both scholars and practitioners seeking to understand the success or failure of whole-school reform efforts. Conceived by Porter and his colleagues (Porter, 1994; Porter, Floden, Freeman, Schmidt, & Schwille, 1988), and used in different contexts to study education reform efforts (Berends, Chun, Schuyler, Stockly, & Briggs, 2002; Clune, 1998; Desimone, 2002a), the theory offers insight into why certain whole-school reform efforts enjoy success, whereas other similar efforts may fail.

The theory postulates that six key features are related to successful implementation: (a) consistency, (b) specificity, (c) authority, (d) power, (e) stability, and (f) comprehensiveness.

Consistency represents the degree of coherence among policies and the extent to which they contradict or reinforce each other. For example, a curriculum may be tied to the school's vision of reform through a guide that links particular parts of the curriculum to specific school goals. Implementation of a policy is easier if the policy is consistent with other reform efforts going on at the school, district, and state, because this uniformity eliminates tensions that require teachers to choose among reforms (Porter et al., 1988). In addition, reforms that build on and complement each other serve to reinforce each other. Two main areas of consistency emerge as being important for successful implementation of comprehensive school reform: (a) consistency with other school initiatives and (b) consistency with state- and district-level reforms and mandates.

Specificity (formerly labeled prescriptiveness) refers to how extensive and detailed a policy is. For example, a curriculum is more specific when accompanied by curriculum frameworks, guidelines, and supplemental materials. According to the policy attributes theory, the more specific a policy is in terms of materials, information, professional development, guidance, and instructions, the more likely teachers will be to implement it (Porter et al., 1988). The logic here is that mechanisms that increase specificity make the policy message clearer, make implementation easier because less interpretation is required, and also serve to reinforce the policy. The CSR implementation research points to three main mechanisms that contribute to the specificity of a whole-school change effort: (a) the locus of development (i.e., whether the model is designed by the school, or is externally developed by a design team), (b) the level and type of professional development provided (e.g., curriculum-based professional development that provides lesson plans vs. philosophically based professional development that provides only general guidelines), and (c) information and monitoring provided by CSR model design teams, districts, and schools.

Policies gain *authority* through becoming law, through becoming part of social or professional norms, and through the backing and support of institutions and individuals, either through expert or through charismatic leadership (Porter et al., 1988). The authoritative aspects of comprehensive school reform implementation fall into three categories: (a) normative authority, which includes teacher participation in decision making, teacher buy-in, participation in networks and collaborative activities, and norms related to race, ethnicity, and income; (b) individual authority, defined as principal leadership; and (c) institutional authority, which includes district leadership, resource support, and parent and community support.

Educational policies have *power* through the rewards and sanctions that they offer to stakeholders (Porter et al., 1988). In the case of comprehensive school reform, power is multilevel and includes differential rewards and sanctions at the state, district, school, and classroom levels. Power operates through the force of the rewards and sanctions associated with the reform effort. Research on the implementation of comprehensive school reform focuses on the contrast between using power and authority in two main areas: (a) choosing a comprehensive school reform design and (b) state, district, and local support of the reform. Previous research has shown that authority is related to sustained, deep implementation, whereas power is related to weak implementation that lasts only as long as the incentives last (Desimone, 2002a).

Stability is the extent to which people, circumstances, and policies remain constant over time. Policies that are part of a stable environment, and that are themselves stable, tend to achieve better implementation success. Three factors related to stability emerge from studies of comprehensive school reform: (a) the mobility of students, teachers, principals, and district leadership; (b) the stability of the policy environment, including the CSR model; and (c) the pace of reform.

Comprehensiveness is the degree to which a whole-school reform effort has each of the other five components in place. When whole-school reforms operate in consistent, stable policy environments, develop teacher support and buy-in through authoritative mechanisms, and are coupled with productive power mechanisms, implementation is deeper and more sustained than in less comprehensive policy environments.

Policies vary in their specificity, consistency, authority, power, stability, and comprehensiveness, and the higher a policy is on one or all of the attributes, the greater the chance of successful implementation (Porter et al., 1988). The theory states that policies that are influential because of their authoritative and thereby persuasive attributes are more likely to become institutionalized than those that exert influence primarily through power. This is presumably because the former persuades teachers, principals, and students that the policy is worthwhile, whereas the latter is effective only as long as the rewards and incentives last.

Further, the set of six policy attributes may vary at the school, district, and state level. This theory provides an analytic foundation from which to draw insights to move us closer to a multilevel theory of school improvement.

Two key factors that affect implementation fall outside this theory: (a) politics and (b) context, specifically grade levels (elementary, middle, or high school), teacher characteristics (e.g., experience), and social, economic, and racial/ethnic factors. Since many of them are fixed (e.g., whether the reform is operating in an elementary or middle school, the teacher's experience and the social/economic and racial characteristics of the school) and not as easy to manipulate as policy variables, this chapter focuses on those variables that scholars and practitioners are able to more easily address in seeking to create more productive learning environments for children.

What Does the Policy Attributes Theory Tell Us About How Whole-School Reform Works?

Applying this theoretical framework to implementation studies of whole-school reform elicits several key themes. One is that *each of the six attributes is related to the strength and type of implementation in a different way.* For example, the specificity of a CSR model is related to implementation fidelity. CSR models that provide more detailed and specific guidelines are more likely to have teachers implementing the model more faithfully. Authority, although possibly the most challenging attribute to achieve, is the attribute that seems to have the most influence on the depth and longevity of implementation (Desimone, 2002a). Genuine teacher buy-in, collaborative planning, and decision making allow ownership of the reform, and principal and district leadership help to integrate the reform into the daily lives of teachers (Cooper, Slavin, & Madden, 1998; Smith et al., 1997). The reform becomes a part of the normative culture. This makes the policy more resilient to weaknesses in other attributes (Datnow, 2000). Although some of the specificity and consistency and power might disappear—for example, professional development might be discontinued, other reforms might be introduced, and incentives might be taken away—if the reform has become part of the teachers' way of thinking, it is more likely to remain (Muncey & McQuillan, 1996). This is consistent with Porter et al.'s (1988) theory, which suggests that policies that operate through power will become ineffective when the policy disappears, whereas policies that operate through authority will remain, since they have their effect through persuading actors that the policy is beneficial to themselves and their students.

Power has been shown to be related to immediate, but often short-term effects (Desimone, 2002a). Districts that mandate reforms through a sanctions system find that schools often respond in a minimalist way and abandon the reform as soon as the sanctions were removed (Berends, Bodilly, & Kirby, 2002). Consistency is related to depth of implementation (Bodilly, 1996; Datnow & Stringfield, 2002) in that conflicting policy messages require teachers to address multiple reforms, which reduces the amount of time they can spend on a CSR model. This is an especially important challenge in the high-stakes accountability environment in which most if not all CSR schools currently exist. Stability plays a role in facilitating the institutionalization of CSR (Berends et al., 2002; Desimone, 2002a). The reform effort needs to be in place for a certain period to become institutionalized, but the mobility of stakeholders and the turbulence of the political environment surrounding the policy make this difficult to achieve (Berends et al., 2002).

A second theme is that *each attribute operates through its relationship with other attributes.* In the context of whole-school reform, the policy attributes are largely interdependent (Desimone, 2002a). For example, consistency can support or weaken authority. If high-stakes testing and CSR are not aligned, teacher commitment and buy-in would be mixed at best, and leaders might be perceived as sending mixed messages. Stability can support authority by providing (a) stable leadership that sends a signal to teachers that there is on-going institutional support for the reform and (b) low teacher turnover that increases the chances that the reform will become part of professional norms. Specificity, too, demonstrates a certain level of authority—when professional development, monitoring, and evaluation are all part of a reform, this demonstrates a joint effort of the school, district, and design team that reflects institutional backing of the reform. In addition, sometimes there is an implicit trade-off between specificity and authority. For example, very prescribed reforms might be easier to implement, but they often lack the buy-in and ownership that teachers feel when they have a role in developing the reform (Cooper et al., 1998; Ross et al., 1997).

Other interdependencies between attributes of comprehensive school reform are evident. For example, specific guidelines, benchmarks, professional development, materials, and so on, provide teachers with practical tools to implement the programs, but these tools are limited by the extent to which they are consistent with other reforms teachers are asked to implement and with the authority of the reform in terms of support from their district and principal. For example, CSRs operate in a standards-based reform environment—no amount of specificity can overcome the tension between performance-based assessments for state tests and CSR models. Also, more practical, on-going monitoring and professional feedback requires more time and so must be supported by attributes of authority, namely, increased time and resources. In addition, district support lends authority to a reform, but such support also contributes to consistency by providing a policy message that is compatible with the school's policy message (Desimone, 2002a).

Similarly, the stability of the environment and the patience with which reformers attempt change contribute to the effectiveness of other attributes (Desimone, 2002a). Policy specificity is more effective if it is provided over an extended period, and the longer the policy environment remains consistent, the more teachers will consider it to be institutionalized (Glennan, 1998). Furthermore, infrequent turnover provides the same stakeholders with a better opportunity to understand and buy-in to the reform (Bodilly, 1998).

A final theme is that *teacher, school, and system reforms should be combined.* Reforms can be characterized as one-teacher-at-a-time (e.g., professional development, curriculum materials), one-school-at-a-time (e.g., CSR), or one-system-at-a-time reforms (e.g., standards-based/systemic reform; Desimone, 2002a). Each has been tried separately and has met with limited success in terms of lasting, large-scale success. For example, one-teacher-at-a-time reforms have had great positive effects on teachers in some cases, but they do not seem to be enough to create a critical mass to turn a school around or to have sustained effects (Sykes et al., 2006). Analyzing the CSR implementation literature using the policy attributes theory provides support for the idea that all three of these types of reforms need to be used simultaneously. For example, the methods for achieving one-teacher-at-a-time rely on specificity of the professional development or materials. Authority relies on schoolwide support and backing characteristic of schoolwide efforts, and consistency relies on coordination of the larger policy system, as reflected in the tenets of standards-based reform. Research in CSR has found that all of these attributes contribute to successful implementation.

Measuring Whole-School Change

Measuring implementation is a key component of both process and impact evaluations (Weiss, 1998). Periodic measurement of implementation benchmarks is useful for monitoring the level and quality of the implementation of a whole-school innovation. To this end, several comprehensive school reform model developers provide an implementation trajectory against which schools can measure their progress and identify areas that need improvement. Measuring implementation is useful in outcome studies because we expect the level of implementation to be related to the magnitude and type of effects on students. We know from decades of research on social programs that within organization implementation varies widely (e.g., Berman & McLaughlin, 1975; Elmore, 1975; Gamoran, 1992). Thus, we cannot assume that each student experiences his or her whole-school reform effort similarly. Measuring implementation and including a variable that measures level and quality of implementation in predicting outcomes in the context of an experimental or quasi-experimental research design adds credibility and explanatory power to inquiries into how and why whole-school works to improve outcomes for students.

In applying the theory of policy attributes to study the implementation of whole-school change, several measurement issues and challenges arise. The first is the operationalization of the attributes to form useful measures for research, evaluation, and practice. On one level, this is a straightforward endeavor. The attributes have been successfully translated into survey measures in a study of standards-based reform (Desimone, 2006b) that could be adapted to the context of whole-school reform. Examples and ideas for adaptation are discussed in the following subsections. However, in thinking about how to operationalize the policy attributes to measure the implementation of whole-school reform, several measurement challenges emerge that must also be addressed. Several apply to the attributes framework, while others are directly relevant to measuring the substance of the intervention. These are also discussed in the following sections.

Consistency

Questions about consistency would ask respondents to judge the level of alignment of various components of the school system (curriculum, assessments, standards, textbooks, see Desimone, 2006b). The goal here would be to find out if the whole-school reform was pushing in the same direction as other policy mechanisms, such as state standards. Also useful in measuring consistency is a tool that allows the mapping of the content of standards, assessments, textbooks, curricula, and teachers' instruction to the same content grid so that a quantitative metric of alignment, or consistency, can be garnered (see Porter, 2002). The same content grid could be used to measure the specificity of the lesson plans or curriculum that accompanies the whole-school reform design. As shown in Table 9.1, the content grid provides details about the cognitive demands (e.g., memorize vs. conjecture) and topics (e.g., multistep equations, inequalities) and their intersection (e.g., memorize inequalities vs. conjecture about the nature of inequalities). When the grid is completed for two different policy documents (e.g., whole-school reform curriculum and state standards), one can see empirically the extent to which each is consistent with the other. For example, a teacher's instruction might cover the same topics as the assessments but the teacher may focus more on higher-level cognitive demands, such as generalize and prove, whereas the assessment might focus more on lower-order cognitive demands, such as memorize and perform procedures. Such a discrepancy would be evident in the content matrix, for example, for the assessment the cell corresponding to *memorize* multistep equation would be completed, whereas for the teacher's self-reported instruction the cell for *conjecture, generalize, prove* multistep equation would be completed.

Developing a Measure of the Consistency of Knowledge Demands of Whole-School Reforms and Teacher Capacity

Another aspect of consistency that may be especially important for the success of whole-school reforms is the consistency between the reform's knowledge demands and teachers' knowledge base. Two intersecting and salient ideas related to explaining weak implementation of CSR are the knowledge demands of CSR and the corresponding lack of teacher knowledge. Implicit hypotheses about the challenging content of whole-school reforms and teachers' inability to faithfully implement them could be directly tested if measures of the knowledge demands of particular reforms were developed and compared to teacher knowledge.

This of course requires adequate measures of teacher knowledge. Recent work has emphasized that growth in teacher's content knowledge is necessary

Table 9.1 Excerpt of Content Grid

	Category of Cognitive Demand			
Time on Topic	Memorize Facts, Definitions, and Formulas	Perform Procedures	Communicate Understanding of Concepts	Conjecture/ Generalize/ Prove	Solve Nonroutine Problems
Topic				
Multiple-step equations				
Inequalities				
Linear equations				
Lines/slope and intercept				
Operations and polynomials				
Quadratic equations				

to make improvements in instructions that foster growth in student learning (Hill, Schilling, & Ball, 2004). In the context of whole-school reform, teacher knowledge of both reform principles and instruction requirements are related to the depth and consistency of implementation. Thus, including measures of teachers' (a) subject-matter knowledge, (b) pedagogical strategies, and (c) understanding of the principles of the particular whole-school reform they are implementing is a critical component to measuring whole-school change. Alternative conceptions of teacher knowledge, such as the division of such knowledge into procedural, foundational, and experiential components (Glazer, 2006) are also crucial to the continued refinement of ideas about how teacher knowledge influences implementation. Current efforts are underway to develop teacher knowledge assessments that can be applied to study the effects of any school reform program (e.g., Bush Ronau, McGattha, & Karp, 2005; Hill et al., 2004), but there is much work left to be done in this area, both in conceptualization and measurement. With solid measures of teacher knowledge and knowledge required to implement the reform and the ability to examine the consistency between the two, we might then be able to determine the extent to which professional development offered to teachers reflects the knowledge demands of the CSR reform. This would help explain implementation successes and failures.

Specificity

While delineating the knowledge demands required of a reform could be considered an aspect of specificity, this construct can also be measured in part by questions designed to elicit detailed information on the type of supporting materials provided to leaders and administrators, and how well delineated the reform is, in terms of the specificity of guidance that schools and teachers receive (see Desimone, 2006b). For example, SFA indicates the exact content and pace teachers should follow, whereas Accelerated Schools is much less specific in terms of what teachers are to do. Much is left for teacher invention, in the case of the latter. Previous research has shown that less-specified models usually have weaker implementation than models that provided detailed implementation guidance (Desimone, 2002b).

Level and Quality of Professional Development

Taking the measurement of the specificity of guidance or professional development one step further, I think that measuring the amount and quality of professional development that is necessary to achieve particular levels of implementation could be quite constructive. Recent research suggests that a substantial number of hours of professional training is necessary—several hours every day for months—to foster significant teacher change (Barnes,

Khorsheed, Rois, & Correnti, 2006). Measuring the links between the number of hours spent in model-related professional development and subsequent teacher change would assist us in thinking about the feasibility of scale up and the role of teacher knowledge in the dynamics of whole-school change.

Determining the Level at Which Different CSR Models Are Effective

Related to looking at links between professional development exposure and teacher change is the idea of examining links between levels of implementation and effects. Rarely do whole-school reform models reach "full" or consistent implementation across all classrooms in a school or all schools in a district. Still, rigorous studies find positive effects on student achievement. So, at what level of implementation does CSR become effective? One hypothesis is that surface or rote implementation of certain whole-school reform efforts is good enough to get substantial results for students. This probably differs across models. SFA, a very prescriptive whole-school reform, might work because teachers are able to implement the fundamentals, even though high-quality implementation is rare (e.g., Barnes et al., 2006). That is, "rote" implementation of SFA may translate into more content exposure and a faster pace of instruction, which may be enough to elicit gains in student achievement. However for less prescriptive models, such as America's Choice, positive effects may require high-quality implementation, which has so far proven elusive (e.g., Nunnery, 1998; Ross, Alberg, & Nunnery, 1999). Building on already available CSR benchmarks for implementation, developing level and quality implementation measures, and using them to help answer the question of "how much is enough" would go a long way to increasing our understanding of thresholds of instructional improvement that garner productive gains for student learning.

Conceptualizing and Measuring Instruction

Another aspect of specificity of a whole-school design is the particular content and teaching practices advocated by the reform. Does the reform specify particular content and pacing, as does SFA, or does it target a broadly defined teaching philosophy, as does Accelerated Schools? How we conceptualize instruction in the context of whole-school reform is central to guiding how to measure it. For example, Glazer (2006) proffers the simple yet profound idea that what counts as instructional evidence depends on how teaching and learning are defined. Work studying CSR implementation does not often acknowledge this important point. For example, when instruction is seen as fixed and discrete it is easier to measure. But when instruction is seen as fluid and subjective and learning as a complex construction, measurement becomes more complicated. Measures of implementation of CSR must make clear the assumptions about how instruction is defined, how this shapes what we measure, and how much change we can reasonably expect, from both teachers and their students.

Authority and Power

Authority measures already exist in many forms, though they usually are not labeled "authority." Factors such as teacher, principal, and district support for reform, buy-in, extent of involvement in developing and implementing the reform, and the degree to which the reform is supported by key policy players (whether the teacher, principal, school board, district superintendent, or governor) all measure aspects of authority. Likewise, questions about the rewards and sanctions associated with particular actions measure the power construct. Previous studies of comprehensive school reform have already tapped into both the authority and power constructs, studying the importance of teacher buy-in and the threat of sanctions in pushing teachers' decisions toward reform adoption and the subsequent quality of implementation (e.g., Datnow, 2000).

Stability

Operationalizing stability should include discrete quantifiable measures of stability, such as principal, teacher, and student mobility, and how long a particular reform has been in place. In addition, it is crucial to measure a respondent's perceptions about how long the current reform will last. The stability of the policy environment is influenced by previous experiences with the fluctuation of reform, and respondents' perceptions of stability can be just as important if not more important than actual stability, in terms of its relationship to implementation (Desimone, 2002a).

Distinguishing True From Perceived Policy Attributes

This issue of perceived versus actual stability leads to another issue in measuring the policy attributes. A fundamental measurement issue is the distinction between "true" and "perceived" policy attributes. Although a true set of policy attributes exists and might be measured through policy document analysis and meeting minutes, arguably, it is how respondents *perceive* the policies that affect respondent actions. For example, even if a policy document exists that says teachers will be rewarded or sanctioned if they follow a CSR model, if teachers are unaware of this provision or if they know their principal will not enforce it, then we would not expect the provision to affect their behavior. Thus, rather than conceiving respondent variation in perceptions of policies as pure measurement error, it may be more productive to consider it as an indication of their knowledge and understanding of the policy.

Applying a Framework to Guide Measurement

An overarching measurement issue in whole-school reform is the need for studies to be grounded in a similar conceptual framework. Currently studies of whole-school reform implementation do not use a core set of guidelines or framework. Using a more explicit conceptual framework to describe the process, mechanisms, and timeline for school change would be helpful. Such a framework would better allow the translation of findings across studies and identification of key elements of the implementation system. Such a framework might have the policy attributes as its core, in addition to key implementation benchmarks.

The framework could also provide methodology guidance, to help drive the constant challenge of choosing appropriate methodologies for studying various aspects of whole-school reform implementation and effects. Research comparing surveys, logs, interviews, and observations of teacher's instruction has demonstrated that each method is differentially appropriate for measuring particular areas of teacher behaviors and understandings of how to implement reforms (Desimone, 2006a). For example, measuring specific behaviors and practices, such as grouping students, and the coverage of particular content are adequately measured by teacher logs and surveys. Aspects of instruction that are more subjective but still central to whole-school reform initiatives, such as the quality of execution of higher-order questioning, teacher-student interactions, and use of student misunderstandings, are better measured through classroom observations by trained experts. Thus, in measuring the implementation of whole-school reform efforts, careful attention must be paid to ensure that the source of data is appropriately matched to each aspect of implementation. This requires a multimethod framework, which matches data sources to the type and quality of data needed for measuring specific aspects of implementation.

Exemplars of Whole-School Change

While there are particular models that have withstood the test of time, are operating successfully in many schools, and have been shown in rigorous research to have beneficial effects on student learning (e.g., SFA), the implementation literature has taught us that even these whole-school reform models are not "school proof" or "teacher proof" in that implementation failures abound, even with "successful" models. Turning again to the policy attributes theory, perhaps a more productive way of conceptualizing exemplars, rather than identifying particular models as they are designed, is to define an exemplar CSR design as one that contains high-quality aspects of each of the policy attributes *as it is implemented.*

Since whole-school designs are interactive, use different professional development providers, and work with different principals in different district and school contexts, no one model will be successful in all of these environments. That is, stability is important, but the CSR designer has no control over the stability of the policy environment of an adopting school or district. On the other hand, CSR models do attempt to integrate as a firm part of their design specific elements that correspond to the policy framework presented here. One example is that many whole-school designs require a schoolwide consensus vote before adoption, to ensure support and buy-in (authority). Though research has shown that voting on the adoption of a school reform is not a straightforward measure of buy-in because of behind-the-scenes pressure to vote a certain way (Datnow, 2000), the voting requirement is an attempt to institutionalize an important component of successful implementation— authority. Thus, rather than considering particular designs as exemplars, I would advocate for conceptualization of exemplar designs as those most closely matched to the theoretical framework presented here, as they are implemented in particular schools.

The policy attributes, however, are separate from the substance of a whole-school design. A design might be powerful, authoritative, consistent, specific, and stable in implementation, but the core substance of the intervention might not be useful for increasing student learning. Thus, one might argue that exemplary designs should be designated based on their demonstrated effects on student achievement. Given this criterion, SFA would qualify as an exemplary design, since it has at least some rigorous experimental research that supports its effects on student achievement (Borman et al., 2005a, 2005b).

I take an alternative view. Nearly all major whole-school reform designs are based on previous research about what works to help students achieve and thus have the potential to have positive impacts. But we know from studies of these designs that they rarely enjoy high-quality implementation, which is likely necessary for those positive impacts to manifest themselves. Thus, I argue that the policy attributes are a useful tool to measure the quality of implementation, an essential component to an "exemplary" design and one that is usually the factor standing between good intentions and good outcomes.

Promising Future Directions

Examining implementation research of the past decade, including several major recent studies, highlights what we know and indicates productive avenues for further exploration. Below I describe several promising directions for whole-school reform.

Studying the Cognitive Demands
Placed on Teachers

There has been much talk of the importance of pedagogical content knowledge and content knowledge and work on developing assessments but little work linking teacher's content knowledge to the effective implementation of particular reforms. How do teachers make decisions about what to teach in the context of implementing a whole-school reform design? To what extent do the bounds of their content knowledge dictate the level of implementation they achieve? Which parts of whole-school reform models require the most professional development/coaching/teacher invention? With which aspects of the models do teachers struggle? Detailed questions focused on understanding the intersection of the cognitive requirements of whole-school reforms and how teachers translate those demands, given their level of knowledge, would shed light on implementation variation. These questions also provide practical implications for the continued improvement of the professional development offered to teachers as part of CSR designs.

Bridging Views of Teaching
as Inferential and Prescriptive

CSR models are predicated on the idea that there are certain aspects of instruction—curriculum, organization, pacing, and so on—that we know work for many students. Recent studies of CSR models identify a breakdown in implementation when teachers cannot rely explicitly on the curriculum guidelines and model-related professional development but instead are required to "infer" what their practice should be. This raises a potentially important question about the relationship between the known technologies of teaching and inferential practices. For example, are there "known" prerequisites (e.g., content knowledge, experience) to being able to invest and extrapolate successful teaching practices from more abstract curricular principles? Would inferential requirements be appropriate only for teachers with sufficient content knowledge and skills, whereas more prescriptive designs are appropriate for less knowledgeable and skilled teachers? One view of instruction is that something unique is needed for each child and that this varies by teacher and content. This is in contrast to a view that there are core instructional content and technologies that work for most students, at most times, with most teachers. What are the significant relationships/bridges between these two views, as they relate to whole-school reforms that are designed to foster consistent teaching across classrooms for teachers with varying ability and experience levels?

Providing Insight Into How Best to Foster
Research-Based Practices That Violate
Conventional Wisdom

A compelling and intractable issue in school reform is that implementation is related to teacher beliefs about the reform. Teachers resist changing when reforms are not intuitive or go against their knowledge of best practice. However, sometimes conventional wisdom about best practice conflicts with research-based ideas. One example is spiraling—moving to new material before a student has mastered current material. Spiraling is a core component of SFA, and many teachers are not comfortable with it, given that it violates their notions of the importance of mastery (Massell & Barnes, 2006). Whole-school reform would benefit from greater insight into the best ways to approach fostering implementation of research-based practice that goes against teachers' conventional wisdom.

Indicate How We Can Teach Teachers
to Implement CSR Reforms Well (or, What
Causes Deep Implementation?)

Teachers follow the aspects of the models that are specified and delineated but fall short of good implementation when they are required to invent their own practices (Barnes et al., 2006), which all models require at least to some extent (Glazer, 2006). Should models require less invention? What are the trade-offs in advocating for more work-intensive, inferential reforms that are more cognitively demanding of teachers? Are the benefits of ambitious instruction so great that they are worth us not being able to do it well? Easy to implement models may have a modest effect on gains in achievement, whereas harder to implement models have bigger effects, but if we cannot achieve the full implementation necessary for those big effects, should we focus on reforms that treat subject matter discretely but that can be implemented well? Should we match reforms to teacher capacity (or at least have a growth model for implementation that accounts for a learning curve)? Brian Rowan has suggested (1990) that certain types of teaching may be more effective in particular environments. Similarly, if a teacher does not have the knowledge necessary to implement a particular whole-school reform well, might it be more effective for her to use a more discrete form of instruction (i.e., a less ambitious whole-school reform model)?

What Are Implementation Challenges, Given
Our High-Stakes Accountability Context?

I highlighted previously the conflict between whole-school reform and performance on standardized tests, where results are needed more quickly than is usually possible given the time it takes to achieve adequate CSR implementation. Current work indicates the same sort of tensions—teachers abandoning the curriculum of whole-school reform to spend time preparing their students for state standardized tests. What do we know about the extent to which the mix of CSR curriculum and test preparation works to help students achieve on standardized tests? How do teachers manage the discontinuity between the demands of the reform and the demands of our current accountability environment?

Identifying Necessary Leadership Qualities

Several CSR studies focus on principal and district leadership of reform efforts. Have we learned enough to suggest a typology or profile of types of district/school management that might serve as an analytic and practical model? Do we know which leadership strategies work for particular models in particular contexts? For example, successful CSR leaders need to be able to negotiate simultaneous bottom-up and top-down forces (Barnes et al., 2006b). Extending that and similar ideas to develop a framework for leadership for whole-school change would provide practical insight to inform the identification and development of successful whole-school change leaders.

The Policy Attributes Theory Reprise

The policy attributes theory presented here could provide a useful framework for monitoring and assessing local implementation and scale-up efforts. Schools and districts could monitor implementation by measuring their whole-school effort's: (a) consistency with other reforms and consistency between the reform's knowledge demands and teacher capacity; (b) specificity in terms of guidance and professional development offered and teaching requirements of the reform and links between specific implementation levels and effects; (c) authority of the reform operationalized as teacher, principal, and district support and buy-in; (d) power as measured by the actual and perceived rewards and sanctions associated with successful implementation; and (e) stability of relevant actors and policies, as well as (f) the comprehensiveness of the implementation system conceptualized as the degree to which each of the other five attributes are being implemented.

It would be useful to study how the policy attributes can be fostered and what their individual and interactive strengths and effects are on quality of implementation, including how they work in conflict and concert. If the policy attributes theory (or a similar framework) were applied to a series of whole-school reform studies, it could serve as a powerful analytic framework with which to integrate findings to develop a theory of implementation grounded in knowledge of how school improvement occurs. It could also serve as a foundational tool to allow us to better link studies of different whole-school reforms and to guide the use of appropriate methodologies for studying whole-school reform. Use of such a conceptual framework would force us to integrate what we already know about how to make whole-school reform work with new efforts to improve implementation success and, in the process, help increase the chances of schools reaching their potential to provide productive environments for children and youth.

References

Barnes, C., Khorsheed, K., Rios, D., & Correnti, R. (2006). *Learning by design: Developing the know-how to improve teaching and learning in high poverty schools.* Paper presented in the Annual Meeting of the American Educational Research Association, San Francisco.

Berends, M. (2000). Teacher-reported effects of New American Schools design: Exploring relationships to teacher background and school context. *Education Evaluation and Policy Analysis, 22*(1), 65-82.

Berends, M., Bodilly, S. J., & Kirby, S. N. (2002). *Facing the challenges of whole-school reform: New American Schools after a decade.* Santa Monica, CA: RAND.

Berends, M., Chun, J., Schuyler, G., Stockly, S., & Briggs, R. J. (2002). *Challenges of conflicting school reforms: Effects of New American Schools in a high-poverty district.* Santa Monica, CA: RAND.

Berman, P., & McLaughlin, M. W. (1978). *Federal programs supporting educational change. Vol. VIII: Implementing and sustaining innovations.* Santa Monica, CA: RAND (ED 159 289).

Bodilly, S. J. (1996). *Lessons from New American Schools Development Corporation's demonstration phase.* Santa Monica, CA: RAND.

Bodilly, S. J. (1998). *Lessons from New American Schools' scale-up phase: Prospects for bringing designs to multiple schools.* Santa Monica, CA: RAND.

Borman, G., Slavin, R., Cheung, A., Chamberlain, A., Madden, N., & Chambers, B. (2005a). The national randomized field trail of Success for All: Second-year outcomes. *American Educational Research Journal, 42*(4), 673-696.

Borman, G., Slavin, R., Cheung, A., Chamberlain, A., Madden, N., & Chambers, B. (2005b). Success for All: First-year results from the national randomized field trial. *Educational Evaluation and Policy Analysis, 27*(1), 1-22.

Bush, W. S., Ronau, R., McGattha, M., & Karp, K. (2005, April). *Diagnostic mathematics assessments for middle school teachers.* Presented at the American Education Research Association Annual meeting in Montreal, Canada.

Clune, W. (1998). *Toward a theory of systemic reform: The case of nine NSF statewide systemic initiatives.* Research Monograph No. 16. Madison, WI: National Institute for Science Education.

Cooper, R., Slavin, R. E., & Madden, N. A. (1998, March 24-28). *Success for All: Improving the quality of implementation of whole-school change through the use of a national reform network.* Revised version of paper presented at the Annual Meeting of the American Educational Research Association, Chicago.

Datnow, A. (2000). Power and politics in the adoption of whole school reform models. *Educational Evaluation and Policy Analysis, 22*(4), 357-374.

Datnow, A., & Stringfield, S. (2000). Working together for reliable school reform. *Journal of Education for Students Placed at Risk, 5*(1&2), 183-204.

Desimone, L. (2002a). How can Comprehensive School Reform models be successfully implemented? *Review of Educational Research, 72*(3), 433-479.

Desimone, L. (2002b). Reinventing Evaluation: Editor's introduction. *Peabody Journal of Education, 77*(4), 1-5.

Desimone, L. (2006a). *How can we best measure teacher's professional development and its effects on teachers and students?* Working paper.

Desimone, L. (2006b). Consider the source: Response differences among teachers, principals and districts on survey questions about their education policy environment. *Educational Policy, 20*(4), 640-676.

Elmore, R. F. (1975). Design of the follow through experiment. In A. M. Rivlin & P. M. Timpane (Eds.), *Planned variation in education: Should we give up or try harder?* (pp. 23-45). Washington, DC: Brookings Institution (ED 114 986).

Gamoran, A. (1992). Social factors in education. In M. Alkin (Ed.), *Encyclopedia of educational research* (6th ed., pp. 1222-1229). New York: Macmillan.

Glazer, J. L. (2006, April). *How instructional designs mediate the knowledge demands of teaching.* Paper presented in the Annual Meeting of the American Educational Research Association, San Francisco.

Glennan, T. K., Jr. (1998). *New American Schools after six years.* Santa Monica, CA: RAND.

Herman, R., Aladjem, D., McMahon, P., Masem, E., Mulligan, I., O'Malley, A., et al. (1999). *An educators' guide to school wide reform.* Arlington, VA: Educational Research Service.

Hill, H. C., Schilling, S., & Ball, D. (2004). Developing measures of teachers' mathematical knowledge for teaching. *Elementary School Journal, 105*(1), 11-31.

Massell, D., & Barnes, C. (2006, April). *Student data for instructional improvement: Comparative CSR strategies.* Paper presented in the Annual Meeting of the American Educational Research Association, San Francisco.

Muncey, D. E., & McQuillan, P. J. (1996). *Reform and resistance in schools and classrooms: An ethnographic view of the Coalition of Essential Schools.* New Haven: Yale University Press.

Nunnery, J. A. (1998, May). Reform ideology and the locus of development problem in educational restructuring: Enduring lessons from studies of educational innovation. *Education and Urban Society, 30*(3), 277-295.

Porter, A. C. (1994). National standards and school improvement in the 1990s: Issues and promise. *American Journal of Education, 102*, 421-449.

Porter, A. C. (2002, October). Measuring the content of instruction: Uses in research and practice. *Educational Researcher, 31*(7), 3-14.

Porter, A. C., Floden, R., Freeman, D., Schmidt, W., & Schwille, J. (1988). Content determinants in elementary school mathematics. In D. Grouws & T. Cooney (Eds.), *Perspectives on research on effective mathematics teaching* (pp. 96-113). Reston, VA: The National Council of Teachers of Mathematics.

Purkey, S. C., & Smith, M. S. (1983, March). Effective schools: A review. *Elementary School Journal, 83*(4), 427-452.

Ross, S. M., Alberg, M., & Nunnery, J. (1999). Selection and evaluation of locally developed versus externally developed schoolwide programs. In G. Orfield & E. H. DeBray (Eds.), *Hard work for good schools: Facts not fads in Title I reform* (pp. 147-158). Cambridge: Harvard University, The Civil Rights Project.

Ross, S., Troutman, A., Horgan, D., Maxwell, S., Laitinen, R., & Lowther, D. (1997). The success of schools in implementing eight restructuring designs: A synthesis of first-year evaluation outcomes. *School Effectiveness and School Improvement, 8*(1), 95-124.

Rowan, B. (1990). Commitment and control: Alternative strategies for the organizational design of schools. *Review of Research in Education, 16,* 353-389.

Slavin, R. E. (1983). Realities and remedies. *Elementary School Journal, 84*(2), 131-138.

Smith, L. J., Maxwell, S., Lowther, D., Hacker, D., Bol, L., & Nunnery J. (1997, March). Activities in schools and programs experiencing the most, and least, early implementation successes. *School Effectiveness and School Improvement, 8*(1), 125-150.

Sykes, G., Anagnostopoulos, D., Cannata, M., Chard, L., Frank K., McCrory, R., et al. (2006). *National board certified teachers as organizational resource institution.* East Lansing, MI: Michigan State University.

Tyack, D., & Cuban, L. (1995). *Tinkering toward utopia: A century of public school reform.* Cambridge, MA: Harvard University Press.

Weiss, C. (1998). *Evaluation research: Methods for studying programs and policies.* Upper Saddle River, NJ: Prentice Hall.

PART III

CHANGING COMMUNITY ORGANIZATIONS

Chapter 10

Building the Capacity of Small Community-Based Organizations to Better Serve Youth

ROBIN LIN MILLER, SHANNON K. E. KOBES, AND JASON C. FORNEY

Community-based organizations (CBOs) enable members of our society to improve human well-being and advocate on behalf of those whose needs are not well met by other types of institutions (Frederickson & London, 2000; Lipsky & Smith, 1989-1990). In light of the central role that CBOs can play in promoting the quality of citizens' lives, fostering their optimal functioning serves an essential purpose toward the larger aim of social betterment.

A principal focus of current efforts to improve CBOs concerns the development of their organizational capacity. Organizational capacity efforts are those in which an internal or an outside entity uses organizational development or other strategies to enhance specific organizational competencies. What constitutes organizational capacity is often implied by the choice of focus of capacity-building intervention efforts (e.g., developing competence to conduct program evaluation) and by the specific social problem area of interest (e.g., developing competence to deliver particular types of evidence-based programs).

In this chapter, we develop a framework for understanding CBO capacity and for guiding efforts to develop it in youth-serving CBOs. We focus specifically on small CBOs, drawing on our own experiences over the past 20 years of working with CBOs in the fields of violence against women, HIV/AIDS, and gay, lesbian, bisexual, and transgender concerns. Although the strategies we describe are broadly applicable and should work equally well across a range of CBOs, the application of these strategies to youth-serving CBOs is less well documented than in CBOs representing other constituents. When possible, we illustrate these strategies with examples drawn from youth-serving CBOs. When we lack examples from youth-serving CBOs, we use examples from CBOs that include youth among constituents. We begin by identifying what sets apart CBOs, including those that represent youth, from other types of organizations.

Defining Features of CBOs

The label "CBO" is often loosely applied to any nonprofit organization operating in a local community setting. Yet, CBOs are unique among nonprofit organizational forms and are infrequently the focus of organizational theory and research. CBOs are citizen-driven organizations that pursue social change in the names of communities that are neglected by the mainstream (Altman, 1994; Marwell, 2004), such as youth of color residing in a specific neighborhood or city. CBOs are distinguished from other types of nonprofit human service organizations by the fact that they act on the behalf of their local community, increase attention to and address the needs of their community, and develop and empower their community (Altman, 1994; Marwell, 2004). The CBO mission is carried out by providing direct services, engaging in community-building endeavors, and influencing local political and policy outcomes (Marwell, 2004). In youth-serving CBOs, youth often play a meaningful role in setting the agenda, articulating youth's needs, and shaping organizational activities. For example, The Center for Teen Empowerment in Massachusetts (http:// www.teenempowerment.com) engages in youth organizing to help youth initiate local efforts at social change. Teen Empowerment's youth organizers select their own goals for social change and the means by which it will be attained. The youth organizers have initiated actions such as community-police dialogues and a local peace conference.

The locally focused community and advocacy orientation of a CBO highlights the centrality of social and political values to the organization's values. CBOs possess distinct and discernible ethical and value stances toward their constituents, the particular social changes they desire to achieve on their behalf, and how they think change can best be brought about. Moreover, those youth and adults who participate in a CBO's operation are likely to possess values that align closely with those of the organization, so the collective value framework guiding the organization becomes of central importance to its ability to sustain itself. Values provide the backdrop against which all organizational competencies must be considered and in which any effort at change will take place.

Challenges to Capacity Building for CBOs

The dangers and challenges of providing capacity development services to CBOs are multiple and highlight the boundary conditions for efforts at change. Change efforts must be appropriate to and fit the political and social environment in which the organization functions and must be appropriate to the organization's size and resources and its stage of development. We briefly address each of these conditions for establishing the fit between capacity-building efforts and organizational circumstances.

Sensitivity to the Political and Social Fit of Capacity Building

In CBOs, unlike other organizational environments, capacity-building efforts run the risk of undoing what makes a CBO community based and an advocate for its constituents, in this case, youth. Capacity development is a professionalizing exercise to some degree and may paradoxically contribute to a CBO becoming a traditional service provider. For instance, capacity-building efforts can co-opt the CBO's community-building and community-management missions by being overly focused on "professional" ways of providing services and on adult-directed activities and decision making. Capacity building could mechanize work in ways that are incongruous with core organizational philosophical principles such as responsiveness, innovation, and flexibility or emphasize priorities that are weakly related to the organization's overarching political purpose to advance the rights and well-being of its youth community.

CBOs may place high value on the facets of their organizations that identify them as community based and as not a mainstream youth service. CBOs want their community to have resources and services directed to their youth, but part of the raison d'etre of a CBO is to make sure that youth have a say in what and how needs are to be met. Like all CBOs, youth-serving CBOs want to be able to determine what capacities they would like to build, rather than have outsiders do so. Successful capacity building should maintain community-based decision making and not undermine youth's voice and participation in capacity building. It should also be consonant with the community-building aspect of a CBO and fit with its larger efforts toward social change to benefit youth.

Size and Resources

As we have previously stated, CBOs are typically rooted in local, citizen-driven movements, are staffed by indigenous adult and youth community workers, and are small organizational settings. For instance, it is not unusual among CBOs to have no more than one or two paid employees. CBOs are often financially vulnerable, with small shifts in funding priorities having large impacts on these organizations' financial health. CBOs may not have resources that other organizations have, such as desks and computers for every employee, organization-wide access to the Internet, and adequate space or supplies. Committed people, paid and unpaid, youth and adult, are typically the most highly prized and plentiful resource.

These features of CBOs have important implications for the scale along which we consider capacity and set the limits to applying knowledge developed from other types of organizations. CBOs may not be able to afford (or welcome) outside capacity-building assistance, so capacity-building approaches rooted in expert-delivered organizational development consultation may be difficult to apply. Indeed, some research suggests that CBOs are most likely to pursue capacity building without outside help and that some of these organizations may reject the idea of capacity building altogether (Light, 2004). Many typical efforts to build and measure capacity need to be reconsidered in light of the small scale and often low and unstable resource base of the CBO.

Stage of Development

CBOs evolve dynamically over time, responding to change in social conditions surrounding the problems of concern to their youth community and the local economics of community-based life. Consequently, which capacities are most important and how each applies to the CBO will depend upon its stage of development and the state of the problem with which it is concerned.

Organizations move through life cycles of growth and decline, with particular competencies of greater importance at some stages than at others (Griener, 1972; Riger, 1984), while also contending with changing environmental conditions (Oliver, 1991). For instance, leadership capacities may be of the utmost importance at an organization's initiation, as it is vision and leadership that will attract and maintain organizational adherents. These skills may also be especially important when the organization's approach is locally contentious or at points of major transition. At other moments in time, skills at routinizing projects may be more important to develop than particular leadership skills, either because of internal organizational needs for stability or because of external demands. The life cycle and environment transactional principles highlight that capacity is dynamic; any particular capacity may be of greater or less importance at any particular stage of an organization's life or in particular circumstances. Those who seek to intervene in CBOs are wise to consider how an organization's present mixture of competencies facilitates its success relative to its current stage of growth or decline and present context.

Organizational Capacity and Development

Our framework for understanding the targets of organizational capacity development derives from Hannan and Carroll (1995). According to these authors, organizations have three distinguishing facets.

1. Organizations are durable social structures, designed to persist over time and routinely and continuously carry out specific actions.
2. They are reliable in so far as they are intended to be good at doing the same thing in the same way over and over.
3. They are internally and externally accountable for performing in accordance with agreed-on standards and procedures.

Although the features of durability, reliability, and accountability may be embodied differently in a CBO than in a corporate setting, any organization must have these capacities to serve its function well (see Table 10.1).

In our extension of this framework to the youth-serving CBO, we see these features as situated within the framework of the values that contribute to the specific structures, activities, and culture the organization has evolved to meet its goals. Change in core values may prompt changes within capacity domains. By the same token, change in a domain may be resisted if it goes against the core value framework.

Approaches to Change

In this section, we identify six approaches to organizational change that have been applied to CBOs, including those that represent youth. For each approach, we describe the action to induce change, propose why the strategy can be reasoned to influence organizational functioning, and discuss what kinds of organizational changes one might expect to occur as a result of engaging each strategy.

Education and Skills-Development Training and Technical Assistance

Education, training, and technical assistance approaches to organizational change are fairly common. The actions and activities that typify this approach to change may be especially common for CBOs because these approaches can be carried out in ways that are low cost, take little staff time relative to other alternatives, and can be offered in a variety of formats that minimally interfere with the day-to-day business of getting work done.

In this strategy, select members of an organization participate in time-limited instruction to enhance their individual knowledge of a well-defined

Table 10.1. Organizational Capacities of CBOs

Domain and Purpose	Capacity	Definition	Challenges for Small CBOs
Durability—Enables survival over time	Environmental scanning	Ability to scan the environment and stay abreast of new developments. Routine acquisition of information about how the field is changing and challenges and opportunities ahead (Correia & Wilson, 2001; Kearns, 2000; Miller, Bedney, & Guenther-Grey, 2003).	CBOs may lack the person power to routinely scan the environment and the burden of collecting information may be too great for an already busy CBO staff. CBOs may have limited contact with and access to influential information sources, such as people who are in the know or networking events.
	Innovation	Ability to adjust to changing times, experiment, and create. (Johnson, Carol, Center, & Daley, 2004; Zeldin, Camino, & Mook, 2005).	CBOs may lack the time and resources necessary to design and implement new innovations or face pressure to do things as other types of institutions do.
	Resources acquisition	Ability to acquire human and nonhuman resources efficiently and effectively (Miller et al., 2003).	CBOs may not have the kinds of resources needed to develop more resources, such as professional development staff.
	Leadership	Ability to attract and maintain qualified and competent board/executive leadership (Foster-Fishman, Berkowitz, Lounsbury, Jacobson, & Allen, 2001; Kearns, 2000; Miller et al., 2003).	CBOs are dependent upon the intrinsic rewards associated with working in the setting to attract and maintain dedicated and skilled leaders. Financial incentives and employee and Board perquisites may be very limited.
	Communication	Ability to communicate effectively to internal and external agents (Arsenault, 1998; Foster-Fishman et al., 2001; Harper, Bangi, et al., 2004).	Local competition for resources and mistrust may hinder a CBO's willingness and ability to communicate with others. Internal communication problems may arise from low use of technology and overburdening of staff.
	Cooperation	Ability to network and work cooperatively with others to avoid unnecessary duplication and maximize resources (Arsenault, 1998; Foster-Fishman et al., 2001; Harper & Caver, 1999; Harper, Lardon, et al., 2004; Kearns, 2000).	CBOs may not have the time, energy, history, or trust of other providers to engage in cooperative ventures. Value clashes and competition over resources among CBOs may also limit cooperation.

Category	Ability	Potential limitation
Vision	Ability to craft unique and compelling vision that mobilizes and bonds community to the agency and its mission (Kearns, 2000).	CBOs may not take the time to carefully craft a clear statement of vision. Over time, CBOs may allow their vision to drift in response to availability of new resources or turnover.
Reliability—Enables consistently high performance		
Program development	Ability to define problems, their causes, and turn prospective solutions into logical, feasible, and clear plans of action (Miller et al., 2003; Shediac-Rizkallah & Bone, 1998).	CBOs may lack the time and resources to study problems systematically and engage in planful action.
Program management	Ability to make sure that plans of action are carried out as intended, adjusted as required, and that problems are addressed in a timely and competent fashion (Miller et al., 2003).	CBOs may lack adequate personnel to carry out plans as intended and respond to implementation problems rapidly.
Resource management	Ability to manage and conserve resources over time and across the implementation of multiple activities (Foster-Fishman et al., 2001; Miller et al., 2003).	CBOs' modest and fluctuating resources may make managing and conserving resources difficult.
Human resource management	Ability to appropriately delegate tasks, supervise paid and nonpaid personnel, provide appropriate supports and feedback, and honor personnel contributions (Foster-Fishman et al., 2001; Miller et al., 2003).	CBOs may lack personnel dedicated to perform HR duties and to provide close supervision of frontline paid and unpaid workers.
Information systems management	Ability to properly collect and use client and service use data to inform program management (Carrilio, 2005; Mitchell, Florin, & Stevenson, 2002).	CBOs may lack computers and technologically advanced personnel to develop and maintain updated and running information systems.
Program evaluation	Ability to collect and use information to improve programs and evaluate program merits relative to agreed-upon goals (Foster-Fishman et al., 2001; Miller et al., 2003; Patton, 2004).	CBOs may lack the knowledge, ability, and resources to conduct evaluation.
Accountability—Enables demonstration that goals are met		
Executive management	Ability of the board and executive leadership to meet its obligations as stewards of the organization's programs (Miller et al., 2003; Saidel, 2002).	CBO leadership may not have adequate knowledge of financial, policy, and legal operational issues.

topic or engage in hands-on skill development training in an area. The flexibility of the approach is among its appeals. Training, technical assistance, and education may be provided in-house or at a location off site, to individuals or to groups, online or face-to-face, via a packaged program or a program developed specifically for or tailored to the specific needs and existing knowledge and skill levels of an organization, in single or multiple sessions, or as a one-shot or an ongoing effort. Typically, education, training, and technical assistance efforts are used to improve employees' knowledge and skill in well-defined topical areas, such as program development and evaluation, financial development and fundraising, and human resource management.

An exemplary training approach to organizational change may be found in Project REP (Youth-led Research, Evaluation, and Planning), an organizational change effort initiated by Youth in Focus, a California CBO devoted to youth empowerment (www.youthinfocus.net). Project REP trains youth served by the organization to design and conduct evaluations as a means to promote youth development and empowerment, while simultaneously encouraging its own organizational development and capacity (London, Zimmerman, & Erbstein, 2003). After training, youth conduct actual program evaluations within and outside the agency on their own or alongside adult teams. The youth evaluators have conducted multiple projects that have led to change in local policy, service configurations, and increased opportunities for youth to have a voice and become involved in local initiatives. The project has led to documented growth in organizational capacity in vital areas such as vision, internal and external collaboration, and networking. The project has also created what its creators call a "youth leadership ladder" by which youth are prepared to assume staff and leadership roles in CBOs.

Training, education, and technical assistance approaches to organizational change assume that when individual staff posses desired competencies, then each will perform his or her job capably. As a result of staff improving their abilities, organizations can function more efficiently and effectively. It is in this sense that education, technical assistance, and training are "trickle-up" strategies of organizational change. It is for the same reason that these strategies are believed to work that they are also limited as a way to change an organization. Education, technical assistance, and training, when these activities succeed, change individuals directly and may only indirectly change the organizations for which they work, if at all. More important, when a well-trained individual leaves an organization, that person will take the benefits of training with himself or herself and may leave little behind. In a very small CBO, the departure of a single well-trained staff person can noticeably depress an organization's short-term capacity. As a strategy for sustained change, training, education, and technical assistance may be severely limited unless continual training, technical assistance, and education opportunities are made available and used.

Participatory Team-Based Organizational and Program Improvement

A second approach to enhancing CBO capacity involves engaging groups of employees and other stakeholders, such as youth, in a collaborative organizational change and improvement initiative designed to develop a sustainable learning environment. The goal in these approaches is to maximize the use of everyone's capacities, perspectives, and insights to advance the organization's success. This approach draws on systems approaches to change (Ackoff, 1981; Checkland, 1981; Churchman, 1979; Flood, 1999; Kim, 2001; Midgley, 2000; Senge, 1990) and organizational action-research paradigms (Argyris & Schon, 1985, 1996). It has been applied frequently within the context of corporate environments and is rapidly gaining currency as a potent way to change CBOs.

Relative to education, technical assistance, and training, developing an organizational learning community as a vehicle for change is time consuming and demanding of staff and other participants. It requires high levels of commitment, engagement, and leadership to succeed. It also requires skilled facilitation, as the success of the approach hinges on the ability of the group to engage in a very particular and specialized form of collective problem solving and constructive dialogue.

Although there are many specific approaches to and ways in which to engage this strategy, the essence of the participatory team-based strategy requires that a collaborative team be formed to address a specific problem. The teams' mission is to study and reflect on the problem in pursuit of actionable strategies for change. The problem may be of any type from deciding how to respond to changing external conditions, such as an increasing number of gay and lesbian youth having poor experiences in the foster care system, to close examination of an internal problem, such as the need to rejuvenate aspects of programming that seem stale or to have lost their cutting edge. One hallmark of this approach to change is that as part of its deliberations, the group pushes itself to identify, examine, and challenge its guiding assumptions about the problem and the boundaries of these assumptions. The process works best when the team can begin to see many different views of the same thing and understand the implications of setting the boundaries around the problem in any one place or viewing it from any one position. A second hallmark of the approach is that the group ultimately develops its ability to function as a collective local learning community through the process and can apply these new learning skills to other collective problem-solving endeavors. Expert facilitators use a variety of techniques and exercises, such as scenario planning, to develop sustainable, well-functioning learning teams.

Midgley (2000, 2006) describes an example of this approach applied to a consortium of providers who believed that their local service response to youth who were on the streets was inadequate. The project used an action-research model as a vehicle for assisting the group to view the problem from many points of view and to develop a vision for change. The first phase of the effort involved developing a picture of how young people on the streets viewed the situation. In this phase, Midgely and colleagues developed a portrait of the reality of street youth's lives through a series of interviews. The focus on youth's view and values as a point of departure was purposefully selected to push the team to examine the phenomenon from a point of view that they did not ordinarily adopt. The second phase involved a series of workshops in which young people on the streets, former runaway and throwaway youth, and adults working in various roles with youth visioned what ought to be and explored the gaps between the real as youth experienced it and the ideal. In the third phase of the effort, the vision from the second phase was translated into an innovative action plan for the community. These first three phases of work occurred over 9 months, illustrating the time- and labor-intensive process of building a learning community. Midgely notes significant change resulting from the three-phase initial work including new patterns of communication and collaboration among key actors in street youth's daily lives (e.g., police, social services) and the development and implementation of new programming based on a refined value system in which mutual trust, respect, and valuing of youth are at the core.

The participatory team-based approach to change works by shifting the culture of local organizational units to a critically analytic, collaborative, and reflective approach to practice. If successful, local learning teams become able to identify and critically examine the range of choices available to them, see previously unseen organizational blind spots and traps, and attain insights on the gaps between reality and the ideal. Teams also come to place high value on collective opportunities to innovate, experiment, and change so as to bring the organization and its work closer to the collective ideal. Although the approach is in part centered on developing the group learning ability of individual employees and other stakeholders, because of its team-based and participatory nature, this approach to organizational change has greater capacity to trickle up and to sustain itself beyond the life of any one member of the initial team. The organizational learning approach is especially appropriate when change efforts focus on planning, innovation, communication, cooperation, and environmental scanning, as these are integral to the approach.

Coaching

Coaching is a third, trickle-up approach to organizational change. In this approach, a knowledgeable party works one-on-one with one or more members of an organization to guide them through a task, providing feedback and encouragement. The coaching approach improves organizational performance by giving individuals and teams information on performance and specific, immediate advice on how performance might be improved. By setting in motion a process by which individuals have ready access to feedback, mentorship, and praise, coaching helps individuals to adjust their behaviors rapidly.

The Socratic nature of some approaches to empowerment evaluation typifies a coaching approach (see Fetterman, 1994; Miller & Campbell, 2006). Miller describes an empowerment evaluation with a small CBO serving adult and youth nighttime street communities in Chicago, Illinois (Wandersman et al., 2003). Miller was invited to work with the group to help them develop their capacity to self-evaluate their nighttime street ministries, youth shelter, and youth shelter advocacy network. For the various street ministries, Miller acted as a coach, working alongside the staff 2 nights a week from 7 p.m. until 2 a.m. for 18 months. She observed and provided a sounding board to help the group reflect on their practice and its implications for organizational policy and evaluation. She offered feedback on the spot as well as in weekly staff meetings. These coaching interactions and the process of ongoing reflection and feedback resulted in multiple organizational changes, including new volunteer training requirements and training content, new volunteer management practices, an evaluation system, and a culture of evaluative thinking. (For other examples of coaching approaches with youth-serving CBOs, see Harper and colleagues' 2004 reports on work with Project VIDA, an HIV-focused, youth-serving CBO in Chicago.)

Like the other approaches previously described, coaching assumes that when an individual receives targeted mentoring and feedback on the performance of a specific task coupled with encouragement, deserved praise, and advice on how to improve, the individual's performance will increase measurably. By improving individual or group performance, the organization's performance will improve in turn. Coaching has the advantage of being suitable to many targets of change, including leadership, program and organizational management, and policy and program implementation. Coaching clearly requires the long-term presence of a coach to work. It may also result principally in changes to an individual's ways of working, rather than impact the organization at large.

Strategic Planning

A strategic plan documents what an organization intends to accomplish and how it intends to do so over a clearly defined period of time. The primary benefit of a strategic plan is that it allows an organization to identify clear links between its stated mission and its programmatic goals and objectives. Strategic plans also help organizations to develop short- and mid-term action plans that take into account what is realistic to accomplish, given the resources and capacity available.

Strategic plans can be useful focusing devices because they offer a tool to prioritize and establish for what and to whom an organization is willing to be held to account. By providing a focus for prioritizing how effort and resources will be directed, strategic plans can become a means to organizational change and a way to prevent mission drift. The process of planning can also be beneficial to organizational actors by creating an opportunity to participate in crafting the short-term vision of the organization and the opportunity to recommit to the larger mission.

Strategic plans are suited to the tasks of shoring up the vision and managing resources well. One example of a template for creating a visioning process and document may be found in the Community Toolbox at http://ctb.ku.edu/. Cooperrider's and colleagues' appreciative inquiry approach provides another example of a popular approach to strategic planning (see http://appreciativeinquiry.case.edu/). The Center for Teen Empowerment, described earlier, has evolved an effective model for including youth in strategic planning efforts (see http://www.teenempowerment/com).

Organizational Restructuring and Resource Reallocation

In organizational restructuring and resource reallocation, an organization reconstitutes the structural arrangement of and resources available to some portion of the organization with an eye toward improving communication and cooperation, responding more effectively to critical service needs, or creating a more efficient organization. For instance, two or more units may be combined into one because they overlap in function or are consistently dependent upon one another to conduct their work, so would be better off being singly administered and in close communication. Alternatively, functions may be divided out to reflect their growth or emerging importance. Rather than combine units or create new units, a restructuring change could involve altering reporting relationships among units to improve coordination or oversight or to decrease or increase a unit's independence, responsibility, and authority. Finally, change could involve providing a particular unit with increased resources to reflect its importance or develop its capacity or decreasing its resources to reflect that it is no longer a priority.

This approach is most applicable with organizations that are large enough to have distinct functional units and to those that are facing growth or shrinkage. Unfortunately, for many CBOs restructuring and resource reallocation occurs as a reactive strategy to manage loss of funds and shifts in funding priorities rather than as a proactive strategy of organizational development. In whatever form it takes, restructuring and resource reallocation are typically targeted toward capacities such as cooperation, communication, resource management, and executive management.

One example of a restructuring effort is the Gay Men's Health Crisis's creation of an agency-wide Department of Evaluation. Gay Men's Health Crisis (GMHC) is a very large CBO serving New York City's HIV-affected communities including children, youth, young adult, and adult populations. From very early after its foundation, GMHC supported ad hoc research and evaluation activity performed by consultants. By the mid-1980s, several departments had one or more part- or full-time evaluators on staff. By the early 1990s, internal demand for evaluation services grew sharply, as did evaluation requirements in grants. In response to new demand and in recognition of the value of evaluation to inform agency decision making, GMHC created a single Department of Evaluation to provide services to every department. As part of this restructuring, all evaluators were housed in a single unit headed by an evaluator. The new department reported to the executive director to preserve its independence and increase its authority. Its director was added to the agency's management team so that evaluation was salient during their deliberations on agency policy and direction. The department also received a substantial investment from the Board to support its services.

Policy Development and Implementation

The final strategy to promote change in an organization is policy development and implementation. Policies tell employees, volunteers, and youth what behaviors are and are not acceptable within the setting and can set the tone for an organization's climate. Polices provide guidance on what kind of place the organization desires to be for its members by specifying rules of conduct, member rights, and the basis for rewards and sanctions. Policies are also essential to protect the organization and its staff and youth's safety and confidentiality. Policies may address any area of organizational life from volunteer appreciation to computer use to work-family leave practices to Board functioning to program procedures to client records.

We work with a small youth drop-in center that has recently set new policies to promote physical safety in its facility. The center has traditionally had and enforced policies to create a desirable positive climate, such as forbidding the use of foul language and being drunk or high while using center space. The center has not had explicit and evenly enforced policies around things such as carrying weapons while in the center or requiring youth to register to use the center, operating on an honor system. So, until recently, it was possible for a youth to use the center without anyone establishing that he or she was weapon-free and for youth to be in the center without anyone knowing who he or she is. Two violent incidents prompted the center to create and enforce new policies, including that all youth must register by providing the center with a minimum of information and legal identification prior to being allowed in center space. In addition to improving actual and perceived safety, the new registration policy has had unplanned beneficial consequences for the organization, including accurate documentation of unduplicated service use and basic characteristics of youth who come to the center.

Approaches to Measurement

Measuring the impact of capacity-building efforts in the context of a CBO is challenging, given the very small number of staff and work units that are typical of CBO settings. Perhaps the most common method of assessing change in organizational capacity is the use of survey methods to track changes in staff skills, knowledge, and perceptions. However, given the small size of a CBO, this approach may be of limited use. CBOs may have too few staff to aggregate individual-level questionnaire data. At best, questionnaires may be used as self-assessment devices on which staff may monitor their own progress. For most small CBOs, qualitative methods that draw on interviews, observations, and document analysis are most suitable to capture organizational change. We identify several common ways in which these methods may be used to document change in CBOs.

Town Hall Meetings and Retreats

Town hall meetings and retreats can be used to gauge change in how an organization is performing. Town hall meetings and retreats provide an opportunity for parents, youth, community members, staff, and management to reflect together on how well the organization is doing in improving its capacity. Often, staff and management at CBOs are too busy to engage in meaningful discussions about these topics among themselves or with key stakeholders. Fetterman's taking-stock approach (Fetterman & Wandersman, 2005) provides one useful structure for having a diverse group of adult and youth organizational stakeholders assess how the organization is doing relative to a set of goals for change. Fetterman, for example, has regularly involved youth participants in applying the approach in school settings (see Fetterman, 2005, for an example. Also, see the Community Tool Box for more information on self-evaluation procedures http://ctb.ku.edu/tools/en/part_j.htm).

Ethnographic Audits

Ethnographic audits are focused investigations of a particular area of organizational functioning. Audits may be conducted by staff or by outside researchers. For the CBO, conducting a self-audit may be a cost-effective means of measuring their current capacity as well as assessing organization change over time. Audits may include both qualitative and quantitative methodology. For example, an organization may conduct quantitative fiscal audits to evaluate the management and allocation of resources. Ethnographic audits may include participant observation, key-informant interviews, focus groups, and unstructured interviews with staff, youth, and other stakeholders, such as parents (Fetterman, 1991). Youth can be trained to carry out many of these data collection, analysis, interpretation, and reporting activities, as the success of Project REP exemplifies.

Case Studies

The use of case studies to evaluate organizational change can be especially useful to obtain a holistic picture of the change process and its results. Case studies are a method for studying a single case (e.g., an organization) or a small set of multiple cases (e.g., four departments in an organization) using multiple methods of data collection (Stake, 1995, 2005; Yin, 1989). Case studies may include participant observation, interviews, and review of archival documents. Case studies take into account the context surrounding the case of interest and facilitate close examination of the particular history and events in the case at hand. A case study approach is best done by a researcher who is trained in case study and mixed-methods research, though youth may be able to participate in defining questions, collecting data, data analysis, and data interpretation and reporting.

Conclusion

The state of scholarship on CBO capacity development is in its infancy, particularly among youth-focused CBOs. Challenges to measurement provide one reason why so little is known about CBO capacity and how it can be changed. For this reason, we see advances in measurement among the most important areas for future work in this field. One area of promise applies cluster evaluation (Barley & Jenness, 1993) and meta-evaluation techniques (Stufflebeam, 2001) to CBO case studies, both of which allow for building a knowledge base across cases of capacity building practice. For instance, Miller and Campell (2006) used meta-evaluation to describe various approaches to empowerment evaluation practice and the organizational outcomes associated with each form of practice. The data for this meta-evaluation comprised 47 case studies.

A second promising approach draws on systems methodologies, such as critical systems heuristics, systems dynamics, agent-based modeling, and soft systems methodology (see Williams & Imam, 2007, for an anthology on systems approaches to intervention and evaluation). These methods typically combine the intervention and assessment process, though can be used to represent how a system behaves in the absence of an intervention effort. For example, system dynamics is often used to develop a solution to an identified problem facing an organization by developing a model of the problem and testing out dynamic hypotheses virtually (Sterman, 2000). Systems dynamics can use any kind of data, including anecdotal data, to develop a testable computer model of the underlying processes that give rise to the organizational behavior of interest (see, e.g., Hirsch, Levine, & Miller, 2007; Miller, Levine, Khamarko, Valenti, & McNall, 2006).

Future work must concern itself with the role of youth in the process of developing and assessing capacity in youth-oriented CBOs. Given the centrality of youth empowerment to many youth-focused CBOs, developing youth-engaged capacity interventions and assessing whether and how these build youth and organizational capacity would be especially beneficial.

Finally, better knowledge of how to intervene in the CBO context hinges on documenting internal efforts at capacity development. Internally directed efforts at CBO capacity building are believed to be more common than expert-directed interventions (Light, 2004). Researchers could learn from communities what capacity building might entail, how it can be conducted, and what works in the CBO context by focused study of indigenous capacity-building efforts.

References

Ackoff, R. L. (1981). *Creating the corporate future.* New York: Wiley.

Altman, D. (1994). *Power and community: Organizational and cultural responses to AIDS.* London: Taylor & Francis.

Argyris, C. & Schon, D. (1985). *Strategy, change, and defensive routines.* Cambridge, MA: Ballinger.

Argyris, C., & Schon, D. (1996). *Organizational learning II.* New York: Addison-Wesley.

Arsenault, J. (1998). *Forging nonprofit alliances.* San Francisco: Jossey-Bass.

Barley, Z. A. & Jenness, M. (1993). Cluster evaluation: A method to strengthen evaluation in smaller programs with similar purposes. *Evaluation Practice, 14,* 141-147.

Carrilio, T. (2005). Management information systems: Why are they underutilized in the social services? *Administration in Social Work, 29,* 43-61.

Checkland, P. B. (1981). *Systems thinking, systems practice.* Chicester: John Wiley & Sons.

Churchman, C. W. (1979). *The systems approach and its enemies.* New York: Basic Books.

Correia, Z., & Wilson, T. D. (2001). Factors influencing environmental scanning in the organizational context. *Information Research, 7.* Retrieved May 2006, from http//InformationR.net/ir/7-1/paper121.html

Fetterman, D. (1994). Empowerment evaluation. *Evaluation Practice, 15*(1), 1-15.

Fetterman, D. M. (Ed.). (1991). *Auditing as institutional research: A qualitative focus.* San Francisco: Jossey-Bass.

Fetterman, D. M. (2005). Empowerment evaluation: From the digital divide to academic distress. In D. Fetterman & A. Wandersman (Eds.), *Empowerment evaluation principles in practice* (pp. 92-122). New York: Guilford Press.

Fetterman, D. M., & Wandersman, A. (Eds.). (2005). *Empowerment evaluation principles in practice.* New York: Guilford Press.

Flood, R. L. (1999). *Rethinking the fifth discipline: Learning within the unknowable.* New York, NY: Routledge.

Foster-Fishman, P., Berkowitz, S., Lounsbury, D., Jacobson, S., & Allen, N. (2001). Building collaborative capacity in community coalitions: A review and integrative framework. *American Journal of Community Psychology, 29,* 241-261.

Frederickson, P., & London, R. (2000). Disconnect in the hollow state: The pivotal role of organizational capacity in community-based development organizations. *Public Administration Review, 60,* 230-239.

Greiner, L. E. (1972). Evolution and revolution as organizations grow. *Harvard Business Review, 50,* 37-46.

Hannan, M. T., & Carroll, R. G. R. (1995). An introduction to organizational ecology. In F. R. Carroll & M. T. Hannan (eds.), *Organizations in industry: Strategy, structure, and selection* (pp. 17-31). New York: Oxford University Press.

Harper, G. W., Bangi, A. K., Contreras, R., Pedraza, A., Tolliver, M., & Vess, L. (2004). Diverse phases of collaboration: Working together to improve community-based HIV interventions for adolescents. *American Journal of Community Psychology, 33,* 193-204.

Harper, G. W., & Carver, L. J. (1999). "Out-of-the-mainstream" youth as partners in collaboration research: Exploring the benefits and challenges. *Health Education & Behavior, 26,* 250-265.

Harper, G. W., Lardon, C., Rappaport, J., Bangi, A. K., Contreras, R., & Pedraza, A. (2004). Community narratives: The use of narrative ethnography in participatory community research. In L. A. Jason, C. B. Keys, Y. Suarez-Balcazar, R. R. Taylor, & M. I. Davis (Eds.), *Participatory community research: Theories and methods in action* (pp. 199-218). Washington, DC: American Psychological Association.

Hirsch, G. B., Levine, R. L., & Miller, R. L. (2007). Using system dynamics modeling to understand the impact of social change initiatives. *American Journal of Community Psychology, 39,* 239-353.

Johnson, K., Carol, H., Center, H., & Daley, C. (2004). Building capacity and sustainable prevention innovations: A sustainability planning model. *Evaluation and Program Planning, 27,* 135-149.

Kearns, K. (2000). *Private sector strategies for social sector success.* San Francisco: Jossey-Bass.

Kim, D. H. (2001). *Organization for learning: Strategies for knowledge creation and enduring change.* Waltham, MA: Pegasus Communications.

Light, P. C. (2004). *Sustaining nonprofit performance: The case for capacity building and the evidence to support it.* Washington, DC: Bookings Institution Press.

Lipsky, M., & Smith, S. R. (1989-1990). Nonprofit organizations, government, and the welfare state. *Political Science Quarterly, 104*, 625-648.

London, J. K., Zimmerman, K., & Erbstein, N. (2003). Youth-led research and evaluation: Tools for youth, organizational, and community development. *New Directions for Evaluation, 98*, 33-46.

Marwell, N. P. (2004). Privatizing the welfare state: Nonprofit CBOs as political actors. *American Sociological Review, 69*, 265-291.

Midgley, G. (2000). *Systemic intervention: Philosophy, methodology, and practice.* New York: Kluwer Academic/Plenum Publishers.

Midgley, G. (2006). Systemic intervention for public health. *American Journal of Public Health, 96*, 466-472.

Miller, R., Bedney, B., & Guenther-Grey, C. (2003). Assessing organizational capacity to deliver HIV prevention services collaboratively: Tales from the field. *Health Education & Behavior, 30*, 582-600.

Miller, R. L., & Campbell, R. (2006). Taking stock of empowerment evaluation: An empirical review. *American Journal of Evaluation, 27*, 296-319.

Miller, R. L., Levine, R., Khamarko, K., Valenti, M. T., & McNall, M. A. (2006, July). Recruiting clients to a community-based HIV-prevention program: A dynamic model. *Proceedings of the International Conference of the System Dynamics Society*, Nijmegen, The Netherlands.

Mitchell, R., Florin, P., & Stevenson, J. (2002). Supporting community-based prevention and health promotion initiatives: Developing effective technical assistance systems. *Health Education & Behavior, 29*, 620-639.

Oliver, C. (1991). Strategic responses to institutional processes. *Academy of Management Review, 16*, 145-179.

Patton, M. Q. (1994). Developmental evaluation. *Evaluation Practice, 15*(3), 311-319.

Riger, S. (1984). Vehicles for empowerment: The case of feminist movement organizations. *Prevention in Human Services, 3*, 99-117.

Saidel, J. (2002). *Guide to the literature on Governance: An annotated bibliography.* Washington, DC: BoardSource.

Senge, P. (1990). *The fifth discipline: The art and practice of the learning organization.* New York, NY: Doubleday.

Shediac-Rizkallah, M., & Bone, L. (1998). Planning for the sustainability of community-based health programs: Conceptual frameworks and future directions for research, practice, and policy. *Heath Education Research, 13*, 87-108.

Stake, R. E. (1995). *The art of case study research.* Newbury Park, CA: Sage Publications.

Stake, R. E. (2005). Qualitative case studies. In N. K. Denzin & Y. S. Lincoln (Eds.), *The Sage handbook of qualitative research* (3rd ed., pp. 443-466). Newbury Park, CA: Sage Publications.

Sterman, J. D. (2000). *Business dynamics: Systems thinking and modeling for a complex world.* Boston, MA: Irwin-McGraw-Hill.

Stufflebeam, D. L. (2001). The meta-evaluation imperative. *American Journal of Evaluation, 22*, 183-209.

Wandersman, A., Keener, D, Snell-Johns, J., Miller, R. L., Flaspohler, P., Dye, M. L., et al. (2003). Empowerment evaluation: Principles and action. In L.A. Jason,

C. B. Keys, Y. Suarez-Balcazar, R. R. Taylor, & M. I. Davis (Eds.), *Participatory community research: Theories and methods in action* (pp. 139-156). Washington, DC: American Psychological Association.

Williams, B., & Imam, I. (Eds) (2007). *Systems concepts in evaluation: An expert anthology*. Inverness, CA: EdgePress.

Yin, R. K. (1994). *Case study research: Design and methods* (2nd ed.). Newbury Park, CA: Sage Publications.

Zeldin, S., Camino, L., & Mook, C. (2005). The adoption of innovation in youth organizations: Creating the conditions for youth-adult partnerships. *Journal of Community Psychology, 33*, 121-135.

Chapter 11

Quality Accountability: Improving Fidelity of Broad Developmentally Focused Interventions

CHARLES SMITH AND TOM AKIVA

Over the last decade the High/Scope Educational Research Foundation has developed and validated the Youth Program Quality Assessment for out-of-school time (OST) programs and several methodologies for its use (High/Scope Educational Research Foundation, 2005; Smith, 2005a; Smith & Hohmann, 2005).[1] This experience has shaped our ideas about what program quality is, how it works, and how OST organizations can consistently produce core developmental experiences for youth (Akiva, 2005, 2007; Smith et al., 2006). As a result of our experience collecting structured observations in a wide variety of youth work and education settings, we frame the quality issue in this way: a high-quality program provides youth with access to key experiences (see Figure 11.1) that advance developmental and learning outcomes. However, many out-of-school-time settings miss opportunities to provide these key experiences for the youth who attend. The cause of this underperformance is frequently systemic, due to existing structures, practices, and policies across the after-school sector. In this chapter, we present the Youth Program Quality Intervention (YPQI), an assessment-driven, multilevel intervention model designed to raise quality in OST programs and thereby raise the level of access to key developmental and learning experiences for the youth who attend.

The current emphasis on evidence-based programs and practices has supported the development and validation of narrowly focused intervention models that address specific issues for specific groups (e.g., print decoding skills for early elementary students or smoking prevention for adolescents).

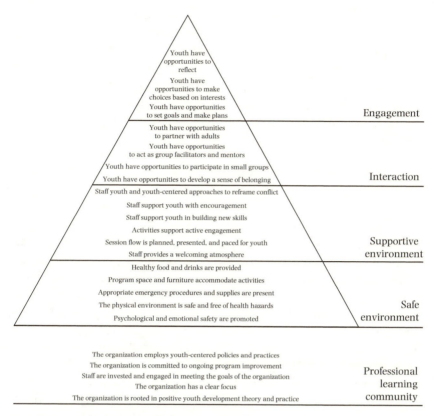

Figure 11.1. Pyramid of Youth Program Quality.

The pyramid, from top to bottom, contains the following levels and items:

Engagement
- Youth have opportunities to reflect
- Youth have opportunities to make choices based on interests
- Youth have opportunities to set goals and make plans

Interaction
- Youth have opportunities to partner with adults
- Youth have opportunities to act as group facilitators and mentors
- Youth have opportunities to participate in small groups
- Youth have opportunities to develop a sense of belonging

Supportive environment
- Staff youth and youth-centered approaches to reframe conflict
- Staff support youth with encouragement
- Staff support youth in building new skills
- Activities support active engagement
- Session flow is planned, presented, and paced for youth
- Staff provides a welcoming atmosphere

Safe environment
- Healthy food and drinks are provided
- Program space and furniture accommodate activities
- Appropriate emergency procedures and supplies are present
- The physical environment is safe and free of health hazards
- Psychological and emotional safety are promoted

Professional learning community
- The organization employs youth-centered policies and practices
- The organization is committed to ongoing program improvement
- Staff are invested and engaged in meeting the goals of the organization
- The organization has a clear focus
- The organization is rooted in positive youth development theory and practice

Unlike narrow intervention models designed to produce effects at the level of individual children, the YPQI is a setting-level intervention that makes ecological groupings of staff and youth its focal concern. The program brings networks of OST programs through a process of identifying and addressing strengths and areas for improvement based on use of the Youth Program Quality Assessment—a diagnostic assessment of program quality (High/Scope Educational Research Foundation, 2005). In the language of education policy, the YPQI represents a *quality accountability system* focused on continuous quality improvement. In the prevention and youth development fields, however, the Youth Program Quality Assessment might be described as a fidelity measure for *broad developmentally focused interventions*[2] like after-school, service learning, or community-based youth programs based loosely on the philosophy of positive youth development.

Whether framed as a quality accountability system or as a fidelity tool for broad developmentally focused interventions, the Youth Program Quality Assessment and the wider YPQI model meet a need for vehicles to help move good program intentions to a reality of high quality and developmental value-addedness in the fields of youth development, prevention, and education. Recent reviews of research suggest that lack of attention to implementation and fidelity present a substantial threat to successful dissemination of evidence-based practices and programs (Fixsen, Naoom, Blasé, Friedman, & Wallace, 2005; National Research Council and Institutes of Medicine, 2000; U.S. Department of Health and Human Services, 2002).

Characteristics of Effective Accountability Systems

Several characteristics of accountability systems support the difficult translation of accountability policies into on-the-ground performance change. The first key characteristic is that programs must count the things that matter and give weight to what matters most. A dilemma in the field of public administration is that it is much easier to hold civil servants accountable for rules of operation than for performance, and indeed, holding staff accountable for operational rules may actually hinder their pursuit of higher performance (as one example see discussion in Behn, 2001). In the OST field, the focus on operation over performance is evident in licensing requirements, accreditation guidelines, quality standards, and monitoring procedures by funding agencies. Each of these is typically weighted toward structural characteristics (staff-student ratios, emergency exit plans, parent outreach, business procedures, budget justifications) with little attention given to the quality of staff and youth performances that more directly shape the crucible of development where youth and adults come together (National Institute of Child Health and Human Development; Early Child Care Research Network [NICHD ECCRN] 2002; La Paro, Pianta, & Stuhlman, 2004). Accountability data often lack validity in the sense of meaningfulness because they do not emphasize the things that have the most impact on the quality of youth experiences— especially staff performance.

The second key characteristic is to focus on assessing/measuring/counting things in a manner that fits an applied organizational context. In the education field, performance accountability based on student achievement data has become ubiquitous. However, the lack of alignment between aggregate achievement indicators and the holistic enterprise of schooling— because teaching is not limited to simple knowledge transmission, school experiences provide more than academic learning, and schools produce learning outside of classrooms too—creates a disconnect between achievement indicators and staff ability to respond to the data (Bryk & Hermanson, 1993; Halverson, Grigg, Prichett, & Thomas, 2005). Student performance data lack validity in the sense of usefulness because it is difficult to apply aggregate achievement data to individual persons and discrete processes in a school. In the OST sector, programs are frequently held accountable for child and community-level outcomes that are nearly impossible to link to specific staff roles and organizational decisions.

When program staff are held accountable for issues that they do not control or do not understand how to change, the likelihood of counterproductive accountability behaviors—resistance, avoidance, and minimum compliance—is increased. The goal of effective accountability policy is staff engagement with data that leads to positive change in staff performance. This points to a third key characteristic: staff incentives to engage in the process are critical to successful transition from data to performances change. Although financial incentives are an obvious first choice, these are frequently not available. Rather, we focus on cooperative incentives that come from the experience of having useful feedback, encouragement to improve your craft, and a sense of shared effort on the part of a team working toward a shared purpose.[3]

In the next three sections, we address each of these issues. First, we examine evidence that the Youth Program Quality Assessment actually measures key performances of staff and youth. Second, we sketch out a simple theory of organizational structure that supports application of quality accountability data in ways that make sense to setting participants. Finally, we describe systems applications of the YPQI elements with a focus on incentives built into each that support staff engagement and intentionality.

An Empirical Definition of Quality

The quality pyramid presented in Figure 11.1 is the product of an extensive instrument development and validation project, the Youth Program Quality Assessment Validation Study. The original validation sample consisted of 1,635 youth nested within 164 program offerings, which were in turn nested within 51 organizations of diverse auspice, purpose, and location.[4] The Youth Program Quality Assessment contains two assessment booklets; one involves observation and the other is interview based. The observational domains and scales are described in the top four levels of Figure 11.1. The interview items of interest are described in the bottom level of Figure 11.1.

Since each level of the pyramid represents a validated multi-item measurement construct, it is possible to provide an empirical definition of quality in the OST sector by drawing upon findings from our prior and current work using the Youth Program Quality Assessment. Findings for diverse samples of programs in the OST sector include the following:

- *Quality scores are low at the top of the pyramid.* Programs are not providing all children who attend with access to key developmental experiences related to peer interaction and task engagement. For example, in the original validation study sample, 53% of settings did not provide youth opportunities to lead groups, and in 47% of settings, youth were not given opportunities to work in small groups (Smith, 2005b; Smith & Hohmann, 2005).

- *Quality scores have a hierarchical structure.* Scores are highest in safety and then become progressively lower going up the pyramid. This hierarchical pattern is consistent across several quality samples from different sectors of the OST field (Smith, 2005b; Smith & Hohmann, 2005).
- *Quality is rooted in the performances of individual staff.* Quality ratings collected on different days for the same staff member's program offering (a group with the same staff, kids, and purpose) were consistent over time (Smith, 2004).
- *Lower quality performances exist in most organizations.* Variance in quality scores was often of equal or greater magnitude between staff *within* the same organization and *across* all organizations in our samples (Smith, 2005b; Smith & Hohmann, 2005).
- *Program content is not related to quality.* No relationships or only weak relationships were found between the type of content offered (art, academic, sports, etc.) and quality scores (Smith, 2005b).
- *Items at the top of the pyramid are related to self-reported youth outcomes.* In multivariate and multilevel models, the items at the top of the pyramid are positively related to youth survey reports for safety, interest, sense of growth, and skill building (Smith & Hohmann, 2005).

These findings begin to provide an empirical definition of quality in the OST field. First, programs appear to be underperforming in the delivery of key developmental experiences to youth who attend and this is true across setting types and content areas. Second, quality in OST programs depends upon the quality of individual staff performances, regardless of the level of aggregation at which data is reported. Finally, the fact that only items at the top of the pyramid are related to youth-reported outcomes suggests that positive setting change entails building a foundation of safety and positive relationships *and* moving on to higher order items related to group interaction and task engagement.[5]

Theory of Setting Structure and Dynamics

With an emerging empirical definition for quality in the OST field, we also needed an applied theory of organizational structure and dynamics that maps quality scores onto the real organizations where data is collected. Both psychometric and consequential validity concerns lead to our recognition of the multilevel, nested structure of OST settings, as single global quality ratings were neither psychometrically ideal nor highly meaningful to individual staff.

Behavior settings theory (Barker, 1968; Schoggen, 1989) provided a setting-level framework that fit the multilevel organizational contexts where we were collecting data. A behavior setting is a small-scale social system that includes people, patterns, and resources. The structural and material characteristics of settings—*setting features*—have a profound impact on the human roles that develop, and consequently, the actions that are taken by the people who inhabit the setting. By thinking of OST programs as behaviors settings, we could break these organizations into experiential units—ongoing groupings of staff and youth—that better fit our quality data. We were also able to root program change in the data by thinking about setting features that would produce individual staff and youth behaviors (roles) that yielded higher levels of point-of-service quality. Finally, behavior settings theory helped us to sort out participant roles that correspond to different setting levels so that quality accountability could be seen as a multilevel application with distinct decision and communication roles at each level.

In OST networks, there are typically three levels of behavior settings represented by the three ovals in Figure 11.2. The point of service (POS) is where staff and youth come together and, in our work, is defined by the contents of the pyramid (Figure 11.1). The POS as a behavior setting happens in a program offering; sometimes that grouping is every youth and adult present at the site, and sometimes it is a subgrouping. In most OST organizations, there are multiple offerings (e.g., photography club at 3:30 on Tuesdays led by staff X) so a typical model of quality is structured by several staff-dependent quality performances nested within an organizational site. The POS is the location of key staff and youth performances that produce developmental gains for youth and *POS quality should be a primary locus of concern for setting-change interventions and accountability policies.*

The professional learning community (PLC)—which should exist for the primary purpose of creating high POS quality—is where managers and frontline staff come together to make decisions about program delivery. The

Figure 11.2. Levels of Quality.

PLC occurs not only in formal staff meetings but also during the range of moments when staff meet to talk about how they will design and deliver a program. Substantial evidence exists in both the school day and social work administration literatures that effective PLCs improve organizational learning (Bryk et al., 1999; InPraxis Group, 2006), professional practice (Desimone, Porter, Garet, Yoon, & Birman, 2002; Halverson et al., 2005; Mason, 2003), job satisfaction (Jaskyte, 2003; Kayser, Walker, & Demaio, 2000), and staff retention (Smith & Ingersoll, 2004). In these studies, PLC-level setting features included teacher training, quality improvement circles, clear values leadership by managers, and orientation and induction procedures.

In the three quality accountability systems that we discuss below, use of the Youth Program Quality Assessment was one of the key PLC-level setting features introduced to support setting change. Evidence from school day research suggests that observational assessment can be a powerful PLC-level setting feature that drives behavior related to instructional process (Pianta, 2003; see review in Hilberg, Waxman, & Tharp, 2003) and quality assessment is often described as a missing link between program implementation and reliable effects in early intervention and youth development programs (National Research Council and Institute of Medicine, 2000, pp. 359-362; National Research Council and Institute of Medicine, 2002, p. 254).

Indeed, a key issue that setting-change interventions in the OST field must address is that many PLCs do not currently focus on their primary purpose— raising quality at the POS—and do not employ setting features, such as quality assessment, to drive the behavior of frontline staff and youth. From both our field experience and recent survey data from several hundred after-school staff we conclude that OST managers do not feel primary responsibility for the development of staff skills related to items at the top of the pyramid, do not share quality data that is available with staff, and do not use existing quality standards to communicate POS-related values to frontline staff (Smith et al., 2006).

The outermost oval in Figure 11.2 depicts the system accountability environment (SAE). Evidence from education research suggests that SAE is a level of setting that can impact the PLC and POS if an accountability and improvement system actually exists beyond paper (Carnoy & Loeb, 2002) and if the participants in these settings are open to accountability pressure (Talbert & McGlaughlin, 1999). Each of the setting-change interventions described in the next section entails creation of an SAE to direct the priorities of program mangers toward POS values and behaviors described in the Youth Program Quality Assessment.

Systems for Setting Change

In this section, we provide three case summaries of setting-change interventions in OST systems. Each of the projects rests upon shared beliefs among network decision makers that decided to adopt the Youth Program Quality Assessment as a core PLC-level setting feature.[6] First, network decision makers usually decide to adopt the Youth Program Quality Assessment (or other instruments like it) because they believe that the *Youth Program Quality Assessment assesses the right things* and is well aligned with a generic positive youth development philosophy that the adopters share. Second, network decision makers believe that uniformity of assessment across programs *supports shared expectations and communities of practice* that clarify program values and staff practices for all stakeholders. Third, most network decision makers also believe that the use of an observational assessment *creates accountability and improvement incentives*. It empowers staff because collecting and interpreting data promotes learning about the professional craft of youth work.

Despite these shared beliefs, the three case summaries describe systems that differ substantially in terms of the stakes and purposes that are attached to the data. Higher stakes systems are characterized by the use of trained reliable assessors, shared findings with program regulators (and sometimes the public), and consequences that are outside the control of program staff. Each of the three cases adopts a different level of stakes, although each is explicitly thought of as accountability *and improvement* system, meaning that the emphasis is upon retaining and improving low quality sites rather than eliminating them.

Case 1: Low Stakes Accountability in a Large, Statewide 21st Century After-School System

In Case 1, the Youth Program Quality Assessment is the cornerstone of a "low stakes accountability" system wherein programs are held accountable for a documented improvement process, rather than an individual program's quality scores. Each fall, staff teams at all 21st century Community Learning Center sites in the state are required to complete a Youth Program Quality Assessment self-assessment, generate an automated report, and develop a program improvement plan based on the data. Assessments and improvement plans from all these sites are compiled for year-end reports to the state to document trends, program improvement areas, and steps taken to address low scores. The primary purpose of the system is staff learning and continuous improvement. The strengths of Case 1 are

- The system provides incentives to engage the quality assessment process: only internal program staff see the results for individual programs and the process yields a single site-team report so that no individual staff performances are singled out.
- The system is relatively inexpensive to administer on a large scale since it entails only 1 day of training and all data collection is conducted using

current staff. Further, each site receives a user manual if training is not possible.

The primary weaknesses of Case 1 are

- Self-assessment teams tend to produce imprecise data with a predictable positive bias.
- Since self-assessment is a good faith effort, it is possible for programs simply to complete the report without ever conducting the observation or, as is more likely, managers complete the assessment without involving line staff in the process.
- Because the quality data is generated through self-assessment it does not serve as an accurate baseline against which to measure system progress into the future.

Case 1 is entering its second year. We have received feedback from a pilot group of program leaders that the self-assessment process is valuable and that they are successfully improvising with the self-assessment methodology as their circumstances require. Over half of the programs that were required to bring the assessment online in year 1 (81 sites) returned completed self-assessments to the statewide program evaluator. The state department of education has begun to provide some aligned in-service training workshops to address items with low-scoring statewide trends. Our evidence suggests that many program directors and their staff have high engagement with this system and many others are enacting minimum compliance or avoidance.[7]

Case 2: Medium Stakes Accountability in Two Statewide After-School Networks

The Case 2 intervention is designed to generate an annual quality baseline against which to measure progress, to provide support to programs, to use data for improvement, and to use baseline data for advocacy and policy work. In Case 2, 21st century program directors and VISTA (Volunteers In Service To America) workers (federally funded community development organizers) complete a 2-day external assessment training and conduct external assessment at every 21st century site (no data collector will observe their own site; so they are not self-assessments) each year until a more formal assessment infrastructure is built. Each program director is responsible for completing one rating at one site, producing the automated quality report (using free software), and sending it via e-mail to both the site and the state Department of Education. The strengths of Case 2 are

- Trained external assessors produce data with high enough precision to support use as a baseline and for planning targeted investments in quality improvement.

- The cost of training and data collection was covered within existing funding.
- Department of Education is offering statewide training in response to the quality findings.

The primary weaknesses of Case 2 are

- Frontline staff in the participating programs have not been trained to conduct the self-assessment process simultaneously with the external assessment. Simultaneous self-assessment and outside assessment reduces fears on the part of frontline staff about the assessment process, and disparities between self and externally produced quality ratings are powerful learning opportunities.

In Case 2, after data were collected, several youth work focus areas were identified—areas in which several programs scored lower than desired. A 2-day training summit was then held in which 21st century directors and staff could select various workshops to attend—each of which was aligned with scales from the Youth Program Quality Assessment (see Figure 11.1). These workshops were highly attended and well received and buy-in appears to be very high across this system. These workshops were primarily geared toward the POS (with the exception of a short "planning with data" segment geared toward PLCs); however, the event itself was a PLC event, allowing administrators and staff to interact with each other and with others from across the state.

Case 3: Higher Stakes Accountability in a County-Based Network of School-Age and School-Based After-School Programs

The Case 3 intervention is designed to provide maximum support and accountability for program quality by combining the relative strengths of the Case 1 and Case 2 approaches with additional training days for program directors on how to use quality data to drive program change and reliability checks to ensure the highest quality of external data. Each year, programs conduct their own self-assessment and develop an improvement plan that is guided and followed-up by quality coaches from a local intermediary. Each year, all programs are also visited by external assessors who report to both the sites and the program improvement intermediary in the county. Ultimately, external assessment scores may be publicly available through a five-star rating system; however, the system will be low stakes for several years as programs become more comfortable with the external assessment process. The primary strengths of Case 3 are as follows:

- Annual combined self-assessment and external assessment produce both a precise quality baseline for future comparison and strong learning opportunities. Discrepancies between self-assessment and external assessment are very strong indicators of training needs and great opportunities for professional reflection on purposes and practices.

- Annual follow-up and coaching for each program that participates in the quality improvement system increases likelihood of successful improvement action.
- Ample resources are directed to overcoming potential obstacles. Three full-time "program quality advisors" employed by the intermediary agency work very closely with participating OST programs to increase the interventions' efficacy.
- Training for program directors on how to use quality data with their staff is provided.
- Capacity for a peer coaching system is being developed and will support expansion from 38 pilot sites to many more of the over 200 OST programs in the county.

The primary weakness for this system is that it is more expensive to operate and may require funds outside of existing budget lines for staff salaries and annual professional development.

Case 3 is now regularly offering half-day training workshops aligned with scales. These workshops are not required but may be attended by programs participating in the pilot. These workshops have had very high registration numbers in comparison to other voluntary workshops the intermediary leads.

A Generic Program Quality Intervention

Each of Cases 1-3 is a variation on the generic model in Figure 11.3 called the YPQI. In each adaptation of the intervention sequence, the project was kicked off by a series of presentations to decision makers and a pilot data collection to generate local learning and feedback. Next, substantial numbers of program staff were trained to conduct the self-assessment, external assessment, or both. After training and successful data collection, automated quality reports were produced for each site and program improvement planning from data occurred. Finally, with additional technical assistance, coaching, or training, program improvements were implemented based on the original diagnostic data. Note that training and technical assistance related to youth work methods—the traditional focus of program improvement policies—did not occur until the end of the YPQI sequence. As a provider of training in youth work methods, we have become very skeptical of the effects that flow from training in youth work methods when it is delivered outside of the context of a multilevel effort that provides both system-level supports and individual-level diagnostic data about staff performances.

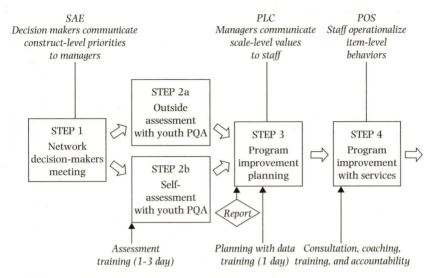

Figure 11.3. Generic Model for Setting Change.

Levels of Decision and Communication

At each stage, important messages are communicated across appropriate levels. Network decision makers articulate program *priorities* to managers ("you are accountable for POS quality as assessed by the Youth Program Quality Assessment") by inviting High/Scope Educational Research Foundation to leadership meetings, deciding to adopt the Youth Program Quality Assessment and hold training, and using data for decisions about investment. Once program managers have received this communication about priorities, they must apply the message within their organizational context and articulate specific POS quality *values* to staff ("we have high scores in the Youth Program Quality Assessment items about reflection, and this area is a central purpose of our program") when they bring staff together around scoring and interpretation of data from their programs. Frontline staff work on *behaviors* that bring youth into contact with key developmental experiences ("program activities will lead to tangible products or performances") when they select items from the Program Quality Assessment and decide how to operationalize them through their craft knowledge as youth workers.

The three-level structure of this model addresses the characteristics of effective accountability systems described earlier in this chapter. The Youth Program Quality Assessment assesses the quality of critical staff and youth performances (characteristic 1) and throughout the intervention YPQI stakeholders continually interact with the Youth Program Quality Assessment rubrics, clear descriptions of best practice (see Figure 11.4 for an example). The YPQI is geared to help program staff understand the program quality performance indicators and to make changes to address weaknesses

III. Interaction

III-L. Youth have opportunities to develop a sense of belonging.

Note: **Structured** *refers to the quality of being intentional, planned, and/or named; it does not refer to informal conversation.*

Indicators			Supporting evidence
1 Youth have no opportunities to get to know each other (beyond self-selected pairs or small cliques).	3 Youth have informal opportunities to get to know each other (e.g., youth engage in informal conversations before, during, or after session).	5 Youth have structured opportunities to get to know each other (e.g., there are team-building activities, introductions, personal updates, welcomes of new group members, icebreakers, and a variety of groupings for activities).	☐

Figure 11.4. Example PQA Item.

(characteristic 2). Finally, the system—whatever resources and level of stakes exist in a particular network—is designed to maximize incentives to engage with data through clarification of role expectations and priorities, engendering team efforts, and improvement of a professional craft (characteristic 3).

In the YPQI model, messages not only flow from left to right—as decisions and communications about priorities, values, and behaviors—but also from right to left. If the appropriate incentives are in place right-to-left feedback can inform, change, and strengthen the overall system. For example, the intermediary in Case 3 originally aimed for a high stakes system but as the project developed network decision makers listened to the messages from managers and modified their plans for how quickly higher stakes uses of quality data will be brought on line. However, if the accountability system is poorly constructed, right-to-left feedback takes the form of resistance, avoidance, or minimum compliance. Here, an example comes from Case 1 where network decision makers at the Department of Education created a low stakes system necessitated by the state's history of intensive local control by individual school districts. However, due to both the scale of the system and a sense of being overburdened by numerous reporting and evaluation requirements, some program managers did not adequately receive the message of priority for POS quality from network decision makers. Consequently, a substantial percentage of program managers decided to save time by completing the assessment without participation of frontline staff—a central focus of the low stakes approach.

Network decision makers, the key players in step one of Figure 11.3, typically make decisions about regulation, funding streams, and monitoring. Network decision makers in Cases 1-3 included lead consultants from state Department of Education and state Department of Human Services, agency directors in county and city government, staff from intermediary organizations and their funders, and influential directors of youth serving programs of both local and national origin. One of the key decisions made by network decision makers in each of Cases 1-3 was how to deal with the potential for uniform assessment across policy silos in the Departments of Education and Human Services that are not typically coordinated but which both fund after-school programs. Specifically, a key area of decision concerned how quality assessment fits with existing statewide licensing requirements under the Human Services side of state government. Another key decision for network decision makers concerned participation in the effort by national organizations such as Boys and Girls Clubs, Campfire, or the YMCA because these organizations typically had quality assessments or other evaluation tools provided/required by the national parent organization. Finally, a key decision about level of effort arose at each site for philanthropic organizations that were committed to the expenditure of evaluation resources for measurement of child and community-level outcomes rather than process measurement like the Youth Program Quality Assessment.

Managers, the key players in step 2 of Figure 11.3, go by a variety of terms—project coordinator, program director, or site supervisor. We consider program managers to be the people who manage the people who work with youth. Buy-in from site managers is perhaps the single most important support to success of the YPQI. One of the keys to achieving buy-in is the presence of a clear message from the system level. Among all of the competing priorities for time, managers need clear messages from their leadership that quality assessment and improvement policy will be taken seriously. This means that deadlines are clear, sufficient support is available, and feedback will be forthcoming. If no one outside of the program ever looks at the data or reads the improvement plans, sufficient priority is not being communicated.

When managers appear to be too busy or uncommitted to quality accountability, this message is readily apparent to even the most well intentioned of their staff working at the POS. Quality assessments provide opportunities for managers to be intentional with their staff about specific program values and behaviors. Unless managers are given clear messages from higher up, their ability to focus staff on POS quality may get lost in the shuffle of numerous competing demands and their staff may shift to minimum compliance or even avoidance/resistance of quality assessment practices.

In Case 3, after most programs conducted self-assessment, we led program managers from 38 programs through a day of training called, "Planning with Data." In this training, program managers received outside observer scores reports for their programs (3-8 observational ratings aggregated to one program score), and selected 3-5 *scales* to improve. They stated which scales to change, how they would change them, and how they would measure success. We strongly encouraged them to bring program staff into the improvement process after the training. Program managers then carried out these improvement plans with ongoing help from the local intermediary organization.

Through this process, program managers communicate to their staff the general message that "point-of-service quality matters" and also provide more specific messages about what areas are currently targeted for improvement. For example, one Case 3 organization chose "Improve opportunities for youth planning and goal setting" as an improvement area and developed plans to have staff include some youth planning component in every activity.

The model in Figure 11.3 ultimately depends on the performance of frontline staff at the POS. However, by targeting change at the three levels (also depicted in Figure 11.2), the chances for meaningful, sustainable change greatly increase. If diagnostic quality data are successfully turned into planning and action, then real performance change can happen at the POS. Every item in the Youth Program Quality Assessment is made up of 2-6 items—actual descriptions of behavior. If step 4 of Figure 11.3 (program improvement with services) is effective, it makes every other step worthwhile.

Steps to Performance Change

The overall vision of the YPQI relies on participants overcoming several potential obstacles, by going through a series of steps.[8] The first step involves initial engagement with the assessment process, a potential obstacle since assessment and observation often carry negative connotations. It is critically important for managers to build a sense of safety by making sure that staff (a) are aware of reliability and validity of the assessment tool and data collection methods, (b) understand that only they and their supervisors will see individual scores, if individual scores are produced, (c) work in teams to build comfort of sharing information about individual performances, and (d) understand exactly what they are being held accountable for and how they will be supported for success by acknowledging and building from strengths.

The next step comes when participants—particularly in systems using external assessment—receive a quality report. In a recent Planning from Data training session, we presented youth workers with their individual quality ratings without fully preparing them. Many of these youth workers reacted with defensiveness and resistance to the validity of the data, and we were never able to overcome this resistance and engage with the improvement process. In contrast, in many other situations where we have adequately prepared participants to receive data, their ability to select improvement areas and develop plans has been consistently successful.

In the third step, participants must overcome the tendency to set unrealistic or insufficiently specific improvement goals. We have found that in the Planning from Data workshop, participants are able to set appropriate, reachable goals. The fourth and final potential obstacle, which in some cases can be the greatest, is the challenge of turning plans into action. A strong SAE coupled with strong program supports such as technical assistance and coaching improve the odds for actual performance change because they ensure encouragement and behavioral modeling for staff to try new things and receive immediate, strength-based feedback.

We have found that safety items are often easiest to improve, although youth workers themselves do not always have control to make such changes. For example, if a first aid kit is missing, it is simple to obtain one, but this responsibility usually goes to the program manager or to some other person responsible for the physical space. Generally, more tangible program improvement goals are likely to lead to more immediate and successful improvement efforts than more abstract ones. For example, if a program sets an improvement goal with scale III-M, "Youth have opportunities to participate in small groups," it is reasonably tangible to implement a change and have staff begin to offer more small group experiences. In contrast, when a program wants to work in scale III-L, "Youth have opportunities to develop a sense of belonging," it is less tangible and harder to recognize success. This is why the Youth Program Quality Assessment is structured around very specific descriptors of positive staff behaviors (see Figure 11.4), in order to translate less tangible concepts into concrete behaviors.

Efficacy of the YPQI and Plans for Future Research

According to one recent and extensive research review, there have been no experimental studies of assessment or evaluation-driven interventions like the YPQI (Fixsen et al., 2005, p. 53), although there have been a few quasi-experimental studies that have found gains in program quality to be associated with participation in program accreditation processes (Bryant, Maxwell, & Burchinal, 1999; Hall & Cassidy, 2002; Whitebook, Sakai, & Howes, 1997). The YPQI employs several characteristics of effective practice in the literature on implementation of evidence-based practices and programs in the human services (Fixsen et al., 2005). The YPQI

- begins with the commitment of system-level decision makers;
- is multilevel, with performance data at the individual and organization levels;

- uses metrics that are easily interpreted and feedback reports that are quickly produced;
- produces alignment between values leadership by managers and behavior change by line staff;
- empowers managers to be selective at key moments such as hiring and participation in improvement planning;
- introduces consulting and coaching before extensive methods training.

Our plans for future research are to test rigorously the efficacy of the YPQI model. Reliable baseline estimates of program quality across dozens of sites have been produced in both Cases 2 and 3 above so that it will be possible to capture pre-to-post change in both samples. Finally, High/Scope Educational Research Foundation will be conducting an experimental trial of the YPQI beginning in fall 2006. In addition, we are currently validating a set of PLC-level quality constructs to complement the Youth Program Quality Assessment as an assessment at the POS level.

Conclusion

Although the ultimate purposes of OST programs are frequently a subject of contention (Halpern, 2005), we believe that the notion of a broad developmentally focused intervention captures the essence of purpose in a majority of out-of-school programming. Precisely because of the lack of clarity in this designation, and its close association with the widely shared philosophy of positive youth development, we believe that tools like the Youth Program Quality Assessment make sense as fidelity measures for settings of this type. However, due to the existing scale of implementation of broad developmentally focused programs—as after-school systems, service initiatives, community and faith-based programs, and prevention programs—the quality assessment is perhaps best seen as the cornerstone of larger quality accountability systems that apply to statewide and regional networks of OST providers.

This line of thought implies a couple of new twists in the current politics of evidence-based practice in the OST field. First, we are suggesting that intervention models focused on setting-level change are important. Setting-level interventions are likely to open the black box of human interaction and relationship that form the core of all education and human service programs. We need to know whether adults delivering service to youth are actually delivering the service. We also need to know if the organizations and systems in which the moment of adult-youth interaction is contextualized are helping or hindering the efforts of staff at the POS. Second, we are suggesting that accountability assessments, practices, and policies should be held more accountable. We need to test the consequential validity of measurement and evaluation as these practices come to occupy an increasing share of total investment in youth programs and policies.

Notes

1. The development and validation of the Youth Program Quality Assessment was funded by the W.T. Grant Foundation with supplementary support from the Michigan Department of Education and Skillman Foundation. The general logic of the discussion that follows also applies to other quality assessment tools in field.

2. Broad developmentally focused interventions like the Perry Preschool Intervention (Schweinhart, Barnes, & Weikart, 1993) and the Teen Outreach Program (Allen, Philliber, Herrling, & Kuperminc, 1997) achieve a condition of multifinality in the generation of outcomes, that is they provide rich multifaceted experiences that meet numerous developmental needs and produce multiple positive outcomes that may differ across the children and youth that participate.

3. For a discussion of the importance of staff motivation or "will" to improve see Cohen, Raudenbush, and Ball (2003). On cooperative accountability, see Behn (2001). The importance of a public discourse in the interpretation of accountability data is discussed in Bryk (1993).

4. See several reports posted at the High/Scope website (Smith, 2005a, 2005b; Smith & Hohmann, 2005) at http://www.youth.highscope.org

5. Figure 11.1 suggests an interesting parallel between the pyramid structure and Maslow's hierarchy of needs. In Maslow's hierarchy, more basic needs (deficiency and belonging needs) had to be at least partially satisfied before working to achieve a sense of actualization (Maslow, 1943). See discussion in Smith et al. (2006).

6. This description of shared beliefs comes from several data sources: anecdotal experiences of High/Scope Educational Research Foundations trainers and consultants, customer satisfaction surveys (n = approximately 1,700) that follow training projects, and 16 interviews with lead contacts at several implementation sites.

7. Because this state has a tradition of strong local control in local districts, we view this level of implementation as very positive. From our perspective, the real test of viability will be how many of the high engagement sites are still using the process in 3 years.

8. The steps described roughly correspond to the steps of change in the transtheoretical model of behavior change developed by Prochaska (1982).

References

Akiva, T. (2005, Fall/Winter). Turning training into results: The new youth program quality assessment. *High/Scope ReSource, 24*(2), 21-24.

Akiva, T. (2007, Spring). Getting to engagement: Building an effective after-school program. *High/Scope ReSource, 26*(1), 13-16.

Allen, J. P., Philliber, S., Herrling, S., & Kuperminc, G. P. (1997). Preventing teen pregnancy and academic failure: Experimental evaluation of a developmentally based approach. *Child Development, 68*(4), 729-742.

Barker, R. G. (1968). *Ecological psychology.* Stanford, CA: Stanford University Press.

Behn, R. D. (2001). *Rethinking democratic accountability.* Washington, DC: Brookings Institution Press.

Bryant, D. M., Maxwell, K. L., & Burchinal, M. (1999). Effects of a community initiative on the quality of child care. *Early Childhood Research Quarterly, 14*(4), 449-464.

Bryk, A. S., Camburn, E., & Seashore-Louis, K. (1999). Professional community in Chicago elementary schools: Facilitating factors and organizational consequences. *Educational Administration Quarterly, 35,* 751-781.

Bryk, A. S., & Hermanson, K. L. (1993). Educational indicator systems: Observations on their structure, interpretation, and use. *Review of Research in Education, 19,* 451-484.

Carnoy, M., & Loeb, S. (2002). Does external accountability affect student outcomes? A cross-state analysis. *Educational Evaluation and Policy Analysis, 24*(4), 305-331.

Cohen, D. K., Raudenbush, S. W., & Ball, D. L. (2003). Resources, instruction and research. *Educational Evaluation and Policy Analysis, 25*(2), 119-142.

Desimone, L. M., Porter, A. C., Garet, M. S., Yoon, K. S., & Birman, B. F. (2002). Effects of professional development on teachers' instruction: Results from a three-year longitudinal study. *Educational Evaluation and Policy Analysis, 24*(2), 81-112.

Fixsen, D. L., Naoom, S. F., Blasé, K. A., Friedman, R. M., & Wallace. F. (2005). *Implementation research: A synthesis of the literature.* Tampa, FL: University of South Florida, Louis de la Parte Florida Mental Health Institute, The National Implementation Research Network (FMHI Publication #231).

Hall, A. H., & Cassidy, D. J. (2002). An assessment of the North Carolina school-age child care accreditation initiative. *Journal of Research in Childhood Education, 17*(1), 84-96.

Halpern, D. (2005). *Confronting the big lie: The need to reframe expectations of afterschool programs.* Chicago, IL: Ericson Institute.

Halverson, R., Grigg, J., Prichett, R., & Thomas, C. (2005). *The new instructional leadership: Creating data-driven instructional systems in schools.* Madison, WI: Wisconsin Center for Education Research, University of Wisconsin-Madison.

Hilberg, R. S., Waxman. H. C., & Tharp, R. G. (2003). Introduction: Purposes and perspectives on classroom observation research. In H. C. Waxman, R. G. Tharp, & R. S. Hilberg (Eds.), *Observational research in U.S. classrooms.* Cambridge: Cambridge University Press.

InPraxis Group Inc. (2006). *Professional learning communities: An exploration.* Edmonton, Alberta: Alberta Education, School Improvement Branch.

Jaskyte, K. (2003). Assessing changes in employee's perceptions of leadership, job design, and organizational arrangements in their job satisfaction and commitment. *Administration in Social Work, 27*(4), 25-39.

Kayser, K., Walker, D., & Demaio, J. (2000). Understanding social workers' sense of competence within the context of organizational change. *Administration in Social Work, 24*(4), 1-20.

La Paro, K. M., Pianta, R. C., & Stuhlman, M. (2004). The classroom assessment scoring system: Findings from the prekindergarten year. *The Elementary School Journal, 104*(5), 409-426.

Maslow, A. H. (1943). A theory of human motivation. *Psychological Review, 50*, 370-396.

Mason, S. A. (2003). *Learning from data: The roles of professional learning communities.* University of Wisconsin-Madison, Madison, WI. Paper presented at the American Research Education Conference in April 2003.

National Institute of Child health and Human Development; Early Child Care Research Network (2002). The relation of global first-grade classroom environment to structural classroom features and teacher and student behaviors. *The Elementary School Journal, 102*(5), 367-387.

National Research Council and Institute of Medicine. (2000). From neurons to neighborhoods: The science of early childhood development. Committee on Integrating the Science of Early Childhood Development. In J. P. Shonkoff & D. A. Phillips (Eds.), *Board on children, youth and families, commission on behavioral and social sciences and education.* Washington, DC: National Academy Press.

National Research Council and Institute of Medicine. (2002). Community programs to promote youth development. Committee on Community-Level Programs for Youth. In J. Eccles & J. A. Gootman (Eds.), *Board on children, youth, and families, division of behavioral and social sciences and education.* Washington, DC: National Academy Press.

Pianta, R. (2003). Standardized classroom observations from pre-k to third grade: A mechanism for improving quality classroom experiences during the p-3 years. Unpublished paper.

Prochaska, J. O., & DiClemente, C. C. (1982). Transtheoretical therapy toward a more integrative model of change. *Psychotherapy: Theory, Research and Practice, 19*(3), 276-287.

Schoggen, P. (1989). *Behavior settings: A revision and extension of Roger G. Barker's ecological psychology.* Stanford, CA: Stanford University Press.

Schweinhart, L. J., Barnes, H. V., & Weikart, D. P. (1993). *Significant benefits: The High/Scope Perry Preschool study through age 27.* Ypsilanti, MI: High/Scope Press.

Smith, C. (2004). *Youth Program Quality Assessment Validation Study: Wave-1 findings for reliability and validity analyses.* Report to the W.T. Grant Foundation.

Smith, C. (2005a). *Findings from the self-assessment pilot in Michigan 21st century learning centers.* Ypsilanti, MI: High/Scope Educational Research Foundation. Retrieved November 8, 2007, from http://youth.highscope.org

Smith, C. (2005b). *What matters for after-school quality? Presentation to the W.T. Grant Foundation After-school Grantees Meeting,* December 19, 2005. Retrieved November 8, 2007, from http://youth.highscope.org

Smith, C., Akiva, T., Arrieux, D., & Jones, M. (2006). Improving quality at the point of service. In D. A. Blythe & J. A. Walker (Eds.), *Rethinking programs for youth in the middle years* (Vol. 112, pp. 93-108). San Francisco, CA: Jossey-Bass.

Smith, C., & Hohmann, C. (2005). *Full findings from the Youth PQA Validation Study.* Ypsilanti, MI: High/Scope Educational Research Foundation. Retrieved November 8, 2007, from http://youth.highscope.org

Smith, T. M., & Ingersoll, R. M. (2004). What are the effects of introduction and mentoring on beginning teacher turnover? *American Educational Research Journal, 41*(3), 681-714.

Talbert, T. E., & McGlaughlin, M. W. (1999). Assessing the school environment: Embedded contexts and bottom-up research strategies. In Sarah Friedman and Theodore Wachs (Eds.), *Measuring environment across the lifespan: Emerging methods and concepts.* Washington, DC: American Psychological Association.

U.S. Department of Health and Human Services. 2002. *Finding the balance: Program fidelity and adaptation in substance abuse prevention.* Washington, DC: Substance Abuse and Mental health Services Administration and Center for Substance Abuse prevention.

Whitebook, M., Sakai, L., & Howes, C. (1997). *NAEYC accreditation as a strategy for improving child care quality: An assessment.* Washington, DC: National Center for the Early Childhood Workforce.

Chapter 12

Altering Patterns of Relationship and Participation: Youth Organizing as a Setting-Level Intervention

PAUL W. SPEER

Youth-focused community organizing provides a valuable context for understanding setting-level interventions. It is important to distinguish at the outset between the structure of community organization and the process of community organizing. The terms are sometimes used interchangeably, but these are distinct concepts and yet both have relevance for youth (Speer & Perkins, 2002).

Community organization may be thought of from a community perspective, that is, what are the youth-serving organizations that compose a community? This contemplates a community's social ecology, which is the number and variety of organizations throughout a community and the relationships among these organizations. Community organizations are most often nonprofit agencies that provide services to youth in neighborhoods and that are located in communities. Youth-serving community organizations may include Boys and Girls Clubs, Boy and Girl Scouts, after-school programs, sports clubs, church groups, 4-H clubs, and the like (Brown & Theobald, 1998).

In contrast, community organizing is conceptualized more as a process—the process of developing leadership among youth and the process of building power for young people—with the goal of creating change. Community organizing is best described as seeking empowerment, both as a process and as an outcome (Mondros & Wilson, 1994; Speer & Hughey, 1995; Swift & Levin, 1987). Significantly, community organizing, as a process, is practiced in some but not all community organizations; organizations that practice community organizing, then, are a subset of the total number of community organizations within a community. In addition, some youth-serving community organizations set out with the goal of service provision but have expanded the services they provide to include community organizing. Therefore, along the spectrum of community organizations, some organizations exclusively exist to practice empowerment through organizing, some other organizations engage as an afterthought or secondary endeavor in some organizing, and still other community organizations practice no organizing.

Both community organizations, which provide important services to youth, and community organizing efforts, which encourage leadership and empowerment, hold as a key goal the development of individual youth. One common method for encouraging youth development is active civic participation and engagement. There are four common approaches to fostering youth civic engagement: civic education, service learning, political action/advocacy, and youth development (Gibson, 2001). Civic education typically focuses on classroom instruction, whereas service learning typically combines experience in community settings with classroom instruction. Alternatively, political action engages youth in some form of explicit political or social act, with varying levels of explicit instruction but most often with no such analysis or guidance. Finally, the youth development approach views civic engagement developmentally: civic engagement is seen as an outgrowth of the development of personal identity, compassion, tolerance, and responsibility. Among these four approaches to civic engagement, political action most closely resembles community organizing, but youth-serving agencies that support political action do not necessarily engage in community organizing if they do not also work to develop leadership among youth. Therefore, community organizations that do not participate in community organizing may still work to increase civic participation—through, for example, mentoring, social services, or community services (Yates & Youniss, 1999).

There are several critical dimensions to youth-focused community organizing. For one thing, in youth organizing, a key focus is on political action and advocacy, but this advocacy is done as a group or collectively, and revolves typically around issues that impact youth directly (Hosang, 2003). That is, the political work is conducted not on behalf of others but instead on behalf of the youth themselves. In addition, the process of youth organizing requires that the youth work to research and critically analyze the mechanisms and causes of the problems they seek to ameliorate. Finally, youth organizing emphasizes acting on problems by changing the environment, rather than presupposing that individuals should adapt to environmental circumstances. This effort to change the world—to influence and alter the policies and practices of the organizations and institutions of which youth are a part—is a critical dimension to community organizing.

Context of Change: PICO

To explore further the specific context of youth organizing, this chapter examines the People Improving Communities through Organizing (PICO) National Network. PICO is a nationwide federation of community organizing groups. PICO uses a congregation-based model of organizing, drawing on religious congregations of various faiths as their base for integrating and working with members of the community. Although it organizes in predominantly faith-based settings, PICO also works with neighborhoods, school parent-teacher organizations, and other associations. To grasp how youth-focused community organizing operates within PICO, it is first important to understand PICO's particular community organizing model.

PICO started in 1972 as a neighborhood-based community organization but evolved into a congregation-based model in 1984 (Reitzes & Reitzes, 1987). PICO is not a religious organization but it draws upon faith communities because they often represent the most viable institutions in urban areas. In addition, faith traditions and their concomitant set of values can serve uniquely as both a unifying orientation for community collaboration and a critical position from which to critique and challenge dominant market ideologies.

PICO adheres to a model of organizing, based on a set of principles that guide the organizing process (Speer & Hughey, 1995). Whereas other approaches may serialize or progress in fixed steps, PICO applies principles of community organizing in a dialectic way that attends to the dynamics of the community context. That is, the organizing process unfolds in a fluid context, and organizing, in the PICO model, requires the perpetual review of the organizing principles due to the constant flux in community environments.

One thing that distinguishes PICO from other organizing efforts, whether it is congregation- or neighborhood-based organizing, is that it is primarily focused at the level of the single, individual organization. A focus on individual organizations joining collectively as a coalition of organizations is secondary for PICO. To develop power effectively, an organizing effort must mobilize large numbers of people who work to influence policy decisions at, usually, a municipal level. Individual religious congregations, neighborhoods, or schools are unlikely, by themselves, to have the capacity to make such an impact. Consequently, most community organizing models utilize a coalition structure of local organizations, whether that is composed of congregations, schools, neighborhoods, or similar groups, and this coalition of individual groups then works together to make policy change within a larger jurisdiction. In contrast, in the PICO model, individual congregations work independently on issues that are affecting them. Recurrently, PICO congregations confront policies that affect most or all participating congregations, and in such circumstances, the multiple congregations collaborate in a federated effort to push for policy change. Nevertheless, the PICO model approach keeps the organizing most active at the level of the single organizational unit. Federated efforts continue in PICO, but the model stresses the need to perpetually maintain organizing at the level of the local, individual organization—most often the congregation. This is one of the most distinguishing features of PICO in the context of national organizing, but it is also important for understanding setting-level change. Because of this emphasis on individual organizations, PICO—more than other community organizing efforts—is focused on immediate settings and how organizing can alter those settings.

PICO's organizing begins when a community expresses interest in having organizing. Typically, clergy from a community contact PICO and express an interest in having PICO organize in their community. PICO then conducts an assessment by visiting the community for several days and having conversations with many individuals, predominantly clergy, to learn about their perceived needs, their expectations, and their commitment. If the inquiring community's needs match what PICO sees as its capacity to offer, PICO will request a local effort to raise funding for 2 years of an organizer's salary, at which time organizing will begin.

Organizing Process

Important dimensions of PICO's organizing process have been described elsewhere (Keddy, 2001; Reitzes & Reitzes, 1987; Speer & Hughey, 1995; Wood, 2002). Three aspects are most critical for understanding how the PICO approach alters settings: relationship development, leadership development, and action.

PICO describes its work as "reweaving the fabric of relationships" in a setting. This means, according to PICO, that a key problem in most communities is that relationships are thin and that people within settings need to be reconnected with one another. In PICO, this is accomplished through the one-to-one conversation. In a one-to-one conversation, individuals visit with one another to talk about issues that are affecting them. Importantly, the one-to-one is more than just visiting with other individuals; it is about listening carefully to others, as they share their stories, experiences, and events that their families have experienced. In listening to such stories, and comprehending their impact, participants in the organizing process begin to understand the issues confronted by the community. When listening to many such stories, about, for example, the lack of affordable medicine, the way businesses are preying on immigrants, a rash of car thefts, or the lack of access to capital for home purchases, one goal is to find the patterns that emerge from these stories. For PICO, however, the most important aspect to this process is the building of relationships among members of the community (Speer, Hughey, Gensheimer, & Adams-Leavitt,

1995). By focusing on people and the pain they experience in their daily lives, individuals within congregations or any organized community begin to focus on the common human qualities that all people share—pain, fear, joy, or hope. The sharing of these emotions between people serves to reconnect people, and the ongoing process of these one-to-ones serves to build relationships. For PICO, it is the building of relationships, more than any particular issue, that has value, and in the end, this value transcends the importance of any specific organizing issue. The PICO approach seeks to build a quality of power that lies primarily in those relationships, and when relationships are developed among people, they offer the potential for long-term strength. Because relationships can atrophy and diminish over time, the one-to-one is viewed as an ongoing process for sustaining these relationships.

Leadership development is a second critical dimension of PICO's process and a key aspect of how PICO alters settings. Although leadership is key in most community organizing efforts, it is PICO's intentionality and leadership development method that makes their process worthy of study. PICO is perpetually developing leaders through what Maton and Salem (1995) term "opportunity role structure." In PICO, organizers purposefully work to create settings with many distinct roles that individuals must fill in the organizing process. That means that at any particular organizing event, there are numerous distinct, specific roles for participants to perform (i.e., role as chairperson for the meeting, role as questioner of public officials, role of timekeeper, role of arranging the meeting facility, role of "pinning" an invited official down with an unequivocal answer to the group's question). Filling these roles provides individuals with opportunities to participate and learn. Importantly, such experiential learning has benefits for those filling such roles—they build confidence in their own skills, they deepen relationships with others in their organization with whom they are working, and they develop an understanding of power dynamics within the broader community as they interface with officials and community representatives. The PICO organization benefits as well from offering multiple roles; drawing from the efforts of numerous participants rather than relying on a single individual adds to the short-term efficacy and long-term viability of the organizing effort.

PICO is also purposeful in leadership development with regard to the rotation of roles within the organizational setting. Organizers work to make sure that individuals obtain experience in multiple roles. Exposure to different roles enhances learning but it also maintains openness within the culture of the organizing process. In important public meetings, it can be easy to rely heavily on a few very competent and capable leaders, but overreliance on such individuals limits the development of individual leaders and, thus, the efficacy and power of the organization (Maton & Salem, 1995; Peterson & Speer, 2000; Speer & Hughey, 1995). Furthermore, organizations that have the same individuals serving in important roles over time communicate, if unintentionally, a fixed or closed nature within the group. That is, organizations where a handful of individuals are perpetually in the same leadership positions communicate a hierarchy—some are "in" and some are "out"—that stifles new leaders from developing. PICO stresses that as new individuals participate in organizing, they intuit their own "place" in the process—that is, they are outsiders and they are aware of who has power in the organization. On the other hand, there is a leadership structure—there are individuals who are clearly taking on responsibilities and who feel owner-ship of the process. What is important in the PICO model is that organizations develop an explicit culture of openness so that many people develop as lead-ers, that a diverse set of skills is developed across a large number of people, and that the cultivation of new leaders is perpetual, expanding, and ongoing. Partly because of their model and partly because they work primarily with low- and moderate-income families, PICO stresses the need for perpetual openness and the constant addition of new leaders into their organizing. Because of the economic strata of those involved in PICO organizing, long-term involvement is never guaranteed. Individuals taking leadership roles in the organizing often must abandon their involvement in organizing to attend to household demands, such as caring for an elderly parent or taking a second job. Turnover in organizing is not sought, but it is expected, and openness, therefore, is a critical part of leadership development in the PICO model.

A third key aspect of PICO's organizing model is action. The relationship and leadership dimensions of the organizing process are amplified as the orga-nizing works through efforts to impact community issues (Speer et al., 2003). Action is a term that is associated with public meetings to pressure for specific policy change, but such events are preceded with an organizing process or "cycle of organizing" (Keddy, 2001; Speer & Hughey, 1995). First, assessment of a community's concerns and issues is accomplished through listening in many one-to-one conversations. Once patterns emerge in those one-to-ones about issues affecting a community, research is initiated to understand the causes and consequences of those identified concerns and issues. Action represents the organizational effort to rectify the identified causes of the issue. Finally, evaluation or reflection entails efforts to judge the impacts of the orga-nizing effort, strengths and weaknesses of the organization, and consideration of what was learned through this organizing process. Despite the emphasis on developing relationships and leadership, issue work is important and becomes the backdrop through which these other dimensions unfold.

PICO Theory of Change

The PICO network's theory of change is anchored in an understanding that power comes through organization and that organizing requires the building of solid, sustainable organizations. PICO's approach to building organizations starts with existing organizations—usually congregations—and works to transform these organizational settings so that they are capable of exercising social power in a community context.

Because the settings that PICO organizes are voluntary, their organizational structure must be different from structures that are anchored in, say, financial or compulsory relationships. PICO recognizes that in voluntary settings, participants must make choices and that participation will be sustained when the process is open and freely chosen by participants. In such an environment, the role of the staff organizer is very important. It is easy for an organizing process to dissolve into a "staff-directed" project; in contrast, the role of the organizer is to train leaders and to encourage development of an organizational culture, which shares a collective consciousness about their organizing process.

Changing a voluntary setting is based on an open process, but the congregational context provides PICO organizing a values base from which to build organization. Because congregational settings share a common adherence to a set of values that seek justice and human dignity, this unifying vision can help support the organizing process. Organizing in settings without such a common basis is much more susceptible to infighting and decline.

PICO's theory of change is that conditions in communities that contribute to human suffering (poor housing, lack of access to health care, unsafe neighborhoods, etc.) are the result of powerlessness by those affected by those problems. To change these conditions, those in society with relatively little power must develop and exercise power to advocate on behalf of their own interests. Making society aware of injustice or oppression will never change conditions; only the exercise of power will make change. To exercise power, those who are relatively powerless must come together and act through organization. Organizations have power to the extent that large numbers of individuals work in a coordinated manner over a sustained period of time. To accomplish this in a voluntary setting is a challenge, particularly among those who have limited economic capacities. PICO utilizes congregations as its organizing base because congregations are anchored in values that prioritize issues of justice and because there is a level of social capital and cohesion already in place within these settings.

Despite the existing level of social capital in congregations, PICO's theory of change also holds that many in these organizational settings are out of relationship with one another. PICO asserts that through organizing they seek to "reweave the fabric of relationships" in organizational settings. To create change, then, the belief is that organizing must work with congregations (or other organizational settings) and reconnect individuals within those settings. By altering that pattern and frequency of interpersonal communication within a setting over time—the social regularity (Seidman, 1990)—organizing settings will have the critical capacity necessary to exercise social power. The PICO model is somewhat unique in that it intentionally seeks to intervene upon settings by expanding the frequency and breadth of interactions within a setting. Their theory of change holds that by altering settings in this way, organizations will increase power and, with it, their capacity to make change.

Theory of Change in PICO Youth Organizing

The PICO organizing process was designed to involve primarily low- and moderate-income residents in organizing as a way to cultivate social power capable of altering decision making and collective resources at a community level of analysis. This organizing process does not exclude youth, but in practice, adults are involved almost exclusively. However, several PICO organizations have developed separate components of their organizations that work exclusively with youth. Organizations that have launched youth organizing have done so because adults involved in organizing have pushed their organizations to focus on youth organizing (Stahlhut, 2003). Generally, the perspective held by PICO federations who now have youth organizing is that it is as youth that individuals first become cognizant of the broad forces that mold and shape society. Particularly for low- and moderate-income youth, recognition of the relative powerlessness individuals possess comes into focus in youth and this realization is an opportunity to act and learn that one's voice can be expressed. Youth organizing, then, holds that by exposing youth to ideas and experiences in which they confront social power and the influence this power has had on their own lived experience, it offers the possibility of awakening their own sense of sociological understanding, as well as their individual capacities and skills. This is not to say that youth will cultivate what Mills (1959) termed a "sociological imagination," but that organizing can stimulate a contemplation of the larger social picture and one's relationship to it. Youth organizing, then, offers a mechanism for both stimulating an understanding of the relationship between oneself and the broader social environment and a way to participate in altering the shape of that environment.

As in its organizing of adults, PICO organizing of youth seeks to create settings where the pattern of interactions within a setting is altered from what the youth typically experience. Commonly, youth spend their time in settings where activities are planned and outcomes defined in advance. Exposure to such settings is not inappropriate; what may be needed, however, are opportunities for youth to participate in a variety of settings, some of which allow or even demand that youth be responsible and self-directed. In many respects, this parallels the concept of "initiative" (Larson, Hansen, & Walker, 2005).

Youth community organizing is not without some level of definition or predetermined goal. Specifically, youth organizing is designed to engage youth in forms of civic participation, broadly conceived (Youniss et al., 2002). Although this type of activity is not suitable to all youth, it is an important phenomenon to study because it is relatively infrequent and the method of engaging youth offers important insights into how to structure settings that may translate beyond the goal of civic engagement.

Organizing Processes Specific to Youth

There are several features to organizing that have been tailored to better align PICO's approach with the interests of youth. These unique features were not designed into organizing efforts with youth but have developed from experience in youth organizing (Stahlhut, 2003).

In PICO's typical organizing model, one-to-one conversations are the fundamental building block of the organization. These conversations build relationships within and across communities. This relationship development process has proved no less important for youth (Larson & Walker, 2005), but youth frequently find the process of reaching out to peripheral acquaintances or strangers to be a barrier that is difficult to overcome. In youth organizing, developing a brief survey has become a technique to rise above this barrier; youth are much more comfortable asking people questions from a survey and then transitioning this form of specific questioning into a dynamic, give-and-take form of questioning and, ultimately, relationship building. Importantly, these conversations are anchored on listening—listening to the experiences and interests of other youth. What are kids talking about? What makes them angry? Where do they see contradictions?

The biggest challenge in youth organizing is to get youth to expand beyond their own personal networks and cliques. This reaching out to others is a challenge in all organizing, but it has proven a greater challenge in youth organizing. Many youth want to work within their own extended networks and feel that this should suffice. In contrast, there are youth that through this organizing process understand the need to bridge boundaries within the organizing setting—these youth often become the most effective organizers.

PICO organizations involved in youth organizing have come to believe that having youth as organizers is a critical component to the success of their efforts; that is, youth organizing is youth-led rather than adult-led (Youniss et al., 2002; Stahlhut, 2003). Youth are hired by the PICO organizations to be organizers. These youth staff are trained by adult staff in the PICO model, but having youth work with youth has proven an effective method of engagement. In these efforts, youth staff are supervised by the adult director of the organization, just as adult organizers are supervised by the director. Importantly, the experience of young people involved in organizing is that youth organizing staff do all the organizing—they conduct trainings, facilitate team meetings, and help coordinate organizing actions. Importantly, the organizer draws heavily on a Socratic method of teaching and reflection on experience. So rather than "instruction" or functioning in a directive manner, the organizer raises questions and asks youth to reflect on the experiences they have had in the organizing—What did you hear in your conversations with other youth? What did we learn from the school superintendent? What are our alternatives? Why did we decide to do that? Ultimately, youth understand that they have defined their own issues and frequently these issues reflect the worldview of youth; organizing issues have included better parking at school and getting toilet paper and soap in school bathrooms. But issues have also included increasing access to college and reinstatement of advanced placement science classes in a high school that dropped those courses because of the poor physical condition of the school's science labs.

Another aspect of organizing that has been tailored to match the experience with youth organizing is that youth interests change rapidly. The organizing process for youth has been pushed to cycle faster than for adults because youth involvement can change rapidly due to the pull of many competing interests in adolescence.

Most youth organizing takes place in schools, sometimes community centers, and only rarely in congregational settings. Youth spend most of their time at school and the focal point of much of their concerns is the school experience. This makes the school setting a natural one for organizing. In relation to this, it is also important to youth that no parents are involved in organizing. Parents are especially unwelcome, but adults in general are not involved in the youth organizing experience. One lesson that has been learned by youth organizing efforts by many in the PICO network is that when youth begin to push to make changes in their school or community, they must have an adult present in meetings, negotiations, or even information sessions with authority figures. Principals, city council members, and other officials do not take youth seriously when they interact only with youth. Youth organizers have learned from experience to invite an adult whom they respect—usually someone outside the setting (i.e., often a pastor rather than a teacher within a school setting)—to be present in any meetings with officials. The adult does not do anything, nor is he or she prepared to do anything, but it raises a level of accountability for the officials youth are meeting with.

Measurement of Setting-Level Change in Youth Organizing Contexts

Change in youth organizing settings may be measured uniquely and powerfully through network analysis. Specifically, the thesis in youth organizing is that participants in the organizing process will alter their typical communication patterns—their interactions with peers through the one-to-one relationship building process. In other words, the organizing process will rework the social regularity of peer interactions in youth networks (Seidman, 1990). Network measures capture change at the setting level, and the pattern of relationships at the setting level is where PICO organizing seeks to impact youth. Youth in particular find it difficult to reach out beyond their personal networks to speak with youth they do not know. When young people do extend beyond their existing networks, organizing is successful; when they do not, organizing is much less effective. Although PICO's youth organizing does not use network analysis directly, they draw on concepts that can be directly linked to network concepts and, at times, they directly employ network tools, such as sociograms, as an analytic means to understand whom they are reaching and whom they are missing in the organizing process. The thesis in PICO's youth organizing is that altering the pattern of relationships in youth settings is the key mechanism in modifying communication that, in turn, will impact attitudes, perceptions, and, ultimately, the behavioral activities of civic engagement that organizing calls "action."

In youth organizing, data gathering about networks can consist of surveying students to find out whom they talk with about school issues. As noted previously, this type of data collection is comfortable for young people. Once gathered, this data can be entered into matrices, which can then be analyzed through network analysis.

The key network indices that correspond to PICO's theory of change in youth settings are betweenness, centralization, and reach. Betweenness measures the extent to which a few individuals within the setting are the only connection among large numbers of other individuals in the setting. If a setting has individual actors possessing a high level of betweenness, this would mean that the setting is dependent upon a small number of individuals who are brokers throughout the setting. Betweenness measures the number of individuals who are in positions to be brokers within a setting—there may be few or many in such a position. The organizing process values those individuals with high betweenness, but at the same time, the process seeks to connect people in a setting who are unconnected, thus reducing the influence of those valued brokers. Therefore, over time, successful organizing within a setting will reduce the level of betweenness in the setting. Centralization in a network may be considered a more global measure of betweenness—it means the extent to which a setting is dominated by a small number of actors. Rather than examining the number of positions in a network that can be considered "brokers," it measures the overall reliance a setting has to those in central roles within the setting. Are there individuals through whom most information flows in a setting? If so, there is a high degree of centralization. In youth organizing, the interests of youth tend to change more rapidly than for adults. If a setting is highly dependent on a small number of youth, even one or two departures can quickly fragment the setting. Successful youth organizing will establish relationships across diverse young people so that the setting is decentralized; this means that when some youth do not maintain involvement in the organizing, the communication throughout the setting will not breakdown. Reach refers to the extent to which relationships in a setting are direct or indirect. It is unlikely that in any setting every individual will develop a relationship with every other individual, but organizing works to build relationships within settings so that there are fewer isolated cliques within the setting. Reach measures how many individuals one must communicate with to be able to connect with everyone in a network. Therefore, A may have a relationship with B, and B have a relationship with C—thus, A can "reach" C by communicating via B. How many people, on average, must individuals in a setting communicate with to reach everyone in a setting? Network analysis has found that, despite the common notion of "six degrees of separation," one's influence, or even one's understanding of potential influence, diminishes dramatically beyond two or three people. Therefore, the reweaving of relationships in youth organizing should reduce the average number of individuals one must talk to for one to be able to "reach" everyone in the setting. These three measures of setting structures—betweenness, centralization, and reach—are all measures of density within settings. Although these measures are similar, they do represent different facets of the overall setting structure that youth organizing seeks to alter.

The most popular theories in network analysis emphasize weak ties, that is, the strength of weak ties (Granovetter, 1973) and structural holes (Burt, 2000). Weak ties are those with whom we are familiar, but not close to—these connections have value because they frequently offer information and access to resources that we are not knowledgeable about. Structural holes are the connections between clusters of densely connected individuals—these are often connections between organizations. However, this chapter is emphasizing just the opposite in youth settings. Certainly weak ties are important and valuable aspects of networks; weak ties and structural holes have known benefits for individuals (such as a job seeker or salesperson), and they can have great value in the organizing process. Hughey and Speer (2002) describe how community organizations can exploit weak ties and structural holes to leverage power as they act to make policy change. In community organizing within individual organizations, however, with the outcome targeted at the exercise of collective power, weak ties outside the organization must be balanced with the need to develop strong ties within it. In the context of organizing, benefits are sought for the collective, a collective where members are relatively weak. In this context, strong ties are important.

Krackhardt (1992) addresses strong ties, noting the importance of interaction, affection, and time as elements of strong ties, what he terms *philos*.

Krackhardt goes on to describe the importance of such relationships for social change, and his research parallels much in the PICO model of organizing:

> When it comes to major change, change that may threaten the status quo in terms of power and the standard routines of how decisions are made, then resistance to that change must be addressed before predictions can be made about the success of that change effort. A major resource that is required to bring about such change is trust in the propagators of that change. Change is a product of strong, affective, and time-honored relationships. Change is a product of *philos*. (Krackhardt, 1992)

PICO's youth organizing model seeks ways to encourage youth to develop relationships beyond the friendships and cliques that constrain their normal interactions. When youth stretch themselves in this way, particularly young people who are in a powerless position both by age and class, they come to realize the common barriers they all face, and this realization helps deepen relationships. For PICO, the depth of these relationships corresponds proportionally with the degree to which organizations can yield participation in the exercise of power to make changes in the environment. Reframed in the language of social science, altering the pattern of relationships is the independent variable; increasing participation is the dependent variable. To measure the impact of this independent variable, network analysis can measure the change in structure of the settings where youth organizing is practiced.

Exemplars from MOP/CCISCO

Metro Organizations for People (MOP) is a PICO Network organization in Denver, Colorado, which has been active in youth organizing for almost 3 years. MOP has five youth organizations: four in schools and one in a community center. MOP's youth organizing was started in Denver's West High School, through an idea presented by several youth at a MOP organized congregation (an organizing effort composed predominantly of adults). For an idea of the characteristics of this school where youth organizing was started, the district's website describes West High as 89% Hispanic; 73% receiving reduced lunch; and 18% meeting state reading standards, well below the 65% state level.

Early in organizing work at this high school, the students found the idea of organizing appealing because it seemed more interesting than the student council, which had been the only other school outlet for student-directed activity and was commonly viewed as simply planning the school's social calendar. The youth organizing effort quickly identified an issue that surfaced in their one-to-ones: the inadequacy of the school bathrooms. Specifically, the school's bathrooms lacked toilet paper and soap. In line with the organizing process, the work of this youth organizing group culminated in an all-school assembly. There, the youth organizing group presented their data and research to the assistant superintendent about the school's budget cuts and the unacceptability of inadequate bathrooms. Not only were maintenance and supplies in the bathrooms improved, but also the assembly launched an interest and energy in organizing throughout the school. Since that time, the youth at West High and the other youth organizing groups in Denver have taken on larger issues. In the last year, the biggest issue they have addressed has been access to college for low-income students. Last summer, the students had 25 research meetings with state legislators, the attorney general, lobbyists, and others. They are now pressing the State Board of Education to authorize courses for college credit.

Substantial issues addressed in youth organizing have been undertaken by CCISCO (Contra Costa Interfaith Supporting Community Organization), the PICO affiliate in Contra Costa County, just across the Bay from San Francisco. Since 1999, a cadre of teenagers have been hired each year and trained to organize their peers in ten different communities. The part-time youth organizers have trained over 350 youth leaders who have organized community action meetings to win major benefits for their own communities. In 2002, CCISCO youth leaders organized a countywide action meeting involving over 500 youth, and the focus of the action was closing the achievement gap between Latino and African American students and the broader student community. Because of the action, youth leaders won commitments from three different school district superintendents across the county to work with youth to prioritize and implement policies to close the achievement gap. Some results from these public actions have included doubling the number of credentialed teachers in Richmond's Kennedy High School, thereby dramatically reducing the annual turnover of teachers, and improving teaching and learning in a challenged school where only one in five students graduate college ready. At Mt. Diablo Unified School District, youth leaders campaigned to implement a reform of the English Language Development program that was automatically placing students with Spanish surnames into remedial English classes regardless of their English language proficiency with little effort to return these students into mainstream classes. This reform has resulted in an 800% increase in transfers to mainstream courses (41 in 2003—prior to the youth intervention—to 376 in 2006) and has allowed reclassified students to take additional elective and college preparatory classes. In Bay Point, a low-income immigrant community with a 60% high school dropout rate, youth leaders campaigned to win an after-school youth center with computer labs and recreational opportunities for teenagers, and in Concord's school system, $500,000 is being used to improve an athletic field for youth.

Implications

Youth-focused community organizing has achieved significant community outcomes, but it also offers potential impacts on the developmental outcomes for participating youth. Although the nature of organizing contexts varies, targeting interventions at the level of settings offers promise to promote positive developmental outcomes for youth. Finally, future research should employ network analysis methodologies as an important tool for measuring the impact of setting-level interventions.

References

Brown, B. B., & Theobald, W. (1998). Learning contexts beyond the classroom: Extracurricular activities, community organizations, and peer groups. In K. Borman & B. Schneider (Eds.), *The adolescent years: Social influences and educational challenges* (pp. 109-1410). Chicago, IL: The University of Chicago Press.

Burt, R. S. (2000). *Structural holes: The social structure of competition.* Cambridge, MA: Harvard University Press.

Gibson, C. (2001). *From inspiration of participation: A review of perspectives on youth civic engagement.* New York: Grantmaker Forum on Community and National Service.

Granovetter, M. S. (1973). The strength of weak ties. *American Journal of Sociology, 78*(6), 1360-1380.

Hosang, D. (2003). Youth and community organizing today. *Social Policy, 34*(2/3), 66-70.

Hughey, J., & Speer, P. W. (2002). Community, sense of community and networks. In A. Fisher, C. Sonn, & B. Bishop (Eds.), *Psychological sense of community: Research, applications and implications* (pp. 69-84). New York: Kluwer Academic/ Plenum Publishers.

Keddy, J. (2001). Human dignity and grassroots leadership development. *Social Policy, 31*(4), 48-55.

Krackhardt, D. (1992). The strength of strong ties: The importance of Philos in organizations. In N. Nohria & R. G. Eccles (Eds.), *Networks and organizations: Structure, form, and action.* Boston: Harvard Business School Press.

Larson, R., Hansen, D., & Walker, K. (2005). Everybody's gotta give: Development of initiative and teamwork within a youth program. In J. L. Mahoney, R. W. Larson, & J. S. Eccles (Eds.), *Organized activities as contexts of development: Extracurricular activities, after-school and community programs* (pp. 159-183). Mahwah, NJ: Lawrence Erlbaum Associates.

Larson, R., & Walker, K. (2005). Processes of positive development: Classic theories. In P. A. Witt & L. L. Caldwell (Eds.), *Recreation and youth development* (pp. 131-148). State College, PA: Venture Publishing.

Maton, K. I., & Salem, D. A. (1995). Organizational characteristics of empowering community settings. *American Journal of Community Psychology, 23*, 631-656.

Mills, C. W. (1959). *The sociological imagination*. New York: Oxford University Press.

Mondros, J. B., & Wilson, S. M. (1994). *Organizing for power and empowerment*. New York: Columbia University Press.

Peterson, N. A., & Speer, P. W. (2000). Linking organizational characteristics to psychological empowerment: Contextual issues in empowerment theory. *Administration in Social Work, 24*(4), 39-58.

Reitzes, D. C., & Reitzes, D. C. (1987). The Alinsky legacy: Alive and kicking. In L. Kriesberg (Ed.), *Social movements, conflicts and change*. Greenwich, CT: Jai Press, Inc.

Seidman, E. (1990). Pursuing the meaning and utility of social regularities for community psychology. In P. Tolan, C. Keys, F. Chertok, & L. Jason (Eds.), *Researching community psychology: Issues of theory and methods* (pp. 91-100). Washington, DC: American Psychological Association.

Speer, P. W., & Hughey, J. (1995). Community organizing: An ecological route to empowerment and power. *American Journal of Community Psychology, 23*, 729-748.

Speer, P. W., Hughey, J., Gensheimer, L. K., & Adams-Leavitt, W. (1995). Organizing for power: A comparative case study. *Journal of Community Psychology, 23*, 57-73.

Speer, P. W., Ontkush, M., Schmitt, B., Raman, P., Jackson, C., Rengert, K. M., et al. (2003). The intentional exercise of power: Community organizing in Camden, New Jersey. *Journal of Community and Applied Social Psychology, 13*, 399-408.

Speer, P. W., & Perkins, D. D. (2002). Community-based organizations, agencies and groups. In J. Guthrie (Ed.), *Encyclopedia of education* (2nd ed., pp. 431-441). New York: Macmillian Reference USA.

Stahlhut, D. (2003). The people closest to the problem. *Social Policy, 34*(2/3), 71-74.

Swift, C., & Levin, G. (1987). Empowerment: An emerging mental health technology. *Journal of Primary Prevention, 8*, 71-94.

Wood, R. L. (2002). *Faith in action: Religion, race, and democratic organizing in America*. Chicago: University of Chicago Press.

Yates, M., & Youniss, J. (Eds.). (1999). *Roots of civic identity: International perspectives on community service and activism in youth*. Cambridge: Cambridge University Press.

Youniss, J., Bales, S., Christmas-Best, V., Diversi, M., McLaughlin, M., & Sibereisen, R. (2002). Youth civic engagement in the twenty-first century. *Journal of Research on Adolescence, 12*(1), 121-148.

Chapter 13

The Ethnic System of Supplementary Education: Nonprofit and For-Profit Institutions in Los Angeles' Chinese Immigrant Community

MIN ZHOU

I nformal social settings outside of school are as important as formal educational settings for children's learning and achievement. In the United States, informal settings are often organized by ethnicity and socioeconomic status (SES) to mediate the processes of individual learning, which consequently lead to intergroup differences in educational outcomes. This chapter examines how a particular type of informal social setting is created and structured by the ethnic community to generate resources for school success. By looking specifically into the nonprofit and for-profit institutions serving young children and youth in Los Angeles' Chinese immigrant community, I unfold an ethnic system of supplementary education that not only offers tangible support but also reinforces cultural norms in pushing immigrant children to succeed in school.[1]

Behind the Ethnic Success Story: Community Forces and the Ethnic Social Environment

The 2000 U.S. Census shows that nearly three-quarters (73%) of U.S.-born Chinese Americans between ages 25 and 34 (and half of U.S.-born Asian Americans) have attained at least a bachelor's degree, compared to 15% of African Americans and 30% of whites (Xie & Goyette, 2004). What is more striking is that the children of Chinese immigrants, who are from low-income immigrant or refugee families, live in Chinatowns, and attend urban public schools in poor neighborhoods, also manage to show up as their high school valedictorians or in freshmen classes of prestigious colleges and universities in disproportionately large numbers. The high educational achievement among Chinese Americans and other Asian Americans seems to have continually perpetuated the model minority stereotype. However, what is behind the ethnic success story is more complicated than what statistical data suggest. For a long time, educators and researchers have sought to explain the unequal educational outcomes of different ethnic minorities by focusing on either cultural factors—an ethnic group's traits, qualities, and behavioral patterns—or on structural factors—a group's unique historical encounters of domination and subjugation, socioeconomic backgrounds, immigration selectivity, labor market conditions, and residential patterns. For example, some studies have found that residential segregation and social exclusion of poor African Americans give rise to distinct values and norms that are at odds with those of mainstream society in regard to work, money, education, home, and family life (Wilson, 1996), or even to an oppositional collective social identity that entails a willful refusal of mainstream norms and values relating to school success (Fordham, 1996; Fukuyama, 1993; Kohl, 1994; Ogbu, 1974). These values and norms in turn lead to a set of self-defeating behavioral problems, such as labor-force nonparticipation, out-of-wedlock births, welfare dependency, school failure, drug addiction, and chronic lawlessness (Lewis, 1966; Wilson, 1996). Other studies, in contrast, have found that low-income families of racial/ethnic minorities tend to concentrate in poverty-stricken and unsafe inner-city neighborhoods. Parents who lack human capital (e.g., education, professional job skills, and English proficiency for immigrants) have few options other than to send their children to dilapidated urban schools that have inadequate facilities and resources, poorly trained and inexperienced teachers, and large proportions of low-achieving students, hence putting children at a much higher risk of school failure (Anyon, 1997; Kozol, 2005; Massey & Denton, 1995; Olsen, 1997; Suarez-Orozco & Suarez-Orozco, 2001; Varenne & McDermott, 1998). These explanations, however, largely overlook certain ethnic social settings, which create resources conducive to education for co-ethnic group members to the exclusion of non-co-ethnic members, who may share the same neighborhood and the same access to public education.

In my view, ethnicity cannot be simply viewed as either a cultural or a structural measure. Rather, it encompasses values, norms, and behavioral patterns that are constantly interacting with both internal and external structural exigencies, such as group-specific contexts of exit and reception.[2] In American society, the concept of ethnicity is inherently interacted with social class. That is, the educational experience of Chinese Americans in Los Angeles may not be the same as that of Mexican Americans in the same metropolis, because the children of these two ethnic groups grow up in different informal social settings. One particular type of such settings is what I term the ethnic social environment.

What is in the ethnic social environment that affects education? We know that social class shapes both formal and informal social settings and has a powerful impact on children's educational experience and their future life chances (Gordon, Bridglall, & Meroe, 2005). Children of middle-class and upper-middle-class backgrounds have access to quality public schools in their neighborhoods or to private schools that are more resourceful. These children are also exposed to informal social settings in support of academic achievement, such as families with highly educated and well-informed parents practicing "concerted cultivation" (Lareau, 2003), and communities in which positive and caring adult role models are next door and various preschool education, afterschool tutoring, and extracurricular activities are around the corner (Zhou et al., 2000). Children of low-income families, in contrast, live in homes and communities with fewer human capital, cultural capital, and social capital resources conducive to education. They have to attend poor urban schools that are often understaffed and insufficiently funded. Moreover, their lived experiences growing up in socioeconomically disadvantaged cultural communities are usually not reflected in school curricula, readers, textbooks, and other learning materials (Scribner and Cole, 1991). Furthermore, they are disproportionately tracked into low-ability and low-performing classes (Kozol, 2005; Olsen, 1997; Xiong & Zhou, 2005). Such incongruous formal educational settings are further exacerbated by seemingly disruptive informal social settings plagued by extreme poverty, high crime, social disorganization, and economic disinvestment (Allen & Boykin, 1992; Boykin & Allen, 1991; Ogbu, 1974; Portes & Rumbaut, 2006).

However, informal social settings are also mediated by race or ethnicity to reinforce or undercut class disadvantages (Gordon et al., 2005). Native-born African American parents, Latino immigrant parents, and Asian immigrant parents in low-income neighborhoods all stress the value of education for their children, and the children of these racial groups all agree that education is imperative in securing a good job (Carter, 2005; Lareau, 2003; Varenne & McDermott, 1998). Yet, only the children of Asian immigrants as a group seem to have gained an upper hand in actualizing that value and show higher rates of academic success than other minority groups (Portes & MacLeod, 1996; Steinberg, 1996). It seems that what determines a child's learning and development is not merely social class but also what Ogbu and his associates call "community forces," which also affect informal social settings in ethnic-specific ways.

According to Ogbu and his associates, community forces are the products of sociocultural adaptation embedded within a cultural community, which entails specific beliefs, interpretations, and coping strategies that a racial/ethnic group adopts in response to often hostile societal treatment or social exclusion (Fong, 2003; Fordham & Ogbu, 1986; Ogbu, 1974; Ogbu & Simon, 1998). Ethnic minorities can turn their distinctive heritages into a kind of ethnic armor and establish a sense of collective dignity. This strategy enables them to cope psychologically, even in the face of discrimination and exclusion, or to accept and internalize socially imposed inferiority as part of their collective self-definition and to develop an "oppositional outlook" toward the dominant group and mainstream institutions, including education (Fordham, 1996; Ogbu & Simon, 1998).

While community forces refer to a common cultural heritage along with a set of shared values, beliefs, behavioral standards, and coping strategies with which members of a cultural community are generally identified, I argue that these community forces must arise from and be supported by the social structures of an ethnic community. Thus, the ethnic community should neither be simply understood as a neighborhood where a particular ethnic group's members and/or businesses concentrate nor as a geographically unbounded racial or ethnic identity in the abstract. Rather, it contains various ethnic structures, such as economic organizations, sociocultural institutions, and interpersonal networks that have been established, operated, and maintained by group members. Because community forces dictate the orientation, coping strategies, and corresponding behaviors of different ethnic groups in regard to mobility goals and means of achieving these goals, informal social settings created and regulated by these forces are likely to facilitate or hinder educational achievement and other long-term mobility goals independent of social class factors (Fernandez-Kelly, 1995; Fordham, 1996).

The informal social settings with which the children of Chinese immigrants are in daily contact may be understood through ethnic social structures in the immigrant community, including various economic, social, and cultural organizations as well as the social networks arising from co-ethnic members' participation in these ethnic organizations. Therefore, an examination of specific ethnic social structures can provide insight into how ethnicity interacts with social class to create a particular social environment to promote academic achievement of immigrant children. The aim of this chapter is not to explain the differences in educational outcomes between Chinese and other ethnic groups but rather to describe a particular type of informal setting to which a successful group of immigrant children is routinely exposed. I try to find out why the children of Chinese immigrants, regardless of socioeconomic backgrounds, excel and succeed in the educational arena in disproportionately large numbers. I do so through an in-depth examination of how nonprofit and for-profit ethnic institutions serving children and youth are developed to form an ethnic system of supplementary education in the Chinese immigrant community in Los Angeles.[3]

The Formation of the Ethnic Social
Environment Conducive to Education

Cultural Values and Norms for
Educational Achievement

While education is generally considered a primary means to upward social mobility in all American families, the educational value is emphasized in some unique ways in the immigrant Chinese family as it is transplanted in the new homeland. First, the children's educational success is very much tied to face saving for the traditional Chinese family. Parents in China and Chinese immigrant parents in the United States often explicitly or implicitly remind their children that achievement is a duty and an obligation to the family rather than to an individual goal and that, if they fail, they will bring shame to the family. This time-honored face-saving norm has been carried over to America to form a community force that drives both children and parents in the area of education. Children are under pressure to excel in every step along the path to a good college education. Their success is not only bragged about by parents among relatives, friends, and co-ethnic coworkers but also featured in Chinese language newspapers, club/organization news-letters, and even radio and television programs. Parents, on the other hand, are under pressure to facilitate their children's education not just to honor family and to vindicate their own sacrifices associated with immigration but also to show to their community that they are *good* parents.

Chinese immigrant parents also take a pragmatic stance on educa-tion. They see education not only as the most effectively means to success in society but also the *only* means (Sue & Okazaki, 1990). The parents are keenly aware of their own limitations as immigrants and the larger struc-tural constraints, such as limited family wealth even among middle-income immigrants, lack of access to social networks connecting to the mainstream economy and various social and political institutions, and entry barriers to certain occupations because of racial stereotyping and discrimination. Their own experience tells them that a good education in certain fields would be a safe bet for their children to get good jobs in the future. These fields include science, math, engineering, and medicine, as well as business and law to a lesser extent. Therefore, in practice, the parents are concerned more about their children's academic coursework, grades, majors, and college rankings than about the children's well-rounded learning experience. They would discourage their children's interests in pursuing history, literature, music, dance, sports, or anything that they consider unlikely to lead to well-paying, stable jobs but pressure their children to get involved in these academic fields and extracurricular activities only to the extent that such involvement would enhance the children's chance of getting into Ivy League colleges and other prestigious universities. Even though the children often get frustrated by the fact that their parents choose the type of education for them and make decisions for their future, many of them end up internalizing their parents' educational values.

Cultural values and norms are one thing. Everyday practices and outcomes are quite another. How does the immigrant family ensure that norms are effective and that values are actualized? In American society, the immigrant family alone cannot ensure that the children excel in school, as opposed to being just like everybody else on average, even if that family has sufficient socioeconomic resources. The U.S.-born or U.S.-raised children can readily fight back if they feel that their immigrant parents are imposing on them old-world norms and values that are at odds with those of American mainstream. In the Chinese immigrant community, there are specific ethnic social structures, in the form of nonprofit and for-profit institutions, in support of education. Next, I describe a growing ethnic system of supplementary education composed of Chinese language schools and a range of for-profit ethnic institutions serving young children and youth from immigrant families.

Chinese Language Schools

Chinese language schools have been an integral part of the ethnic community in the Chinese Diaspora worldwide. In the United States, Chinese language schools date back to the late 1880s.[4] Just like other ethnic language schools in the immigrant German, Scandinavian, Jewish, and Japanese communities, Chinese language schools initially aimed to preserve language and cultural heritage in the second and succeeding generations (Acherman, 1989; Beatty, 1995; Harada, 1934; Onishi, 1948; Shimada, 1998; Svensrud, 1933). They were cultural institutions independent of the public school system and were often regarded as competing with rather than supplementary to a child's formal schooling (Leung, 1975). From the passage of the Chinese Exclusion Act of 1882 to the outbreak of World War II, most Chinese immigrants were confined to Chinatowns and so were Chinese language schools. As an old saying goes, "Wherever there is a visible Chinese enclave, there is at least one Chinese language school."

Chinese language schools before World War II were among the very few ethnic institutions serving children. According to earlier studies of Chinese language schools in San Francisco's Chinatown, early schools were mostly private and financed primarily by tuition ($4-$5 a month) or donations from churches, temples, family associations, and Chinese businesses. Each school was governed by a board consisting of mostly elite members from ethnic organizations and businesses in Chinatown (Fan, 1976; Fong, 2003; Foreman, 1958; Tom, 1941). Schools typically had 1-2 part-time teachers, instruction was in Cantonese, and classes were held daily for 3-4 hour in the evenings and Saturday mornings, usually in the basement of a teacher's home or in a room inside a family association building. Teachers were not certified in any formal way. Their pedagogical approaches typically emphasized cramming, spoon-feeding, or mechanical memorizing, which were popular teaching methods of the time in China. Before World War II, there were about a dozen Chinese language schools in San Francisco's Chinatown serving nearly 2,000 K-12 children, four in Los Angeles' Chinatown and at least one in New York and other major cities where the Chinese population was visibly present (Foreman, 1958; Ma, 1945; Tom, 1941).

Early Chinese language schools aimed primarily to train children to be proficient in Chinese language and culture and were thus perceived by mainstream America as competing with public education and inhibiting assimilation. There was some truth to such perceptions. Under legal and social exclusion, Chinatown's children attended segregated public schools during regular school hours on weekdays and spent many more hours after school, on weekends, and during summer vacations learning Chinese in ethnic language schools. Immigrant parents believed that proficiency in the Chinese language was more practical for their children than educational success in American schools, since their children's future options were limited to either returning to China or finding jobs in Chinatowns (Leung, 1975; Wong, 1988). Parents also believed that a strong Chinese identity and ethnic pride instilled in the children through Chinese cultural and moral teachings were necessary to help the children cope with racism and discrimination. Children attended Chinese language schools in their neighborhoods after regular school as a matter of course with little questioning. Even though most children lacked enthusiasm and interest, many of them did recognize the practical value of Chinese schooling, as their future prospects were largely limited to Chinatowns or China (Chun, 2004). Like other ethnic organizations in Chinatown, earlier Chinese language schools had very little contact with mainstream institutions and education in ethnic language schools was supplementary but *not* complementary to public schooling. In some sense, the findings from past research about the lack of effects or significantly negative effects of Chinese schooling on academic performance and physical and mental health of immigrant Chinese children seemed to have missed the point that public education and assimilation at that time were issues irrelevant to the excluded Chinese.

The repeal of the Chinese Exclusion Act in 1943 marked a new era for Chinese Americans. For the first time in history, immigrant Chinese and their offspring were legally allowed and encouraged to participate in American society. While Chinatowns still concentrated the majority of the Chinese in the United States, residential movements out of the enclave among those from more affluent families and among the upwardly mobile young adults grew into an irreversible trend. Chinese language schools, however, suffered from stagnant growth and even decline, as mainstream American society became more open to immigrant Chinese families and their children and put greater pressure on them to assimilate. The children, especially adolescents, started to question the necessity of Chinese schooling and the practical value of Chinese language proficiency. Their schoolteachers posed similar questions about Chinese learning and indirectly encouraged the children to break away from the ethnic language schools under the rationale that such ethnic education would place too much burden on their young minds and serve to confuse and ultimately impede their social and intellectual development. Indeed, some earlier studies designed from this rationale found that ethnic language school attendees were more likely than the nonattendees to show unfavorable outcomes such as sleepiness, eye strain, a lack of outdoor and leisure activities, low academic performance on standardized tests, a lack of leadership quality, and a double identity dilemma (feeling part Chinese, part American, but belonging to neither; Fan, 1976; Ma, 1945).[5] Other factors that caused Chinese language schools to decline included the aging of the teachers, who were mostly non-English speaking and slow to adjust to changes, the rigidity of the curriculum and teaching methods, residential dispersion, and the opening of various educational and vocational opportunities outside Chinatown. Thus, going to Chinese school became a burden on the child and a source of parent-child conflict. Yet, the children continued to attend Chinese language schools because their parents made them, but most dropped out by the sixth grade. Parents were ambivalent as well. While they wanted their children to learn English and excel in school, many feared that they would lose their children if their children became too Americanized.

A significant turning point in the development of Chinese language schools occurred in the late 1960s. The growth momentum continued in the 1980s and peaked in the mid-1990s as a direct result of phenomenal Chinese immigration. Between 1961 and 2000, nearly 1.5 million immigrants were admitted as permanent residents from China, Hong Kong, Taiwan, and other parts of the world. The new arrivals are no longer only the poor, uneducated peasants from villages of Canton that traditionally sent emigrants to the United States. Many are cosmopolitan urbanites, college-educated professionals, skilled workers, and independent entrepreneurs. Upon arrival in the United States, a majority of them manage to bypass Chinatowns to settle directly in more affluent outer areas or suburbs in traditional gateway cities as well as in new multiethnic, immigrant-dominant suburban municipalities. The latter have been referred to as "ethnoburbs" (Li, 1997). Today, more than half of the Chinese immigrants live in suburbs and those who remain in Chinatowns have shrunk in relative numbers. For example, less than 3% of Los Angeles' ethnic Chinese population lives in Chinatown as of 2000.

The openness in mainstream American society does not automatically guarantee desirable outcomes of economic mobility and social integration. Decades of legal exclusion, social isolation, discrimination, and persistent racial stereotyping have left the Chinese with practically one feasible channel—public education. Whereas children's education was never an issue for survival in a society full of bachelors and sojourners, it has now become an urgent and central issue for the immigrant family and the entire ethnic group. As immigrant families and the ethnic community redefine their goals, the ethnic community and its social and cultural institutions are simultaneously transformed to meet new demands. Consequently, the past 30 years have witnessed a revival and rapid growth of ethnic institutions in Chinatowns and new Chinese ethnoburbs.

Contemporary Chinese language schools are registered as nonprofit ethnic organizations. These language schools have evolved to a much broader range of functions beyond language and culture to facilitate, rather than compete with, children's education (Fong, 2003; Lai, 2000, 2001, 2004; Leung, 1975). The 1995 survey conducted by the National Council of Associations of Chinese Language Schools (NCACLS) counted a total of 634 registered Chinese language schools in the United States (223 in California) with 5,542 teachers serving 82,675 K-12 students (Lai, 2004; Wang, 1996). Even though the number of Chinese language schools has not changed much in Los Angeles' Chinatown, the number in Chinese ethnoburbs in San Gabriel Valley and other suburbs in Los Angeles' metropolitan area has increased exponentially (Fong, 2003). As of the summer of 2006, Southern California Council of Chinese Schools listed 106 member schools: 7 in the City of Los Angeles (3 in Chinatown) and 88 in Los Angeles's suburbs.[6]

Unlike traditional Chinese language schools, contemporary Chinese language schools are afterschools, offering ethnic language instruction as well as a range of elective classes, such as Chinese Geography and History, Chinese painting and calligraphy, Chinese and western style chess, crafts, cartoon, music and performing arts, computer, basketball and badminton, kung fu, lion and dragon dance, and Chinese cooking and cuisine. Some schools, those in Chinatown or Chinese ethnoburbs in particular, run classes 7 days a week, from 3:00 to 6:30 p.m. daily after regular school hours and half-a-day on weekends. The majority of the suburban schools are weekend schools, using space in local public schools or churches. Students usually spend 2 hours on Chinese language learning and one or more hours on regular school homework or other selected specialties. Many schools also offer academic tutoring, standardized test preparation (e.g., SAT, SATII, AP, etc.), math and science drill, and special skill training seminars such as speech, classic poetry reading, debate, and leadership. For example, Thousand Oaks Chinese School, founded in an affluent white suburb northwest of Los Angeles, started with just 8 students and one teacher in 1975 and has grown into a school of 560 students and 50 teachers in 2005 in its 30 language classes and 20 enrichment or cultural classes, ranging from SAT preparation for the Chinese subject test, calculation with an abacus, calligraphy, dancing, and ping pong. Some Chinese schools are accredited institutions for extra credits in Chinese language to fulfill the foreign language requirement in regular high schools. As nonprofit institutions, Chinese languages schools charge tuitions, ranging from a low of $150 per child per semester to a high of $450 and depend largely on parental volunteerism in fund raising and administration. Teachers are college-educated Chinese immigrants, who may or may not have prior teaching experience or teaching certification. They are recruited mainly through informal referrals within the ethnic network.

Each school has a Parent-Teacher Association (PTA), and parental involvement is expected. Suburban Chinese schools also organize a variety of parent-run activities for parents and adults, giving parents an option to stay in school rather than drive back and forth to drop off and pick up their children. These parent-run activities include a variety of seminars on parenting, doing business, real estate or other financial investments, and family financial management; information sessions on how to help children select Advanced Placement (AP) courses, prepare for standardized tests, and apply for colleges and college financial aid; and leisure classes such as t'ai chi chuan, chorus singing, and folk dancing.

Chinese schools in the United States at any given time enroll only about 10-25% of the school-age children (5-14-year-old) of Chinese ancestry (Lai, 2004). However, most of the children of Chinese immigrants have been to a Chinese school or a Chinese language class at some point in their preteen years. In fact, "going to Chinese school" is a common Chinese American experience.

For-Profit Educational Institutions: Afterschool Tutoring, Academic Drill, College Preparation, and Enrichment

The development of Chinese language schools has also paralleled the rapid development of for-profit ethnic afterschool institutions geared solely toward educational achievement and college admissions since the late 1980s, such as *buxiban and kumon*, academic cram schools, college preparatory centers, and enrichment programs, as well as early childhood intellectual development programs. The *Southern California Chinese Consumer Yellow Pages* listed 135 academic afterschool tutoring establishments, including *buxibans* and *kumons*, 50 art schools/centers, 90 music/dancing studios, and 14 daycare and preschools (*California Chinese Consumer Yellow Pages*, 2004). There are also hundreds of private home afterschools not listed in phone directories. Many of these unlisted home afterschools are run by stay-at-home mothers who take care of three to five children of the same ages as their own children, which can be found in the advertisement section of nationally circulated or local Chinese language newspapers.

These private afterschools have been incorporated into the region's burgeoning Chinese enclave economy. Like other Chinese ethnic businesses, they concentrate in Chinatown and Chinese ethnoburbs in Los Angeles' San Gabriel Valley. They vary in scale, specialty, quality, and formality, ranging from transnational enterprises with headquarters or branches in Taiwan and mainland China with highly specialized curricula and formal structures to one-person or mom-and-pop operations that are more informal and less structured. Some of these private institutions offer comprehensive academic programs like Chinese language schools but others tend to be highly specialized and have concrete objectives that are often more academically oriented than linguistically oriented. For example, many private institutions offer English, math, chemistry, physics tutoring, and intensive drilling courses that aim solely to help children perform better in formal schools, even though some of the instruction or tutoring may be bilingual. Thus, their core curricula are supplementary to, rather than competing with, the public school curricula. These for-profit programs are also embedded in nonprofit Chinese language schools as well as in other ethnic organizations serving immigrants, such as family, kin, and district associations and churches. Like nonprofit Chinese schools, teachers may or may not have prior teaching experiences and are recruited through informal co-ethnic network. But for some specialized programs, such as those tutoring SAT verbal, writing, and English skills, these institutions would prefer recruiting non-Chinese certified teachers who are teaching at formal schools. Programs with certified teachers from formal schools tend to be the most expensive. Unlike nonprofit Chinese schools, for-profit institutions often do not require parental involvement and do not have programs for parents.

Students enrolled in ethnic afterschools are almost exclusively Chinese from immigrant families of varied socioeconomic backgrounds. Daily programs tend to draw students who live nearby, while weekend programs tend to draw students from both the local community and elsewhere in greater Los Angeles. Driving through the commercial corridor of Monterey Park, Alhambra, and San Gabriel, the growing Chinese ethnoburbs east of Los Angeles, one can easily see the flashy bilingual signs of these establishments, such as "Little Harvard," "Ivy League School," "Stanford-to-Be Prep School," "IQ180," "Hope Buxiban," "Little Ph.D. Early Learning Center" (a preschool), and "Brain Child" (a daycare center).

Major Chinese language newspapers, such as the *Chinese Daily News*, *Sing Tao Daily*, and *China Press*, publish weekly education editions with success stories, educational news and commentaries, and relevant information, such as standardized tests' schedules, high school and college ranking, application deadlines of major schools, programs, and tests. For-profit institutions also place advertisements in the Chinese language newspapers (Zhou & Cai, 2002). Chinese language advertisements are targeted more to the parent than to the child, making such promises as to "bring out the best in *your* child," "turn *your* child into a well-rounded superstar," and "escort your child into *your* dream school" [emphases added] as well as to "improve your test scores by 100 points" and "open the door to UC admission." Many Chinese youth whom I interviewed agreed that going to a Chinese school or a Chinese-run *buxiban* or *kumon* program had been a shared experience of being Chinese American, even though they generally disliked the fact that they were made to attend these ethnic institutions by their parents (Zhou & Kim, 2006; Zhou & Li, 2003). Unlike nonprofit Chinese language schools, for-profit institutions rarely offer seminars and activities for parents. However, parents become acquainted with one another during brief drop-off or pick-up times.

As the ethnic system of supplementary education takes root in the Chinese immigrant community, offering various academic and cultural enrichment programs and afterschool care, the children of Chinese immigrants are drawn by community forces into an ethnic social environment with ample resources in support of the mission that "every student is a success."

Intangible Benefits, Costs, and Trade-offs

Tangible resources, in terms of availability and access, offered by the ethnic systems of supplementary education seem obvious. There are intangible benefits too. Nonprofit and for-profit ethnic institutions do not merely provide educationally relevant services supplementary to public education but also serve as a locus of social support and control, network building, and social capital formation.

First, the ethnic system of supplementary education provides an important physical site where formerly unrelated immigrants (and parents) come to socialize and rebuild social ties. Reconnecting with co-ethnics often helps ease psychological and social isolation associated with uprooting. Even though parental interaction occurs mostly during drop-off and pick-up times or in parent-run activities, these brief moments are important for the formation of co-ethnic ties. These co-ethnic ties may not be strong ties but they nonetheless serve as bridge ties that connect immigrants to, rather than isolate them from, the mainstream society by making their social life richer and more comfortable.

Second, the ethnic system of supplementary education serves as an intermediate ground between the immigrant home and American school, helping immigrant parents—especially those who do not speak English well—learn about and navigate the American education system and make the best of the system in serving their children even when they are unable to get involved personally in formal schools and their PTAs. Through these ethnic institutions, immigrant parents are indirectly but effectively connected to formal schools and are well informed about specific factors crucial to their children's educational success. They also readily exchange valuable information about child rearing and share success stories or failure lessons. Such co-ethnic interaction reaffirms the educational goal of the immigrant family while putting pressure on, and even creating competition among, parents. In this sense, social capital arising from participation in Chinese language schools, afterschools, and other ethnic institutions is extremely valuable in promoting academic achievement by offering an alternative for parental involvement.

Third, the ethnic system of supplementary education fosters a sense of civic duty in immigrants who are often criticized for their lack of civic participation in mainstream U.S. society. In nonprofit institutions, many parents volunteer their time and energy for tasks ranging from decision making to fundraising to serving as teaching assistants, event organizers, chauffeurs, security guards, and janitors. Parents also take the initiative in organizing community events such as ethnic and American holiday celebrations.

The intangible benefits for children are also multifold. First, Chinese language schools and other relevant ethnic institutions offer an alternative space where children can express and share their feelings of growing up in immigrant Chinese families. A Chinese schoolteacher we interviewed said:

> It is very important to allow youths to express themselves in their own terms without any parental pressures. Chinese parents usually have very high expectations of their children. When children find it difficult to meet these expectations and do not have an outlet for their frustration and anxiety, they tend to become alienated and lost on the streets. But when they are around others who have similar experiences, they are more likely to let out their feelings and come to terms with their current situation.

Second, these ethnic institutions provide unique opportunities for immigrant children to form different peer networks, giving them greater leverage in negotiating parent-child relations at home. In immigrant families, parents are usually more comfortable and less strict with their children when they hang out with co-ethnic friends. This is because they either know the parents or feel that they can communicate with co-ethnic parents if things should go wrong. When children are doing things that would cause their parents anxiety, they can use their co-ethnic friendship network as an effective bargaining chip to avoid conflict. In the case of interracial dating, for example, a Chinese girl may simply tell her mother that she will be studying with so-and-so from

Chinese school (whose parents are family friends), while spending time with her non-Chinese boyfriend.

Third, these ethnic institutions nurture ethnic identity and pride that may otherwise be rejected by the children because of the pressure to assimilate. In ethnic language schools and other ethnic school settings, children are exposed to something quite different from what they learn in their formal schools. For example, they read classical folk stories and Confucian sayings about family values, behavioral and moral guidelines, and the importance of schooling. They listen to or sing ethnic folk songs, which reveal various aspects of their cultural heritage. Such cultural exposure reinforces family values and heightens a sense of ethnic identity, helping children to relate to their parents' or their ancestor's "stuff" without feeling embarrassed. More important, being part of this particular ethnic environment helps alleviate bicultural conflicts that are rampant in many immigrant families. Many children we interviewed, especially the older ones, reported that they did not like being made to go to these ethnic institutions and to do extra work but that they reluctantly did so without rebelling because other co-ethnic children were doing the same. As Betty Lee Sung (1987) observed in her study of immigrant children in New York City's Chinatown, bicultural conflicts are

[M]oderated to a large degree because there are other Chinese children around to mitigate the dilemmas that they encounter. When they are among their own, the Chinese ways are better known and better accepted. The Chinese customs and traditions are not denigrated to the degree that they would be if the immigrant child was the only one to face the conflict on his or her own. (p. 126)

However, the ethnic effect is by no means uniformly positive. Overemphasis on educational achievement comes with costs. Tremendous pressure on both children and parents for school achievement can lead to intense intergenerational conflict, rebellious behavior, alienation from the networks that are supposed to assist them, and even withdrawal from formal schools. Alienated children easily fall prey to street gangs and are also vulnerable to suicide. Ironically, pressures and conflicts in a resourceful ethnic environment can also serve to fulfill parental expectations. Children are motivated to learn and do well in school because they believe that education is the only way to escape their parents' control. This motivation, while arising from parental pressure and being reinforced through their participation in the ethnic institutions, often leads to desirable outcomes.

What are the trade-offs? Chinese immigrants perceive education as the only feasible means of social mobility that would yield observable returns. They tend to be extremely pragmatic and realistic about what to do and what not to do. The trade-off is often viewed as a sacrifice that not only parents but also children are expected to make. A nonprofit program organizer summed it up in these words:

> Well, tremendous pressures create problems for sure. However, you've got to realize that we are not living in an ideal environment. Without these pressures, you would probably see as much adolescent rebellion in the family, but a much *larger* [emphasis in tone] proportion of kids failing. Our goal is to get these kids out into college, and for that, we have been very successful.

For the majority, expected outcomes seem well worth the sacrifice. But for a small minority, undesirable outcomes, such as depression, running away, and even suicide, can be devastating to families. It should also be noted that access to the ethnic system of supplementary education is more restricted for working-class families than for middle-class families in the Chinese immigrant community. While Chinese language schools are accessible and for-profit afterschool programs have varied price tags and are thus affordable to most families, high-quality academic and specialized enrichment programs tend to be more expensive and less affordable for working-class families. Many high-quality private *buxibans*, college preparatory schools, music and dance lessons, and other enrichment programs, which rival mainstream institutions such as the Princeton Review and Kaplan, are extremely expensive. However, a high demand for afterschool services from immigrant parents' with higher than average SES and high rates of self-employment in the immigrant community stimulate new business opportunities for prospective co-ethnic entrepreneurs aiming at serving working-class immigrant families. When working-class families are exposed to this kind of informal setting where education becomes a basic need, they are under pressure to provide for their children's education in the same way as they do for their children's food and clothing.

Concluding Remarks: Lessons From the Immigrant Chinese Experience

This chapter aims to address the question of whether it is culture or structure that promotes the educational achievement of immigrant children. Existing quantitative data and anecdotal evidence show that the children of Chinese immigrants, even those from poor immigrant families and attending inadequate inner-city schools, are doing exceptionally well in school and that they fare better than other native-born racial groups, including whites. One explanation for their success leans on the cultural influence of Confucianism while the other focuses on immigration selectivity. This case study of the ethnic system of supplementary education in the Chinese immigrant community shows that "culture" and "structure" intersect to create an ethnic social environment promoting school success.

The Chinese case is unique in several significant ways, and each indicates the culture-structure interaction.[7] First, the Confucian value on education adapts to contemporary mobility aspirations and expectations to affect educational practices in China and immigrant Chinese families in the United States. In present-day China, a good college education is viewed as the single most important means to upward social mobility. Many families, urban families in particular, are doing everything possible and necessary to ensure that their children eventually get into prestigious universities. Since the best educational opportunities are relatively scarce, aspiring college-bound students must compete with one another through the annual national college entrance examination. Often times, students only have one chance to take this exam; as a popular saying suggests, "*one* exam [the national college entrance exam] determines a child's future." Consequently, a family's educational drive is geared almost entirely toward academic outcomes to the neglect of the subtleties and intricacies in a child's learning process and often at the expense of the child's well-rounded development. Meanwhile, a wide range of private *buxibans*, exam cram schools, enrichment programs, and English language programs emerge to fill the growing demand, serving preschoolers and K-12 graders. Some preschool child development centers for 2 to 5-year-olds even have rigorous academic curricula, including math, Chinese, English, music and dance, and are staffed with foreigner experts. These homeland practices and afterschool institutions are believed to be effective and thus get transferred into America, as Chinese immigrants strive to push their children to success in school.

Second, immigrant selectivity, which draws a tremendous amount of human capital and financial resources, and structural barriers, which deter many highly educated and economically resourceful immigrants from assimilating into the mainstream American economy, combine to boost the growth of the Chinese enclave economy. As the demand for educational services from Chinese immigrant families grows, various nonprofit and for-profit institutions emerge to form an ethnic system of supplementary education. Once the ethnic system of supplementary education takes root, it further stimulates new demands for more and better services; hence the rise of an ethnic social environment in which educational values are reaffirmed and tangible resources conducive to school success are easily accessible.

Third, the visibility of a co-ethnic middle class in the Chinese immigrant community provides role models as well as opportunities for co-ethnic interaction across class lines. Unlike traditional immigrant enclaves that concentrate new arrivals of low-SES backgrounds and native racial ethnic minorities, contemporary Chinese immigrant communities tend to grow in suburbs (or ethnoburbs) and comprise immigrants of varied SES backgrounds. Even in inner-city Chinatowns where poor and low-SES immigrant families tend to concentrate, there is a significant presence of co-ethnic middle-class members who go there on a regular basis to work, do business, shop, or entertain, and participate in various activities of the ethnic institutions. The co-ethnic middle class serves two main functions. On the one hand, the sheer presence of a disproportionately large number of highly educated professionals, particularly those who have been incorporated into the mainstream American economy, provides role models to show that education would pay off. On the other hand, the return of middle-class co-ethnics, who are residentially assimilated, to the ethnic enclave provides opportunities for mixed-class interaction. Social ties formed from mixed-class co-ethnic interaction tend to transcend class boundaries to become instrumental bridge ties, which heightens the significance of Bourdieu's conception of social capital. That is, social capital consists of not only products of embedded social networks or relationships, but processes that reproduce access, or lack of access, to power and resources.

Several lessons may be drawn from the Chinese American experience. First, the Chinese case suggests that informal social settings are as important as, if not more important than, formal social settings such as schools to affect children's educational achievement. Within the Chinese immigrant community, a well-established Chinese system of supplementary education makes available and accessible resources in helping promote and actualize the educational value. However, there is a lack of institutional mechanisms within the ethnic system of supplementary education to deal with problems, especially intergenerational conflicts, mental stress, depression, and excessive peer pressures from unhealthy competition. There is also a lack of interconnectedness between these ethnic educational institutions and other nonprofit social service organizations already existing in the community. Moreover, the utility of ethnic resources and social capital may be effective only to a certain point, that is, to ensure that immigrant children graduate from high school and get into prestigious colleges. But beyond high school, these ethnic resources may become constraining. For example, many children of Chinese immigrants tend to concentrate in science and engineering not only because their families want them to do so but also because their co-ethnic friends are doing so. After graduating from college, they often lack the type of social networks that facilitate their job placement and occupational mobility. In these respects, there is much room for improvement in the existing ethnic systems of supplementary education.

Second, the ethnic Chinese system of supplementary education is not easily transferable to other ethnic or immigrant minority groups because of variations in immigration histories, group-level socioeconomic characteristics, patterns of incorporation and community organization, and host society reception. While it is unrealistic to expect other minority groups to follow suit, it may be possible to open up ethnic resources to non-co-ethnic members through greater interethnic cooperation and public assistance. For example, nonprofit interethnic organizations can help make available educationally relevant afterschool services, particularly for-profit services, provided by ethnic Chinese to other Asian and Latino immigrants who are likely to share the same locale. The state can provide financial assistance to families in need to access private afterschool services.

Third, ethnic entrepreneurship in the area of education may offer an alternative path to publicly funded afterschool programs. As the Chinese case shows, nonprofit organizations and for-profit organizations are interconnected to foster informal social settings conducive to education. The state should continue to improve existing afterschool programs while also providing incentives to potential entrepreneurs to develop private afterschools and other educationally related programs (such as tutoring, music, sports, etc.), especially in disadvantaged neighborhoods.

In summary, the Chinese ethnic system of supplementary education may not be a direct causal factor for the extraordinary educational achievement of the children of Chinese immigrants but it does provide an informal social setting in which educationally relevant resources are both available and accessible. This kind of informal social setting is not necessarily intrinsic to a specific culture of origin. Rather, it results from the culture-structure interaction, which is unique to a national-origin group's migration selectivity, premigration SES, the strength of a preexisting ethnic community, and the host society's reception. Most immigrant families, Chinese and non-Chinese alike, place high value on education and consider it the most important path to upward social mobility. However, value cannot be actualized without the support of the family *and* the ethnic community. But the ability of the family and that of the ethnic community to influence children vary by national origins and generations. National-origin groups that constitute a significant middle class with valuable resources (i.e., education, job skills, and financial assets) upon arrival in the United States have a leg up in the race to move ahead in their new homeland, while others lacking group resources trail behind. Educators and policymakers should be careful not to attribute school success or failure merely to culture, or to structure, but to the culture-structure interaction.

Notes

This chapter draws material from the author's published work in "Ethnic language schools and the development of supplementary education in the immigrant

Chinese community in the United States," *New Directions for Youth Development: Understanding the Social Worlds of Immigrant Youth*, Winter 2003, pp. 57-73 (coauthored with Xiyuan Li) and "Community forces, social capital, and educational achievement: The case of supplementary education in the Chinese and Korean immigrant communities," *Harvard Educational Review*, 76, 2006, pp. 1-29 (coauthored with Susan Kim).

1. I draw on the conception of supplementary education developed by Gordon and his colleagues to frame my study of ethnic organizations serving youth and children (Gordon et al., 2005).

2. Contexts of exit and reception are group-level measures (Portes & Rumbaut, 2006). Variables for contexts of exit may include premigration socioeconomic characteristics (education, occupation, income, etc.), homeland educational practices, and conditions of exit (regular or undocumented migrant status, refugee status, etc.). Variables for contexts of reception may include government policy toward a specific national origin or ethnic group, public attitude, and the organization of the preexisting co-ethnic community.

3. The data on which this chapter is based are drawn from multiple sources: (a) I extract relevant data from a multisite ethnography of immigrant neighborhoods in Los Angeles, in which Chinatown was selected as one of the main research sites. In this study, neighborhood-based ethnic institutions (including nonprofits, for-profit establishments, and other locally based social structures) were closely observed and face-to-face or phone interviews were conducted to examine how social organization at the neighborhood level affects immigrant children's school adaptation. Relevant data include intensive field observations in ethnic language schools, private afterschools, and educational institutions as well as interviews with ethnic language schools' principals, parents, and adolescent participants in Chinatown. (b) I use data from two other ethnographic case studies: a weekend Chinese language school in a white middle-class suburb west of Los Angeles and a private afterschool in a Chinese ethnoburb east of Los Angeles. (c) I conducted content analyses of Chinese language newspapers or other media accounts, advertisements, and curricular materials. The ethnic newspapers circulating in the Chinese immigrant community heavily advertise the academic schools such as the SAT prep schools as well as the language schools during the beginning of the school year. In addition, there are sections in the newspapers that cover education related topics on a weekly basis. Some of the articles in the education sections are translations of what has been published by the *Los Angeles Times* or popular mainstream magazines such as *Newsweek* on such topics as best U.S. colleges, college admissions guidelines, admission rates, graduation rates, and so forth. Thus, content analysis gives me a unique viewpoint of what kind of information has been available to the Chinese immigrant community when it comes to education and how ethnic institutions are interacting with individuals involved in them.

4. Some noted that Chinese language schools dated as far back as the late 1840s, at the time when Chinese laborers started to arrive in the United States in large numbers (Wang, 1996).

5. These same studies also found favorable outcomes among Chinese school attendees, in terms of general health, posture, nutrition, and grade point averages.

These conflicting results imply that Chinese schooling is complex leading to multidimentional outcomes. I also suspect that the association between Chinese school attendance and the lack of leadership quality may have been spurious.

6. Compiled by the author from the Southern California Council of Chinese Schools' Web site: http://scccs.com/member/MemWeb.htm (viewed on July 31, 2006). The numbers do not include the less structured, private and weekend Chinese language classes.

7. Now in the United States, only the Korean immigrant community presents a comparable ethnic system of supplementary education (Bhattacharyya, 2005; Zhou & Kim, 2006).

References

Acherman, W. I. (1989). Strangers to the tradition: Idea and constraint in American Jewish education. In A. S. Himmerlfarb & S. D. Pergola (Eds.), *Jewish education worldwide: Cross cultural perspectives* (pp. 71-116). New York: University Press of America.

Allen, B. A., & Boykin, A. W. (1992). African American children and the educational process: Alleviating cultural discontinuity through prescriptive pedagogy. *School Psychology Review, 21*(4), 586-596.

Anyon, J. (1997). *Ghetto schooling: A political economy of urban educational reform.* New York: Teachers College Press, Teachers College, Columbia University.

Beatty, B. (1995). *Preschool education in America: The culture of young children from the colonial era to the present.* New Haven: Yale University Press.

Bhattacharyya, M. (2005). Community support for supplementary education. In E. W. Gordon, B. L. Bridglall, & A. S. Meroe (Eds.), *Supplementary education: The hidden curriculum of high academic achievement* (pp. 249-272). Denver: Rowman and Littlefield.

Boykin, A. W., & Allen, B. A. (1991). The influence of contextual factors on Afro-American and European-American children's performance. *International Journal of Psychology, 26*(3), 373-387.

Carter, P. L. (2005). *Keepin' it real: School success beyond black and white.* New York: Oxford University Press.

Chinese Consumer Yellow Pages. (2004). *Southern California Chinese consumer yellow pages.* Rosemead, CA: Chinese Consumer Yellow Pages.

Chun, Gloria Heyung. (2004). Shifting ethnic identity and consciousness: U.S.-born Chinese American youth in the 1930s and 1950s. In J. Lee & M. Zhou (Eds.), *Asian American youth: Culture, identity and ethnicity* (pp. 113-141). New York: Routledge.

Fan, C. Y. (1976). The Chinese language schools of San Francisco in relation to family integration and cultural identity. Unpublished doctoral dissertation, Duke University.

Fernandez-Kelly, M. P. (1995). Towanda's triumph: Social and cultural capital in the transition to adulthood in the urban ghetto. *International Journal of Urban and Regional Research, 18*(1), 89-111.

Fong, J. C. (2003). *Complementary education and culture in the global/local Chinese community.* San Francisco: China Books and Periodicals.

Fordham, S. (1996). *Blacked out: Dilemmas of race, identity, and success at Capital High*. Chicago: University of Chicago Press.

Fordham, S., & Ogbu, J. U. (1986). Black students' school success: Coping with the "burden of 'acting White.'" *Urban Review, 18*, 176-206.

Foreman, H. S. (1958). *A study of Chinese language schools*. Unpublished master's thesis, San Francisco State College.

Fukuyama, F. (1993). Immigrants and family values. *Commentary, 95*, 26-32.

Gordon, E. W., Bridglall, B. L., & Meroe, A. S. (Eds.). 2005. *Supplementary education: The hidden curriculum of high academic achievement*. Lanham: Rowman & Littlefield Publishers.

Harada, K. G. (1934). *A Survey of Japanese language schools in Hawaii*. M.A. thesis, University of Hawaii.

Kohl, H. (1994). *"I won't learn from you" and other thoughts on creative maladjustment*. New York: New Press.

Kozol, J. (2005). *The shame of the nation: The restoration of apartheid schooling in America*. New York: Crown Publishers.

Lareau, A. (2003). *Unequal childhoods: Class, race, and family life*. Berkeley: University of California Press.

Lai, H. M. (2000). Retention of the Chinese heritage: Language schools in America before World War II. *Chinese America: History and perspectives, 2000*. San Francisco: Chinese Historical Society of America.

Lai, H. M. (2001). Retention of the Chinese heritage: Language schools in America, World War II to present. *Chinese America: History and perspectives, 2000*. San Francisco: Chinese Historical Society of America.

Lai, H. M. (2004). *Becoming Chinese American: A history of communities and institutions*. Walnut Creak: AltaMira Press.

Leung, E. K. (1975). *A sociological study of the Chinese language schools in the San Francisco Bay Area*. Unpublished doctoral dissertation, University of Missouri, Columbia.

Lewis, O. (1966). The culture of poverty. *Scientific American, 215*(4), 19-25.

Li, W. (1997). *Spatial transformation of an urban ethnic community from Chinatown to Chinese ethnoburb in Los Angeles*. Unpublished doctoral dissertation, University of Southern California.

Ma, Y. Y. (1945). *Effects of attendance at Chinese language schools upon San Francisco children*. Unpublished doctoral dissertation, University of California, Los Angeles.

Ogbu, J. U. (1974). *The next generation: An ethnography of education in an urban neighborhood*. New York: Academic Press.

Ogbu, J. U., & Simon, H. D. (1998). Voluntary and involuntary minorities: A cultural-ecological theory of school performance with implication for education. *Anthropology and Educational Quarterly, 29*, 155-188.

Olsen, L. (1997). *Made in America: Immigrant students in our public schools*. New York: The New Press.

Onishi, K. (1948). *A study of the attitudes of the Japanese in Hawaii toward Japanese language schools*. M.A. thesis, University of Hawaii.

Portes, A., & MacLeod, D. (1996). The educational progress of children of immigrants: The roles of class, ethnicity, and school context, *Sociology of Education, 69*(4), 255-275.

Portes, A., & Rumbaut, R. (2006). *Immigrant America: A portrait* (3rd ed). Berkeley, CA: University California Press.

Scribner, S., & Cole, M. (1973). Cognitive consequences of formal and informal education. *Science, 182*(4112), 553-559.

Shimada, N. (1998). Wartime dissolution and revival of the Japanese language schools in Hawaii's: Persistence of ethnic culture. *Journal of Asian American Studies, 1*(2), 121-151.

Steinberg, L. (1996). *Beyond the classroom: Why school reform has failed and what parents need to do.* New York: Simon & Schuster.

Sue, S., & Okazaki, S. (1990). Asian American educational achievement: A phenomenon in search of an explanation. *American Psychologist, 45*, 913-920.

Svensrud, M. (1933). Attitudes of the Japanese toward their language schools. *Sociology and Social Research, 17*(Jan-Feb), 259-271.

Suarez-Orozco, C., & Suarez-Orozco, M. M. (2001). Children of immigration. *Harvard Educational Review, 71*(3), 599-602.

Sung, B. L. (1987). *The adjustment experience of Chinese immigrant children in New York City.* New York: Center for Migration Studies.

Tom, K. F. (1941). Functions of the Chinese language schools. *Sociology and Social Research, 25*, 557-561.

Varenne, H., & McDermott, R. (1998). *Successful failure: The school America builds.* Boulder, CO: Westview Press.

Wang, X. (1996). *A view from within: A case study of Chinese heritage community language schools in the United States* (Monograph series). National Foreign Language Center, Johns Hopkins University, Baltimore.

Wilson, W. J. (1996). *When work disappears: The world of the new urban poor.* New York: Vintage Books.

Wong, S. C. (1988). The language situation of Chinese Americans. In S. L. McKay & S. C. Wong (Eds.), *Language diversity: problem or resource?* (pp. 193-228). New York: Newbury House.

Xie, Y., & Goyette, K. A. (2004). *The American People, Census 2000: A demographic portrait of Asian Americans.* New York: Russell Sage Foundation Press & Washington, DC: Population Reference Bureau.

Xiong, Y. S., & Zhou, M. (2005). Selective testing and tracking for minority students in California. In D. J. B. Mitchell (Ed.), *California policy options.* Los Angeles: UCLA Lewis Center.

Zhou, M. (2004). Are Asian Americans becoming White? *Context, 3*, 29-37.

Zhou, M., Adefuin, J., Chung, A., & Roach, E. (2000). *How community matters for immigrant children: Structural constraints and resources in Chinatown, Koreatown, and Pico-Union, Los Angeles.* Project final report. Berkeley, CA: California Policy Research Center.

Zhou, M., & Cai, G. (2002). The Chinese language media in the United States: Immigration and assimilation in American life. *Qualitative Sociology, 25*, 419-440.

Zhou, M., & Kim, S. S. (2006). Community forces, social capital, and educational achievement: The case of supplementary education in the Chinese and Korean immigrant communities. *Harvard Educational Review, 76*(1), 1-29.

Zhou, M., & Li, X. (2003). Ethnic language schools and the development of supplementary education in the immigrant Chinese community in the United States. In C. Suarez-Orozco & I. L. G. Todorova (Eds.), *New directions for youth development: Understanding the social worlds of immigrant youth* (pp. 57-73). San Francisco: Jossey-Bass.

PART IV

CHANGING LARGER SOCIAL STRUCTURES

Chapter 14
Socioeconomic School Integration

RICHARD D. KAHLENBERG

Forty years ago, James Coleman's massive study, *Equality of Educational Opportunity*, found that the single most important predictor of a student's academic achievement is his or her family's socioeconomic status and the second most powerful predictor is the socioeconomic status of the student population in the school he or she attends. Coleman's findings have been replicated repeatedly in the research literature and continue to hold up today (Coleman, 1966; Kahlenberg, 2001, pp. 25-35). Virtually, everything that educators talk about as desirable in a school—high standards and expectations, good teachers, active parents, a safe and orderly environment, a stable student and teacher population—is more likely found in economically mixed schools than in high-poverty schools.

However, efforts to shape the social setting of the school—through student assignment policies influencing the socioeconomic status of the student body—have largely been taken off the education reform table for decades. Instead, liberals have called primarily for increasing resources spent on education; conservatives have backed changes in school governance, such as private school vouchers and charter schools; and centrists have backed standards-based reform. Socioeconomic school integration—the logical policy step that flows from Coleman's research and its progeny—has been mostly off the radar screen. The wars over compulsory busing for racial desegregation in the 1970s have understandably left policymakers wary of the political implications of promoting any kind of school integration.

Very recently, however, there are some signs of change. With new pressure to close the racial and economic achievement gaps under the federal No Child Left Behind Act of 2001, a small but growing number of school districts have begun trying to create the optimal economic mix of students in public schools through alternatives to compulsory busing. This chapter will (a) describe the research underlying socioeconomic school integration programs; (b) offer a theory on how to create economic integration in schools; (c) articulate the ingredients of successful socioeconomic integration plans; (d) describe how to measure the degree of economic school integration and its success or failure; (e) outline exemplars of efforts to create economic school integration; and (f) consider the current status of the literature and promising future directions.

The Research Underpinning Programs of Economic School Integration

All students—rich, poor, white, black, Latino, and Asian—perform at higher academic levels in schools with strong middle-class populations than they do in high-poverty schools. Research consistently suggests that although it is possible to make schools with high concentrations of poverty work—we all know of such individual schools—it is extremely uncommon. A recent study by Professor Douglas Harris of University of Wisconsin for example, found that middle-class schools (those with less than 50% of students eligible for free and reduced-price lunch) are 22 times as likely to be consistently high performing as high-poverty schools (those with 50% or more of students eligible for subsidized lunch) (Harris, 2006).

Middle-class schools perform better in part because middle-class students on average have access to better health care and nutrition, and they come to school better prepared (Rothstein, 2004). But the vastly different educational environments, typically found in middle-class and high-poverty schools, also have a profound effect on achievement. On the 2005 National Assessment of Educational Progress (NAEP) given to fourth graders in math, for example, low-income students attending more affluent schools scored substantially better (239) than low-income students in high-poverty schools with 75% or more low income (219). This 20-point difference is the rough equivalent of 2 years learning. Indeed, *low-income* students who are given a chance to attend more affluent schools performed more than half a year better, on average, than *middle-income* students who attend high-poverty schools (231) (National Center of Education Statistics [NCES], 2006). At the high-school level, similar results are found. In 2005, for example, Professor Russell Rumberger and his colleague Gregory J. Palardy from the University of California found that a school's socioeconomic status had as much impact on the achievement growth of high-school students as a student's individual economic status (Rumberger & Palardy, 2005).

Why does it matter whether a child attends a middle-class or high-poverty school? While money matters a great deal in education, people matter more. Consider the three main sets of actors in a school: students, parents, and faculty (teachers and principals). Research suggests that students learn a great deal from their peers, so it is an advantage to have classmates who are academically engaged and aspire to go on to college. Peers in middle-income schools are more likely to do homework, less likely to watch TV, less likely to cut class, and more likely to graduate—all of which have been found to influence the behavior of classmates. Middle-class schools report disorder problems half as often as low-income schools, so more learning goes on. It is also an advantage to have high achieving peers, whose knowledge is shared informally with classmates all day long. Middle-class peers come to schools with twice the vocabulary of low-income children, for example, so any given child is more likely to expand his or her vocabulary in a middle-class school through informal interaction (Kahlenberg, 2001, pp. 50-58).

Parents are also an important part of the school community, and research finds that it is an advantage to attend a school where parents are actively involved, volunteer in the classroom, and hold school officials accountable. Research repeatedly finds that middle-class parents are more likely to be involved in schools. Not having to work three jobs and having a car makes it easier to help out, and it is not surprising that in middle-class schools parents are four times as likely to be members of the parents teachers association (PTA) (Kahlenberg, 2001, pp. 62-64).

Finally, research finds that the best teachers, on average, are attracted to middle-class schools. Nationally, teachers in middle-class schools are more likely to be licensed, to be teaching in their field of expertise, to have high teacher test scores, to have more teaching experience, and to have more formal education. Generally, teachers consider it a promotion to move from poor to middle-class schools, and many of the best teachers transfer into middle-income schools at the first opportunity. Moreover, teachers in middle-class schools are more likely to have high expectations. Research has found that the grade C in a middle-income school is equivalent to the grade A in a low-income school, that is, on standardized tests, students receiving As in high-poverty schools score at the same level as students receiving Cs in middle-class schools. Middle-class schools are also more likely to offer Advanced Placement (AP) classes and high-level math (Kahlenberg, 2001, pp. 67-74).

It is important to note that research finds that socioeconomic school integration is a more powerful lever for raising academic achievement than racial integration per se. Racial desegregation raised black achievement in certain areas (like Charlotte, North Carolina, where middle-class whites and low-income blacks were integrated) but not in others (like Boston, where low-income whites and low-income blacks were integrated). Research finds that the academic benefits of racial desegregation came not from giving African American students a chance to sit next to whites but from giving poor students of all races a chance to attend predominantly middle-class institutions (Kahlenberg, 2001, pp. 35-37).

At the same time, socioeconomic integration often produces a fair amount of racial integration, which has important societal benefits, apart from the question of academic achievement. Racial school integration can produce more tolerant adults and more enlightened citizens in our democracy. African American students are more likely to be low incomed than white students, and they are far more likely to attend high-poverty schools than whites. Segregated African American schools are five times more likely to be poverty concentrated schools than segregated white schools, so breaking up concentrations of poverty may yield a substantial racial integration dividend (Orfield & Lee, 2006). A study by Duncan Chaplin of the Urban Institute found that integrating poor and nonpoor students results in 55.6% as much black/white integration as poor/nonpoor integration at the district level. If integration occurs at the metropolitan level, 79.9% as much black/white integration occurs as poor/nonpoor integration (Chaplin, 2002). Research involving socioeconomic integration in Wake County (Raleigh), North Carolina found that 2 years after the district moved from a policy of racial integration to a policy of socioeconomic integration in 2000, 63.3% of schools remained racially desegregated compared with 64.6% of schools under the racial policy (Flinspach & Banks, 2005).

Are middle-class children hurt by attending economically mixed schools? The research suggests that sprinkling a few middle-class kids into a school of highly concentrated poverty will likely hurt their academic achievement, but as long as a majority of the students are middle class (not eligible for free and reduced-price lunch), middle-class student achievement does not decline with the presence of some low-income students. Studies find that integration is not a zero sum game, in which gains for low-income students are offset by declines in middle-class achievement. This is true in part because the majority set the tone in a school, and because research finds that middle-class children are less affected by school influences (for good or ill) than low-income children (Kahlenberg, 2001, pp. 37-42).

A Theory of How to Create Economic School Integration Through Controlled Public School Choice

For many years, policymakers have employed three basic alternatives for student assignment, none of which is fully satisfactory in achieving socioeconomic school integration. One option is a system of neighborhood schools, in which students are assigned to the school that is geographically closest to their home. Given high levels of residential segregation, by socioeconomic status and race, the neighborhood school option usually results in high levels of school segregation.

A second option, pursued to dismantle racial segregation in the 1970s and 1980s, relied on compulsory school busing. Students were mandatorily assigned to schools, in often distant neighborhoods, with the goal of achieving a racial mix at the schools found at the end of the bus ride. Compulsory busing gave little say to parents about their child's schooling, and it often accelerated white and middle-class flight from public school systems. Today, compulsory busing is mostly a thing of the past, and in many jurisdictions even proponents of busing are disappointed with the degree of actual integration produced.

A third option, which seeks to avoid the segregation of neighborhood schools on the one hand and white and middle-class flight on the other, is the use of "magnet schools." These schools, usually located in distressed neighborhoods, draw upon not only the local population of students but also upon middle-class white student populations who choose to travel to the schools for their distinctive educational offerings (e.g., a Montessori school or a math/science theme). Magnet schools are often effective in creating economic and racial integration, but they give rise to a new inequality: Resources are expended on a relatively small number of special schools that are often superior to the regular system of public schools attended by the vast majority of students.

To avoid the pitfalls of these three options, Charles Willie of Harvard University and Michael Alvesl, a private consultant formerly associated with Brown University, devised a fourth option, known as "controlled public school choice," in which *all* schools in a district are "magnetized," taking on distinctive themes or pedagogical approaches (Willie & Alves, 1996). In these districts, there are no neighborhood schools; instead, all parents choose from a variety of offerings, ranking their preferences. The use of universal choice is important because it not only avoids the inequality between magnets and nonmagnets, but also avoids problems of stratification that arise under systems in which middle-class parents tend to actively exercise choice while low-income parents tend to "choose not to choose." Under controlled public school choice, the school district honors parental choices with an eye to ensuring that the schools are also integrated within a certain percentage point range of the socioeconomic balance of the school district as a whole (Table 14.1).

Ingredients of Successful Socioeconomic Integration Plans

There are several ingredients that distinguish highly successful socioeconomic integration plans using controlled choice from less successful plans as outlined in the following subsections.

Table 14.1. Alternatives for Student Assignment

Policy Advantages	Neighborhood Schools	Compulsory Busing	Magnet Schools	Controlled Choice
Consciously seeks to integrate schools	No	Yes	Yes	Yes
Seeks to reduce white middle-class flight	Yes	No	Yes	Yes
Provides a systemwide approach to student assignment	Yes	Yes	No	Yes

Create Incentives for Middle-Class Families to Engage in Socioeconomic Integration

Some parents may choose to send their children to economically integrated schools because they believe that their children will benefit from exposure to diversity, but experience suggests many more will need additional incentives. When La Crosse, Wisconsin, sought to integrate its schools socioeconomically by changing the boundaries between schools, there was very strong resistance from some members of the community, who generated a great deal of political turmoil. Middle-class parents with political clout found the new policy disadvantageous for their own children and hence had little affirmative reason to embrace the plan. The school board that enacted the policy was recalled, and the superintendent's job was in jeopardy. (Over time, as children became accustomed to socioeconomically integrated schools and thrived in them, a pro-integration school board was returned to power, and the superintendent's position became secure, Mial, 2002.)

In Cambridge, Massachusetts, in contrast, integration policies (initially centering around race and subsequently around socioeconomic status) lured middle-class families into integrated schools (indeed back into the public school system as a whole) through a system of magnet schools that offered distinctive pedagogical approaches and themes (Fiske, 2002). Cambridge magnetized all of the schools in the early 1980s and the public schools saw a 32% increase in new white students and a 13% increase in new minority students over 4 years. The overall share of school-aged students attending public schools rose from 75% to 88% over a 6-year period (Wells & Crain, 2005). Likewise, Wake County, North Carolina was successful in attracting waiting lists of middle-class families, when it turned virtually all the schools in the city of Raleigh into magnet schools (Kahlenberg, 2006; Silberman, 2002).

Successful magnet schools offer the basic curriculum to all students—reading, math, and the like—but on top of the basic academic program offer a plus. That plus can come in the form of a pedagogical approach (Montessori, Multiple Intelligence, multiage classrooms) or a theme (math/science, the arts). The point is not that any particular magnet theme would be attractive to everyone—it will not be—but that it will be attractive to some significant number of families in the community because it fits the individual needs of their children.

Some parents might like a "Core Knowledge" School associated with the theories of educator E. D. Hirsch, Jr. who emphasizes learning broad swaths of academic material; an Essential School associated with the theories of educator Theodore Sizer, who emphasizes in-depth knowledge of a smaller number of topics; or a Multiple Intelligences School associated with the theories of educator Howard Gardner, who says each person has eight intelligences—linguistic, logical-mathematical, spatial, musical, bodily kines-thetic, interpersonal, intrapersonal, and naturalistic—and that conventional schools tend to ignore several of these. A Montessori school, with its emphasis on active learning and multiage class groupings, might be attractive to some families, whereas a school which emphasizes the environment and outdoor activities might be attractive to others.

Involve Key Stakeholders

Socioeconomic school integration works best when there is strong community support from key sectors, including teachers, parents, and community leaders. In La Crosse, Wisconsin, teachers were instrumental in pushing for socioeconomic school integration because they knew they could do their jobs more effectively if concentrations of poverty were not allowed to persist. Teachers went to principals, who went to the superintendent, who went to the school board to enact the policy. Teachers were an important source of support for socioeconomic integration when the plan came under political attack from others (Mial, 2002).

Successful socioeconomic integration plans also involve parents. In setting up a system of magnet schools, a number of communities have used surveys of parents in the community to find out what sorts of schools would be attractive to them (U.S. Department of Education, 2004). If a survey suggests that parents are especially enthusiastic about a Montessori elementary school, one should be established as an option. The survey can also be used to help marry socioeconomic integration and choice. If a Montessori school proves especially attractive among upper-middle-class parents, for example, the school can be located in an economically distressed community to draw in part from the local student population and in part on more affluent families willing to travel for the special program offered.

In addition, successful districts involve the larger community in setting up a system of magnet schools and pursuing socioeconomic integration plans. School districts can tap into local resources—like hospitals, museums, and colleges—which might form partnerships with magnet schools. And the business community, which has a strong stake in attracting employees to an area through good schools and which relies on the public schools to produce its future workers, is often a source of support for integration plans. Business leaders know that employees need to get along with people from different backgrounds and that segregated schools do not generally bring out the full potential of low-income students. Business officials have often been the key champions of integrated schooling (Freivogel, 2002; Mial, 2002; Silberman, 2002).

Adjust Magnet Offerings Depending on Demand

Successful socioeconomic integration plans are dynamic and adjust the magnet school offerings depending on consumer demand. In most school systems, some magnet schools are likely to be overchosen year after year and others may be underchosen. The oversubscribed schools should be franchised. Families, who might turn to private school because a public school with an arts focus is continually oversubscribed, for example, should be offered the chance to attend a second newly created arts school. Over time, severely underchosen schools that have failed to attract families should be closed and reopened with a more desirable program. For school boards that face inevitable community outrage whenever schools need to be closed, or whenever boundaries are changed, it is desirable to have an objective way to make decisions about closing schools; those that are most underchosen are the least justified in staying open.

Provide Free Transportation and Good Information to Parents

Successful universal magnet programs provide reasonable transportation free of cost to students. Failing to provide free transportation effectively denies choice to lower income families. Likewise, successful programs ensure that parents are well informed about the choices available. Special outreach is made to low-income communities through a variety of community organizations, social service agencies, parents' groups, and religious congregations in the community to educate parents about their options and help them mobilize to have a strong voice in school district matters.

Make Bus Rides Manageable

Long bus rides are not good for children, and they are potentially disastrous to the political viability of socioeconomic integration programs. In jurisdictions that cover large geographic areas, complete choice among all of a district's schools would mean excessively long bus rides for students. To avoid this problem, successful socioeconomic integration programs divide districts into smaller zones within which students are given a menu of school options. The zones are drawn to be demographically balanced so that even within smaller geographic areas, the chances for socioeconomic integration are maximized.

Admit Students to Magnets by Lottery, With Priorities to Walkers, Siblings, and Those Who Contribute to Economic Diversity

Although magnet school applicants should generally be admitted by lottery, successful systems build in three priorities: for walkers, for siblings, and for students who will contribute to the economic diversity in a school.

Most people agree that a family which lives across the street from (or in close proximity to) a school should receive a priority in admissions. Likewise, it is better not to break up families into different schools, so siblings should be given a priority. For the reasons outlined earlier, steps should also be taken to create a healthy economic mix at all schools to ensure that magnets contribute to socioeconomic integration rather than further segregation.

Although some school districts have long provided a priority in school assignment based on a student's race, there are two reasons to focus on a student's socioeconomic status. Most importantly, the drivers of academic achievement are keyed to the economic mix in a school, not to the racial mix per se. Moreover, there are legal complications to using race in student assignment. In June 2007, the U.S. Supreme Court struck down policies using race in student assignment in Louisville, Kentucky and Seattle, Washington. Although there are serious legal problems associated with using race, there are no similar obstacles to considering a student's socioeconomic status. Even the most conservative Supreme Court justices have indicated that although the use of race by government officials is subject to "strict scrutiny" by courts, government actors can use socioeconomic status as long as there is a "rational basis" for doing so—a far easier standard to meet.

Avoid Within-School Segregation

There is some evidence that within racially and economically diverse school buildings, classrooms are sometimes "resegregated" through tracking and ability grouping. The solution to this problem is complicated, and there is a sensible middle ground between systems of complete tracking and universally heterogeneous groupings. Many educators come down in the middle, in favor of ability grouping in some classes (e.g., math but not civics) and in some grades (middle and high schools but not elementary school). The Japanese, for example, have no ability grouping in the early grades but a great deal of it in the upper grades. Research suggests that such ability grouping should be fluid, so that students who are ready to move up to a more challenging group are permitted to do so; and it should be carefully calibrated, so that a student who is slow in reading but fast in math is placed appropriately in both classes, rather than being rigidly tracked into honors or general education path across the board. Strong protections must be put in place to avoid grouping that reflects racial or economic class bias.

Employ Effective Teaching Techniques for Heterogeneous Populations

There is a growing body of research suggesting that in schools with heterogeneous achievement groups, the old-fashioned teacher lecturing will not work well. Instead, research suggests that cooperative learning—in which students work in heterogeneous groups and help teach one another—is more effective. Evidence confirms that the best way to learn is to teach: to explain a concept to others requires a higher level of understanding. Indeed, Uri Treisman has found that the greater reliance of Chinese American students on study groups at Berkeley helps explain the group's relative academic success in math (Treisman, 1992).

It is also important that in socioeconomically integrated schools, all students, including those from low-income families, be made to feel welcome. Research has found that students may perform poorly if they are concerned about fulfilling a negative stereotype about a group of which they are a part (Steele, Spencer, & Aronson, 2002). In order to be successful, districts pursuing socioeconomic school integration have to examine some of the new research identifying ways to avoid the problem of "stereotype threat" and ensure that students experience the opposite phenomenon: a classroom marked by "identity safety" (Davies, Spencer, & Steele, 2005).

Use Interdistrict School Choice When Necessary

Controlled choice is normally employed within a single school district. But given the evidence, outlined earlier, that student performance may decline in schools with populations greater than 50% low income, interdistrict public school choice makes sense in certain cases. In some jurisdictions (about 14% nationally), it will be impossible to get to the goal of 50% or more middle-class student populations in every school because the entire district student population is majority low income. But high-poverty districts are often surrounded by more affluent suburban districts. Nationally, roughly 60% of students are middle class, and creative efforts to integrate schools across existing school district lines can be pursued. Today, an estimated 500,000 students cross school district lines each day through interdistrict public school choice programs. Relatively few of these are involved in programs of socioeconomic integration, but the willingness of parents to send their children to schools outside their district highlights the inherent attraction of good schools in an environment where choice is permitted (Kahlenberg, 2006).

How to Measure the Degree of Economic Integration in Schools

There are many ways to measure the socioeconomic diversity of a school, a district, or a given region within a district, but the most commonly used indicator is eligibility for free and reduced-price meals. Under the federal school lunch program, students from families making less than 185% of the poverty line are eligible for free or reduced-price meals. In the 2007-2008 school year, the cutoff for subsidized lunch is an annual income of $38,203 for a family of four. Other measures of socioeconomic status are available. In pursuing socioeconomic integration, San Francisco schools, for example, ask applicants about such factors as their mother's educational background. But free and reduced-price meals eligibility is the most readily available socioeconomic indicator and requires no new collection of data from parents. Students who are eligible for subsidized lunch are considered "low income," whereas those not eligible for free or reduced-price lunch are considered "middle class."

At the middle- and high-school level, subsidized lunch data are sometimes considered less reliable than at the elementary school level because some students fear being stigmatized for participating in the program. In such cases, some school districts use as a criterion—whether a student has *ever* received free or reduced-price lunch in his or her public schooling.

One other question arises: Should individual *classrooms* be measured by free and reduced lunch percentages? It seems reasonable to keep track of such data as a way of monitoring against bias. Enormous differences among different classrooms within schools raise a red flag of potential bias. But in general, there is more reason to permit reasonable variations in economic diversity by classroom than by school. A student who works hard and wins a place in the highest academic track should not be penalized in the name of proportional economic balance. By contrast, "tracking" by school building—where students from low-income families are sent to entire schools where expectations are held low—is far more difficult to justify because no student can be said to have "earned" the right to attend a particular nonselective school.

Ultimately, the success or failure of a school district's socioeconomic integration plan will be measured by the degree to which it improves outcomes in traditional indicators such as academic achievement, graduation rates, and adult earnings. But there are several proximate mediators of the effects of socioeconomic integration on achievement. We might want to know the degree to which students are more or less academically engaged (e.g., changes in truancy and suspension rates). Likewise, what is the effect of socioeconomic integration on PTA membership, the number of hours that parents volunteer in schools, and the like? What is the effect of socioeconomic integration on teacher turnover rates and the ability of the school district to attract and retain highly qualified teachers (measured by teacher test scores, experience, and education credentials)? What is the effect on teacher expectations of students and on the rigor of the curriculum employed?

Exemplars of Efforts to Create Economic School Integration

Nationally, a growing number of districts are pursuing policies of socioeconomic school integration, breaking up concentrations of poverty and giving more students a chance to attend economically mixed schools. In the 1990s, there were only a couple of districts pursuing socioeconomic integration; today, there are about 40 districts that use socioeconomic status as a factor in student assignment. The list includes districts that are urban and suburban, southern, northern, eastern, and western: from Wake County (Raleigh), North Carolina to San Francisco, California; from La Crosse, Wisconsin to Cambridge, Massachusetts; from St. Lucie County, Florida to Rochester, New York and to San Jose, California. In all, more than 2.5 million students live in school districts with some form of socioeconomic integration plan in place, up from 20,000 students in 1999 (Kahlenberg, 2007). (See also Appendix for list of school districts pursuing socioeconomic integration.)

Cambridge, Massachusetts is perhaps the best example of a jurisdiction using controlled choice to achieve socioeconomic integration. In Cambridge, all K-8 schools have been designated as magnet schools. Parents rank their preferences among schools, and the district honors choices in a way to ensure that all schools are within ±10% points of the system's average eligibility for free and reduced-price lunch. In Cambridge, school officials have managed to honor both economic integration and parental choice, with some 90% of families receiving one of their first three choices of schools (Fiske, 2002).

Wake County, North Carolina, which includes the city of Raleigh and the surrounding suburbs in a single district, uses an extensive system of magnet schools in Raleigh to reach its goal that no school has more than 40% of students eligible for free and reduced-price lunch or more than 25% reading below grade level. In Wake County, low-income and minority students perform better than low-income and minority students in other North Carolina districts that fail to break up concentrations of poverty. On the 2005 High School End of Course exams, for example, 63.7% of low-income students in Wake County passed compared with 48.7% in Durham County, 47.8% in Guilford County, and 47.8% in Mecklenburg County (Kahlenberg, 2006).

The Current Status of the Literature and Promising Future Directions

The policy of economic school integration rests on a well-established solid base of empirical research on the negative consequences of concentrated school poverty and the positive effects of racial and economic school integration. Going forward, research should focus on case studies of the fledgling movement of school districts specifically pursuing socioeconomic integration, assessing the effects of the programs on achievement and detailing the way in which political obstacles were surmounted.

Advocates of private school vouchers have poured many millions of dollars into studies of the practice (many of which show, to the chagrin of supporters, negligible academic gains). A comparable effort is needed to evaluate socioeconomic school integration, a practice that is far more likely to be found successful.

Research would seek to provide further evidence on several important questions. How cost-effective are socioeconomic school integration experiments in raising student achievement compared with other reforms (e.g., reducing class size)? At precisely, what point does the rising presence of low-income students in a school begin to hurt the academic achievement of middle-class students? Does socioeconomic diversity enrich classroom discussions for all students as supporters hypothesize?

In addition, further research is needed on the politics of socioeconomic school integration. Instituting a policy of socioeconomic integration requires heavy political lifting, and there has been some opposition in every jurisdiction that uses the program. How have school officials addressed political resistance to socioeconomic integration in various districts? What are the most effective ways for magnet schools and controlled public school choice to be used to achieve "buy in" from middle-class families who might be fearful of integration? What are the best pedagogical techniques available for teaching in economically mixed classrooms? How can "identity safety" for low-income students be maximized?

A consortium or network of school districts pursuing socioeconomic school integration might be an important vehicle for this research. Today, individual districts come to the idea of socioeconomic integration largely on their own, and each finds itself reinventing the wheel. A consortium for socioeconomic school integration, modeled after a group such as the Minority Student Achievement Network, might provide an opportunity for districts to share best practices and commission carefully designed research to measure the costs and benefits of socioeconomic integration to student achievement.

No district has found it easy to get past the community opposition to socioeconomic integration, and yet none has been able to learn from the experience of other districts, except through individual opportunistic contacts. Examples of best, and worst, practices are accumulating rapidly with no institution to collect and organize them. By the same token, a track record of effects on achievement is accumulating with inadequate scientific data collection efforts and scholarly analysis.

Policymakers have long known that changing the school setting for children through socioeconomic integration represents a promising alternative for narrowing the academic achievement gap between economic and racial groups and making better use of the untapped talents of low-income and minority students. There is now, for the first time in many years, a growing chance to study communities engaged in changing those settings through a system of controlled public school choice rather than compulsory busing. It remains to be seen whether researchers will capitalize on this opportunity.

Appendix: School Districts Pursuing Socioeconomic Integration

A. Districtwide socioeconomic plans
Cambridge School District, Massachusetts (6,103)
Christina School District, Wilmington, Delaware (19,364)
Coweta County Public School District, Georgia (19,685)
La Crosse School District, Wisconsin (7,300)
McKinney Independent School District, Texas (19,743)
Moorpark United School District, California (7,773)
Rochester City School District, New York (34,000)
San Jose Unified School District, California (31,874)
St. Lucie County Public School District, Florida (34,786)
Wake County School District, North Carolina (109,424)
Williamsburg-James County School District, Virginia (9,402).

B. Socioeconomic status used as a factor in student assignment to some of the schools
Austin Independent School District, Texas (79,707)
Baltimore Public School District, Maryland (108,523)
Berkeley Unified School District, California (8,904)
Brandywine Public School District, Delaware (10,602)

Charles County School District, Maryland (25,610)
Charlotte-Mecklenburg Public School District, North Carolina (114,071)
Clark County Public School District, Nevada (270,607)
Duval County Public School District, Florida (128,023)
Eugene Public School District, Oregon (18,207)
Fresno Unified School District, Florida (80,760)
Greenville County Public School District, South Carolina (64,245)
Guilford County Public School District, North Carolina (66,971)
Hamilton County Public School District (Chattanooga), Tennessee (40,655)
Manatee County School District, Florida (40,006)
Manchester School District, Connecticut (7,800)
Miami-Dade Public School District, Florida (369,223)
Montgomery County Public School District, Maryland (139,311)
New York City Public Schools: Community School Districts 10, 13, 14, 15, 20 and 21, New York (206,151)
Omaha Public School District, Nebraska (46,035)
Palm Beach County School District, Florida (169,381)
Portland Public School District, Oregon (44,169)
Proviso Township High Schools, Illinois (4,852)
Rock Hill Public School District of York County, South Carolina (16,179)
Rutherford County/Murfreesboro School District, Tennessee (32,959)
San Francisco Unified School District, California (56,236)
Seminole County Public Schools, Florida (21,457)
South Orange-Maplewood Public School District, New Jersey (6,559)
Springdale Public School District, Arkansas (13,678)

References

Chaplin, D. (2002). Estimating the impact of economic integration of schools on racial integration. In *Divided we fail: Coming together through public school choice—Report of The Century Foundation Task Force on the common school.* New York: The Century Foundation Press, 2002.

Coleman, J. S. (1966). *Equality of educational opportunity.* Washington, DC: U.S. Government Printing Office.

Davies, P. G., Spencer, S. J., & Steele, C. M. (2005). Clearing the air: Identity safety moderates the effects of stereotype threat on women's leadership aspirations. *Journal of Personality and Social Psychology, 88,* 276-287.

Fiske, E. B. (2002). Controlled choice in Cambridge, Massachusetts. In *Divided we fail: Coming together through public school choice—Report of The Century Foundation Task Force on the common school.* New York: The Century Foundation Press, 2002.

Flinspach, S. L., & Banks, K. E. (2005). Moving beyond race: Socioeconomic diversity as a race-neutral approach to desegregation in the Wake County public schools. In J. C. Boger & G. Orfield (Eds.), *School Resegregation: Must the South Turn Back?* Chapel Hill, NC: University of North Carolina Press.

Freivogel, W. (2002). St. Louis: Desegregation and school choice in the land of Dred Scott. In *Divided we fail: Coming together through public school choice—report of The Century Foundation Task Force on the common school.* New York: The Century Foundation Press.

Harris, D. N. (2006). *Ending the blame game on educational inequity: A study of 'High Flying' schools and NCLB.* Education Policy Research Unit, Arizona State University.

Kahlenberg, R. D. (2001). *All together now: Creating middle-class schools through public school choice.* Washington, DC: Brookings Institution Press.

Kahlenberg, R. D. (2006). Helping children move from bad schools to good ones. *Security and Opportunity Agenda.* The Century Foundation. Retrieved November 15, 2007, from www.tcf.org/list.asp?type=PB&pubid=565

Kahlenberg, R. D. (2007). *Rescuing Brown v. Board of Education: Profiles of Twelve Districts Pursuing Socioeconomic School Integration.* The Century Foundation. Retrieved November 5, 2007, from http://www.tcf.org/list.asp?type=PB&pubid=618

Mial, R. (2002). La Crosse: One school district's drive to create socioeconomic balance. In *Divided we fail: Coming together through public school choice— Report of The Century Foundation Task Force on the common school.* New York: The Century Foundation Press, 2002.

National Center of Education Statistics. (2006). *Condition of education, 2006.* Washington, DC: U.S. Department of Education.

Orfield, G., & Lee, C. (2006). *Racial transformation and the changing nature of segregation.* Cambridge, MA: The Civil Rights Project at Harvard University.

Rothstein, R. (2004). *Class in schools: Using social, economic, and educational reform to close the Black-White achievement gap.* Washington, DC: Economic Policy Institute.

Rumberger, R. W., & Palardy, G. J. (2005). Does segregation still matter? the impact of student composition on academic achievement in high school. *Teachers College Record, 107*(9), 1999-2045.

Silberman, T. (2002). Wake County schools: A question of balance. In *Divided we fail: Coming together through public school choice—Report of The Century Foundation Task Force on the common school.* New York: The Century Foundation Press, 2002.

Steele, C. M., Spencer, S., & Aronson, J. (2002). Contending with group image: the psychology of stereotype and social identity threat. In M. Zanna (Ed.), *Advances in Experimental Social Psychology, 34,* 379-440.

Treisman, U. (1992, November). Studying students studying calculus. *College Mathematics Journal, 23,* 362-372.

U.S. Department of Education. (2004). *Creating successful magnet school programs.* Washington, DC: Government Printing Office.

Wells, A. S., & Crain, R. L. (2005). Where school desegregation and school choice policies collide. In J. T. Scott (Ed.), *School choice and diversity: What the evidence says* (pp. 59-76). New York: Teachers College Press.

Willie, C., & Alves, M. (1996). *Controlled choice: A new approach to school desegregated education and school improvement.* Providence, RI: Education Alliance Press and the New England Desegregation Assistance Center, Brown University.

Chapter 15

The Co-Construction of Educational Reform: The Intersection of Federal, State, and Local Contexts

AMANDA DATNOW

This chapter begins by offering a theory of how district, state, and federal contexts shape the success of educational reform efforts at the school level. As I will demonstrate, the connections among these contextual levels are important, as they give some insight into why policies developed at "higher" levels of the system may or may not be implemented as intended when they reach the local level.

More specifically, I will expand on what colleagues and I have called the "co-construction" theory of reform implementation (see Datnow, Hubbard, & Mehan, 2002 for a full explanation of the theory). Explanations for the roots of variation in implementation and how to study it tend to be influenced by two dominant approaches: the technical-rational perspective and the mutual adaptation or what we extend and call a "co-construction" perspective (Snyder, Bolin, & Zumwalt, 1992).

The technical-rational perspective is the most extensively used approach for studying reform policy implementation. It operates on classical management theory, which places a premium on planning, organization, command, coordination, and control (Morgan, 1986). Many educational reforms originated by the U.S. government circa 1965 until 1980 (e.g., Follow Through, Education for All Handicapped Students, Vocational Education) exemplify this perspective. Following this line of thinking, the causal arrow of change travels in one direction—from active, thoughtful designers to passive, pragmatic implementers. This would exemplify what Elmore (1980) calls "forward mapping," noting that it is problematic because it assumes that policymakers control the organization, political, and technical processes that affect implementation.

Early studies of reform implementation that exemplify the technical-rational perspective include Hall and Loucks (1979) and Gross, Giaquinta, and Bernstein (1971). In these studies, implementation is measured according to an objectified standard: fidelity to the policy. The technical-rational perspective is more likely to see local variation in implementation as problematic or as a dilemma rather than as inevitable (Snyder et al., 1992). Organizational models of school improvement that developed in response to these technical-rational models do not suffice for understanding policy or reform implementation (Fullan, 1991; Louis, 1994). Because their focus is on school-level strategies for self-renewal and improvement, they downplay the actions that initiated reform and the governmental, community, and district actions that occurred away from and before the school attempted reform.

Later, context began to be seen as part and parcel of the school change process. The phrase "mutual adaptation" was first coined by Berman and McLaughlin (1978) in the Rand Change Agent Study to characterize this dynamic conception of context. Berman and McLaughlin argued that implementation should be seen as "a mutually adaptive process between the user and the institutional setting—that specific project goals and methods be made concrete over time by the participants themselves" (McLaughlin, 1976 cited in Snyder et al., 1992). As Berman and McLaughlin imply, not only was mutual adaptation inevitable, it was also desirable. Negotiation, flexibility, and adjustment on the part of educators and reform designers were keys to successful reform (Snyder et al., 1992).

In Datnow et al. (2002), we argue that reform is a co-constructed, conditional process or borrowing from Hall and McGinty (1997), "a web of interrelated conditions and consequences, where the consequences of actions in one context may become the conditions for the next" (p. 461).

We believe that formulating implementation as a co-constructed process coupled with qualitative research is helpful in making sense of the complex, and often messy, process of school reform. Even when policies are seemingly straightforward, they are implemented very differently across localities, schools, and classrooms (Elmore & Sykes, 1992).

Our theory also builds upon work in the sociocultural tradition, especially Rogoff (1995) and Tharp (1997) who identify personal, interpersonal, and community "levels" or "planes" of interaction and McLaughlin and Talbert (1993) who depict organizations as successively contextualized layers. We extend this work by explicitly calling attention to the political and economic conditions that enable possibilities and impose constraints on education in general and school reform in particular. Moreover, because contexts are inevitably connected to other contexts (Sarason, 1997), contexts throughout the social system must be considered (Datnow et al., 2002, p. 12).

Most studies that look across contextual levels take an *embedded* sense of context. If we were to take an embedded sense of context, we would assume that events at higher levels of the context occur first and are more important analytically. We might also assume that policies originating in "higher" levels of context cause or determine actions at lower levels. However, this may limit our understanding of educational reform, as we will explain. In the theory of co-construction, the causal arrow of change travels in multiple directions among active participants in all domains of the system and over time. This conceptualization makes the reform process flexible, with people who have "different intentions/interests and interpretations [and who] enter into the process at different points along the [reform] course. Thus many actors negotiate with and adjust to one another within and across contexts" (Hall & McGinty, 1997, p. 4). As with Elmore's (1980) "backward mapping" concept, we also do not assume that policy is the only, or even major, influence on people's behavior. Individuals at the local level do indeed make decisions that affect not only policy implementation, but sometimes also the policy itself (as we have seen with the amendments to No Child Left Behind [NCLB]). This emphasis upon multidimensionality marks the co-construction perspective of reform implementation and departs from the technically driven, unidirectional focus of the technical-rational perspective. We believe this approach is helpful in making sense of educational reform and the connections that exist between contextual levels (Datnow et al., 2002).

Data-Driven Decision Making: An Example of the Co-Construction of Reform

This chapter will bring to life the co-construction perspective of reform implementation, and specifically the connections among federal, state, district, and school levels, through an examination of a current reform movement, Data-Driven Decision Making (DDDM). This reform effort, in ideal circumstances, demonstrates the positive ways in which actors at various levels might successfully co-construct reform.

Background

With the advent of NCLB, the push for increased accountability and improved student achievement in U.S. schools has never been greater. The theory of action underlying NCLB requires that educators know how to analyze, interpret, and use data so that they can make informed decisions in all areas of education, ranging from professional development to student learning. When school-level educators become knowledgeable about data use, they can more effectively review their existing capacities, identify weaknesses, and better chart plans for improvement (Earl & Katz, 2005). DDDM is also critical to identifying and finding ways to close achievement gaps between white and minority students (Bay Area School Reform Collaborative, 2003; Olsen, 1997).

Previous research, though largely without comparison groups, suggests that DDDM has the potential to increase student performance (Alwin, 2002; Doyle, 2003; Johnson, 1999, 2000; Lafee, 2002; McIntire, 2002). A recent national study of the impact of NCLB reveals that districts are indeed allocating resources to increase the use of student achievement data to inform instruction in schools identified as needing improvement (Center on Education Policy, 2004). Student achievement data can be used for various purposes, including evaluating progress toward state and district standards, monitoring student progress, evaluating where assessments converge and diverge, and judging the efficacy of local curriculum and instructional practices (Crommey, 2000).

However, data need to be actively used to improve instruction in schools, and individual schools often lack the capacity to implement what research suggests (Wohlstetter, Van Kirk, Robertson, & Mohrman, 1997). Systems can play a key role in helping schools build the skills and capacity to use data for decision making. Summarizing findings across several major recent studies of school districts, Anderson (2003) writes:

> Successful districts in the current era of standards, standardized testing, and demands for evidence of the quality of performance, invest considerable human, financial and technical resources in developing their capacity to assess the performance of students, teachers and schools, and to utilize these assessments to inform decision-making about needs and strategies for improvement, and progress towards goals at the classroom, school, and district levels. (p. 9)

Quite simply, high performing districts make decisions based on data, not on instinct (Supovitz & Taylor, 2003; Togneri & Anderson, 2003).

Similarly, in the charter school arena, Education Management Organizations (EMOs) and Charter Management Organizations (CMOs) have also sought to build capacity in schools and districts, and several expressly utilize DDDM as one of their key pillars. It is not surprising that some EMOs and CMOs utilize DDDM, as this is a practice that has foundations in the field of business and management. EMOs and CMOs operate schools according to a specified school organization and instructional model (Colby, Smith, & Shelton, 2005).

Methods

As the above discussion suggests, using data to improve decision making is a promising systemic reform strategy. However, there is a dearth of rigorous research conducted thus far on this practice. Recently, the NewSchools Venture Fund in San Francisco set an agenda to help fill this research gap. In response to their agenda, we[1] conducted a qualitative case study of four high performing school systems to capture the details of data-driven instructional decision making. Our study included two mid-sized urban school districts and two nonprofit CMOs. These particular school systems were chosen on the basis of being leaders in using data for instructional decision-making, which seems to have led to improved student achievement over time. We chose exemplary districts/systems so that other school systems could potentially learn from the successes of their experiences in using data.

In collaboration with NewSchools, we chose these systems from a list of over 25 systems that had been recommended as fitting our criteria. We narrowed down the list of possible sites after reviewing system websites, speaking with experts in the field, and conducting phone interviews with system leaders. While acknowledging the successes they had experienced in becoming more data-driven, all system leaders also were careful to note that their work was "in progress."

Our study included the following four systems (Table 15.1):

These systems have obvious differences in size, history, and mission. Garden Grove and Aldine are mid-sized, urban public school districts that have been in operation for many years. Both have histories of steadily improving student achievement over the past decade. Aspire and Achievement First are relatively new organizations, the former having been founded in 1998 and the latter in 2003. They are both networks of charter schools that operate central offices that function as quasi-school districts, providing oversight in accounting, curriculum, governance, and organization. All four systems comprise primarily of schools in urban locations and/or those serving large numbers of low-income students and/or students of color.

Table 15.1.   Data Sources

System	Number of Schools	Location	Type
Garden Grove Unified School District	70	California	Regular public school district
Aldine Independent School District	63	Texas	Regular public school district
Achievement First	6	New York; Connecticut	Nonprofit charter management organization
Aspire Public Schools	14	California	Nonprofit charter management organization

We studied two schools in each of the four systems. These schools were recommended to us by system personnel because of their high level of engagement in DDDM. Our study included six elementary schools, one middle school, and one high school serving ninth graders only. The Appendix gives a detailed demographic picture of the schools and the systems.

Our site visits to the systems and schools took place between March and May, 2006. We interviewed two to three system/district administrators, including the superintendent, assistant superintendent (in three of the four systems) or chief academic officer, and the director of research and/or assessment. At each school, we interviewed the principal, often an assistant principal, and a minimum of five teachers across grade levels. We also interviewed lead teachers, where possible. We conducted approximately 70 interviews across the four systems and schools. At each school, we also conducted informal observations of the school and classrooms and relevant meetings. We also gathered a plethora of documents at the school and system levels that were pertinent to our study.

As our discussion will make clear, there is more than one way to be a data-driven system. Although there are some common features among them, all of the systems and schools approached DDDM differently—and all achieved successes in the process. I will attempt to highlight the choices and tradeoffs made by the systems and schools, as I flesh out the co-construction framework described earlier.

Conceptual Framework

Our study is guided by the co-construction framework in which federal and state accountability contexts and elements of the system context help to set the stage for data-driven practices at the school level. When we observe the movement towards DDDM, we see that schools, districts, states, and the federal government all have a role in co-constructing the success of this reform. See Figure 15.1 for a graphic representation of the framework.

Federal and State Context

As Figure 15.1 shows, the broader federal and state accountability policies that form the outermost box provide an important frame for the work that happens inside the box, namely at the system and school levels. The federal government holds states, districts, and schools accountable for student performance. States set curriculum standards and also hold schools and districts accountable. These policies help to provide what we call political leverage or what people in districts have called "air cover" for their efforts.

Although the crux of the work around data use takes place at the school and district levels, some district leaders pointed to NCLB as having provided

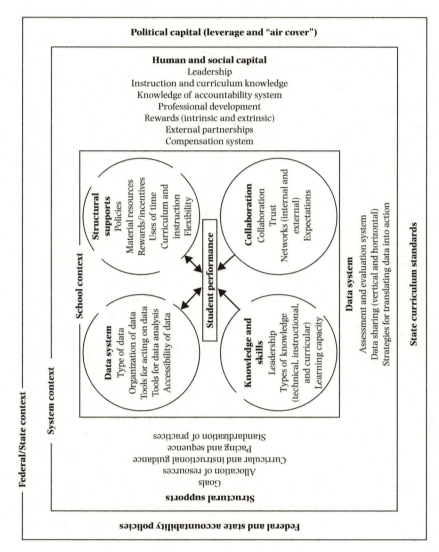

Figure 15.1. Conceptual Framework.

the political leverage they needed in order to stimulate improvement at the school level. All systems set goals that were strongly influenced by and tightly interwoven with state and federal accountability systems. As one principal stated, "Accountability is a strong force for change. It truly is the change agent." This fit well with district agendas. As one district administrator explained, she had long hoped to increase the use of assessment data to inform instructional decision making because she believed this would help teachers improve their practice and close achievement gaps. She explained: "Even if the state system goes away, and NCLB goes away, . . . this is going to stay in our district. We will create our own system because this is good and it's the way our kids get equal access to kids in more affluent areas."

Even though NCLB helped to catalyze change, school and district administrators and teachers also struggled with balancing the demands of NCLB with their other goals for student learning. Across the four school systems, teachers indicated dissatisfaction with current measures of student performance. In Achievement First schools, teachers expressed a desire for the system to move beyond quantifiable data gathered from tests to more qualitative data gathered informally. Educators in Aspire schools mentioned that they would like to see more sophisticated assessments for reading and math that were aligned with state tests; they would also like to have teachers engaged in more systematic data collection and analysis of student behavior as it relates to academic progress.

Educators across the four school systems also expressed the need to go beyond the demands of NCLB and state accountability systems, and integrate assessments that would measure critical thinking skills. At one Aldine school, for example, the staff hoped that the school system would move toward working more on higher-order thinking skills and developing assessments that required students to construct more open-ended responses. Similarly, the superintendent of Achievement First noted that interim assessments should be seen as "standards-plus." That is, they must include everything on the state standards but they could indeed include more. The challenge, however, as he explained, was to make sure that schools demonstrate consistent mastery of the standards before adding items that capture higher-level skills. He also noted that higher-level skills can be more difficult to measure.

In sum, while being a lever for change efforts in the districts, school and district leaders still struggled to figure out how to meet the demands of NCLB and their state assessments, while not narrowing their curriculum, assessments, and goals for student learning. Using the co-construction framework, one might say that although the policy mandates of NCLB and state accountability systems flowed in a downward direction to districts and schools, at the local level, educators attempted to find ways for NCLB to enhance their work. At the same time, they often bumped up against the limits of the narrowing of curriculum and student goals that could result if they focused only on NCLB.

District and School System Context

As we move to the system context box in Figure 15.1, we see important features of the district or school system context. First, there are the structural scaffolds that systems establish that help provide the conditions for DDDM at the school level. These include (a) the establishment of goals for student achievement and (b) the development of a system-wide curriculum. Establishing meaningful and challenging goals for student performance was a precondition to effective DDDM in all of the systems. The systems we studied approached goal setting in a number of different ways; however, all melded the need to meet larger accountability demands with goals tailored to the needs of their system. For most systems, taking the time and space to develop specific goals geared toward their needs ended up being a pivotal aspect of using data purposefully. Setting up system goals enabled school leaders to grapple and reflect on their history, their current progress, and future plans. Thus, goal setting was a critical step to beginning the process of continuous improvement.

The Garden Grove superintendent explained that their movement into DDDM began when they decided to focus on developing reasonable, objectively measurable goals. With the state's accountability system as leverage for change, Garden Grove School began to assess its strengths and weaknesses with regard to student achievement. The first strategy was to work on ensuring that the curriculum and instruction were aligned to the state standards. The district's administrative team began the next hurdle of establishing meaningful, measurable goals. As part of this process, they came to the realization that the team was ill-equipped and lacked the capacity to write strong goals. With the aid of a consultant from WestEd Regional Educational Laboratory, the district leadership underwent the process of developing and refining goals that spanned several years. In order to make appropriate goals, Garden Grove school district looked closely at past performance data. By doing so, they discussed what the superintendent described as "the big challenge"—the groups of students whose needs were being unmet by the district.

Criteria for the goals were set, including the requirement that they be meaningful and measurable at all levels: student, classroom, school, and district. Generalized objectives such as "all students become lifelong learners" were avoided because they did not enable the district to assess whether or not the goals were being met. Site administrators and teachers from schools representing all levels of the district were part of the final development and refinement process, hence jointly constructing the goals for students. All in all, it took 3 years before the goals were finalized and documented so they could be shared throughout the district.

The district now has two main goals: (a) All students will progress through the bands on the California Standards Test (CST) scores annually (e.g., if a student is performing at the "basic" level, he/she will perform at the "proficient" level within a year). Within 5 years, the district also expected all students to be performing at least at the proficient level. (b) All English language learners will progress through the California English Language Development Test (CELDT) levels annually. As evidence of the district's ability to maintain focus, all district and school staff members whom we interviewed were able to clearly articulate the goals.

DDDM was also greatly facilitated by clear, grade-by-grade, system-wide curriculum, high-quality materials aligned to the curriculum, and curriculum guides suggesting the breadth and depth of content to be taught. Both districts, Garden Grove and Aldine, had put into place system-wide curriculum, accompanied by a pacing plan and instructional materials. Implementation of the curriculum was closely monitored for several years before DDDM came to the forefront of their policy agendas. For example, Aldine developed a pacing plan in 1997 and framed it as "you're going to follow it, and it's non-negotiable." The plan follows the state standards and is divided into 6-week periods. At the same time, the district curriculum has flexibility built into to it. As a district administrator shared, "the text does not drive the curriculum, and you're not going to walk in and find everybody using the same things in the book at the same time." A teacher reinforced, "The district gives us lesson plans, but they don't tell us how to teach them."

The existence and implementation of a system-wide curriculum appeared to facilitate DDDM, as it allowed all teachers to be "on the same page," in their discussions on data about student learning. On the other hand, the tradeoff is less autonomy for teachers at the local level. As one teacher said, "Curricular and instructional alignment can be especially positive for new and lower-performing teachers, but sometimes the higher performing teachers almost feel hamstrung by it." Overall, however, the benefits appeared to outweigh the disadvantages, and system leaders were generally in agreement that a system-wide curriculum was essential to being data-driven. However, it seems that a balance could be struck, with a district plan that allowed for some flexibility.

The system also played a critical role in establishing effective, easy-to-use data management and assessment systems. Given the current federal and state accountability contexts, it is not surprising that most school systems can be considered "data rich." However, having data alone does not ensure the DDDM will take place. In order to conduct analysis and use data to create action plans, systems had to grapple with organizing data in an accessible format and presenting it a comprehensible manner. Therefore, systems had to figure out how to organize, prioritize, and manage data. Investing in a user-friendly data management system was among the most important actions systems took, in becoming more data-driven. Particularly for teachers and school site leaders, timely and useful reports of student achievement data on benchmarks and other assessments were integral to an effective data management system. Three of the four school systems in this study had data management systems (such as Data Director and EduSoft) that allowed them to easily run reports displaying student results on interim and state assessments and sometimes other assessments as well. Achievement First was the only system that required teachers to score the tests themselves and enter the data into a Microsoft Excel template. The template was then given to the principal, who compiled class- and school-level reports. Achievement First was in the process of developing a customized, automated system that would be used to score, store, and analyze benchmark assessment data.

As these systems asked more sophisticated questions related to their data, their tools for managing data needed to keep pace. Each school system struggled in its own way with integrating multiple types of data into one comprehensive management system because achievement data, student demographic information, report cards, and discipline data were typically organized separately from one another and in varying formats.

District and school leaders also indicated that they struggled with prioritizing the multitude of types of data that they were collecting. For example, one leader in the Aspire home office believed that the organization as a whole needed to have a broader conversation about how to manage and use data. In Aldine, the director of assessment mentioned that people had trouble discerning the importance of different types of data and identifying key information that made data interpretation difficult. Teachers in various school systems remarked that, given their access to a diverse array of data, they did not always know how to decide which data were most or least significant. Similarly, Garden Grove struggled with how to prioritize different data. The superintendent emphasized the importance of focusing on high-yield areas rather than trying to hit every target and missing them all. Thus, all of these school systems are grappling with using data appropriately, effectively, and efficiently.

For most systems, direct aid was provided to struggling teachers. In fact, leaders often believed that it was incumbent upon them to scaffold staff members who were uncomfortable accessing or utilizing data. Administrators might hand out hard copies of the electronic information until individuals became more adept at using the system. In some cases, the leadership team facilitated the use of data by breaking down data by grade level or by classroom as needed. Lead teachers/coaches might also conduct the analysis for teachers and then visit a teacher's classroom to model a lesson. One of Aldine's principals explains that "you have to take it step-by-step because if you don't you can send people over the edge, in terms of their motivation, of their self-confidence and burn them out." Therefore, leaders not only modeled high expectations and professional accountability, but also took responsibility to build DDDM capacity within their schools.

The system also played an important part in creating mechanisms for data sharing and for translating data into action. In concert with structuring, modeling, and scaffolding effective data discussions, systems supported schools by establishing time for teachers to learn from one another. One administrator observed that the key to making data relevant was the working relationships developed between staff because "without collaboration and the collegiality, data is impossible." Teachers heavily relied on one another for support, to learn new instructional strategies, and to help discuss data. In fact, every single participant stressed the importance of having built-in collaboration time as a crucial factor in developing mutual trust and sharing knowledge to improve practice. A common sentiment was that "you can't do it alone." Across many of our conversations with the teachers, "we do it together," was a common refrain.

Most of the school systems devoted frequent and substantial time to reviewing data and planning accordingly. Aldine and Aspire not only had weekly structured data discussion times, but teachers also had daily instructional planning time within grade levels or partner teams. Structured time for data discussions was probably the most important scaffolding for continuous improvement. Most schools had early dismissal for students one day a week in order to provide 2-3 hours of uninterrupted time for data discussions among grade-level teams. In Aspire schools, two meetings per month were devoted to grade-level team data discussions. Another meeting was set up for similar discussion between instructional coaches and teams. The last meeting of the month was used by the principal, leadership team, and coaches to look at data together to decide which teachers needed instructional support or which students needed intervention. All Aldine schools had at least weekly data-centered discussions among grade-level teams of teachers. The administrators considered instructional planning meetings to be "sacred," whereas the administrative meetings were scheduled with more flexibility.

The systems also helped to empower educators for DDDM at the school and district levels through building human and social capital. Professional development regarding data management systems and data use has been an important strategy for building people's capacity in all four systems. In addition to building capacity and creating structures to foster DDDM processes, systems also had to develop tools to help teachers and principals act on data. Although they differed in the degree of comprehensiveness of data sources and management of data, all systems were sensitive to providing immediate feedback on student achievement and progress toward goals presented in an accessible manner.

All the systems created data analysis protocols and goal monitoring reports for administrators, teachers, and in some cases for students as well. Data discussion templates typically began by guiding teachers through a discussion of strengths, areas of weaknesses, grade-level trends, and subgroup trends. The discussion was then followed by a brainstorming session among teachers on instructional and grouping strategies and action plans. Typically, grade-level teams convened together to discuss data facilitated by the grade-level lead teacher. Teachers were asked to prepare for the meetings ahead of time by filling out data summary sheet, and areas were also required to bring in an assessment (e.g., pre/post test, benchmark, or unit test). They then shared what they felt worked well, areas of struggle, and their action plans. During the team meetings, they might share class report graphs or an item analysis graph usually created from data management system. Lastly, the team came to a consensus about actions to take or strategies to implement. An assistant principal at one Aldine school shared that data discussions are key because "data is only good as you understand it and you analyze it, and then it's only good as you do something about it."

Achievement First was the only school system in which data discussions primarily took place between individual teachers and the principal, rather than in small groups of teachers. Principals and teachers would discuss how to organize small groups of students for targeted instruction, which standards needed to be re-taught, and which students were struggling. The superintendent indicated that Achievement First had attempted to start group discussions about data among teachers but found that individual data discussions with the principal are more meaningful. "I think that the beauty of the one-on-one is that you actually physically walk out with a plan for your students," he explained. He added that data sharing among teachers can get complicated because they might not work at the same grade level or on the same subject matter, which tends to make the discussion about "all sorts of stuff" and even "excuse-making" (e.g., the test question was poorly written). Instead, teachers met with the principal and brought with them a tangible 6-week instructional plan based on student achievement data. The principal and teacher would discuss the so-called battle plan, and the principal would then hold the teacher accountable for implementing the plan. One of the limitations of the Battle Plan approach was the time involved for the principal to meet with each one of the teachers individually. This was possible given the relatively small staff size in the Achievement First schools; however, it may be more difficult in schools with larger staffs.

All of the systems recognized that DDDM was enhanced when educators share data not only within schools but across them. Networks helped to strengthen interconnections and spread innovation across sites and levels. Although most data discussions still occurred at the school level or between an individual school and the system office, systems were attempting to structure data discussion across schools through such networks. District and school site leaders often highlighted performance data from other schools with similar student demographics to further emphasize the necessity of monitoring data and making changes. In general, the network configurations themselves seemed to be less important than the collaborative relationships that were developing within them.

Establishing a culture of data use was also critical component of each system's efforts. System leaders found it was essential to create explicit expectations for data use among all principals and teachers. System leaders were keenly aware of the importance of hiring staff who would support their belief in DDDM. In some ways, the CMOs had a distinct advantage here. Because they were starting schools "from scratch," they could hire teachers and principals who brought in their expectation of DDDM. During the interview process, teachers were probed on their comfort with and openness toward using data. Many of the teachers hired in Aspire and Achievement First schools were new to the profession and thus incorporated DDDM from the beginning.

The school districts, Aldine and Garden Grove, obviously had to cultivate an interest in DDDM with a wider variety of teachers, many of whom had been in the system for some time. They tried to create an atmosphere around data that would gain buy-in from different staff members, as the superintendent in Garden Grove explained, "by making data non-threatening." She added, "Just like for doctors, lab reports are not a bad thing." Instead of blaming a teacher or a school for poor performance on the tests, district leaders focused on examining the data. Gaps evidenced by tests were addressed in a manner that invited help from the district.

Sometimes creating a safe culture of data use meant slowly starting to share data. For example, in Garden Grove, at first the focus was to examine the district as a whole. Next, the district began to produce school-level reports in which the school was compared to the rest of the district. Today, data examination is centered at individual school sites and school-level data were shared between schools. At the school level, teachers only had access to their own class data; the principal and data team had access to all of the teachers' data.

In all four school systems, schools and central offices collaborated closely in order to make improvements. Schools were held accountable for results, but the main responsibility of the central office was to support schools and provide resources. In other words, a trusting relationship was built, based on mutual accountability and with a two-way communication flow between schools and central offices.

School Context

The school context box is where everything comes together. In concert with system-wide goals, schools formulated goals specific to the needs of their students and communities. Often, schools would establish schoolwide goals, then grade-level goals, classroom goals, and in some cases, individual student goals. Again, the emphasis was on making goals meaningful at the local context. Ultimately, both at the system and school levels, goals were tied to improving learning and instruction. In particular, state and federal accountability policies played a central role in framing student achievement; however, the four systems moved beyond, simply reacting to accountability demands and worked at creating meaningful goals that embodied principles of continuous improvement.

As noted above, in keeping with district policies, schools provided time for meeting to discuss data, flexibility for re-teaching, and curriculum and material resources in order to facilitate data-driven instruction. Schools also developed their own assessments and tools for acting on data, which were often created by teachers working together. Teachers were also leading the way in fostering *student*-level discussions by developing data analysis tools. At Aldine, departments have created several tools such as Student Analysis Sheet that includes item analysis and student reflection questions (e.g., What was your target score?; On a scale of 1-5 how much effort did you put in?; What skills do you need to work on?; and What will you do to improve those skills?). A Student Reflection Form has also been created that includes prompts such as, "Briefly explain your grade in term of effort and mastery level. What is your goal for the next assessment? What can you do differently for the next test to achieve the goal? How can I help you be successful?"

In one Aspire school, all of the teachers with whom we spoke mentioned analyzing assessments with their students. Some teachers graphed their class results for student discussions. One teacher used the class results of one benchmark assessment to conduct a math lesson on median and mode. Another teacher made biweekly graphs of math, reading, and writing benchmark scores, showing the class average and the names of students who performed above the goal of 85% proficiency. He also highlighted students who did not make the 85% benchmark level but who still made huge gains. During student conferences held two or three times a year, teachers reviewed assessments with students and their parents to establish and monitor goals based on a "Personalized Student Learning Plan." Another teacher created a student-led conference form with sample goals and strategies, which included goal statements (e.g., I will earn a score of 20 or above on our spelling paragraph) and a list of strategies (e.g., I will practice writing the spelling paragraph every night).

Similar to the systems, schools also functioned as places to build human and social capital in the form of building the knowledge and skills of teachers, a process which happened through professional development, instructional leadership, and networking among teachers. Although most teachers said they had attended training on the use of data and received ongoing coaching from school site administrators, helping teachers to use data appropriately and thoughtfully remained an ongoing effort. Expressing a sentiment echoed by several teachers across these school systems, one teacher in Aldine remarked that gathering and disaggregating data was not the problem, but having training on what to do with the data and how to read it more carefully would be welcomed. When asked about what schools should avoid, a teacher stated, "Don't just throw the data out there and expect the teachers to be able to pick it up and run with it." Principals from district schools indicated that they needed to develop skills and capacity to have "quality conversations" around data.

Building teacher capacity for effective data use seemed to go hand-in-hand with building instructional knowledge and skills. Some teachers expressed frustration about assessing so frequently; they constantly asked, "How am I supposed to teach differently?" Although the use of data could pinpoint areas for improvement and areas of strength, data alone could not help improve student learning. Without professional development to build instructional knowledge for re-teaching, differentiating instruction, and providing scaffolding for students, teachers did not have the tools to utilize data to make improvements. Teachers desired more opportunities to observe other schools and learn from other teachers in order to build a broader repertoire of instructional strategies from which to choose.

Schools also played a critical role in providing the expectations for data-driven instruction among teachers, as well as creating a climate of trust and collaboration so that teachers could work in professional learning communities to improve their practice. In alignment with the system, school site leaders also took up the task of fostering a culture of data use. Principals were adept at conveying the systems' messages on how to approach data. One principal told her staff that data are a resource for asking questions and help to make improvements. She shared that when a teacher expresses sentiments such as, "This is so depressing, I worked so hard, and these are my scores." She responded with, "Don't go there. Don't look at it that way. What we need to do then is to say, okay what can we do differently next time?" All in all, teachers viewed data as absolutely relevant and necessary. One teacher exclaimed, "I don't know what I ever did without it." Teachers commented that data were helpful because now teachers were not "shooting darts blindfolded." One teacher mentioned that data "open your eyes more" because they help teachers realize that teaching does not always lead to learning. Teachers believed that using data caused them to reflect more on their instructional strategies in relation to their students progress, and many of the teachers we interviewed said that they were differentiating instruction more now, that they knew which students needed help in particular areas.

Most schools had at least one designated person who assisted with data management and use. Informally, leadership team members and other teachers at school sites became "data experts." Across all the systems, teachers named one or two teachers to whom they specifically turned to assist them with using the data system, such as inputting results, analyzing results, and creating reports. In some districts, such as Garden Grove, these teachers were designated members of the school's data team, who had received district training in the use of data. In other cases, they were teacher leaders, such as the reading coach at one Aspire school. Sometimes they were simply teachers who had a keen interest in using data and analyzing results, not those in a formal designated role.

Thus, we see that when it comes to DDDM, implementation is a system-wide activity, even when the desired change is mainly at the school level. However, the various policy levels have varying degrees of influence, and varying levels of connection with each other, depending on local circumstances. In DDDM, reform success is a joint accomplishment, or co-construction, of individuals and policies at multiple levels of the system.

Methodological Issues

What does the co-construction theory imply for measurement of school reform implementation, at the local, district, and state levels? The knowledge gained from the aforementioned example of DDDM has been gained through careful qualitative data analysis. Some of the knowledge presented could also be gathered through surveys of educators, which could help to provide a more comprehensive look at the use of data across the system. Clearly, change processes and linkages between contextual levels (e.g., federal, state, district, school) cannot be adequately assessed with the randomized experiment techniques currently being touted as the gold standard in educational research. That said, it would be interesting to compare schools where educators had access to training and tools to assist in data use, versus those that do not, if such an experiment could be structured. Random assignment to these conditions, however, may prove tricky as most districts are working hard to make sure that all of their schools are engaged in district-wide reform initiatives.

Educational reform is complex and must be assessed in a variety of ways that includes both quantitative and qualitative data and most likely, case-study methods. For the purpose of understanding context specifically, the case-study approach can be used to study settings purposefully selected to represent the contextual conditions that are deemed relevant to the questions under study. Ethnographies of districts using data would also be interesting but would likely require a focus in depth in one or two sites.

In order to fully understand the co-construction of a multilevel reform such as DDDM, researchers would ideally gather detailed, longitudinal case-study data on the district, state, community, and other systemic linkages that might influence school-level reform efforts. Multiple schools and school systems would be involved. The study might employ a mixed-methods design that supplements the qualitative data with valid and reliable measures of student achievement over at least a 3-year period. Survey data gathered from teachers and principals would also be very useful in assessing the extent to which educators at the school level have been engaged in reform efforts. For example, in a study of DDDM, teachers and principals could be asked about the presence of systemic structural supports (e.g., collaboration time, networks), professional development, and resources devoted to assist in their use of data. They could also be surveyed on how and for what purposes they used data in instructional decision making.

Future Directions

Examining the co-construction of reform and the linkages across the educational system would likely provide insights that can inform the fields of educational research, policy development, and evaluation. However, there is a dearth of empirical research that has as its primary goal identifying or describing such linkages. This gap in the reform literature reflects a systemic weakness in understanding why reform efforts have not been more successfully sustained. Clearly, educational reform involves formal structures, such as district offices, state policies, and so on. It also involves both formal and informal linkages among those structures (Datnow, Lasky, Stringfield, & Teddlie, 2006). Yet, reform involves a dynamic relationship, not just among structures but also among cultures and people's actions in many interlocking settings. It is this intersection of culture, structure, and individual agency across contexts that helps us better understand how to build positive instances of educational reform.

Although there are not many, there are some recent research studies that attempt to address the intersection of educational reform across contexts, rather than simply focusing on one level of the system. One example is Hubbard, Stein, and Mehan's (2006) book, *Reform as Learning*, which focuses on educational reform in San Diego City Schools over a period of several years. The book not only foregrounds the role of the district but also includes detailed ethnographic data of how multiple levels of the system (including the community and state contexts) intersect to produce reform at the school level. A second example is the book of Oakes, Lipton, Ryan, and Quartz (2002), *Becoming Good American Schools*, which draws on longitudinal, comparative case-study research to tell the stories of 16 schools in four states that engaged in detracking and other reforms. The case studies illuminate the connections between school-level efforts, district change, community values regarding equity and excellence, and state policy agendas. More multilevel studies of this type are needed.

Appendix: Characteristics of the School Systems

			Race/Ethnicity					Free-Lunch Status	ELL Status	
	Grades	Size	African American (%)	Asian or Pacific Islander (%)	Latino (%)	White (%)	Native American (%)	Eligible (%)	ELL (%)	Location
California										
Garden Grove	K-12	50,030	1	31	52	16	<1	61	47	
School A	K-6	583	0	72	11	17	<1	33	25	Urban
School B	K-3, 4-6	1,230	<1	23	68	8	<1	73	56	Urban
Aspire		3,600								
School A	K-8	409	20	3	77	7	0	86	66	Urban
School B	K-5	350	9	8	29	46	0	37	23	Suburban
Connecticut										
Achievement First	K-8	989								
School A	5-8	264	63	0	37	2	0	73	0	Urban
School B	K-2	151	73		26	<1	0	77	2	Urban
Texas										
Aldine	PK-12	56,127	32	2	61	6	<1	78	14	
School A	9	893	23	2	71	4	0	80		Urban Fringe
School B	K-4	633	17	<1	79	4	0	87	63	Urban Fringe

Note. All data reported are for 2004-2005. Figures have been rounded to the nearest percent.
ELL = English Language Learner.

Notes

This work reported herein was supported by a grant from NewSchools Venture Fund, with funding they received from The William and Flora Hewlett Foundation and the Bill and Melinda Gates Foundation. I am grateful to my colleagues at NewSchools, notably Joanne Weiss, Marisa White, Ramona Thomas, Julie Peterson, Misha Simmonds, and Jennifer Carolan for assisting me in this effort. However, I wish to note the contents of this report do not necessarily reflect the positions or policies of NewSchools or of foundations. I wish to express my sincere thanks to the educators who gave generously of their time and effort to participate in this study. I also wish to thank my research team at the Center on Educational Governance at the University of Southern California, including Priscilla Wohlstetter, Dominic Brewer, Guilbert Hentschke, Vicki Park, Courtney Malloy, Lindsey Moss, Michelle Nayfack, Ally Kuzin, Cassandra Davis, and Paul Galvin.

1. The study was led by me as Principal Investigator, Priscilla Wohlstetter as Co-Principal Investigator, and a team of researchers at the Center on Educational Governance at USC, most notably Vicki Park.

References

Alwin, L. (2002). The will and the way of data use. *School Administrator, 59*(11), 11.

Anderson, S. (2003). *The school district role in educational change: A review of the literature.* Ontario: International Centre for Educational Change, Ontario Institute of Studies in Education.

Bay Area School Reform Collaborative. (2003). *After the test: Using data to close the achievement gap.* San Francisco: Author.

Berman, P., & McLaughlin, M. W. (1978). *Federal programs supporting educational change, Vol. VIII.* Santa Monica, CA: Rand.

Center on Education Policy. (2004). *From the capital to the classroom: Year 2 of the No Child Left Behind Act.* Washington, DC: Author.

Colby, S., Smith, K., & Shelton, J. (2005). *Expanding the supply of high quality public schools.* San Francisco, CA: The Bridgespan group.

Crommey, A. (2000). *Using student assessment data: What can we learn from schools?* Oak Brook, IL: North Central Regional Educational Laboratory.

Datnow, A., Hubbard, L., & Mehan, H. (2002). *Extending educational reform: From one school to many.* London: Routledge Falmer Press.

Datnow A., Lasky S., Stringfield S. C., & Teddie C. (2006) *Integrating educational systems for successful reform in diverse contexts.* New York: Cambridge University Press.

Doyle, D. P. (2003). Data-driven decision-making: Is it the mantra of the month or does it have staying power? *T.H.E. Journal, 30*(10), 19-21.

Earl, L., & Katz, S. (2005). *Leading schools in a data rich world.* Thousand Oaks, CA: Corwin Press.

Elmore, R. (1980). Backward mapping: Implementation research and policy decisions. *Political Science Quarterly, 94,* 601-616.

Elmore, R. E., & Sykes, G. (1992). Curriculum policy. In P. Jackson (Ed.), *Handbook of research on curriculum* (pp. 185-215). New York: Macmillan.

Fullan, M. G. (1991). *The new meaning of educational change* (2nd ed.) New York: Teachers College Press.

Gross, N., Gaicquinta, J., & Bernstein, M. (1971). *Implementing organizational innovations: A sociological analysis of planned educational change.* New York: Basic books.

Hall, G. & Loucks, S. (1979). *Implementing innovations in schools: A concerns-based approach.* Austin, TX: Research and Development Center for Teacher Education, University of Texas.

Hall, P. M., & McGinty, P. J. W. (1997). Policy as the transformation of intentions: Producing program from statutes. *The Sociological Quarterly, 38,* 439-467.

Hubbard, L., Stein, M. K., & Mehan, H. (2006). *Reform as learning: When school reform collides with school culture and community politics.* New York: Routledge.

Johnson, J. H. (1999). Educators as researchers. *Schools in the Middle, 9*(1), 38-41.

Johnson, J. H. (2000). Data-driven school improvement. *Journal of School Improvement, 1*(1), XX.

Lafee, S. (2002). Data-driven districts. *School Administrator, 59*(11), 6-7, 9-10, 12, 14-15.

Louis, K. S. (1994). Improving urban and disadvantaged schools: Dissemination and utilization perspectives. *Knowledge and Policy, 4,* 34-54.

McIntire, T. (2002). The administrator's guide to data-driven decision making. *Technology and Learning, 22*(11), 18-33.

McLaughlin, M., & Talbert, J. E. (1993). *Contexts that matter for teaching and learning.* Stanford, CA: Stanford University Center for Research on the Context of Secondary School Teaching.

Morgan, G. (1986). *Images of organization.* Newbury Park, CA: Sage Publications.

Oakes, J., Lipton, M., Ryan, S., & Quartz, K. (2002). *Becoming good American schools: The struggle for civic virtue in educational reform.* New York: Jossey-Bass.

Rogoff, B. (1995). Observing sociocultural activity on three planes: Participatory appropriation, guided participation, and apprenticeship. In J. V. Wertsch, P. Del Rio, & A. Alvarez (Eds.), *Sociocultural studies of mind* (pp. 139-164). Cambridge: Cambridge University Press.

Sarason, S. (1997). Revisiting the creation of settings. *Mind, culture, and activity, 4,* 175-182.

Snyder, J., Bolin, F., & Zumwalt, K. (1992). Curriculum implementation. In P. Jackson (Ed.), *Handbook of research on curriculum* (pp. 402-435). New York: Macmillan.

Supovitz, J., & Taylor B. S. (2003). *The impacts of standards-based reform in Duval County, Florida, 1999-2002.* Philadelphia, PA: Consortium for Policy Research in Education.

Tharp, R. G. (1997). *From at risk to excellence: Research, theory, and principles for practice, research report #1.* Santa Cruz, CA: Center for Research on Education, Diversity and Excellence.

Togneri, W., & Anderson, S. (2003). *Beyond islands of excellence: What districts can do to improve instruction and achievement in all schools.* Washington, DC: Learning First Alliance.

Wohlstetter, P., Van Kirk, A. N., Robertson, P. J., & Mohrman, S. A. (1997). *Organizing for successful school-based management.* Alexandria, VA: Association for Supervision and Curriculum Development.

Chapter 16

Using Community Epidemiologic Data to Improve Social Settings: The *Communities That Care* Prevention System

ABIGAIL A. FAGAN, J. DAVID HAWKINS, AND RICHARD F. CATALANO

Community coalitions seek to promote the healthy development of young people through collaborative action (Butterfoss, Goodman, & Wandersman, 1993; Wandersman, 2003). Some community coalitions do so by targeting elevated (multiple) risk and protective factors predictive of substance use, delinquency, violence, and other poor outcomes with multifaceted components that operate across multiple settings (Hawkins, Catalano, & Arthur, 2002; Spoth & Greenberg, 2005; St Pierre, 2001). Such community-based initiatives allow intervention approaches to be tailored to local needs, as identified by community members. When guided by a common vision that inspires and motivates community members, coalitions can bring diverse stakeholders and key leaders together to create a more positive context that promotes healthy youth development. Community coalitions can also increase political alliances, foster communication among community members, and coordinate human and financial resources (Hallfors, Cho, Livert, & Kadushin, 2002; Lasker, 2000; Mitchell, Florin, & Stevenson, 2002; St Pierre, 2001).

Findings from research trials suggest that community-wide risk reduction interventions can prevent alcohol and tobacco use among adolescents (Biglan & Taylor, 2000; Perry et al., 1996, 2000; Wagenaar et al., 2000). However, some community coalition initiatives have failed to produce significant improvements in outcomes (Flewelling et al., 2005; Hallfors et al., 2002; Spoth & Greenberg, 2005). For example, a quasi-experimental evaluation of the effectiveness of 12 coalitions participating in the Robert Wood Johnson Foundation's *Fighting Back* initiative found no significant reductions in youth and adult substance use, even though the coalitions were well funded and employed comprehensive prevention and intervention strategies. The lack of positive findings led the authors to recommend several strategies for improving the effectiveness of community coalitions, including having clearly defined, focused, and manageable goals; using high-quality data to make decisions; selecting programs that have been shown to be effective; and carefully monitoring the quality of implementation of prevention activities (Hallfors et al., 2002). A review of coalitions by Flewelling et al. (2005) attributed coalition ineffectiveness to community members' lack of interest in the effort, emphasizing the need for coalitions to better engage members and foster community ownership of prevention activities.

The Communities That Care (CTC) prevention operating system seeks to address these issues through a five-phase model that includes (a) assessing community readiness to undertake collaborative prevention efforts; (b) forming a diverse and representative prevention coalition; (c) using epidemiologic data to assess prevention needs; (d) choosing evidence-based prevention policies, practices, and programs based on these data; and (e) implementing the new strategies with fidelity, in a manner congruent with the programs' theory, content, and methods of delivery. CTC activities are planned and carried out by the CTC Community Board, a prevention coalition of community stakeholders who work together to promote positive youth outcomes. Board members participate in a series of six CTC training workshops in which they build their coalition and learn the skills needed to install the CTC system, increase the likelihood of healthy youth development, and decrease the likelihood of problem behaviors, including substance use, delinquency, and violence (Hawkins & Catalano, 1992; Hawkins et al., 2002).

CTC is guided theoretically by the social development model (Catalano & Hawkins, 1996; Hawkins & Weis, 1985). The model posits that bonding to prosocial others (Garmezy, 1985; Rutter, 1980; Werner, 1989) and having clear norms against antisocial behavior (Elliott, Huizinga, & Menard, 1989) are protective factors that inhibit the development of antisocial behaviors. The social development model maintains that bonding is created when people are provided opportunities to contribute to prosocial groups, have the skills to become successfully involved in these opportunities, and are recognized for their contributions. Interventions that strengthen individuals' opportunities, skills, and recognition are likely to enhance their bonding to positive social groups and their adoption of prosocial norms for behavior.

The social development model guides the community mobilization component of CTC. The CTC system creates opportunities for all interested community stakeholders to develop a common vision for positive youth development based on prevention science (Coie et al., 1993). CTC trainings help coalition members actualize this vision by building skills in assessing epidemiologic levels of risk and protection, matching needs with effective prevention programs, and implementing programs with fidelity. The CTC system also provides benchmarks to mark progress toward the community vision and suggests appropriate recognition activities when these goals are achieved. By increasing opportunities, skills, and recognition for community stakeholders to work together, CTC seeks to promote closer social bonds among coalition members and a stronger commitment to implementing effective preventive interventions. Greater bonding and commitment are hypothesized to lead to greater collaboration among community members and to improved implementation of youth development and preventive interventions chosen by the CTC Community Board (Hawkins et al., 2002).

The CTC process is grounded in the use of epidemiologic data collected, in part, through an anonymous, school-wide survey of students, the CTC Youth Survey (Arthur, Hawkins, Pollard, Catalano, & Baglioni, 2002; Glaser, Van Horn, Arthur, Hawkins, & Catalano, 2005). This instrument measures community, family, school, peer, and individual risk and protective factors as well as youth behaviors including drug use, delinquency, and school problems. When implemented community wide, the survey is used to create a profile of community levels of risk and protection. Based on this information, Board members prioritize elevated risk and depressed protective factors for attention and select evidence-based prevention policies and programs that address these factors. After programs are launched, communities readminister the survey every 2 years to monitor the effectiveness of their prevention efforts in changing community levels of prioritized risk and protective factors and behaviors.

Communities using the CTC model are expected to experience better collaboration among decision makers and service providers, and greater adoption and implementation of effective prevention programs that are matched to community needs. Through a data-driven and community-operated strategic approach to prevention, CTC seeks to bring about change in the major settings affecting young people—schools, families, community service organizations, and ultimately, the community itself—by ensuring that tested and effective policies and programs for reducing risk and enhancing protection are available and implemented across these settings (Hawkins et al., 2002). This chapter describes these community change processes more fully using examples from 12 intervention communities implementing CTC as part of the Community Youth Development Study (CYDS).

Research Methods

The Community Youth Development Study

The CYDS is a 5-year community-randomized trial involving 24 small- to medium-sized towns in seven states. The primary goal of the study is to test

CTC's ability to reduce risk factors, increase protective factors, and decrease levels of drug use, violence, and other adolescent problem behaviors. The study also investigates the degree to which CTC increases the use of epidemiologic data to prioritize specific risk and protective factors for preventive action and the selection and implementation of tested and effective prevention programs across community settings.

Study communities range in size from 1,500 to 50,000 residents. Communities are not suburbs of larger cities, have clear geographic boundaries, and all have their own governmental, educational, and law enforcement structures. In fall 2002, 12 communities were randomly assigned to implement CTC, while 12 sites were assigned to the control condition to provide prevention services as usual. The 12 intervention communities received training and technical assistance in the CTC system, funding for a full-time CTC coordinator, and up to $75,000 annually to replicate tested and effective prevention programs targeting students and their families in grades 5 through 9. Training and technical assistance were provided by certified CTC trainers from the Channing Bete Company, at that time the distributor of CTC, and research staff from the Social Development Research Group at the University of Washington.

The CTC Youth Survey

The CTC Youth Survey risk and protective factors scales have been found to be reliable and valid across gender and ethnicity (African American, Asian American, Latino, Native American, and European American), and for students in grades 6 through 12 (Arthur et al., 2002; Glaser et al., 2005). The development of the survey, items included in the scales, and the psychometric properties and criterion validity of the scales have been reported elsewhere (Arthur et al., 2002, 2007; Glaser et al., 2005).

All communities in the study administered the survey in 1998, 2000, 2002, and 2004 to a census of consenting 6th-, 8th-, 10th-, and 12th-grade public school students. Teachers administered the survey during one classroom period and ensured the anonymity of students' responses. Multiple screening criteria identified students whose responses suggested inconsistent or dishonest reporting. Dichotomous measures of each risk and protective factor differentiated students reporting high and low levels of risk and protection. The prevalence of each problem behavior was calculated as the percentage of students reporting that activity (Arthur et al., 2007). Student survey data were aggregated to calculate community levels of risk, protection, and problem behaviors by grade and year.

Figure 16.1 depicts the relative distribution of risk factors reported by eighth-grade students in one intervention community. Similar community profiles of risk factors, protective factors, and problem behaviors were

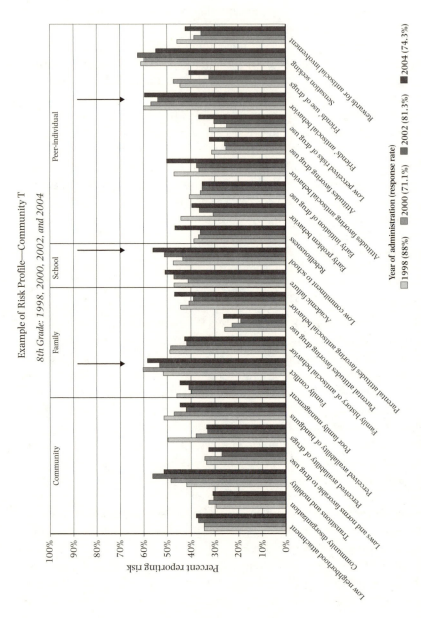

Figure 16.1. Risk Factor Profile for Community "T" (Source: The CTC Youth Survey, Administered in Public Schools to Eighth-Grade Students in 1998, 2000, 2002, and 2004).

generated for all years of survey administration and separately for each grade of students in all study communities.

Results

Prior analyses have found that all intervention sites successfully accomplished the major activities associated with Phases 1 through 4 of CTC during the first 18 months of the study (Quinby et al., in press) and implemented prevention programs with a high degree of fidelity during Phase 5 (Fagan, Hawkins, Hanson, & Arthur, in press). This chapter focuses on the degree to which the use of the CTC Youth Survey led to changes in community settings affecting young people, specifically investigating processes by which CTC Community Boards analyzed their community-level student survey data, prioritized risk and protective factors for intervention, and selected tested and effective prevention programs to be installed in family, school, and community settings.

Phases 1 and 2: Assessing Readiness and Creating a Community Board

The first steps in the CTC process involve an assessment of "readiness" to adopt the CTC system (Phase 1) and creation of a diverse, representative CTC Community Board (Phase 2). In order to participate in the research study, the school superintendent, the mayor or city manager, and the lead law enforcement officer in each participating community signed letters promising participation in the study's required data collection efforts. Of 26 communities eligible for this study, the 24 included here submitted signed letters after visits from University of Washington researchers to explain the project and answer questions. During the first two CTC training workshops, community stakeholders in CTC communities identified attitudinal and structural readiness issues that could inhibit successful implementation of the CTC system. Potential readiness issues included concerns that some community members did not see adolescent problem behaviors as preventable or as a priority for community action, concerns about the history of collaboration among community youth-serving organizations, and concerns about the strength of school district support for administering the CTC Youth Survey. In some study communities, stakeholders noted that many residents viewed teenage alcohol use as normative and not necessarily a concern. Several communities identified individuals and agencies whose participation would benefit the CTC effort but who would be difficult to engage in CTC. While readiness challenges existed, none was so serious as to prevent progress, and all CTC Boards outlined steps to address identified readiness issues.

During Phase 2, all 12 intervention sites formed CTC Community Boards. Eighteen months after beginning the CTC process, 376 volunteers were participating in CTC Boards ranging in size from 18 to 76 members. School personnel and human service agencies were particularly well represented. Other members included elected officials, youth, parents, law enforcement personnel, public health officials, faith leaders, business representatives, and other residents (Quinby et al., in press). Board members attended the CTC *Community Board Orientation* to learn the key principles of the CTC system and to create a vision statement that would guide the development of their prevention coalition and associated prevention activities.

Phase 3: Conducting a Community-Level Risk and Resource Assessment

During Phase 3, each Community Board analyzed survey data collected from 1998 to 2002 from their 6th-, 8th-, 10th-, and 12th-grade students. Between 67% and 85% of all eligible public school students in these grades participated in the survey in 2002, suggesting that the survey information was representative of most students in the participating communities. Board members attended the CTC *Community Assessment Training* to learn skills to assess data trends and identify risk and protective factors that were consistently elevated or depressed over time. Based on these assessments, each Board prioritized between two and seven factors to target with prevention activities.

Prior work has shown variation in community levels of risk and protection (Hawkins, Van Horn, & Arthur, 2004), and communities' priorities varied in this study. However, as shown in Table 16.1, some risk factors were elevated across communities and were selected by a majority. Ten of twelve communities prioritized the risk factor "low commitment to school" and seven prioritized "friends who engage in problem behaviors." Other factors were selected less consistently, and nine risk and protective factors were not chosen for action by any intervention site in this study.

The assessment process encouraged community stakeholders to focus on changing community conditions that have been shown by research to be associated with youth problem behaviors and that were prevalent in their community. Thus, each CTC Board's efforts were grounded in survey data that identified specific changes that were needed in each community setting. However, Board members did not determine priorities based solely on the prevalence of risk and protective factors. Decisions also were based on Board members' assessment of community norms and resources and on their own attitudes regarding specific risk and protective factors.

For example, Board members in Community T, whose data are depicted in Figure 16.1, prioritized three elevated risk factors for action: family conflict,

Table 16.1. Risk and Protective Factors Prioritized by CTC Communities in 2004

Risk and Protective Factor, by Domain	Number of Communities
Community	
Extreme economic deprivation	1
Low neighborhood attachment and community disorganization	3
Community laws and norms favorable toward drug use, firearms, and crime	2
Availability of drugs	2
Community recognition for prosocial involvement	5
Community opportunities for prosocial involvement	2
Family	
Family management problems	4
Family conflict	2
Favorable parental attitudes toward the problem behavior	1
School	
Low commitment to school	10
Academic failure beginning in late elementary school	3
School recognition for prosocial involvement	2
School opportunities for prosocial involvement	2
Peer-Individual	
Friends who engage in the problem behavior	7
Favorable attitudes toward the problem behavior	4
Rebelliousness	3
Sensation seeking	3

low commitment to school, and friends who engage in problem behaviors. They considered two other elevated risk factors but did not prioritize them. Community members attributed high rates of "transitions and mobility" to the town's growing population and the recent opening of several new schools. While recognizing that students who frequently move and change schools were at risk for involvement in problem behavior, Board members felt their prevention resources would be better spent addressing other elevated risk factors. The Board decided not to prioritize the risk factor "sensation seeking" because no program had yet been identified that, when rigorously tested, demonstrated effectiveness in reducing sensation seeking or problem behaviors specifically among sensation seekers. Moreover, some Board members had difficulty perceiving sensation seeking as a problem and argued that it could result in prosocial activities (e.g., skiing or rock climbing) as well as problem behaviors. As another example, in some communities in which hunting was common and gun ownership customary, Board members did not consider elevated levels of "availability of firearms" to be a problem.

As these cases illustrate, risk and protective factors were prioritized because they were elevated, but community norms also influenced the prioritization process. Regardless of the specific factors chosen for attention, each CTC Board reached consensus in seeking to change specific community risk and protective factors. This process of prioritizing specific elevated risks and depressed protective factors is a central element of the CTC system and is hypothesized to increase community commitment to making specified changes community wide that are necessary to affect prioritized factors and ultimately improve youth outcomes. In our view, the development of a community-wide consensus regarding the specific risk and protective factors that need to be addressed community wide is an important change in the community setting itself. Agreement among stakeholders and providers regarding intervention priorities should increase the development and implementation of policies and programs across the community focused on these agreed targets.

After identifying prevention priorities, Board members attended the CTC *Community Resource Assessment Training* to learn how to conduct a resource assessment of current community programs and policies already in place to address the priorities. They used this information to identify factors not currently being adequately addressed, in preparation for selecting new programs that would fill gaps in resources, as well as complement and avoid duplication of existing programs, policies, and practices.

Phases 4 and 5: Selecting and Implementing Evidence-Based Prevention Programs

Phases 4 and 5 of CTC involve the development and implementation of a Community Action Plan that identifies community prevention goals and the prevention programs that will help achieve these goals. Community Board members in all intervention sites attended the CTC *Community Plan Training* (CPT) to create their plans. In the first half of the training, community members set objectives regarding the extent to which they anticipated that prevention efforts would reduce risk, increase protection, and lower rates of problem behaviors. For example, in Community T (whose data are shown in Figure 16.1), Board members specified three risk factor goals:

1. Decrease family conflict from a baseline of 53.2% in 2002 to 48% by 2008.
2. Decrease low commitment to school from a baseline of 51.1% in 2002 to 41.1% by 2008.
3. Decrease friends who engage in problem behaviors from a baseline of 53.3% in 2002 to 45% by 2008.

Board members in the 12 CTC sites wrote similar goal statements regarding the prioritized risk and protective factors and all behavioral outcomes of concern. Stating specific prevention objectives was important in concretizing the community's vision of healthy youth development and in establishing baseline levels that could be tracked over time through repeated administration of the youth survey. CTC Board members were encouraged to share their goals and their progress toward them with the larger community so that all residents understood the scope and direction of prevention efforts.

During the second half of the CPT workshop, communities selected prevention programs that had previously been tested in controlled trials and had been effective in preventing youth health and behavior problems, as described in the *CTC Prevention Strategies Guide* (Hawkins & Catalano, 2004). The *Guide* identified 39 tested programs appropriate for schools, families, and children in grades 5-9, the developmental focus of this test of CTC. Options included parent training programs, school-wide interventions, life skills curricula, mentoring programs, specific after-school activities, and community-based interventions.

As shown in Table 16.2, the 12 CTC communities selected 13 different tested, effective programs to implement during the 2004-2005 school year.

Table 16.2.   Prevention Programs Selected by CTC Communities

Program	Number of Communities	
	2004-2005	*2005-2006*
School-based	6	11
All Stars Core	1	1
Life Skills Training	2	4[a]
Lion's-Quest Skills for Adolescence	2	3
Project Alert	—	1
Olweus Bullying Prevention Program	—	2[a]
Program Development Evaluation Training	1	1
After school	11	13
Participate and Learn Skills (PALS)	1	1
Big Brothers/Big Sisters	2	2
Stay SMART	3	3
Tutoring	4	6
Valued Youth Tutoring Program	1	1
Parent training	11	13
Strengthening Families 10-14	2	3
Guiding Good Choices	6	7[a]
Parents Who Care	2[a]	1
Family Matters	1	1
Parenting Wisely	—	1

[a] Program funded through local resources rather than study funds in one or two communities.

While many programs were chosen by multiple communities, each site selected a unique combination of between one and four prevention programs based on their analyses of local survey data and programs available to target prioritized risk and protective factors. In most cases, communities chose to adopt new prevention programs, though some also chose to expand existing programs. Thus, during the first 18 months of the research study, the 12 CTC intervention communities moved from creating a prevention coalition to implementing new and expanded tested and effective youth development and prevention programs.

As with the prioritization of risk and protective factors, communities based program selection decisions on data and other considerations. In most cases, several programs were available to address the same risk or protective factor. To choose the program(s) most appropriate for their community, during the CPT, Board members assessed programs' core requirements, financial costs (staffing, training and technical assistance, supplies, equipment, administration, transportation, etc.), necessary human resources (e.g., staff and coordinator skills, availability of volunteers, etc.), and local social/political factors that might influence implementation (e.g., community norms, competing programs, current or expected budget crises, cultural fit, etc.). Using these guidelines, Board members selected programs which they thought could be implemented with fidelity, were affordable, and would be supported by program providers, participants, and the broader community. While each community developed its action plan based on a distinct set of circumstances and considerations, all 12 sites achieved the common goal of selecting effective prevention interventions.

To further illustrate the CTC prevention planning processes, we next describe two communities' experiences during this phase. Although the program decisions that were reached and the data they were based upon were community specific, many of the challenges to and facilitating factors for prevention planning were encountered by other communities involved in the study.

Community J: Building on Existing Resources

Community J is composed of six rural small towns whose students attend a common high school but separate elementary schools. The community prioritized six risk and protective factors during Phase 3: extreme economic deprivation, community opportunities for prosocial involvement, low commitment to school, friends who engage in problem behaviors, favorable attitudes toward the problem behavior, and rebelliousness. In Phase 4, the Community Board selected four programs to address four of their six priorities: Life Skills Training (targeting friends who engage in problem behaviors and favorable attitudes toward drug use), Tutoring (targeting low commitment to school),

Big Brothers/Big Sisters (targeting rebelliousness), and Stay SMART (targeting friends who engage and favorable attitudes). The resource assessment showed that all four programs had operated in the community in past years but without reaching significant proportions of students in grades 5-9 or with deviations in fidelity to program requirements. The Board decided that these programs could be expanded and fidelity enhanced, thereby increasing the likelihood of producing community-wide changes in youth outcomes.

The Life Skills Training program had been taught in one of the four elementary schools but implementation was inconsistent over the years and teachers had made some changes to the program's required material. With input from school representatives and endorsement from the school principals and superintendent, the Board voted to expand this program to all elementary schools. This would not only allow a greater number of students to be served but also, the Board hoped, increase program fidelity through increased community support, oversight, and accountability. The Board and schools also agreed to expand after-school tutoring to two of the elementary schools without such services. Tutoring was feasible because schools were eager to nominate tutees and a nearby university could provide tutors who were earning their education degrees.

The Board identified a regional Big Brothers/Big Sisters agency that served few local students. The CTC Board decided to fund half of an existing staff position in the agency to increase recruitment efforts and mentoring matches in the six-town area. The Boys and Girls Club was offering the Stay SMART program in one town on a limited basis, primarily serving the Native American children of that town, which had the smallest population of all six communities. The Board funded this program to forge a stronger partnership with the Club, which was geographically isolated and not always included in prevention efforts. In addition, the Board wanted to expose students from other towns to the Native American culture, and, more generally, to increase interaction between children who would later meet in high school, thereby reducing the potential for a stressful transition to high school.

Community J did not select effective programs to influence their fifth and sixth prioritized community-level factors, because extreme economic deprivation was already being addressed by a different service agency in town, and no effective programs had been identified to address community opportunities for prosocial involvement. Though Community J was unable to address *all* priorities in its initial plan, the Board was satisfied with targeting four priority factors with four prevention programs. They believed they had the human and fiscal resources to effectively implement these services, particularly because by expanding existing programs they avoided some initial costs and organizational obstacles associated with new programming. Community J created a comprehensive initial action plan. Its comprehensiveness reflected in part the already high levels of collaboration among community residents and organizations. Representatives from major service organizations participated in the CTC effort, attended the CPT, and were receptive to working together on prevention program planning and implementation.

Community H: Challenges in Adopting School-Based Programs

Community H is a town of about 17,000 residents located 60 miles from a large metropolitan area. Its Board prioritized five risk and protective factors during Phase 3: family conflict, school opportunities for youths' prosocial involvement, school recognition for youths' prosocial involvement, rebelliousness, and sensation seeking. Because several factors were in the school domain, Community Board members identified potential school-based programs during the CPT. Key school administrators did not attend this workshop, however, and during a subsequent meeting with Board representatives, the school superintendent and two junior high school principals decided they could not endorse new school programming, even though they agreed that students' needs should be addressed. In their view, the *No Child Left Behind Act* of 2002 and a similar state mandate to improve academic test scores left little time in the school day to address other issues or to use staff development days to train teachers in new initiatives. In addition, the administrators thought the new programs overlapped too much with current programming.

Given the school's lack of desire to implement new prevention programming, the CTC Board selected the Strengthening Families Program: For Parents and Youth 10-14 to target one priority risk factor (family conflict). Board members agreed that parent education services would be an asset to community residents, and there was a well-regarded family services agency equipped to offer the program. In addition, the local Boys and Girls Club had a small grant to implement this program, and with additional funding, the Club could collaborate with the family center to serve more families. Representatives from these two agencies were skeptical at first, as they had not successfully partnered in the past, but they agreed to collaborate on this project to benefit the community at large.

The Board considered other programs to address its remaining risk factors. However, there were no programs identified that had been demonstrated to reduce sensation seeking, and the only nonschool options to address rebelliousness were two research-based mentoring programs. Board members determined that they already had a popular local mentoring program and did not want to introduce a competitor. Thus, the final action plan in the first year of the project allowed Community H to target only one of its five priority risk and protective factors.

This community's initial prevention planning experiences were not atypical. Several communities in the study had elevated risk and low protection in the school domain, but many school administrators were reluctant to approve new programming because of mandates to improve academic outcomes and demands on teachers' time. Schools were much more likely to endorse after-school tutoring programs that avoided these problems while still providing structured, individualized assistance to students. As shown in Table 16.2, four of the 12 (33%) communities selected tutoring programs in the first year of the project, and six (50%) selected these programs in the second year. Parent training programs were also widely adopted. Ten of twelve (83%) sites offered parent training over the 2 years, and two of these communities funded multiple parent programs. Parent training was appealing because it allowed sites to address elevated family, peer, and individual-level risk factors. Furthermore, social service providers were well represented on Community Boards and were often passionate advocates of the benefits of universal parent training programs. As has been shown in other research, "champions" who promote a program and persuade others of its value can greatly facilitate the adoption, implementation, and sustainability of a new program (Backer, David, & Soucy, 1995; Elliott & Mihalic, 2004; Ellickson, Petersilia, Caggiano, & Polin, 1983; Miller & Shinn, 2005).

Adoption of school-based programs was likewise facilitated when championed from within the community by CTC Board members, particularly when school administrators actively participated in the CTC process and collaborative prevention planning. When support was lacking, the CTC coordinator and Board members employed several strategies to overcome resistance, including sharing youth survey information with school board members, administrators, and staff via formal presentations and informal discussions. In addition, the CTC coordinator informed school personnel of research, demonstrating that lower levels of risk factors, higher levels of protective factors, and decreased substance use were related to higher standardized achievement test scores (Arthur, Brown, & Briney, 2006). The CTC Board also presented survey results to community groups and publicized program decisions to garner community-wide support for the use of a data-driven approach to preventing adolescent problem behaviors. Increasing public awareness helped engage more community members in local prevention efforts, and sometimes provided an additional impetus for schools to adopt and install new programs as part of the community-wide effort.

As shown in Table 16.2, these efforts paid off. The number of communities using school-based curricula doubled, with five sites choosing school programs in the 2004-2005 school year, and 10 of the 12 sites implementing these programs in 2005-2006 (including Community H).[1] In some cases, schools agreed to adopt programs as pilot efforts either in one of their schools or using staff from other organizations to teach lessons. In two sites with relatively weak initial support, school and community buy-in was so enhanced that local rather than study funding was used to implement programs in the

2005-2006 school year. Thus, as reported by others (Miller & Shinn, 2005; St Pierre, 2001), the community/school partnership was challenging at first, but grew over time through maintaining active communication, building trust and credibility, fostering support on all levels, and promoting a common vision of healthy youth development. Community-specific epidemiologic data on youth risk, protection, and problem behaviors were key to demonstrating a need for specific changes.

The final CTC training, the *Community Plan Implementation Training*, emphasized the importance of implementing selected prevention programs with fidelity and recommended processes for monitoring implementation. As described elsewhere (Fagan et al., in press), the program monitoring system developed for this study relied on program implementers to complete short, written checklists describing their performance, and on community members to periodically observe lessons. Research staff analyzed these data and provided written reports to Community Coordinators and Boards, who, in turn, provided feedback to staff and made implementation changes when necessary to overcome challenges.

High rates of implementation fidelity were achieved during the 2004-2005 school year. Implementers taught the majority of information, adhered to programs' critical components, and delivered the recommended number of sessions with the recommended length and frequency of lessons (Fagan et al., in press). This outcome was anticipated, given that community members spent much time considering program requirements and soliciting support from program implementers prior to implementation. By using a common theoretical framework to select programs, actively monitoring their delivery, and implementing efforts within a community context favorable to prevention efforts (Hawkins et al., 2002), Community Boards helped increase community ownership and accountability for program delivery. By installing programs with fidelity, communities increased their likelihood of achieving the positive effects for participants.

Discussion

This chapter described the CTC prevention operating system and its manualized, data-driven prevention approach that seeks to effect change in social settings. Change in CTC communities begins when community stakeholders agree to focus on empirically identified predictors of youth outcomes (risk and protective factors). As CTC Board members consider data from their community's young people reported on the youth survey, they reach consensus on those factors which will be prioritized for action across the community. This should increase the likelihood that, across settings, actions and interventions are undertaken in a manner that advances the risk reduction and protection enhancement goals shared by all. Where gaps in preventive services are identified, CTC Boards choose tested and effective prevention policies and programs that address the elevated risk factors and depressed protective factors reported by young people. They identify the settings where these new programs or activities should be installed. When installed in appropriate community settings and implemented with fidelity, these new tested and effective prevention programs should result in decreased levels of risk, increased levels of protection, and less youth involvement in problem behaviors.

In the CYDS, Community Board members in all 12 intervention sites used local survey information to select a total of 16 different prevention programs over the first year of implementation. In some cases, existing programs that met evidence-based criteria were strengthened or expanded; in other cases, and over time, new tested and effective programs were adopted. Once selected, programs were implemented with a high degree of adherence to program protocols. In all communities, use of the CTC framework provided a foundation for effective community action.

The CTC process promotes change in social settings. Most obviously, the installation of new effective programs that seek to change targeted family, school, peer group, and community-level risk factors holds the potential to change schools, peer groups, families, and the larger community settings in which young people develop. For example, in our view, moving from resistance to the adoption of an effective middle school curriculum that fosters problem-solving, decision-making, and interpersonal skills and reduces adolescent drug use is a change in the school setting. The school is providing skills in the classroom not previously taught. Providing those skills to all young people in the schools should, in turn, positively affect peer group compositions and interactions among students. As noted earlier, in some communities in this study, the inclusion of new curricula was facilitated by the commitment of the CTC Board to addressing the community's priority risk and protective factors. This community-wide commitment was, itself, a change in the community setting affecting young people's development.

Some of the interventions chosen by communities were designed specifically to make changes in schools or other settings. These included school-wide organizational change programs such as the Program Development Evaluation Program (Gottfredson, 1984) and the Olweus Bullying Prevention Program (Olweus, Limber, & Mihalic, 1999), which seek changes in school norms by having all school administrators and staff promote consistent messages that bullying behavior is not acceptable and will not be tolerated. Parent training programs like Guiding Good Choices® teach parents to set and enforce expectations for children's behavior and teach skills to reduce family conflict and skills to strengthen family bonds (Hawkins & Catalano, 2003). By changing family norms and parental behaviors in these ways, the program seeks to change the family as a social setting for child development, enhancing children's bonds to parents and reducing their likelihood of problem behavior.

In addition to effecting change through the implementation of targeted prevention programs, the CTC process itself promotes community-wide change. It provides diverse community stakeholders with a common language and methodology for planning and conducting prevention activities. Second, it develops consensus regarding priorities for community-wide action focused on elevated risk factors and depressed protective factors. Third, it enhances collaboration across stakeholder groups and organizations through the creation and activation of a prevention coalition. Fourth, through the use of the social development model, the CTC process reinforces progress and success in hopes of promoting a community context that favors prevention efforts. Thus, communities that adopt the CTC model can increase the likelihood of desired outcomes in multiple settings.

It is important to note that the communities described in this chapter may not represent typical CTC sites. The 12 intervention communities likely had a higher-than-average degree of readiness to adopt the CTC system, as they received financial support and technical assistance to participate in the study and conduct prevention programs. Moreover, all sites were part of a prior research study that involved administration of the youth survey, so this challenge did not need to be overcome before CTC implementation. Communities that lack commitment to implement the survey, do not have at least minimal levels of trust and communication between community members, and cannot make healthy youth development a priority will need to address these issues before trying to implement CTC.

All research sites were chosen because they were small- to medium-sized communities with distinct boundaries and their own governmental, educational, and law enforcement structures. While CYDS outcomes may not be generalizable to larger cities or urban communities, prior effectiveness studies of CTC have been conducted in such areas. The CTC framework was adopted by the Office of Juvenile Justice and Delinquency Prevention in the 1990s and was used in cities and counties throughout the United States. An evaluation of this effort found that CTC adoption resulted in improved collaboration, increased involvement of community members in prevention activities, reduced duplication of prevention efforts, increased leveraging of resources for prevention, and increased use of research-based approaches (Office of Juvenile Justice and Delinquency Prevention, 1996). A separate evaluation of CTC in Pennsylvania, including sites in three major metropolitan areas, demonstrated positive youth outcomes. After controlling for community poverty, school districts using CTC experienced lower levels of risk and reduced adolescent substance use and delinquency compared to school districts not using the CTC framework (Feinberg, Greenberg, Olson, & Osgood, 2005).

As emphasized throughout this chapter, successful implementation of the CTC system is grounded in the administration of the student survey and analysis of this data. CTC communities are encouraged to supplement information with official records of problem behaviors, such as arrest reports, teenage pregnancy rates, and school suspension data. Repeated administration of the survey (at least every 2-3 years) allows communities to monitor levels of risk, protection, and problem behaviors over time. Used in conjunction with data from the program monitoring system, community members refine their prevention activities. If data do not demonstrate improvements in student outcomes, communities are advised to make changes to improve prevention activities. Conversely, communities can interpret positive results as evidence that their efforts are working and can use this information to garner additional community support for activities, seek additional funding for prevention efforts, and ultimately increase the likelihood that the new policies and programs installed through the CTC process will be sustained (St Pierre, 2001).

Acknowledgments

This work was supported by a research grant from the National Institute on Drug Abuse (R01 DA015183-01A1) with co-funding from the National Cancer Institute, the National Institute on Child Health and Development, the National Institute on Mental Health, and the Center for Substance Abuse Prevention.

The authors wish to acknowledge the contributions of the communities participating in the Community Youth Development Study.

Note

1. These numbers do not match those in Table 16.2 as some communities implemented more than one school-based program.

References

Arthur, M. W., Briney, J. S., Hawkins, J. D., Abbott, R. D., Brooke-Weiss, B. L., & Catalano, R. F. (2007). Measuring community risk and protection using the Communities That Care Youth Survey. *Evaluation and Program Planning, 30,* 197-211.

Arthur, M. W., Brown, E. C., & Briney, J. S. (2006). *Multilevel examination of the relationships between risk and protective factors in student populations and students' academic test performance.* Report prepared for the Washington State Office of Superintendent of Public Instruction. Seattle: Social Development Research Group, University of Washington. Retrieved February 27, 2007, from http://www1.dshs.wa.gov/pdf/hrsa/dasa/ResearchReports/MERRPFATS0706.pdf

Arthur, M. W., Hawkins, J. D., Pollard, J. A., Catalano, R. F., & Baglioni, A. J. (2002). Measuring risk and protective factors for substance use, delinquency, and other adolescent problem behaviors: The Communities That Care Youth Survey. *Evaluation Review, 26,* 575-601.

Backer, T. E., David, S. L., & Soucy, G. (1995). Introduction. In T. E. Backer, S. L. David, & G. Soucy (Eds.), *Reviewing the behavioral science knowledge base on technology transfer* (pp. 1-20). Rockville, MD: National Institute on Drug Abuse.

Biglan, A., & Taylor, T. K. (2000). Why have we been more successful in reducing tobacco use than violent crime? *American Journal of Community Psychology, 28,* 269-302.

Butterfoss, F. D., Goodman, R. M., & Wandersman, A. (1993). Community coalitions for prevention and health promotion. *Health Education Research, 8,* 315-330.

Catalano, R. F., & Hawkins, J. D. (1996). The Social Development Model: A theory of antisocial behavior. In J. D. Hawkins (Ed.), *Delinquency and crime: Current theories* (pp. 149-197). New York: Cambridge University Press.

Coie, J. D., Watt, N. F., West, S. G., Hawkins, J. D., Asarnow, J. R., Marman, H. J., et al. (1993). The science of prevention: A conceptual framework and some directions for a national research program. *American Psychologist, 48,* 1013-1022.

Ellickson, P., Petersilia, J., Caggiano, M., & Polin, S. (1983). *Implementing new ideas in criminal justice.* Santa Monica, CA: The Rand Corporation.

Elliott, D. S., Huizinga, D., & Menard, S. (1989). *Multiple problem youth: Delinquency, substance use, and mental health problems.* New York: Springer-Verlag.

Elliott, D. S., & Mihalic, S. (2004). Issues in disseminating and replicating effective prevention programs. *Prevention Science, 5,* 47-53.

Fagan, A. A., Hawkins, J. D., Hanson, K., & Arthur, M. W. (in press). Bridging science to practice: Achieving prevention program implementation fidelity in the Community Youth Development Study. *American Journal of Community Psychology.*

Feinberg, M., Greenberg, M., Olson, J., & Osgood, W. (2005). *Preliminary report: CTC impact in Pennsylvania. Findings from the 2001 and 2003 PA Youth Survey.* University Park, PA: College of Health and Human Development, The Pennsylvania State University.

Flewelling, R. L., Austin, D., Hale, K., LaPlante, M., Liebig, M., Piasecki, L., et al. (2005). Implementing research-based substance abuse prevention in communities: Effects of a coalition-based prevention initiative in Vermont. *Journal of Community Psychology, 33,* 333-353.

Garmezy, N. (1985). Stress-resistant children: The search for protective factors. In J. E. Stevenson (Ed.), *Recent research in developmental psychopathology. Journal of Child Psychology and Psychiatry: Vol. 4 [Book Supplement]* (pp. 213-233). Oxford: Pergamon Press.

Glaser, R. R., Van Horn, M. L., Arthur, M. W., Hawkins, J. D., & Catalano, R. F. (2005). Measurement properties of the Communities That Care Youth Survey across demographic groups. *Journal of Quantitative Criminology, 21,* 73-102.

Gottfredson, G. D. (1984). A theory-ridden approach to program evaluation: A method for stimulating researcher-implementer collaboration. *American Psychologist, 39,* 1101-1112.

Hallfors, D., Cho, H., Livert, D., & Kadushin, C. (2002). Fighting back against substance use: Are community coalitions winning? *American Journal of Preventive Medicine, 23,* 237-245.

Hawkins, J. D., & Catalano, R. F. (1992). *Communities That Care: Action for drug abuse prevention.* San Francisco, CA: Jossey-Bass Publishers.

Hawkins, J. D., & Catalano, R. F. (2003). *Guiding good choices.* South Deerfield, MA: Channing Bete Company.

Hawkins, J. D., & Catalano, R. F. (2004). *Communities That Care prevention strategies guide.* South Deerfield, MA: Channing Bete Company, Inc. Retrieved November 10, 2007, from http://ncadi.samhsa.gov/features/ctc/resources.aspx

Hawkins, J. D., Catalano, R. F., & Arthur, M. W. (2002). Promoting science-based prevention in communities. *Addictive Behaviors, 27,* 951-976.

Hawkins, J. D., Van Horn, M. L., & Arthur, M. W. (2004). Community variation in risk and protective factors and substance use outcomes. *Prevention Science, 5,* 213-220.

Hawkins, J. D., & Weis, J. G. (1985). The social development model: An integrated approach to delinquency prevention. *Journal of Primary Prevention, 6,* 73-97.

Lasker, R. D. (2000, April-May). *Track 3. Promoting collaborations that improve health.* Presented at the Community-Campus Partnerships for Health's 4th Annual Conference, Washington, DC.

Miller, R. L., & Shinn, M. (2005). Learning from communities: Overcoming difficulties in dissemination of prevention and promotion efforts. *American Journal of Community Psychology, 35,* 169-183.

Mitchell, R., Florin, P., & Stevenson, J. F. (2002). Supporting community-based prevention and health promotion initiatives: Developing effective technical assistance systems. *Health Education and Behavior, 29,* 620-639.

Office of Juvenile Justice and Delinquency Prevention. (1996). *1996 Report to Congress. Title V incentive grants for local delinquency prevention programs.* Washington, DC: Author.

Olweus, D., Limber, S., & Mihalic, S. F. (1999). Bullying prevention program. In D. S. Elliott (Ed.), *Blueprints for Violence Prevention: Book 9.* Boulder, CO: University of Colorado, Institute of Behavioral Science, Center for the Study and Prevention of Violence.

Perry, C. L., Williams, C. L., Komro, K. A., Veblen-Mortension, S., Forster, J. L., Bernstein-Lachter, R., et al. (2000). Project Northland high school interventions: Community action to reduce adolescent alcohol use. *Health Education and Behavior, 27,* 29-49.

Perry, C. L., Williams, C. L., Veblen Mortenson, S., Toomey, T. L., Komro, K. A., Anstine, P. S., et al. (1996). Project Northland: Outcomes of a communitywide alcohol use prevention program during early adolescence. *American Journal of Public Health, 86,* 956-965.

Quinby, R., Fagan, A. A., Hanson, K., Brooke-Weiss, B. L., Arthur, M. W., & Hawkins, J. D. (in press). Installing the Communities That Care prevention system: Implementation progress and fidelity in a randomized controlled trial. *Journal of Community Psychology.*

Rutter, M. (1980). *Changing youth in a changing society.* Cambridge, MA: Harvard University Press.

Spoth, R. L., & Greenberg, M. T. (2005). Toward a comprehensive strategy for effective practitioner-scientist partnerships and larger-scale community health and well-being. *American Journal of Community Psychology, 35,* 107-126.

St Pierre, T. L. (2001). Strategies for community/school collaborations to prevent youth substance use. *The Journal of Primary Prevention, 21,* 381-398.

Wagenaar, A. C., Murray, D. M., Gehan, J. P., Wolfson, M., Toomey, T. L., Perry, C. L., et al. (2000). Communities mobilizing for change on alcohol: Outcomes from a randomized community trial. *Journal of Studies on Alcohol, 61,* 85-94.

Wandersman, A. (2003). Community science: Bridging the gap between science and practice with community-centered models. *American Journal of Community Psychology, 31,* 227-242.

Werner, E. E. (1989). High-risk children in young adulthood: A longitudinal study from birth to 32 years. *American Journal of Orthopsychiatry, 59,* 72-81.

Chapter 17

The Youth Data Archive: Integrating Data to Assess Social Settings in a Societal Sector Framework

MILBREY McLAUGHLIN AND MARGARET O'BRIEN-STRAIN

T he Youth Data Archive (YDA), a project of the John W. Gardner Center at Stanford University, provides integrated data from public and private youth-serving organizations to inform analyses at the individual, program setting, and community levels. Currently working in three communities and two counties, the YDA links individual-level administrative data from schools and public agencies such as child welfare, health services, and probation with program data from youth development programs offered through community-based youth organizations (CBYOs), as well as other data sources such as survey data or qualitative studies. In doing so, the YDA aims to support policymakers, practitioners, community members, and others in making positive changes in the social settings—the programs, out-of-school activities, institutional contexts—within and through which youth move. At the same time, the YDA is also an instrument to measure the settings themselves.

The overarching theory of change behind the YDA posits that different and better information about the social settings and resources available to youth—and their associated outcomes—will foster better choices and decisions about how to improve those individual and collective settings. The YDA's theory of change has four conceptual building blocks:

1. To successfully change youth development settings, one must account for their embedded context.
2. The relevant context for youth development programs extends to the entire societal sector.[1]

3. Data integration can measure settings at the individual level and provide rich contextual information at the community levels, illuminating the importance of societal sector in determining the success of youth and supporting value-added assessment of individual programs.
4. Setting change as the result of data integration is achieved not through the data itself but rather by creating a structure for building relationships and knowledge.

In this chapter, we first expand on these four tenets and provide details on the YDA's data integration and data-use strategies. We close with a review of the current status of the YDA: What has been accomplished so far? What are the challenges to the YDA's development and effectiveness? What are the next steps and promising directions?

Importance of Context for Youth Development Settings

The field of youth development research has made enormous progress in defining the features of positive developmental settings for youth. As the National Research Council's 2002 *Community Programs to Promote Youth Development* details, empirical and theoretical evidence links features of social settings (safety, appropriate structure, supportive relationships, etc.) to youth development outcomes (physical, intellectual, psychological/emotional, and social) and to positive societal outcomes for youth (academic achievement, employment, civic engagement, noninvolvement in crime; Eccles & Gootman, 2002). However, much less is known about how to foster and sustain change in those settings.

The YDA takes the perspective that strategies to change settings must account for their *embedded contexts*. That is, even successful efforts to change the quality and outcomes of youth programs and organizations are bound to fall short—in terms of their sustainability, replicability, and ability to maximize cumulative benefits—if they focus *only* on internal processes, measures, and opportunities. Youth-serving organizations are embedded within multiple regulatory, normative, and policy settings—environments that affect their missions, resources, political support, and viability. These broader system environments are extremely complex, reflecting the multiple goals of the organizations, the patchwork and unstable funding strategies, dynamic political environments, and complicated relationships with upstream and downstream organizations. Viewing the social settings within and through which youth move as part of a larger system of resources and opportunities carries important implications for both analysis and efforts to change those settings.

Considering interrelationships among various youth development assets, Cook et al. (2002) found small, independent effects of neighborhoods, nuclear families, friendship groups, and schools on early adolescent development and provided support for the conclusion that "more is better"—the more developmentally superior contexts that are available to young people, the better their life chances (see also Eccles & Gootman, 2002). However, Cook et al. also concluded that "Contexts really matter in determining how young people's lives develop, but they do so cumulatively more than singly" and that "pan-contextual improvement requires pan-contextual measures" (p. 1306).[2] Practitioners and others working with youth appreciate that although more is better, the nature and quality of opportunities available to young people matter; not all Boys and Girls Clubs, after-school programs, sports teams, tutoring efforts, or other CBYOs have equally effective offerings and appeal to young people either in terms of content or their operations (Eccles & Gootman, 2002; McLaughlin, Irby, & Langman, 1994).

Just as other programs in the same environment can provide cumulative benefits, the context also can create challenges or barriers that are beyond the control of an individual program. High-stakes education accountability policies, for instance, with their single-minded focus on academic achievement frustrate efforts to provide school-linked resources for programs aimed at social, emotional, or physical outcomes. Community-based organizations in many communities may fail to reach participation goals not for reasons of program quality, but because inadequate local policing and transportation policies discourage teens' attendance. In both of these instances, the character and capacity of social settings serving youth are constrained by aspects of their broader institutional contexts.

The goal of changing social settings in ways that benefit youth, then, presents a challenge not only in understanding how particular projects and programs can be made more effective on their own terms, but also in understanding how particular projects and programs can be made more effective as part of a larger system of resources and opportunities for youth, that is, how to change social settings in ways that make them add up to more for young people *and* facilitate the operation of any single program.

A Societal Sector Framework

The YDA adopts a *societal sector framework* as the strategy for treating settings' embedded contexts as questions for research and unit of analysis. A societal sector framework, as developed by Scott and Meyer (1991), emphasizes function over geography or bureaucratic affiliation; it takes the wider interorganizational systems implicated in providing a given type of service—in this instance, programs and services for youth. This perspective differs from frameworks that cluster together organizations seen as similar in form or focus—for example, schools, CBYOs, health services for youth—or models that emphasize formal linkages, such as categorical policy streams, or informal networks such as professional affiliations. It considers other forces at work in society and urges researchers to look outside the formal policy system to nonformal relationships that extend across categorical or functional boundaries—such as those with nongovernmental organizations, professional organizations, or the private sector—and pursue lessons learned about relationships, contexts and outcomes, while also tracking opportunities associated with the new actors and associations revealed by this broader frame.

For the youth development sector, this approach features the complexity of relationships across all actors and organizations such as other youth-serving organizations, schools, social service agencies, child-protective services, civic leaders, and community agencies. It takes both a vertical and a horizontal view of youth-serving organizations and the agencies with which they interact. A vertical assessment looks at linkages between the "top" of the relevant policy system to consider in what ways and with what consequences macrolevel programs and policies make their way to the "bottom" or community level. A horizontal view focuses on the interrelationships among youth-serving actors at a particular policy level—neighborhood, community, county, or state. Questions prompted by this framework include, for example: How are program resources or outcomes enhanced or constrained by decisions made at the school district level, by the priorities of county government, or by local political support? Are effective collaborations apparent?

Assessing the contribution of a particular youth organization or other youth resource within a societal sector framework moves away from a "main effects" or "impact" approach to program evaluation to consider the *value added* of an organization within the context of other opportunities and resources for youth. For example, what is the value added as measured by youth development outcomes of differently implemented after-school programs? Do some program designs seem particularly beneficial for youth from different cultural, ethnic, or socioeconomic backgrounds? Are benefits seen primarily in combination with youth participation in such youth-serving institutions as health clinics? Or are they most effective when other resources such as a neighborhood policing program also are present? Locating youth-serving organizations in their broader institutional environment mitigates risks of under- or overestimating program effects because youth outcomes can be understood in the context of broader opportunities and resources.

Despite the enormous value of a societal perspective as a strategy to advance the emerging field of youth development, the programs, organizations, and agencies in this sector have been famously Balkanized in their operation and relationships. Major public players in the youth policy arena including organizations in education, health care, social services, and juvenile justice comprise well-recognized and stable systems, and they largely operate in splendid isolation from one another. At the CBYO level, agencies may be closely linked with each of the government systems but they also provide services quite different from those offered through government agencies. In many cases, the same CBYO may contract with several government agencies for similar youth development activities, repackaged as promoting health, education, or crime prevention as required for the funding stream.

Between the government and community-based providers targeting youth, we find that both the norms of practice and services provided are often incompatible and frequently conflict. Beginning in the late 1980s, both youth policy and research on adolescent development entered a new phase, one that departed from a narrow emphasis on remedying "deficits" and uncoordinated institutional supports to focus on the broader context of healthy development and enhanced integration of youth services (Pittman, Irby, & Ferber, 2000). Reformers experienced in working with young people argued that the needs of youth are complex and interwoven and contended that policies and programs intended to benefit them should strive for continuity across sectors (such as education, social service, and juvenile justice), organizations, and age groups. Further, reformers pushed for policies that featured a broadened conception of youth and youth services rather than a focus on "fixing problems." Programs and policies consistent with a youth development point of view acknowledge the broader social and institutional contexts that actively influence individual outcomes and development. Service providers such as CBYOs typically see their mission in positive, youth development terms.

While local public partners often embrace elements of the positive youth development perspective, the requirements imposed by their vertical position—in terms of both funding and performance expectations—lead to a focus on deficits. In particular, publicly funded youth agencies face increasing pressures to meet performance outcomes, where the mandated outcomes of interest are generally framed as avoiding or correcting negative results (e.g., reducing the number of teen pregnancies, the share of children not proficient on test scores, and recidivism in juvenile justice). As local budgets are squeezed, a move toward positive youth development strategies may appear too distant from the required outcomes. Moreover, as part of their larger vertical systems, public agency staff are professionally trained and affiliated within those separate systems, as health professionals, social workers, or educators.

Conceptually, professionally, and pragmatically then, many actors in the youth arena do not see themselves as part of the same sector. Thus, advocates of a societal perspective face the extraordinarily difficult task of mobilizing support across fractured, segmented interests. The Gardner Center YDA is built on the belief that data integration offers an opportunity to address the sometimes conflicting aims of youth-serving organizations and to make the societal perspective meaningful for them.

Data Integration to Measure
Settings and Contexts

The YDA brings a societal sector perspective to the concept of data integration, using integrated data to encourage community-level responsibility and accountability for resources, opportunities, and youth outcomes through coherent, mutually reinforcing policies and programs. By matching individual-level data across programs and over time, we create "event histories" for children and youth that offer a much richer context for understanding participation in any given program.

To illustrate the character and measurement value of such integrated data, Figure 17.1 draws upon the YDA to present simplified event histories for two children who attended the same middle school in 2005. Based solely on the information for 2005, Child 2 appears less needy than Child 1, who is receiving food stamps, Medicaid, and welfare. If we wanted to understand the impact of the family counseling on test scores for children in middle school, however, we might get a very different understanding of Child 2 if we took into account the fact that over the previous 2 years he was the subject of three alleged instances of child abuse and that his family was intermittently on and off public assistance throughout his childhood. On the other hand, his child welfare caseworker may have no idea that he is receiving services through a family center or that he lost connection with his after-school program when he moved to middle school.

Such event histories offer a rich strategy to measure programs and their contexts. First, in the short run, the YDA helps community partners understand the full set of services and opportunities for youth in a community. In particular, it allows us to determine whether multiple agencies are serving the same youth, the paths they take to reach services, and how services can be better coordinated. In addition, it can be used to find gaps in service by types of service, youth characteristics and needs, and geography. Second, over time, the YDA will allow us to measure the cumulative effects of community youth development programs and services on youth outcomes, accounting for the complex dynamics of youth participation in public and private programs. Third, where we can document key features of programs' structures or approaches, such as their reliance on such tools as the Bay Area's Community Network for Youth Development's Framework for Practice, or link survey and observational data on youth development outcomes, the integrated data can document the empirical connections between youth development outcomes and other outcomes such as academic achievement, youth employment, and juvenile justice.

For an individual youth organization, the YDA can help in planning, programming, and evaluation. Take, for example, a local Boys and Girls Club. The YDA can identify where children of the target age group live, what languages they speak, what activities are currently available to them,

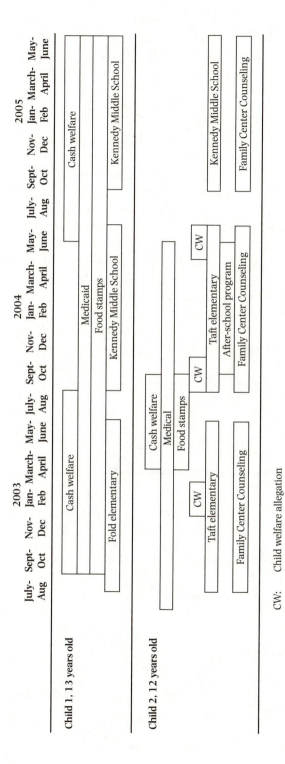

CW: Child welfare allegation

Figure 17.1. Example Event Histories.

and which children are at risk in school or in foster care and are not being reached by any community programs. For programming purposes, the YDA can help point to best practices by determining how programs with similar content—such as science programs—are linked to outcomes like high school completion and whether programs with specific features like higher adult to child ratios fare compared to other similar programs. This naturally extends to the club's own evaluation, but it reduces the burden for the program by capturing information such as school attendance before and after participation and leaving the program's own evaluation to focus on collection of data not available in other systems, such as youth leadership.

At the same time, if we take outcomes observed in administrative data such as reduced recidivism in juvenile justice or greater rates of high school graduation as long-term outcomes, we can use the YDA to expand from a simple logic model for one program to a richer examination of a sequence of programs or a comparison across different programs that differ in their youth development approaches and outcomes, as seen in Figure 17.2.

We are not the first to advocate for a data system that integrates various youth-focused resources and that looks across the agencies, organizations, and programs that target the same population. In fact, there has been a resurgence in data systems work as the cost of information systems has dropped,

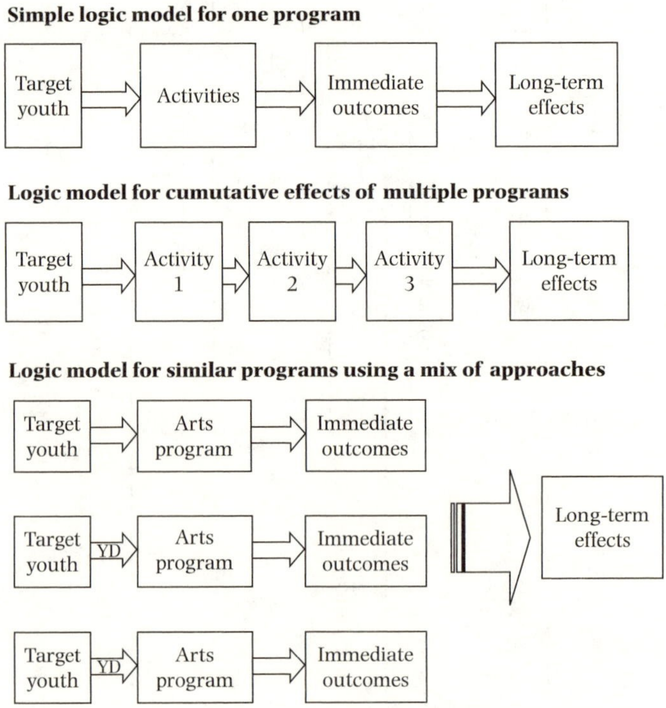

Figure 17.2. Alternative Logic Models Possible With Integrated Data.

their use has become widespread, and the internet has provided greater communications options. At present, there are three common strategies for youth-focused data activities: indicators, geographic information systems (GIS), and integration of public data systems.

A number of communities have adopted "report cards" to give an account of a community's or a state's youth indicators—high school dropouts, asthma rates, and teen births.[3] Philadelphia's efforts supported by funding from the Urban Health Initiative resulted in one of the nation's most comprehensive "report cards;" the city was successful in engaging both public and nonprofit agencies as well as community-based organizations in a system to link client-based data (see Weitzman, Silver, & Brazill, 2005, pp. 14-15). The Annie E. Casey Foundation's work on KIDS COUNT and the related local KIDS COUNT projects provide other sophisticated examples of such indicator projects. States such as New York, Iowa, and Oklahoma compile similar reports to mark the status of their youth. Closely related to such report card efforts, GIS projects combine such indicators with spatial information to highlight status by neighborhood (zip code, census block, political district). The resulting maps can be quite compelling to policymakers and the public, especially on resource allocation by location. As useful as these portraits are as status indicators, they do not address the interrelationships among various youth outcomes or, by extension, the resources and programs associated with them.

Data integration, where information is linked across programs at the client level, provides a much richer ability to show the complexity of youth participation across programs. Because the same public social service or health agency commonly runs many different programs, just achieving data integration within an agency has been an important step. A few jurisdictions have successfully integrated data across public agencies. South Carolina, for example, has made substantial investments in integrated data systems, led by health specialists, but crossing a wide range of state departments. For example, the state linked data from health, mental health, disabilities, education, social services, and vocational rehabilitation departments to develop an unduplicated count of children with special health care needs, along with their service utilization, county of residence, educational performance, and household structure. This information was used to target outreach, prevention, health, and educational programs for these children (Bailey, 2003).

Knowledge Management: Using Data to Build Relationships

Although the technical barriers to data integration are falling, there are still critical challenges in making data integration a tool for change. Weitzman et al. (2005) studied efforts to improve data practice in 15 "distressed cities."

They note the technical, resource, bureaucratic, and access challenges that frustrated efforts in each city and found that "mobilizing political will and local government leadership [were] critical to overcoming these obstacles" (p. 1); they concluded that a comprehensive "data warehouse" holding all public data "remains a phantom; a vision of what might be, rather than what is" (p. 15). Respondents in their study see this vision as stymied by lack of leadership; what's needed is someone to be "in the middle of this in a neutral position" (p. 19).

The challenges are particularly significant for data integration that seeks to give voice to community-based youth-serving organizations and weight to positive youth development. Because public agencies hold the majority of administrative data on youth, the public agencies play a central role in data integration, which can exacerbate the divisions between the public and nonprofit sectors. The nonprofit or community-based perspective is disadvantaged for a number of reasons. First, these systems often rely on substantial hardware and software investments, creating an expensive system owned by the government agencies. Second, with the system owned by the government side, community organizations may be hesitant to share data except in their role as contractors. Third, community organizations rarely have the skills or the standing within the data integration work to use the integrated data for their own analyses, leaving them in the consumer role. Finally, returning to the conflict between the positive youth development perspective of community-based organizations and the problem-solving requirements facing public agencies, the dependence of these systems on administrative data inherently leads to a dominance of the deficit picture rather than a portrait of positive youth skills, attitudes, and strengths.

Thus, although our theory of change holds that different and better information about the character, resources and outcomes of social settings will further better choices and decisions, we also acknowledge the limits [or myth] of information, by itself, leading to positive social setting change. With Brown and Duguid, we recognize that a "tight focus on information, with the implicit assumption that if we look after information, everything else will fall into place, is ultimately a sort of social and moral blindness" (2000, p. 31).

The YDA takes the creation of new knowledge for setting change as problems of knowledge management.[4] Following Brown and Duguid (2000), the YDA project builds on the premise that knowledge and information are not one and the same and that translating information into actionable knowledge requires intentional strategies of convening, negotiating, support, and relationship building among stakeholders. Central to enacting this theory of change, then, are opportunities and supports for users to develop shared understandings about the significance of YDA analyses and data, negotiate implications for action, and agree on appropriate indicators assessments with which to both measure and guide change. The YDA, in other words, assumes the creation of a community of practice within which to consider programs and policies for youth.[5]

We take data linkage as an approach and a tool, not an end in itself. YDA users require a venue in which they can learn to ask questions, engage in candid conversation about implications they see in the data for policy and practice, and make decisions that implicate multiple institutions and programs. To be successful, the YDA must help practitioners, policymakers, and other stakeholders see themselves as part of a broader context and use information provided by the YDA to examine relationships between relevant dimensions of social settings and outcomes for young people. However, to do so, the YDA must be responsive to the incentives that guide decisions about policies and practices, creating opportunities for stakeholders representing diverse interests to start by considering the implications of data for their own organizations and not just the youth-serving sector more generally.

To achieve this, we have incorporated several critical features that speak to the role of relationship building and knowledge management. They include (a) expertise located in the "neutral middle," (b) long-term commitment but near-term products, (c) close oversight by data contributors, and (d) lowered costs and administrative hurdles by structuring for research purposes.

Expertise Located in the "Neutral Middle"

The Gardner Center serves as a neutral third party, holding data for the benefit of the community as a whole rather than giving a preference to the government agencies or to the nonprofit agencies, including those seen as advocates sometimes in opposition to government. In this role, we are responsible for all the technical elements of creating the data archive, including negotiating access to the data; identifying protocols for secure, low-burden data transfer; and data matching. We also provide analytical expertise, so we take the lead in product development, although we are also working to build the capacity of our community partners. Because we have no authority over any of the entities providing data, the negotiation of data access is the greatest ongoing challenge. In fact, this middle role is only feasible because of four factors: First, we have community partners already committed to the concept of community youth development. Second, we are known and trusted in the community. Third, we approach the archive creation as a long-term commitment. Finally, we have been fortunate to obtain grants that provide general start-up support rather than relying on the funding from any one agency or support for a specific analytical task.

Long-term Commitment but Near-Term Products

The Gardner Center's long-term commitment has turned out to be one of the most important features of the project. In planning for a long-term role, we take a stepwise approach to building the archive. As soon as we have data contributed, we seek to develop analyses of interest to contributors, thereby encouraging other agencies to participate. For those who are less comfortable about providing data, we develop strategies for less sensitive initial data transfer. For example, for public mental health programs, we will start with information only on participation in these programs, leaving more detailed case information to later phases and future analyses. Together these strategies allow the project to move forward even when specific agencies are not initially committed to the project or have concerns about data confidentiality. Initial "foot draggers" do not stymie the project but can be given time to feel comfortable with the project and the process. Moreover, because our analyses are not just summary indicators, we can gradually address data issues as they arise. For example, some of our first analyses have examined after-school programs. The staff directing these programs had conducted youth and teacher surveys to capture many of the youth development features of the programs but the surveys were all anonymous and therefore could not be incorporated into the event histories. Seeing how the survey data could be integrated into the larger analysis has led the programs to change their data collection procedures. Similarly, our initial analyses rely on the information currently available, recognizing that the answers may change as additional data comes into the archive. Rather than being a disadvantage, the analyses drawn on less than universal initial data become the basis for conversation about what alternative interpretations might be more accurate, what data would be needed to test the alternative interpretations, and how policymakers might change their views and their actions based on such information. This is exactly the process of knowledge creation we seek in the YDA.

Close Oversight by Data Contributors

A key strategy to ensure that agencies are willing to join the YDA is the establishment of data-use agreements in which agencies do not lose ownership or control of their data. In the communities that have less of an existing collaborative structure, agencies express political worries, concerns that their data in the hands of another public or private youth-serving group could be used to embarrass them or initiate legal action. This worry is not unique to our communities. As Weitzman et al. (2005) observed, in some communities "there is almost a paranoia that runs through it that they are afraid if they work together that someone will see inefficiencies and take money away from them" (p. 19).

To alleviate these concerns, we are establishing two groups in each local community to advise the YDA work—a Policy Committee and a Data Oversight Team, with representatives from every major agency contributing data.[6]

The Policy Committee is largely an extension of ongoing collaborative work in the community. It has two basic roles. First, it generates and approves questions for analysis, including topics proposed by outside researchers. In approving questions for analysis, the contributing agencies approve the use of their data for that topic. Second, the Policy Committee assists with dissemination and outreach. The Data Oversight Team serves as a more technical review panel. One of its tasks is to review findings for accuracy and data interpretation. Especially in the early years of the YDA, we believe this approach is critical to building trust among the partners who provide their data to the initiative. Equally important, we have found this kind of review critical to avoiding misinterpretations that may have enormous impact on the findings. For example, in one county, what appeared to be a sudden drop in the number of foster homes was in fact an artifact of a data cleaning that eliminated all inactive foster homes in 1 month. Administrative changes in the way data are recorded can also greatly affect results without any underlying change in services. The same data interpretation issues exist for data captured on paper forms or in simple spreadsheets as for data from sophisticated government IT systems. The review process will provide a forum for discussing such data issues and, ideally, improving data collection over time. We also hope that this task will create another avenue for collaboration in the communities, as partners talk together around concrete data findings, prompting further questions and new strategies.

Lowered Costs and Administrative Hurdles by Structuring for Research Purposes

Because our purpose in the YDA is to use data to build knowledge for community youth development, we have adopted a data structure that significantly lowers the Information Technology (IT) costs as well as the confidentiality concerns relative to the large relational databases with live lookup and reporting, developed for day-to-day service integration rather than research. These systems not only require greater hardware and software investments (so they are more expensive) but they also usually require client consent procedures. Because our focus is on analyses of broader community issues, including the cumulative value added by youth-serving organizations, we are able to employ simpler file structures designed for policy analysis and research rather than live program administration. Moreover, since we are providing aggregated results—albeit with much greater use of subgroup analysis and other statistical techniques—we fall clearly within the bounds of data use for research purposes, which fall under a different set of confidentiality rules and requirements. Many of the features of the relational databases that are used for policy purposes, such as standard outcome reports, can be built into internet-based collaborative environments. Once the archive is established, the ongoing costs will largely be the staff time for specific analyses, which we expect will be supportable on a low-cost fee basis.

Progress to Date, Challenges, and Next Steps

The YDA currently operates in three communities where we have strong existing connections. To date, we are working with eight public agencies, four school districts, and a handful of community-based organizations in two counties. Table 17.1 lists how the types of data we have compare to the types we have targeted for eventual inclusion in the archive. We continue to work with agencies in each community to add additional participants into the YDA. Particularly with agencies such as public health departments, the commitment to participate in the archive will bring multiple new data sources, such as nurse visitation, teen pregnancy prevention, and school health clinic data.

Our initial analyses have focused on school-based services included after-school programs and mental health counseling. In terms of service coordination, we have examined the share of children in two school districts who receive public assistance or Medicaid or who are involved in the child welfare system. Although these children are more likely than their classmates to reach school-based services, many do not participate. The school district is using this information to improve outreach to Asian language minorities, who appear to be underserved even after controlling for school characteristics and social services participation. While descriptive statistics are the

Table 17.1. Types of Data Ideally Included in Archive

Y	School attendance, grades, and test score	Y	After-school program participation
Y	Child welfare caseload and placement	*	Youth employment service receipt
*	Juvenile probation placement and services	*	Job training participation
Y	TANF participation and services	Y	Sports, arts, and enrichment program participation
Y	Housing assistance		Alcohol and other drug substance abuse services
Y	Public health insurance participation		Teen parenting and pregnancy prevention services
*	Public health insurance claims	Y	Independent living assistance
	Arrest records	Y	Other community-based service participation
*	Mental/behavioral health caseload	*	Early childhood education

Note. Y = Currently in the YDA for one or more community; * = Data use currently being negotiated and/or data sources available through other research.

main analytical tool to determine who is and is not receiving services, we have relied on more sophisticated regression analyses to assess the impact of school-based services. For example, we used a generalized propensity scores approach to identify children in schools without mental health counseling who were most like those children receiving counseling in similar schools that offer these services. This allowed us to use a notional control group to test the impact of the mental health counseling on test scores. We found a small but significant additional boost in test scores year to year for counseling participants once we used this control group strategy to statistically correct for the fact that the most troubled children—who also have unusually low school performance—are most likely to receive services. The ability to control for child welfare history turned out to be an important factor in identifying the control group. An upcoming project will examine the overlap between welfare eligibility and child neglect cases to assess the role of various support services, including cash assistance, food stamps, alcohol and drug treatment, job training, and mental health services, in preventing inadequate care for children and thus keeping children safe at home.

The ongoing challenge for the YDA is exactly that seen in other cities and anticipated by project staff: the slow process of gaining and maintaining data access. While the Gardner Center's long-term commitment has been critical in making progress, the downside of this patience is the fact that staff has turned over at a number of the partner agencies, while the agencies themselves shift data systems over time. In one school district, for example, virtually all of the staff with whom we had negotiated to develop a data-use agreement left the district before data was actually provided under the agreement; we are now negotiating from scratch with new personnel. Another agency that is one of our strongest allies has been required to adopt a new statewide database; thus they have to learn how to work with it internally first and then learn to export data for outside stakeholders like the YDA. These situations are endemic in a project such as the YDA and are largely addressed by maintaining strong relationships at multiple levels of agencies as well as by maintaining key partners such as local foundations.

Other future goals for the YDA include the more systematic inclusion of measures of social settings such as the Community Network for Youth Development's Youth Development Framework for Practice, social setting indicators used by the Boys and Girls Clubs of America, and the Program Quality Assessment measures used in High/Scope. The inclusion of these measures, as well as data on youth perspectives of their resources and opportunities, will rely on new data collection. Such data would allow the YDA to take a "natural experiment" approach to better understand variation in the nature of relevant social settings and how they operate in different local and system contexts. Over time, we hope the YDA will broaden the commitments to community youth development by creating community, county, and regional accounts of resources and opportunities available for youth. Finally, we will be tracking the evolution of the YDA to understand its lessons for knowledge management in a societal sector, including: Which stakeholders use the YDA under what conditions and to what end? What factors contribute to agencies' capacity to use data generally and the YDA in particular? What factors facilitate candid examination of data across sectors, agencies, and programs to address collective responsibilities for effective social settings and youth development? And what factors constrain these discussions?

Notes

1. A societal sector framework, as developed by Scott and Meyer (1991), emphasizes function over geography or bureaucratic affiliation; it takes the wider interorganizational systems implicated in providing a given type of service—in this instance, programs and services for youth.

2. In contrast to Cook et al.'s (2002) conclusion about linearity and additivity, Talbert and McLaughlin (1999) find that aspects of the education institutional environment are not additive but rather interact in ways that mean the same factor acts as a resource at one school site but has no or negative effects for another school site operating in the same district context.

3. The indicator strategy is actually a revitalization of the social indicators movement of the 1960s and 1970s (see e.g., Bauer, 1966; U.S. Office of Management and Budget, 1973).

4. The literature on knowledge management is extensive. See Von Krogh, Ichijo, and Nonkara (2000) and Wenger, McDermott, and Snyder (2002) for useful collections on the topic.

5. We use the concept "community of practice" as elaborated by Wenger (1998) and Wenger et al. (2002).

6. The Kids Integrated Data System (KIDS) run by the Cartographic Modeling Lab at the University of Pennsylvania to link data from Philadelphia city government and the city school district takes a similar governance approach.

References

Bailey, W. P. (2003). Integrated state data systems. In R. M. Weinick & J. Billings (Eds.), *Tools for monitoring the health care safety net*, AHRQ Publication No. 03-0027, September 2003, Agency for Healthcare Research and Quality, Rockville, MD. Retrieved November 8, 2007, from www.ahrq.gov/data/safetynet/tools.htm

Bauer, R. A. (Ed.). (1966). *Social indicators*. Cambridge, MA: The MIT Press.

Brown, J. S., & Duguid, P. (2000). *The social life of information*. Cambridge: Harvard Business School Press.

Cook, T. D., Herman, M. R., Phillips, M., & Settersten, R. A., Jr. (2002, July-August) Some ways in which neighborhoods, nuclear families, friendship groups, and schools jointly affect changes in early adolescent development. *Child Development, 73*(4), 1283-1309.

Eccles, J. S., & Gootman, J. A. (2002). *Community programs to promote youth development.* Washington, DC: National Academy Press.

McLaughlin, M. W., Irby, M. A., & Langman, J. (1994). *Urban sanctuaries: Neighborhood organizations in the lives and futures of inner-city youth.* San Francisco: Jossey-Bass.

Pittman, K, Irby, M., & Ferber, T. (2000). *Unfinished business: Further reflections of a decade of promoting youth development.* Takoma Park, MD: The Forum for Youth Investment.

Scott, W. R., & Meyer, J. W. (1991). The organization of societal sectors: Perceptions and early evidence. In W. W. Powell & P. J. DiMaggio (Eds.), *The new institutionalism in organizational analysis* (pp. 108-140). Chicago: The University of Chicago Press.

Talbert, J. E., & McLaughlin, M. W. (1999). Assessing the school environment: Embedded contexts and bottom-up research strategies. In S. L. Friedman & T. D. Wachs (Eds.), *Measuring environment across the life span: Emerging methods and concepts* (pp. 197-227). Washington, DC: American Psychological Association.

U.S. Office of Management and Budget. (1973). *Social indicators.* Washington, DC: Author.

Von Krough, G., Ichijo, K., & Nonaka, I. (2000). *Enabling knowledge creation.* New York: Oxford University Press.

Weitzman, B. C., Silver, D., & Brazill, C. (2005). Efforts to improve public policy and programs through improved data practices: Experiences in fifteen distressed American cities. *Public Administration Review.* New York, NY: Center for Health & Public Service Research. Retrieved November 8, 2007, from http://wagner.nyu.edu//chpsr/uhi/uhi_bibliography.php

Wenger, E. (1998). *Communities of practice.* New York: Cambridge University Press.

Wenger, E., McDermott, R., & Snyder, W. M. (2002). *A guide to managing knowledge: Cultivating communities of practice.* Cambridge, MA: Harvard Business School Press.

PART V

CROSS-CUTTING THEMES: STRATEGIES
FOR MEASUREMENT AND INTERVENTION

Chapter 18

Measuring and Improving Program Quality: Reliability and Statistical Power

ANDRES MARTINEZ AND STEPHEN W. RAUDENBUSH

T his chapter considers interventions that aim to increase the quality of programs serving youth. These interventions include after-school programs (e.g., Hirsch & Wong, 2005), comprehensive school reform programs (e.g., Borman et al., 2005), teacher professional development programs (e.g., Kinzie et al., 2005), and training programs for coaches (e.g., Smith, 2006), among others. Whether such interventions are athletic, educational, therapeutic, or social, they operate in group settings such as teams, therapy groups, whole schools, or classrooms. One important way to increase program quality is to increase the quality of interactions involving adults and youths within these groups. A "good" team, classroom, or school functions in a way that improves the skill, knowledge, or emotional regulation of the youth who participate in that group. For simplicity we shall refer to the teams, schools, or classrooms as "groups" and the youth who participate in these groups as "persons."

The ultimate aim of the interventions in which we are interested is to change persons—that is, to change outcomes measured at the person level (knowledge, skill, etc.). A study that intends to evaluate the impact of an intervention on persons ought to use valid and reasonably reliable measures of those person-level outcomes. Such person-level measures, however, are not the focus of the current chapter.

Instead, we focus on the measurement of program quality, which is a characteristic of the group rather than the person. The interventions we are concerned with here aim to improve personal outcomes but they aim to do so by improving group quality (e.g., Pianta, La Paro, Payne, Cox, & Bradley,

2002). If such an intervention does not improve group quality, it will not improve the outcomes of persons participating in these groups. Therefore, it is useful to examine impacts of interventions on group quality. However, this can be done only if we know how to measure group quality reliably. If we fail to measure these group outcomes with adequate reliability, the study will lack statistical power to detect intervention effects on group quality. Let us briefly review the rationale for focusing on group quality as an outcome and then consider the importance of reliability and its influence on statistical power.

Why Focus on Group Quality?

The interventions of interest in this chapter are based on a theory that has two parts: a theory of how the intervention changes group quality and a theory of how group quality affects personal outcomes. Knowing whether the intervention affects group quality is essential to understanding when, why, and how an intervention affects personal outcomes.

Consider first a study in which groups were randomly assigned to one of two interventions (treatment vs. control) and that evaluators found no impact on personal outcomes. Assume that the study had adequate statistical power and that the personal outcomes were well measured. Two possibilities emerge.

First, it may be that the intervention improved group quality in all the ways intended but that persons in those groups failed to benefit from such group-quality improvements. For example, suppose a teacher training intervention caused teachers to change their methods of classroom instruction in all the desired ways but that these instructional changes produced no change in student achievement. Clearly, the underlying theory about the link between group quality (in this case, instructional quality) and person outcomes (student achievement) was incorrect.

Second, it may be that the intervention had no impact on group quality. In this case, we have a failure of program theory about how the intervention affects group quality. For example, if a teacher training program had no impact on classroom instruction, we could not have tested a theory about how improved classroom instruction affects student learning.

Now suppose that the evaluators in this case never bothered to measure group quality. Then it would be impossible to distinguish between these two contradictory explanations. The theory about the intervention's impact on group quality could have been wrong, the theory about the impact of group quality on personal outcomes could have been wrong, or both could have been wrong. In sum, it would be difficult to draw any conclusions for the study that might guide future program development.

Next, consider an intervention that did positively affect personal outcomes. Interpreting such a result also depends on knowing whether the intervention changed group quality in the ways intended. If these intended group changes did not occur, then the program must have had its effect on persons through channels that the program designers failed to anticipate. But if the intended changes in the group did occur, we can increase our confidence in the program theory. Knowing which changes in group quality are essential to boost personal outcomes is potentially of great use to others who would adopt the intervention.

The argument here is that assessing the impact of an intervention on group quality is essential in building a science of intervening to improve youth outcomes. In the language of this chapter, knowing how the intervention affects the group is essential even though the ultimate aim is to affect the person. We therefore confine our interest to studies that aim to evaluate the impact of a new intervention on program quality as measured at the level of the group.

The Importance of Reliability at the Group Level

If intervention science requires an understanding of how interventions affect group-level quality, it follows that valid measurement of group-level quality is essential to the advancement of intervention science. The measurement of group settings such as neighborhoods, schools, classrooms, day care centers, or after-school programs is comparatively underdeveloped despite more than a century of intense interest in measuring personal attributes such as cognitive skill and personality. Raudenbush and Sampson (1999) called the science of validly measuring ecological settings "ecometrics" as distinct from the much more thoroughly developed science of measuring psychological attributes, widely known as "psychometrics."

This chapter focuses on one aspect of valid measurement, namely, reliability. Reliability is the consistency of results of applying a measurement procedure under conditions deemed irrelevant to the true value of what is measured. One cannot make valid inferences about group quality based on unreliable data. Reliability is, in short, a necessary if not sufficient condition for valid inference about the quality of a group's functioning. How to insure validity given adequate reliability is a topic of great interest in intervention science but it is beyond the scope of this chapter.

To make these ideas clear, consider the study of classroom quality that will serve as the illustrative example later in this chapter. The supposition is that there exist stable differences between classrooms on some dimension of classroom quality, for example the "emotional climate" of a class. The stable, "true" level of emotional climate of a class is called the *true score*.

In practice, each classroom is observed over 20-minute intervals (called *segments*) on each of one or more days (called *dates*) by one or more trained observers (called *raters*). The coded results are then averaged over segments, dates, and raters to construct an estimate of the true score that we shall call the *observed score*. The observed score will not be equivalent to the true score for several reasons. For starters, the observable emotional climate will likely vary randomly from segment to segment within a date and also from date to date. Because the aim is to discern *stable* differences between classrooms on emotional climate, this short-term random variation is extraneous variation arising from what might be called *temporal instability*.

Next, different raters might vary randomly in their tendency to rate emotional climate favorably, a source of random error known as *rater inconsistency*. In this setting, temporal instability and rater inconsistency combine to generate random *error variance*. This error variance is the variation in the observed scores that is irrelevant to the variation of interest: variation in the stable true scores. The larger the error variance relative to the true-score variance, the less reliable the measure of emotional climate.

Defining Reliability

The variance in the observed scores is the sum of the true-score variance plus the error variance. This is based on the classical measurement model that says simply

$$\text{Observed score} = \text{True score} + \text{Error}. \tag{1}$$

We typically assume that the magnitude of the error does not depend on the value of the true score. We then have a formula for the total variance in the observed scores:

$$\text{Observed-score variance} = \text{True-score variance} + \text{Error variance}. \tag{2}$$

The two simple statements (1) and (2) then generate the traditional formula for the reliability of the observed score, namely the fraction of observed-score variance that is attributable to the variance of the true scores:

$$\begin{aligned}
\text{Reliability} &= \frac{\text{True-score variance}}{\text{Observed-score variance}} \\
&= \frac{\text{True-score variance}}{\text{True-score variance} + \text{Error variance}}.
\end{aligned} \tag{3}$$

One can see from Equation (3) that if error variance diminishes to zero, reliability approaches its maximum of 1.0. This assumes, of course, that there exists some true-score variance to study! If the "objects of measurement," namely the groups, all have the same level of positive emotional climate, then the only variance in the observed scores is error variance and reliability achieves its minimum of 0. In sum, reliability will be high when (a) the groups actually vary a lot in their true scores and (b) the error variance is small.

Reliability and Statistical Power

Let us now imagine a study in which groups are randomly assigned to receive a new intervention (the "treatment condition") versus the standard approach (the "comparison condition"). However, suppose the error variance is very high so that reliability is very low. This low reliability does not bias the evaluation of an intervention in favor of one condition over the other, assuming that temporal instability and rater inconsistency vary randomly over the groups. That is, low reliability does not make it more or less likely that the sample mean of the treatment group will exceed the sample mean of the comparison group. In a thought experiment, imagine the average true score after the intervention is identical in the two groups. Error variance would create a 50-50 chance that the observed treatment mean would exceed the observed control mean.

Although low reliability will not introduce bias, it will weaken the *statistical power* to detect real differences between the treatment conditions when they exist. We define *statistical power* as the probability of detecting a true program impact when in fact such a program impact actually exists.

Imagine for a moment that the intervention really works to improve positive emotional climate so that the mean true score of the groups in the treatment condition exceeds the mean true score in the comparison group. However, suppose that the error variance is excessively large. This "noise" caused by measurement error variance will make it harder to discern the "signal," that is, the difference in true scores generated by the treatment.

Technically, the problem unfolds as follows. In any study comparing two groups, an observed difference between the two groups might arise because there is truly some systematic, underlying causal process that generates a meaningful difference between them. Alternatively, the observed difference could be an artifact of chance: the means of any pair of successive random samples will vary somewhat even if no causal process is at work. The task of statistical significance testing is then to compare the magnitude of any observed difference to the magnitude of differences likely to arise by chance when no causal process is at work. The more variation we can expect by chance, the larger the observed mean difference must be before it can be proclaimed "significant." The role of measurement error in this scenario is to magnify the chance variation that we will see from successive random samples. The larger the measurement error variation, the larger the observed mean differences must be to be proclaimed significant. Therefore, measurement error undermines the power to detect true mean differences.

While the reliability of measurement of the outcome affects statistical power, it is not the only factor affecting power. Power is also affected by the *sample size*, that is, the number of groups assigned to each condition (Bloom, 2005; Raudenbush, 1997; Schochet, 2005). The mean of the observed scores within the treatment condition will tend to become more stable when more groups contribute to that treatment condition mean and similarly for the control condition: more groups in the control condition lead to a more stable control condition mean. As these means become more stable, their mean difference also becomes more stable, and one can more readily discern the differences between the two true-score means by looking at the two observed-score means.

All of this assumes, of course, that the treatment condition really does generate, on average, elevated levels of positive emotional climate. The magnitude of this treatment effect is called the *true effect size*. The larger the true effect size, the greater the statistical power. Of course, most interveners try to make their impact as large as possible by establishing a truly effective intervention. The researcher, however, generally has no control over the effect size, so that source of power is typically unavailable to the researcher.

The two sources of power that *are* amenable to the control of the researcher are thus reliability of measurement of the outcome and sample size. In the next sections, we show how one can spend money to increase reliability and how doing so increases power. However, one might instead spend money to increase the sample size, an alternative route to increased power. In the concluding section we consider the trade-offs associated with these different investment strategies. We also consider how clever design decisions might offset the deleterious effects of low reliability and low sample size on statistical power.

Strategies for Increasing Reliability

As we saw in Equation (3), reliability declines with measurement error variance. In the context of our example, such error variance increases with temporal instability of two types (variation between segments within a date and variation between dates) and with rater inconsistency. This reasoning leads immediately to several possible options for improving reliability:

- If temporal inconsistency attributable to segments is large, make sure to observe multiple segments per day. The more segments observed, the more stable will be the average rating taken over those segments.

- If temporal inconsistency attributable to dates is large, make sure to observe on multiple dates. The more dates observed, the more stable will be the average rating taken over those dates.
- If rater instability is large (lack of agreement between raters), there are two options: (a) make sure each group is observed by multiple raters because deploying more raters will stabilize the average rating taken over those raters or (b) spend more time (and money!) training the raters in order to reduce rater inconsistency.

Each of these provisions potentially involves increased spending. Observing on more segments or days means paying raters to spend more time observing groups; getting more raters per class may mean hiring more raters. These options all increase labor costs. Alternatively, one might make sure that each rater rates a large number of classrooms, each on one occasion (rather than, say, assigning a rater to observe a small number of classrooms, each on multiple occasions). But this last option may increase travel costs and travel time. So the question arises: if the goal is to maximize reliability, how should resources be invested to do so at minimum cost?

The general idea is to spend money on options that will add the most to reliability. Thus, if segments vary a lot within a date but dates do not contribute much to the variation, one should invest more money on multiple segments per date and less money on dates. If raters are highly inconsistent, then one should spend more money training them to be more consistent or one should assign more raters to look at each group, making the average taken over those raters more stable. While the general idea is quite intuitive, its implementation is a little more complex than one might assume. We show in detail how such assessments might be made in the context of an illustrative example.

Illustrative Example

Data are from the National Center for Early Development and Learning (NCEDL) Multi-State Study of Pre-Kindergarten. The study uses the Classroom Assessment Scoring System (CLASS) (Pianta, La Paro, & Hamre, 2004), an instrument being used in various large-scale evaluation studies. CLASS is an assessment system of classroom interactions between teachers and students and is divided into four domains: emotional support, classroom organization, instructional support, and student outcomes (Hamre, Mashburn, Pianta, Locasle-Crouch, & La Paro, 2006; Pianta & Allen, this volume, chapter 2).

The study involves a random sample of 240 childcare centers and, within each center, a random sample of a single classroom. A total of 26 raters participated in 167 observation dates. Classrooms were not simultaneously assessed by multiple raters. Thus, there is never more than one rater per segment.

However, many classrooms were observed by more than one rater, sometimes on the same date. On average, each rater visited about 16 classrooms for 2 or 3 consecutive days and completed between 2 and 8 segments (20-minute observation periods) per visit, generating a total of 6,473 observations for the 240 classrooms. As our outcome, we use the composite measure "emotional climate" that incorporates the assessments of positive climate, negative climate, teacher sensitivity, regard for student perspectives, overcontrol and behavior management. With classrooms as the groups and therefore the unit of measurement (and thus the only source of true variation), the main sources of measurement error will include the raters, the dates, and the segments. Although error variance has these three sources, they combine in a somewhat complex way involving main effects, two-way interaction effects, and three-way interaction effects.

Main Effects

The main effects are simply the effects of average differences between segments, average differences between dates, and average differences between raters. More specifically, the variance attributable to the main effect of segments is

$$\text{Segment noise} = \frac{\text{Segment variance}}{n \text{ of segments}}. \tag{4}$$

Thus Equation (4) says that the noise contributed by the main effect of segments is simply the magnitude of the variation between segments on any given day within any given classroom divided by the "n of segments" that is the number of segments observed on that day. If the segment variance is large, its influence can be counteracted by increasing the number of segments observed on a given day. In contrast, if the segment variance is already very small, increasing the number of segments per day would be a waste of money. In the extreme case, if there were no variation between segments, it would be a complete waste of money to observe more than one segment in any given day!

In a similar vein, the variance attributable to the main effect of dates is

$$\text{Date noise} = \frac{\text{Date variance}}{n \text{ of dates}}. \tag{5}$$

Equation (5) says that the noise contributed by the main effect of dates is the magnitude of the variation between dates for any given classroom divided by the "n of dates" that is the number of dates observed for that classroom. We can reduce "date noise" by increasing the number of dates we observe each classroom.

Finally, the variance attributable to the main effect of raters is

$$\text{Rater noise} = \frac{\text{Rater variance}}{n \text{ of raters}}. \tag{6}$$

Rater variance will be large when some raters are "tougher" than others. That is, one rater may tend, in general, to view each classroom less positively than another rater. One can thus reduce rater noise by assigning multiple raters to rate each classroom (increasing "n of raters"). Alternatively, it may be that better training would reduce rater variance thus reducing rater noise. Intuitively, if raters strongly agree on what they see, rater variance will be small and one need not assign many raters to look at the same classroom.

Two-Way Interaction Effects

Equations (4), (5), and (6) would seem to describe all sources of error variance, namely segment noise, date noise, and rater noise. But life is more complex. Consider rater noise. As mentioned, some raters are, in general, tougher than others. This tendency, may, however, depend on the classroom observed. Rater A may be tougher than Rater B when looking at Mr. Smith's classroom, but more lenient than rater B when looking at Ms. Johnson's classroom. Thus, the "effect" of a rater may depend on the classroom observed. This dependence generates *rater-by-classroom noise*

$$\text{Rater-by-classroom noise} = \frac{\text{Rater-by-classroom variance}}{n \text{ of raters}}. \tag{7}$$

Rater-by-classroom variation is an example of an interaction effect: the impact of one factor depends on the value of the other. Here, "the impact of Rater A relative to Rater B" depends on which classroom is being observed.

The impact of the rater may also depend on the date. Suppose, for example, that Rater A went to an all-night party the day before observing classes and as a result of the ensuing hangover gave unusually low ratings the next day. This scenario would generate *rater-by-date noise*, that is

$$\text{Rater-by-date noise} = \frac{\text{Rater-by-date-variance}}{n \text{ of raters} \times n \text{ of dates}}. \tag{8}$$

Note that if rater-by-date variation is large, its impact on reliability can be reduced by increasing the denominator of Equation (8) which can be done in one of two ways: increase "n of raters," that is, the number of raters who observe a given classroom; or by increasing "n of dates," that is, the number of dates on which a classroom is observed.

Now one might imagine that rater-by-segment noise could also be a problem. This would occur, for example, if the tendency of Rater A to be tougher than Rater B varied as a function of which 20-minute segment was of interest. While such noise might in fact be a problem, this source cannot be estimated using the current data set because in no case did two raters rate the same classroom during the same segment. Therefore, for the current data, the rater-by-segment noise is completely confounded with the segment noise.[1]

The only remaining two-way interaction[2] of interest involves dates and classrooms. A classroom would plausibly exhibit a more favorable emotional climate on 1 day than on another. This generates

$$\text{Date-by-classroom noise} = \frac{\text{Date-by-classroom variance}}{n \text{ of dates}}. \tag{9}$$

Three-Way Interaction

One final source of noise is a three-way interaction effect involving raters, dates, and classrooms. Recall that Rater A had a bad hangover on a given date and therefore tended to rate classrooms very hard that day. This tendency of Rater A to be tough on that day did not, however, apply to Ms. Johnson's class: Rater A tended to see her classroom through rose-colored glasses even on a very bad day! Thus, we have the three-way interaction noise

$$\text{Rater-by-date-by-classroom noise} = \frac{\text{Rater-by-date-by-classroom variance}}{n \text{ of raters} \times n \text{ of dates}}. \tag{10}$$

As indicated by Equation (10), if rater-by-classroom-by-date noise is large, one can reduce it by adding either multiple raters or multiple dates (or both) per classroom.

Summary

The data from our illustrative example enable us to partition the error variance into seven pieces. Thus, we have

$$
\begin{aligned}
\text{Error variance} =\ & \text{Segment noise} + \text{Date noise} + \text{Rater noise} \\
& + \text{Rater-by-classroom noise} \\
& + \text{Rater-by-date noise} \\
& + \text{Date-by-classroom noise} \\
& + \text{Rater-by-date-by-classroom noise.}
\end{aligned}
$$

Each component of noise can be reduced by appropriately revising the deployment of resources (adding raters, dates, or segments, or increasing rater training). How resources can be deployed most cost effectively depends on the magnitude of each source of variation. Thus, adding raters will reduce rater noise, rater-by-classroom noise, and rater-by-date-by-classroom noise. Adding dates will reduce date noise, rater-by-date noise, and rater-by-date-by-classroom noise. Adding segments will reduce segment noise.

Results

Using the analysis of variance, we can estimate each source of variation. Next, we can use the formulas 4-10 to approximate the likely effect of adding raters or dates (or of increasing rater training). The results are displayed in Table 18.1. The two largest sources of estimated variation are true-score variance (i.e., variance between classrooms) and segment variance, both estimated to be 0.47. Given the large variation between segments, it is clear that adding segments will be very helpful in reducing error variance, thereby increasing reliability. The next two largest sources of error variance are rater variance (at 0.17) and rater-by-classroom variance (at 0.15). Each can be reduced by adding raters. In contrast, date noise and rater-by-date noise are very small—there is no need to redeploy resources to reduce these. However, date-by-classroom noise is nontrivial at 0.13. In addition, the three-way interaction is quite modest at 0.07. We can anticipate a modest improvement in reliability by adding dates because the classroom-by-date and three-way interactions are nonnegligible. However, the apparent benefit of adding raters will be greater given the comparatively large values of rater variance and rater-by-classroom variance in addition to the modest-sized three-way

Table 18.1. Estimated Variance Components for Illustrative Example

Source	Variance Estimates[a]
True-score variation	
Classroom variance	0.47
Error variation[b]	
Rater variance	0.17
Date variance	0.00
Segment variance	0.47
Rater-by-classroom variance	0.15
Date-by-classroom variance	0.13
Rater-by-date variance	0.00
Rater-by-date-by-classroom variance	0.07

[a] Maximum likelihood estimates.
[b] Standardized components.

interaction. We now make these intuitions precise by simulating the effects on reliability of adding raters or dates.

Adding Raters

Figure 18.1 shows how the reliability increases as dates per classroom are added, holding constant the number of segments observed. The horizontal axis ranges from 1 to 2 and includes fractional numbers of raters per classroom. It may seem odd to imagine 1.5 raters per classroom, but this is completely plausible in that some classrooms might be rated by only one rater while others could be rated by 2. The horizontal axis then represents the "typical" number of raters per classroom, actually computed as the *harmonic mean*.[3] Note that as the number of raters per classroom increases from 1 to 2, the reliability increases quite a lot. This result is graphed assuming three possible numbers of dates per classroom. (The black dot in the figure represents the expected reliability with 1.51 raters per classroom and 4.21 dates per classroom; these are the actual numbers deployed in the illustrative example.) We see that, given 4.21 dates per classroom on average, reliability increases from about 0.52 to 0.62 when the number of raters increases from 1 to 2.

Adding Dates

Figure 18.1 also allows inspection of the impact of adding more dates per classroom on the overall reliability of the measure. The figure shows that

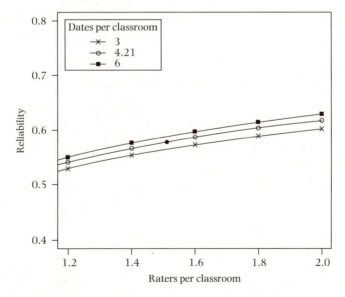

Figure 18.1. Reliability of a Classroom-Level Measure by the Number of Raters per Classroom and the Number of Dates on Which They Rate.

reliability increases very slowly as dates are added. This is because the sources of noise associated with dates are comparatively modest (see Table 18.1).

Increasing Segments

Changing the number of segments per rater visit can have a potentially large effect on reliability (see Figure 18.2). This is easily explained by noting that the variability associated with the segments is relatively large compared to other sources of error. However, the effect of the large segment plus rater-by-segment variability is lessened by the already high segments per rater visit. If raters had completed only 2 observation segments per classroom visit the reliability would have been less than 0.50.

Reliability, Sample Size, and Statistical Power

In evaluations of the impact of an intervention on group quality, statistical power is the probability of discovering a true difference between treatment and control conditions on group quality. In these studies, unreliable measurement of group quality weakens the statistical power of the evaluation. This means that if a new intervention is truly effective in boosting quality of group processes, the study will nonetheless have a poor chance of detecting this effect unless group quality is measured with sufficient reliability. In

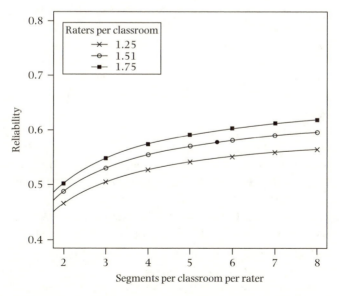

Figure 18.2. Reliability of a Classroom-Level Measure by the Number of Segments per Classroom per Rater and the Number of Raters per Classroom.

effect, poor reliability has the exact opposite effect of increasing the sample size on the chances of discovering a truly effective intervention.

Let us return to our example. Suppose that a researcher is interested in using coaches to help teachers improve the emotional climate of their classrooms. The researcher selects K schools as sites for the study and, within each school, assigns J classrooms to receive either the treatment or the control approach to coaching teachers. How does the reliability of measurement of emotional climate together with sample sizes J and K affect power?

We can gain insight into this problem by examining the *precision* or accuracy with which we can estimate the impact of the treatment. Precision is technically the reciprocal of the squared standard error of the estimated impact of treatment. Suppose for simplicity that the impact of the treatment is the same in each school. Then the precision will be

$$\text{Precision} = \frac{JK \times \text{Reliability}}{4 \times \text{True-score variance}}. \tag{11}$$

As Equation (11) shows, precision increases with the sample sizes K (number of schools) and J (number of classrooms per school). But the benefit of adding classrooms or schools is multiplied by the reliability. Reducing reliability from 1.0 to 0.50 is equivalent to effectively throwing out half the classrooms in the study![4]

A caveat is in order. As mentioned, Equation (11) assumes a constant treatment effect across schools. If the treatment effect varies from school to school, we must add to the precision the factor K divided by the variance of the treatment effect. Nevertheless, measurement reliability still has an appreciable effect on power.

Figure 18.3 displays the effect of increasing the reliability of measurement on statistical power in a hypothetical study in which 6 classrooms are randomly assigned to a treatment or control condition within each of 15 schools.

The average effect size is assumed to be 0.50, 0.75, or 1.0 in units of the standard deviation of the group-quality outcome. These may seem to be large effect sizes, but we are assuming that an intervention effect on program quality must be quite large in order to have a nonnegligible effect on person-level outcomes.

We also assume that the variation of the standardized effect sizes is quite large at 0.05. The impact of reliability is appreciable. For example, suppose the effect size is 0.75. If reliability is 0.70, power will be near 0.80, often regarded a satisfactory level of power. But if reliability is 0.50, power drops to around 0.50, clearly an unsatisfactory level of power. (Note that a power of 0.50 implies that even if the intervention is quite effective in improving classroom emotional climate, the study will have a probability of only 0.50 of detecting this effect.)

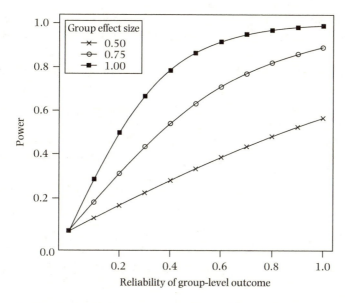

Figure 18.3. Power of a Blocked Group-Randomized Trial to Detect 0.50, 0.75, and 1.00 Group-Level Effect Sizes Taking Into Account Outcome Reliability.

Using the methods described in the previous section, one can diagnose the sources of error variance and redesign the measurement accordingly. For example, adding segments and raters per classroom might appreciably boost power. The alternative to boosting reliability is to increase the sample size by adding schools. Costs should be considered in choosing among these options, but it will often be true that adding schools is quite expensive.

Conclusions

The measurement of group-level outcomes enables researchers to study processes typically associated with program quality (e.g., instructional quality, school climate), thus shifting the focus to the mechanisms by which an intervention generates changes in individual-level outcomes.

Measurement error can substantially reduce the power of a study to detect important program effects on quality. Reducing measurement error increases power to detect significant effects. Measurement error can be reduced by redeploying resources, for example by increasing the number of raters or occasions of observation. Good rater selection and training will also play a key role by reducing error variance attributable to rater inconsistency.

Increasing reliability is not the only strategy for increasing the power to detect treatment effects on group quality. The most common strategy is to increase the sample size. One also may exploit knowledge about pretreatment characteristics of groups that predict the outcome of interest. For example, one might use a group-level covariate in the analysis or "block" groups on a pretreatment covariate prior to randomization (Raudenbush, Martinez, & Spybrook, 2007). The three approaches—increasing reliability of measurement, increasing sample size, and exploiting prior information—can be used together in a cost-effective approach to increasing statistical power.

The approach we suggest has three steps. The first step is to define all important sources of measurement error. The second step is to design a measurement study that quantifies these sources of error. The third step is to consider design options for improving statistical power. This approach allows researchers to make optimal use of any available resources to maximize the reliability of the group-level measures and the power to detect program effects.

Acknowledgments

The work reported has been supported by the William T. Grant Foundation under the grant "Building Capacity for Evaluating Group-Level Interventions." The authors are especially grateful to Bob Granger, Ed Seidman, and Vivian Tseng, from the William T. Grant Foundation, Howard Bloom and Pei Zhu, from MDRC, and Jessaca Spybrook, University of Michigan, for their continued advice and encouragement. We wish to thank Robert C. Pianta and Andrew J. Mashburn for generously lending data from the Multi-State Study of Pre-Kindergarten for the case study presented here and the participants of the joint meeting between the William T. Grant Foundation and the Forum for Youth Investment held in Washington, DC, on December of 2006 for their interest in discussing the ideas here presented.

Notes

1. This confounding will not cause any trouble if there is no plan to dispatch multiple raters to a given classroom on a given date during a given segment. In that case, the number of raters per segment will never exceed 1.0, and rater-by-segment noise as well as segment noise can each be reduced by adding more segments. Thus, if the confounded segment noise + rater-by-segment noise is large, the clearly effective strategy is to add segments.

2. One might also wonder whether segments can interact with classrooms or with dates. They cannot. A segment, by definition, is a 20-minute interval of observation that occurs on a given date in a given classroom. It is therefore impossible to observe the same segment on different dates or in different classrooms, so that no interaction involving segments with raters or dates is definable.

3. The harmonic mean of J quantities for $j = 1, \ldots, J$ is $J/(\Sigma 1/n_j)$, the reciprocal of the average reciprocal of those quantities. The harmonic mean gives a better representation of "typical number of raters" than does the simple average. The latter overestimates the typical number.

4. Computations of the relationship between reliability and power can be replicated using the "Optimal Design" software (Raudenbush, Liu, Spybrook, Martinez, & Congdon, 2006), freely downloadable (with documentation) from the

William T. Grant Foundation's Web site (http://www.wtgrantfoundation.org/) or from http://sitemaker.umich.edu/group-based.

References

Bloom, H. S. (2005). Randomizing groups to evaluate place-based programs. In H. S. Bloom (Ed.), *Learning more from social experiments: Evolving analytic approaches* (pp. 115-172). New York: Russell Sage Foundation.

Borman, G. D., Slavin, R. E., Cheung, A., Chamberlain, A., Madden, N., & Chambers, B. (2005). Success for all: First-year results from the national randomized field trial. *Educational Evaluation and Policy Analysis, 27*(1), 1-22.

Hamre, B. K., Mashburn, A. J., Pianta, R. C., Locasle-Crouch, J., & La Paro, K. M. (2006). *Classroom assessment scoring system technical appendix*. Greensboro, NC. Retrieved January 4, 2008, from http://www.classobservation.com/research/class_tech_manual.pdf

Hirsch, B. J., & Wong, V. (2005). After-school programs. In D. L. DuBois & M. J. Karcher (Eds.), *Handbook of youth mentoring*. Thousand Oaks, CA: Sage.

Kinzie, M., Whitaker, S., Neesen, K., Kelley, M., Matera, M., & Pianta, R. (2005). State wide Web-based professional development & curricula for early childhood educators: Design & infrastructure. In G. Richards (Ed.), *Proceedings of World Conference on E-Learning in Corporate, Government, Healthcare, and Higher Education 2005* (pp. 814-821). Chesapeake, VA: AACE.

Pianta, R. C. & Allen, J. P. (this volume). Building capacity for positive youth development in secondary school classrooms: Changing teachers' interactions with students.

Pianta, R. C., La Paro, K. M., & Hamre, B. (2004). *Classroom assessment scoring system (CLASS)*. Unpublished manuscript.

Pianta, R. C., La Paro, K. M., Payne, C., Cox, M. J., & Bradley, R. (2002). The relationship of kindergarten classroom environment to teacher, family and school characteristics and child outcomes. *The Elementary School Journal, 102*(3), 225-238.

Raudenbush, S. W. (1997). Statistical analysis and optimal design for cluster randomized trials. *Psychological Methods, 2*(2), 173-185.

Raudenbush, S. W., Liu, X.-F., Spybrook, J., Martinez, A., & Congdon, R. (2006). *Optimal design software for multi-level and longitudinal research* (Version 1.77). Retrieved November 15, 2007, from http://sitemaker.umich.edu/group-based or http://www.wtgrantfoundation.org/

Raudenbush, S. W., Martinez, A., & Spybrook, J. (2007). Strategies for improving precision in group-randomized experiments. *Educational Evaluation and Policy Analysis, 29*(1), 5-29.

Raudenbush, S. W., & Sampson, R. J. (1999). Ecometrics: Toward a science of assessing ecological settings, with application to the systematic social observations of neighborhoods. *Sociological Methodology, 29*, 1-41.

Schochet, P. A. (2005). *Statistical power for random assignment evaluations of education programs*. Princeton, NJ: Mathematica Policy Research.

Smith, R. E. (2006). Understanding sport behavior: A cognitive-affective processing systems approach. *Journal of Applied Sport Psychology, 18*(1), 1-27.

Chapter 19

Improving Youth-Serving Social Settings: Intervention Goals and Strategies for Schools, Youth Programs, and Communities

HIROKAZU YOSHIKAWA AND MARYBETH SHINN

I n this book, we aimed to draw together current work on theories and measurement relevant to youth-serving settings. Rather than asking whether and how youth-serving settings enhance positive youth development, we have asked whether and how youth-serving settings can be *improved* to enhance positive youth development. This shift in conceptual focus requires theory and measurement at the setting level, rather than the individual level. In this chapter, we synthesize and draw strategies for improving youth-serving settings from the rich set of data and theory that are presented in this book. We discuss strategies at both the organizational level (i.e., lessons for schools and youth organizations) and at the broader levels of communities, institutions, and public policy.

The National Research Council report on community youth organizations (Eccles & Gootman, 2002) concluded that community programs that enhance youth development provide youth with six kinds of resources: physical and psychological safety; supportive relationships; appropriate structure; opportunities for belonging and skill building; positive social norms; and support for efficacy and mattering. However, the report did not outline what organizations could do to foster these characteristics.

The chapters in this book outline many ways in which either external change agents or "insiders"—adults or youth from a particular organization or community—can facilitate positive qualities of schools and youth organizations. What common goals and accompanying intervention strategies to change social settings emerge across this very diverse set of programs and policies? In this chapter, we summarize three sets of goals and strategies: (a) participatory approaches to setting-level change; (b) increased capacity to use setting-level data, in addition to individual-level data, in daily practice; and (c) enhanced representation and developmental experiences of diverse youth in settings. In each of these three sections, we summarize directions at the organizational level and the broader community, institutional, and policy levels. We conclude the chapter with a discussion of evidence regarding the success of the change strategies presented in the book.

Intervention Goals and Accompanying Strategies

Participatory Approaches to Setting-Level Change in Organizations and Communities

Organizations

Effective schools and organizations have been described as "learning communities" in which support for staff professional development occurs not through periodic workshops, but in much more frequent team meetings and joint preparation time that infuse staff learning in the schools' daily routines (Cochran-Smith & Lytle, 1999; Lee, 2001; Miller, Kobes, & Forney, chapter 10). Chapters in this volume depict both schools and youth organizations as potential learning communities in which not only teachers, but support staff, youth workers, and a variety of levels of administration engage in focused efforts to enhance youths' learning opportunities and social experiences. We term this broader concept the fostering of participatory learning at the organizational level. Several strategies emerged across chapters as key to achieving the goal of increasing participatory learning in organizations.

First, a process of establishing buy-in must occur before the process of participatory learning can take hold. This buy-in must occur at multiple levels, including the organizational leadership, teachers/caregivers, and support staff. As Miller, Kobes, and Forney (chapter 10) state, the most common vehicle for assuring this buy-in is the establishment of a collaborative team with representation from multiple stakeholder groups. This team often engages in initial assessment and goal setting. Several chapters in the volume illustrate the value of engaging multiple stakeholder groups in a youth-serving organization to enhance learning. For example, Weinstein (chapter 5) describes efforts to equalize expectancies across groups of students in a high school. A participatory process, establishing buy-in across administration, teachers, and support staff resulted in an intervention that successfully detracked students at low levels of achievement such that college-preparatory and honors classes were no longer the domain of a select group in the school. In a discussion of successful whole-school reform, Desimone (chapter 9) describes the establishment of buy-in as occurring not only at levels of teachers and administration, but also at the broader levels of district leadership and parent and community support.

For individualized training and professional development within an organization, the relationship between the consultant and teacher or staff person must address this issue of buy-in as well. In the MyTeachingPartner intervention described by Pianta and Allen (chapter 2), for example, the relationship between the coach and teacher is introduced as a personal, supportive, and nonsupervisory relationship. In the Reading, Writing, Respect, and Resolution (4Rs) program described by Jones, Brown, and Aber (chapter 4), buy-in of teachers who implement the curriculum is fostered by alternating attention in the training to classroom conflict and teachers' own experiences of conflict in their lives.

Second, addressing the well-being and perceived needs of stakeholder groups can also be critical to buy-in. The 4Rs program, for example, which focuses on the emotional life of the classroom, includes in its training for teachers modules on stress reduction and support for their own emotion-focused coping. Several programs (e.g., MyTeachingPartner; the 4Rs program) also directly address the issue of behavior management, which is an urgent need expressed by many teachers and staff in schools and community youth organizations. The introduction of a program as one that can concretely help address such a "front-burner" need among a stakeholder group can increase the chances of acceptance and implementation.

Community and Broader Contexts

Similar principles of establishing buy-in are essential at the level of communities and broader contexts. At this wider ecological level, stakeholders themselves represent multiple organizations or institutions.

At the community level, such a participatory process can occur after presentation of evidence-based programs by outsiders or can emerge organically from within communities (Wilson-Ahlstrom & Yohalem, 2007). Fagan, Hawkins, and Catalano (chapter 16) describe a multistage process through which coalitions involving leaders from multiple sectors of the community choose evidence-based prevention strategies tailored to data from their community. First, the Communities That Care (CTC) facilitators assess the readiness of a community to adopt the CTC system. They then help establish a diverse, representative CTC Community Board. In the third phase, the community board prioritizes risk and protective factors for targeting, based on the CTC Community Youth Development survey. Only after this extensive participatory process does the board create an Action Plan based on selection of evidence-based prevention programs targeting the chosen risk factors. At each stage, input from multiple stakeholders is solicited. Although the process is guided throughout by "outsiders" from the CTC intermediary organization, the process ensures high levels of buy-in and participation from community representatives.

Other chapters in the volume described processes through which "insiders"— members of a community, whether youth or adults—generate change in social settings. Participation of multiple stakeholder groups, including youth themselves, in the design of efforts to change settings, emerged as a theme across several intervention examples. Miller, Korbes, and Forney (chapter 10) describe a community-based organization for youth empowerment (Project REP, or youth-led Research, Evaluation, and Planning). Youth were trained to conduct evaluations both within and outside Project REP. After training, youth worked on their own or alongside adults to evaluate a variety of youth programs in California, leading to successful organizational and policy-level change. The model of community organizing described by Speer (PICO, in chapter 12) was initially implemented among adults. It involves initial phases of one-on-one conversations among members of a congregation to discuss social issues and potential targets for change. Gradually, problems emerge from the aggregation of these individual stories about daily lived experience, and organizers select those to work on. In its application to youth organizing, teens were found to be more comfortable starting with a survey-based format and then transitioning to individual conversations. In addition, organizing leaders hired by PICO have been youth, not adults. It may be that when insiders or community members are involved in the generation of change, the change is more sustainable. Evidence on this important question, however, is missing from the research literature.

When setting-level change emerges from communities themselves, a close fit of the ultimate change process with community and cultural norms was often a key component of perceived success. For example, the PICO youth organizing model was tailored to the developmental norms of youth: in contrast to PICO's adult model, youth organizing occurs in much shorter cycles due to the shifting interests of youth. Zhou (chapter 13) describes a system of supplemental schooling that emerged in the Chinese immigrant community in Los Angeles. The schools fit cultural norms emphasizing educational achievement in this community and provide avenues for co-ethnic civic engagement among adults and identity building for youth. Zhou cautions, however, that the organizations may also exacerbate the negative effects of high levels of academic pressure that are also a norm in this community.

At the institutional and policy levels, change can occur through the convergence of senior leadership, vision and buy-in, capacity building, and leveraging of resources. For example, Maton, Hrabowski, Ozdemir, and Wimms (chapter 7) describe the Meyerhoff Program, a successful effort to increase the representation and achievement of minority students in science, technology, engineering, and mathematics at a public university. The program increases representation and retention of students of color via recruitment, admissions, orientation, and provision of a series of supports such as study groups, personal advising relationships, tutoring, and research internships during the academic years and summers. The goals of inclusion and retention were in this case instituted as a campus priority by the senior administration. Change then followed at the department chair and faculty levels. This example highlights the role for institutional leadership in the development of change strategies and contrasts with the more "bottom-up" processes described thus far.

Capacity building often occurs through institutions or umbrella organizations that support multiple schools or youth programs. Larger organizations that support multiple youth-serving organizations are what Schorr (1998) called "intermediary organizations," providing training, organizational assessment, technical assistance, and material or human resources to their component organizations. Among the change strategies described in this volume, several have formal intermediary organizations associated with them. Some are required due to the replication of a program across multiple communities (e.g., the CTC program, chapter 16). Others are voluntary; this distinction is likely important for ultimate organizational change (Wilson-Ahlstrom & Yohalem, 2007). The intermediary organization for the CTC program defines each phase of the process leading to implementation of community-level prevention programs (i.e., facilitates the formation of community coalitions, designs the community youth survey of risk and protective factors that is administered, and selects the programs that are considered sufficiently evidence-based). The CTC organization thus functions as a gatekeeper as well as provider of technical assistance and human as well as financial resources. In other cases, coordination among multiple systems requires an umbrella organization. For example, the Youth Data Archive described by McLaughlin and O'Brien-Strain (chapter 17) requires a central organization with high capacity for data management, synthesis, and analysis to coordinate and pool multiple administrative data sets across systems. The characteristics of intermediary organizations likely have a profound influence on the success of implementation of local youth programs.

Policy theories cite both top-down and bottom-up processes as contributing to successful implementation of school reform at the local level. Desimone (chapter 9), applying Porter's theory of attributes of successful policy implementation to whole-school reform, highlights the tension between authority gained by a school reform approach, which requires buy-in and support from all levels, including teachers, school administrators, and district leadership, and power, which typically sets incentives and sanctions for particular behaviors in a top-down fashion.

Increased Capacity to Use Setting-Level Data, in Addition to Individual-Level Data, in Daily Practice

The use of data to drive improvement in practice is a mantra of the school reform field and is in fact a central goal of No Child Left Behind. Many educators note that the use of data in daily practice in schools and youth organizations is typically anecdotal and reactive. A common practice, for example, is conversation in teacher or team meetings addressing the needs of particular children based on incidents involving those youth in the past week. Although this approach can involve the assemblage of anecdotal data from multiple stakeholder groups in an organization, it is a crisis-driven and largely individual-level process, with little impact on students in a school as a whole. In contrast, data regarding social processes in social settings can also be used more thoughtfully and productively to set goals and monitor change efforts, as described in the introductory chapter. Chapters in this book provide several examples.

Organizations

Data on setting-level processes can stem from assessment of interactions among specific people or groups in a setting (teachers and students; students and students, e.g., in schools), or the nature and organization of human, physical, economic, or temporal resources in a setting (Tseng & Seidman, 2007). In an example of the former, Henry (chapter 3) discusses interventions that provide normative feedback (information on an individual's behavior relative to a group-level norm) concerning particular risk behaviors (drinking; gambling) among college students, with the result of lowering the levels of those risk behaviors. Although this intervention approach has not been tested with younger adolescents, the multiple examples of efficacy with college populations that Henry cites show the potential power of providing both individual- and setting-level behavioral information to youth in an educational setting. Datnow (chapter 15) profiles four school systems with successful approaches to data-driven decision making. Two of the schools fed student assessment data back to students with graphs depicting the overall distribution. Students were encouraged to set goals, much as teachers did themselves, based on the periodic assessments. Data from the Classroom Assessment Scoring System assessment instrument, used in MyTeachingPartner (chapter 2), are useful in that they provide direct feedback on what quality adult-youth interactions look like. This avoids the common problem with sharing solely individual-level assessments with teachers or service providers—a tendency to blame the student (or the student's family!) rather than consider the role of classroom processes such as the teacher-student relationship.

Data on the distribution of resources within a setting can also be used to improve the daily practice of teachers or caregivers. The Youth Program

Quality Assessment described by Smith and Akiva (chapter 11) includes the overall nature of resources in a youth program (e.g., physical structures related to youth safety) and the distribution of resources (e.g., opportunities for youth leadership), in addition to the quality of staff-youth interactions in particular program offerings. Their data showed, for example, that a large percentage of youth programs did not provide opportunities for youth leadership in any of their program offerings. Such information can directly influence efforts to redistribute such opportunities across staff and youth. The Youth Program Quality Assessment can be used for both self-assessments and assessments by external evaluators. Smith and Akiva describe the trade-offs of these two approaches in the phases of initial engagement with assessment, receipt of the quality report, and setting of feasible goals and steps towards achieving them.

Data are critical to setting goals and monitoring change, but they are not by themselves enough. Time, leadership, and resources must be provided to support the use of setting-level data in daily practice. In Weinstein's example (chapter 5) of school-wide efforts to equalize expectancies across groups of students, the core of the participatory process in one high school was a 2-hr weekly meeting. In these meetings, a team of teachers joined the principal, vice-principal, discipline dean, and college advisor, along with the university researchers. Data concerning the unintended effects of the tracking system in this school were shared (e.g., by being tracked into remedial courses early in their high school years, groups of initially low-performing students could successfully complete all high school courses they were offered, yet not be eligible for college). Weinstein reports that this pattern was one of which neither students nor their families were fully aware. These data were used to spur policy changes in the school, giving retroactive college-preparatory credit for successfully completing "remedial" courses in the first year, making honors classes more accessible, and dismantling noncollege preparatory classes in the second year. In the four school systems utilizing data-driven decision making that Datnow describes in chapter 15, one unifying factor was the creation of structured time for discussion of data. Most of the schools provided 2-3 hours a week of uninterrupted meeting time for teams to present and discuss data, develop strategies, and monitor progress (students were typically let out early 1 day a week to accommodate such meeting time). Across the systems, the membership of teams engaging in these discussions varied, with some at the grade level, some structured around coaches and their teams, and some comprised of leadership, including principal, grade chairs, and coaches.

Time and resources to support the use of data in practice are also not enough. Attention must be paid to the kinds of conversations and interactions occurring around data and their interpretation. The quality of discourse in an organization concerning setting-level processes can be tracked to generate change. Pollock in her chapter (chapter 6) distinguishes between everyday discourse about race and equity in schools that can help or harm the experience of students of color. She challenges educators to talk more precisely about student subpopulations, the causes of racial disparities, and the impact of their own behaviors on students of color. For example, what Pollock terms "hyperaggregated" talk diverting direct discussion of race to the needs of "all students" substitutes generalities for discussion of the needs of particular groups. Similarly, discussing a student's assessment data in terms of his or her personal or family characteristics alone can divert attention from how teaching strategies can potentially facilitate the student's learning.

Community and Broader Contexts

At the community and broader levels, the data provided to stakeholder groups to bring about setting-level change more often concern an entire community or jurisdiction. Such data can also be categorized into information pertaining to social processes within a community and the nature and organization of resources. Fagan, Hawkins, and Catalano, in their CTC model (chapter 16), use a youth survey to help communities identify the patterns of risk and protective factors for youth risk behaviors. This population-based data provides a window into social processes. For example, the survey includes measures of school and family attachment, school and community opportunities for prosocial involvement, and peers' risk behaviors as well as attitudes toward those behaviors.

Fagan and colleagues (chapter 16) describe how communities use aggregate individual data (the CTC youth survey). In contrast, McLaughlin and O'Brien-Strain (chapter 17) describe the use of data pertaining to multiple youth-serving service systems in a data archive that combines system-level information with information on particular youth. Administrative data on youth involvement in multiple systems, including school, health, government benefit and social service, child protective, mental health, and community agencies, are integrated in a longitudinal database. The aim of the Youth Data Archive is to address problems stemming from inadequate data management at the service system level. Because data are not shared and readily available to practitioners and administrators, efforts are often wasted or duplicated in youth services. Early detection of multiple service system use, for example, could, with the use of the archive, trigger secondary preventive measures. The capacity of such a data archive to inform the implementation of services within agencies, the effectiveness of communication and coordination of services across them, and ultimately the investment of resources at the community and policy levels, is high. The authors describe efforts in three communities that have begun assembling and using data across systems. Challenges at the systems level in building and maintaining such a complex database include staff turnover and changing data systems in various agencies over time.

Again, data are critical, but insufficient to guide change. Rather, the intervention must create a process to support the use of data to set goals and monitor change efforts. In CTC, facilitators help the community coalition to examine which risk factors are particularly high, and which protective factors particularly low, in their community and prioritize a small number for targeted action. This information is used to guide the choice of evidence-based prevention programs that target the chosen risk and protective factors. In the Youth Data Archive, archive administrators work with the staff of local agencies to learn to use the data in planning.

For schools, district-wide initiatives are crucial in improving system-wide use of data to inform practice. Datnow (chapter 15) describes several factors at the district level that co-occurred with successful data-driven decision making at the school level, among the four districts she and her colleagues studied. These factors included goal setting that avoided generalized objectives such as "all students become lifelong learners" in favor of specific goals relevant to particular groups, such as "all English language learners will progress through the [state standardized assessment] levels annually;" system-wide curricula suggesting the breadth and depth of content to be taught; the establishment of easy-to-use data management systems that teachers could use easily to identify data relevant to particular groups or individuals; and system-wide professional development to help teachers use data. Each approach to what Datnow terms scaffolding of district-level goals when successful took into account the diversity in capacity and skills among teachers. Flexibility was to some degree built into curricula; workshops on using data were provided to teachers with differing levels of comfort in using web-based data systems; and one principal set up individual data discussion plans with each teacher, rather than requiring the discussions to be done in group contexts.

Enhanced Representation and Developmental Experiences of Diverse Youth in Social Settings

Attending to diversity is an important goal of youth-serving organizations. How can this goal be put into practice? Chapters in this book described efforts of two broad types: influencing representation within settings of under- or overrepresented groups, and improving the social and academic experiences of particular marginalized groups. Several chapters in this volume present strategies for how to achieve these goals, with reference to youth of color, immigrant youth, youth from low-income families, and lesbian/gay/bisexual/transgendered (LGBT) youth.

Organizational

The representation of youth of color, youth in poverty, or LGBT youth in organizations can be considered overall (what is the percentage of youth of particular groups in the organization as a whole), or across settings within the organization (how does the relative representation of youth of particular groups differ across different kinds of settings within the organization?). In this section, we discuss efforts within organizations to address representation of the second kind; addressing representation of the first kind is more likely to require change at the community or broader levels, so is discussed in the next section.

Efforts within organizations to address representation of different groups often aim to increase representation in settings where particular groups are underrepresented. Maton and colleagues (chapter 7), for example, described the Meyerhoff initiative to increase representation of students of color in a specific subset of degree programs (science, technology, engineering, and math) where they were underrepresented. This was accomplished through over 10 years of focused effort within a single public university. The Meyerhoff initiative changed policies related to entry (admissions), retention (orientation and student support), and advancement (involvement in activities, like research, that build qualifications for careers postcollege in the target fields).

The experiences of marginalized groups of students can also be a target of setting-level intervention. Basic social processes such as ensuring safety are a concern for some groups; Russell and McGuire's chapter (chapter 8) focuses on LGBT students, who experience feeling unsafe due to multiple kinds of harassment and victimization in schools (verbal, environmental, and physical). They describe efforts that can be led by students or begun by teachers or administrators to address LGBT student safety and well-being in school policy. In schools where LGBT students report that teachers intervene when harassment occurs, these students also feel safer.

Interventions described by Weinstein (chapter 5) focus on both representation of particular groups (disadvantaged students, disproportionately Black or Latino) in college-preparatory classes within high school and on their experiences, specifically, academic and social expectancies transmitted by the school. Weekly team meetings allowed teachers to examine and change the ways that low expectations were perpetuated in school structures (such as tracking) and in their own behavior. Pollock (chapter 6) describes multiple efforts that educators can undertake to increase the quality of race talk in schools, another dimension of social interaction that directly affects the well-being and prospects of students of color. The specificity of subpopulations under discussion (addressing needs of particular Latino immigrant groups, for example, rather than Latinos as a whole) can be increased in everyday discourse about race and ethnicity. She also describes how ascribing achievement gaps to cultural characteristics of parents of particular ethnic groups can be replaced by a more careful analysis of these parents' relationships with other parents, educators, administrators, and institutions such as the media.

The representation of particular groups of students in youth-serving settings across a community or district can also be the target of change. Kahlenberg's chapter on socioeconomic integration of schools presents one in a long history of efforts to desegregate America's schools but this time with a primary emphasis on integration by class, not by race (chapter 14). Kahlenberg presents a strategy at the organizational level to accomplish socioeonomic integration: "magnetizing" all schools in a district, following an approach devised by Willie and Alves (1996). All parents then choose where they would like to send their children, based on curricular foci and organizational and teaching approaches of various schools. He posits that a side benefit of this approach is greater racial integration. In implementing these programs, Kahlenberg highlights the need to provide comprehensive information about schools to parents (particularly those who may be less likely to access it), free transportation across relatively short distances, and admission based on family choice, with some adjustments for distance, siblings, and socioeconomic status. Within the school setting, Kahlenberg also cautions against within-school segregation, which can undo the purpose of the community-level policy. He also describes several exemplars of cities and districts that have accomplished socioeconomic integration, using either "bottom-up" (i.e., driven by teachers) or "top-down" (driven by policy makers or administrators) strategies.

District-wide or state-level coalitions can also help improve the quality of social experiences of stigmatized groups. Russell and McGuire (chapter 8) describe, for example, how a state commission on gay and lesbian youth established in Massachusetts provided the spark not only for advocacy and policy change in that state, but for similar efforts in subsequent years in the states of Washington and California. In California, the work of LGBT youth, advocates, researchers, and educators in developing school safety resources was accompanied by advocacy for a state law to reduce harassment toward and increase the safety of LGBT youth in schools. The California Student Safety and Violence Prevention Act, passed in 2001, was the result of this coalition's work; the law has resulted in state-wide dissemination of school safety policies.

Conclusion: Evidence for Success of Change Efforts

We conclude with comments about the evaluation of efforts to improve settings serving youth. Rigorous evaluations of efforts to change settings are relatively rare and the change efforts portrayed in this book vary in the level of evidence for their success. In some cases, authors such as Pollock (chapter 6) identify an important and widespread setting-level problem and offer suggestions for how to approach it, based on the best available evidence, without waiting for formal research to show that particular efforts work. Similarly, Henry (chapter 3) extrapolates from the success of other interventions targeting setting norms (for drinking, e.g., among college students) to hypothesize that interventions based on collecting and feeding back normative information about aggression can change classroom norms. Additional research is needed to examine the success of these approaches.

In other cases, a well-documented case study of a change effort such as the Meyerhoff program at the University of Maryland Baltimore County (chapter 7) constitutes what mathematicians call an "existence proof." That is, it shows that it is possible, with the right efforts and supports, to create settings where minority students achieve on a par with Caucasian and Asian students in difficult and technical subjects. Maton and colleagues (chapter 7) make no claim that such a program can be replicated everywhere—but the program at least stands as a challenge to other universities and a strong counterargument to those who argue that the blame for lack of comparable success elsewhere lies in students rather than institutions. Similarly, Zhou's case study of supplementary education in Los Angeles Chinese immigrant community (chapter 13) suggests that both cultural and structural accounts of the success of Chinese students in American schools leave out the role of specific settings that may mediate that success. McLaughlin and O'Brien-Strain's Youth Data Archive (chapter 17) and some of the interventions to build capacity of community-based organizations described by Miller et al. (chapter 10) are in the same category of case studies. Not all interventions of a particular type are likely to be equally effective. Understanding the boundary conditions for these change efforts, that is, the circumstances in which they are and are not successful, is an important area for future research.

At the other extreme, some of the interventions described here have been or are currently being subjected to what have been called cluster-, group-, or place-randomized trials (Bloom, 2005; Murray, 1998), in which classrooms, youth programs, schools, or entire communities are randomly assigned to treatment and control conditions to determine whether the intervention succeeds in modifying characteristics of the setting and in turn to fostering positive development for youth. Examples are the MyTeachingPartner intervention (Pianta and Allen, chapter 2), the 4Rs intervention (Jones, Brown, and Aber, chapter 4), some whole-school change efforts, such as Success for All (Borman et al., 2005), and the CTC prevention system (Fagan et al., chapter 16). Martinez and Raudenbush (chapter 18) describe the methodological challenges of these trials and approaches to increasing statistical power through attention to reliability of setting-level measures (see also Bloom, 2005). Only relatively mature interventions are ready for such tests.

Intermediate between chapters that offer as-yet-untested interventions or single case studies and those based on powerful cluster-randomized designs are chapters that use multiple case studies to develop intervention tools and suggest their broader applicability. Examples include the schools where Weinstein works to achieve high expectations for all (chapter 5), the districts and states that have adopted antibullying and harassment policies to increase safety for LGBT students, described by Russell and McGuire (chapter 8), the school systems that use data-driven decision making, described by Datnow (chapter 15), and the school systems that have introduced socioeconomic integration, described by Kahlenberg (chapter 14). Community-based examples include the out-of-school-time programs participating in the Youth Program Quality Intervention described by Smith and Akiva (chapter 11; which is now undergoing a group-randomized trial) or the PICO youth organizing efforts described by Speer (chapter 12). In each case, successive implementations have helped to refine these change efforts and contribute to the accumulation of evidence that they work. Schools and community organizations that participate in these change efforts are neither randomly sampled nor randomly assigned to programs. (One can hardly assign states at random to institute antiharassment policies to protect LGBT students, for example.) Nevertheless, the accretion of evidence for the success of these efforts over time, along with the knowledge gained in each new instantiation, make it more plausible that successful change efforts will spread. Our hope is that the aspirations and evidence presented here will stimulate further research on still more sophisticated efforts to change settings for youth and to make settings responsive to the needs of all of their members.

In sum, the intervention strategies presented in this volume brought about setting-level change by fostering participatory learning processes in organizations and communities; enhancing the representation and developmental experiences of diverse youth; and enhancing settings' capacity to use setting-level data, in addition to individual-level data, in daily practice. These strategies, considered individually, hold promise for enhancing youth well-being in each of their target communities. Considered together, they hold great promise for enriching the field of positive youth development and improving the prospects of America's young people.

References

Bloom, H. (2005). (Ed.). *Learning more from social experiments: Evolving analytic approaches.* New York: Russell Sage Foundation.

Borman, G., Slavin, R., Cheung, A., Chamberlain, A., Madden, N., & Chambers, B. (2005). The national randomized field trial of Success for All: Second-year outcomes. *American Educational Research Journal, 42,* 673-696.

Cochran-Smith, M., & Lytle, S. L. (1999). Relationships of knowledge and practice: Teacher learning in communities. *Review of Research in Education, 24,* 249-305.

Eccles, J., & Gootman, J. A. (2002). (Eds.). *Community programs to promote youth development*. Washington, DC: National Academy Press.

Lee, V. E. (2001). *Restructuring high schools for equity and excellence: What works*. New York: Teachers College Press.

Murray, D. M. (1998). *The design and analysis of group-randomized trials*. New York: Oxford University Press.

Schorr, L. (1998). *Common purpose: Strengthening families and neighborhoods to rebuild America*. New York: Anchor Books.

Tseng, V., & Seidman, E. (2007). A systems framework for understanding social settings. *American Journal of Community Psychology, 39*, 217-228.

Willie, C., & Alves, M. (1996). *Controlled choice: A new approach to school desegregated education and school improvement*. Providence, RI: Education Alliance Press and the New England Desegregation Assistance Center, Brown University.

Wilson-Ahlstrom, A., & Yohalem, N. (2007). *Building quality improvement systems: Lessons from three emerging efforts in the youth service sector*. Washington, DC: Forum for Youth Investment.

Contributors

J. Lawrence Aber is professor of Applied Psychology and Public Policy and academic director of the Institute for Human Development and Contextual Change at the Steinhardt School of Culture, Education, and Human Development, New York University. Aber earned his Ph.D. from Yale University and an A.B. from Harvard University. His basic research examines the influence of poverty and violence, at the family and community levels, on the social, emotional, behavioral, cognitive, and academic development of children and youth. Aber also designs and conducts rigorous evaluations of innovative programs and policies, such as violence prevention, literacy development, welfare reform, and comprehensive services initiatives, for children, youth, and families. He coedited *Neighborhood Poverty: Context and Consequences for Children* (Russell Sage Foundation, 1997), *Assessing the Impact of September 11th, 2001, on Children Youth and Parents; Lessons for Applied Developmental Science* (Erlbaum, 2004) and *Child Development and Social Policy: Knowledge for Action* (APA Publications, 2007). He received a William T. Grant Faculty Scholar award and a Visiting Scholar award from the Russell Sage Foundation.

Tom Akiva manages network program quality projects and conducts training and consultation in youth development. He was part of the development team for the Youth Program Quality Assessment (PQA) and has been involved in major applications of this instrument. From 1998 to 2002, Akiva directed the Institute for IDEAS, Akiva High/Scope Educational Research Foundation's month-long, residential program for teenagers. Akiva received his master's degree in education from the University of Michigan and is certified to teach at the secondary level. He has worked in middle schools and high schools, and has taught university and community college courses in education, social work, and writing. He lives in Ann Arbor, Michigan, with his wife and two perfect daughters.

Joseph P. Allen is professor of Clinical, Developmental, and Community Psychology at the University of Virginia. He received his Ph.D. in clinical and community psychology at Yale University. Allen's research is in the area of adolescent social development. In particular, he studies the development of adolescent autonomy in the family and peer group, as well as interventions that may enhance this development and prevent the onset of serious problem behaviors. He is associate editor of *Child Development* and a former W. T. Grant Faculty Scholar and Spencer Foundation Fellow. His book (with S. T. Hauser and E. Golden) *Out of the Woods: Tales of Resilient Teens* was published by Harvard University Press in 2006.

Joshua L. Brown is an assistant professor of Psychology at Fordham University. Brown completed his Ph.D. in Developmental Psychology from the Department of Human Development at Teachers College, Columbia University, and has worked in program evaluation research in both private and university-based settings. Brown's research focuses on understanding and promoting the social-emotional and academic development of children at risk through the rigorous design and evaluation of school-based intervention programs. His current work includes a longitudinal, experimental study of the impacts of a schoolwide violence prevention and social-emotional learning and literacy intervention on children, teachers, classrooms, and other school micro-contexts in eighteen public elementary schools in New York City.

Richard F. Catalano is professor and director of the Social Development Research Group, School of Social Work, University of Washington. Catalano is the principal investigator on a number of federal grants, which include family-, school-, and community-based prevention approaches to reduce risk while enhancing the protective factors of bonding and promotion of healthy beliefs and clear standards. He received his Ph.D. in Sociology in 1982 from the University of Washington in Seattle, Washington.

Amanda Datnow is associate professor at the Rossier School of Education at the University of Southern California. At USC, she directs the Ph.D. program in Urban Education Policy and is associate director of the Center on Educational Governance. Her research focuses on the politics and policies of school reform, particularly with regard to the professional lives of educators and issues of equity. She has conducted numerous prior studies of comprehensive school reform and studies of other related school change issues. She is currently conducting research on data-driven decision making in urban high schools.

Laura M. Desimone is associate professor at the Graduate School of Education, University of Pennsylvania. She studies education policy effects on teaching and learning in the core academic subjects, policy implementation, and improving methods for studying policy effects (e.g., improving surveys). Before coming to the University of Pennsylvania, Desimone was a professor at Vanderbilt University, and she worked at American Institutes for Research in Washington, DC; the Bush Center in Child Development and Social Policy at Yale University; RAND in Washington, DC; and the Frank Porter Graham Child Development Center at the University of North Carolina, Chapel Hill. She received her Ph.D. in public policy analysis from the University of North Carolina, Chapel Hill.

Abigail A. Fagan is assistant professor at the Department of Criminology and Criminal Justice, University of South Carolina. She received her Ph.D. in Sociology from the University of Colorado at Boulder in 2001, and was formerly an intervention specialist at the Social Development Research Group at the University of Washington. Her research interests include crime prevention strategies, implementation fidelity of prevention programs, gender and crime, sibling influences on crime, and victimization.

Jason C. Forney is a graduate student at Ecological-Community Psychology at Michigan State University. His academic and professional work includes HIV prevention and program evaluation. Currently, he is assisting a local organization in its efforts to improve support services to people living with HIV or AIDS. Prior to his graduate career, Forney served as a project coordinator at Wayne State University in Detroit, Michigan, for a community-based longitudinal study investigating the effects of homelessness on the experiences of adolescents.

J. David Hawkins is endowed professor of Prevention, Social Development Research Group, School of Social Work, University of Washington; past president of the Society for Prevention Research; and a fellow of the American Society of Criminology. His research studies include the Seattle Social Development Project, an ongoing longitudinal study that includes a nested preventive intervention; and the Community Youth Development Study, a randomized controlled trial of the Communities That Care prevention operating system involving 24 communities. He received his Ph.D. in 1975 from Northwestern University.

David B. Henry is associate professor of Psychiatry at the Institute for Juvenile Research of the University of Illinois at Chicago. He is a community psychologist who studies the ecological factors that affect the lives of children, adolescents, and persons with intellectual disabilities. His work includes publications on child development and psychopathology; prevention of violence, substance abuse, and sexual risk; peer influence processes; methodology and statistics; and community attitude toward persons with intellectual disabilities. He serves as mentor and advisor on research methods for several junior and senior faculty at his institution and others. He is married, has two grown children, and makes his home in Chicago, Illinois.

Freeman A. Hrabowski, III, has served as president of UMBC (The University of Maryland, Baltimore County) since May 1992. His research and publications focus on science and math education, with special emphasis on minority participation and performance. He serves as a consultant to the National Science Foundation, the National Institutes of Health, and universities and school systems nationally. Hrabowski also sits on several corporate and civic boards. Examples of recent awards or honors include election to the American Academy of Arts & Sciences and the American Philosophical Society; receiving the prestigious *McGraw Prize in Education* and the U.S. *Presidential Award for Excellence in Science, Mathematics, and Engineering Mentoring*; and being named a Fellow of the American Association for the Advancement of Science. He also holds a number of honorary degrees. Hrabowski has coauthored two books, *Beating the Odds: Raising Academically Successful African American Males* and *Overcoming the Odds: Raising Academically Successful African American Young Women* (Oxford University Press).

Stephanie M. Jones is assistant professor of Education at the Harvard Graduate School of Education. She completed her graduate work in the Psychology Department at Yale University and a postdoctoral fellowship at the Yale Child Study Center. Her research is focused on tracking the longitudinal impact of broad ecological risks, such as poverty and exposure to community violence, on social-emotional problems and competencies in early childhood and adolescence. In addition, Jones is currently conducting a number of policy-relevant, experimental evaluation studies of preschool- and school-based programs, targeting emotional and behavioral problems of children at risk.

Richard D. Kahlenberg is a senior fellow at The Century Foundation, where he writes about education, equal opportunity, and civil rights. He is the author of *Tough Liberal: Albert Shanker and the Battles Over Schools, Unions, Race and Democracy* (Columbia University Press, 2007); *All Together Now: Creating Middle Class Schools through Public School Choice* (Brookings Institution Press, 2001); *The Remedy: Class, Race, and Affirmative Action* (Basic Books, 1996); and *Broken Contract: A Memoir of Harvard Law School* (Hill & Wang/Farrar, Straus & Giroux, 1992). In addition, Kahlenberg is the editor of four Century Foundation books: *America's Untapped Resource: Low-Income Students in Higher Education* (2004); *Public School Choice vs. Private School Vouchers* (2003); *Divided We Fail: Coming Together Through Public School Choice. The Report of The Century Foundation Task Force on the Common School* (2002); and *A Notion at Risk: Preserving Public Education as an Engine for Social Mobility* (2000). He is a graduate of Harvard College and Harvard Law School.

Shannon K. E. Kobes is currently a Ph.D. candidate at the Ecological-Community Psychology program, Department of Psychology, at Michigan State University. She completed a masters in Cognitive and Social Processes from Ball State University. Her scholarly work focuses on the formal and informal systems response to sexual assault, specifically issues related to secondary victimization and coordinated community responses to sexual assault. She is currently assisting in the development of the Capital Area Sexual Assault Response Team in Lansing, Michigan. Prior to her graduate work, she provided direct care to clients at both a nonprofit psychiatric residential treatment center for adolescent females and a nonprofit psychiatric residential treatment center for adults in Omaha, Nebraska.

Andres Martinez is a doctoral student in the combined program in Education and Statistics at the University of Michigan and a visiting research scholar at the University of Chicago. His research interests revolve around program evaluation and the measurement of social settings. He is currently working on a project supported by the William T. Grant Foundation to help build the capacity of social scientists, foundation leaders, and public officials to evaluate group-based interventions aimed at improving the life chances of youth.

Kenneth I. Maton is professor of Psychology and director of the Community-Social Psychology Ph.D. Program in Human Services Psychology at University of Maryland, Baltimore County. His research focuses on empowering community settings, minority youth achievement, and the community psychology of religion. Recent books include *Investing in Children, Youth, Families and Communities: Strengths-Based Research and Policy* (edited volume; American Psychological Association) and *Overcoming the Odds: Raising Academically Successful African American Females* (coauthor; Oxford University Press). Maton is past-president of the Society for Community Research and Action (SCRA; APA Division 27), and the most recent winner of SCRA's Distinguished Contribution to Theory and Research Award. He serves on the editorial boards of *American Journal of Community Psychology, Analysis of Social Issues and Public Policy*, and *Journal of Community Psychology*.

Jenifer K. McGuire is assistant professor of Human Development at Washington State University. She earned a Ph.D. in Human Development and Family Studies at the University of Arizona in 2003 and a master's degree of Public Health from the University of Arizona in 2001. Her research focuses on adolescent health and sexuality, including adolescent sexual behavior, sexuality education, health and well-being among sexual minority youth, and family and social contexts of transgender youth. She was the recipient of an internship award from the Society for the Psychological Study of Social Issues in 2004 for a study of community center supports for transgender youth.

Milbrey McLaughlin is the David Jacks Professor of Education and Public Policy at Stanford University. Professor McLaughlin is codirector of the Center for Research on the Context of Teaching, an interdisciplinary research center engaged in analyses of how teaching and learning are shaped by teachers' organizational, institutional, and social-cultural contexts. McLaughlin is also executive director of the John W. Gardner Center for Youth and Their Communities, a partnership between Stanford University and Bay Area communities to build new practices, knowledge, and capacity for youth development and learning both in communities and at Stanford.

Robin Lin Miller is associate professor in the Ecological-Community Psychology program, Department of Psychology, Michigan State University, and affiliate scientist of the Intervention and Dissemination Core, Center for AIDS Intervention Research, Medical College of Wisconsin. She studies how programs are implemented in community settings and what organizational contingencies govern the application of scientific programs to community-based service provision. She also studies organizational factors that affect how social science knowledge and evidence-based practices are used by and influence community-based organizations. She previously served as director of Evaluation Research at Gay Men's Health Crisis where her work earned her the Marcia Guttentag Award for outstanding career promise from the American Evaluation Association. Robin is currently editor of the *American Journal of Evaluation*. She is a member of the scientific leadership team of the NICHD-funded Adolescent Trials Network, a national clinical trials consortium aimed at reducing exposure to HIV among adolescents. She has consulted to numerous community-based organizations serving disenfranchised youth and young adults.

Margaret O'Brien-Strain is director of the Youth Data Archive at the John W. Gardner Center for Youth and Their Communities at Stanford University and a senior research associate for the SPHERE Institute. O'Brien-Strain received her Ph.D. in Economics from Stanford University and has more than ten years of experience in public policy research and technical assistance. Her research covers a broad range of health, human services, and education policy, including child care subsidies and preschool for all; Medicaid, children's health insurance programs, and health outreach; developmental disabilities; and youth development programs. Much of her work focuses on the interaction and integration of programs at the community level in California, as well as outcomes measurement and using data to improve program design.

Metin Özdemir is a doctoral student in Human Services Psychology (Community/Social Psychology concentration) at the University of Maryland, Baltimore County. He received his B.S. in psychology and M.S. degree in Social Psychology from the Middle East Technical University, Turkey. His research interests revolve around issues related to the ecological context of adolescent and youth positive development, and their participation in the community. Currently, he is working on his dissertation project, which will be an examination of the development of adolescents' self-efficacy beliefs in multiple domains. He remains part of the initiative team of Public Achievement in Turkey, a transformative, civic action tool for people of all ages.

Robert C. Pianta is dean of the Curry School of Education and the director of the Center for Advanced Study of Teaching and Learning (CASTL) at the University of Virginia. He holds the Novartis U.S. Foundation Chair in Education at the Curry School and is a professor in the Department of Psychology. A former special education teacher, he is a developmental, school, and clinical child psychologist who studies how children's experiences at home and in school affect their development and how relationships with teachers and parents, and experiences in classrooms, can help improve outcomes for at-risk children and youth. Pianta is a principal investigator on the MyTeachingPartner, IES Interdisciplinary Doctoral Training Program in Risk and Prevention, and National Institute of Child Health and Human Development Study of Early Child Care and Youth Development grants; a senior investigator with the National Center for Early Development and Learning; and editor of the *Journal of School Psychology*. He has written over two hundred journal articles, chapters, and books on early childhood development, transition to school, school readiness, and parent-child and teacher-child relationships.

Mica Pollock, associate professor at the Harvard Graduate School of Education, studies youth and adults struggling to talk about, think about, and address fundamental questions of racialized inequality and diversity in their daily lives. An anthropologist of education, she examines everyday debates over race in both school and community settings. She is the author of *Colormute: Race Talk Dilemmas in an American School* (Princeton University Press, 2004), which won the 2005 AERA Outstanding Book Award, and *Because of Race: How Americans Debate Harm and Opportunity in Our Schools* (Princeton University Press 2008), an analysis of debates inside the federal government over the treatment of students of color in American schools. She is also the editor of *Everyday Antiracism: Getting Real about Race in School* (The New Press 2008), a volume of concrete antiracist strategies for educators written by 65 experts in race and education studies. Pollock's newest work examines professional development attempts to assist educators to engage issues of race and diversity. Before receiving her M.A. in anthropology and her Ph.D. in anthropology of education from Stanford, Pollock taught at a high school in California.

Stephen W. Raudenbush is the Lewis-Sebring Distinguished Service Professor of Sociology and founding chair of the Committee on Education at the University of Chicago. He is interested in conceptualizing and measuring the social organization of neighborhoods, schools, and classrooms and studying their impact on youth. Evaluation of the reliability and validity of assessments of these social settings borrows from and extends tools from psychometrics, as explained in recent articles in *Science*, *Sociological Methodology*, and *The American Journal of Sociology*. Professor Raudenbush has coauthored a series of articles in *Psychological Methods* on the design of multilevel and longitudinal experiments. His work on causal inference in multilevel settings has recently been published in *Educational Evaluation and Policy Analysis* and in the *Journal of the American Statistical Association*. His book with Anthony S. Bryk, *Hierarchical Linear Models: 2nd Edition* (2002), provides an authoritative account of analytic methods for multilevel data.

Stephen T. Russell is the Fitch Nesbitt Professor of Family and Consumer Sciences, and director of the Frances McClelland Institute for Children, Youth and Families at the University of Arizona. He earned his Ph.D. in sociology from Duke University in 1994. His research focuses on adolescent ethnic and sexual identities, sexuality development, and sexual health. He conducts research on adolescent pregnancy and parenting, and on the health and development of sexual minority youth. Russell is associate editor of the *Journal of Research on Adolescence*; he received a Wayne F. Placek Award from the American Psychological Foundation (2000), was a William T. Grant Foundation Scholar (2001-2006), and is a visiting distinguished professor of Human Sexuality Studies at San Francisco State University.

Marybeth Shinn is professor of Applied Psychology and Public Policy at New York University. She received her Ph.D. in social and community psychology from the University of Michigan. Shinn studies how social contexts, including social settings, neighborhoods, socioeconomic circumstances, and social policies, affect individual well-being. With anthropologist Kim Hopper, she is using capability theory to understand questions about environments that foster capabilities for homeless and mentally ill adults, which parallel questions in the current book about settings that promote youth development. Her other work focuses on causes, consequences, and prevention of homelessness for families and individuals. Shinn was a fellow at the Russell Sage Foundation. She has served as president of the Society for the Psychological Study of Social Issues and the Society for Community Research and Action and has received awards for Distinguished Contributions to Theory and Research and Ethnic Minority Mentoring from the latter group.

Charles Smith is director of High/Scope Educational Research Foundation's Youth Development Group and coordinates development of curriculum, training, publications, and research related to work with youth. Smith has a Ph.D.

in Public Policy from Wayne State University where he helped to develop and implement the Youth Urban Agenda Civic Literacy Project for seven years. His content knowledge includes youth development, civic education, the history of adult education policy, and early childhood education. Smith's research interests are currently focused on the development of quality measures and modeling relationships between instructional practices and developmental outcomes.

Paul W. Speer is associate professor in the Department of Human and Organizational Development, Peabody College, at Vanderbilt University. His research is in the area of community organizing, empowerment, and community change. He currently teaches courses in Action Research, Community Development Theory, and Applied Research Methodology. At this time he is conducting a five-year study of community organizing in Brooklyn and Rochester, New York; Kansas City; and Northern Colorado, and a study of local efforts to intervene on affordable housing policies in Kansas City, Missouri; Rochester, New York; and Nashville, Tennessee.

Rhona S. Weinstein is professor of the Graduate School in the Psychology Department and former director of the Clinical Science Program and Psychology Clinic at the University of California at Berkeley. She was also founding co-director of research and development for CAL Prep, an Early to College Secondary School created through a partnership between UC Berkeley and Aspire Schools. She received her B.A. from McGill University and her Ph.D. from Yale University. Weinstein's research focuses on the multilayered dynamics of academic expectations and self-fulfilling prophecies, as they impact the educational opportunities and the development of minority and poor children, and on the design of interventions to promote school culture change. Her book *Reaching Higher: The Power of Expectations in Schooling* (Harvard University Press, 2002) received the Division K Book Award from the American Educational Research Association and the Virginia and Warren Stone Prize from Harvard University Press. Weinstein has received awards for teaching, institutional excellence, school reform, and science, including the Seymour B Sarason Award and the Distinguished Contributions to Theory and Research in Community Psychology Award from the American Psychological Association.

Harriette Wimms is a doctoral student in Human Services Psychology (clinical/community psychology concentration) at UMBC. She received her B.S. in English from Towson University in 1990, and after working for ten years in publishing, she returned to college to receive her M.S. in Developmental Psychology from Johns Hopkins University in 2000 before entering UMBC. Her master's thesis explores mother-child relationships within the context of a community job-training program. Her dissertation, focusing on the minority pipeline in psychology, utilizes qualitative and quantitative research methods to explore the experiences, perceptions, and aspirations of African American and Latino/a doctoral students. Ms. Wimms is also the proud mother of a two-year-old boy.

Hirokazu Yoshikawa is professor of Education at the Harvard Graduate School of Education. He studies the effects of welfare and antipoverty policies on children; the influence of low-wage work dynamics and conditions on family processes and children; the development of young children in immigrant families; and whole-grade approaches to music education. He has participated in multiple Congressional briefings on child and family policy and human development. He has received three early career awards from the American Psychological Association (the Louise Kidder Award from the Society for the Psychological Study of Social Issues, the Boyd McCandless Award for contributions to Developmental Psychology, and the Minority Fellowship Program's early career award), as well as the Ethnic Minority Mentorship award from the Society for Community Research and Action (Division 27 of the APA). He was recently a member of the National Academy of Sciences Committee on Family and Work Policies. In 2004, he was awarded a fellowship from the Center for Advanced Study in the Behavioral Sciences. He is editor (with Thomas Weisner and Edward Lowe) of *Making it Work: Low-Wage Employment, Family Life, and Child Development* (Russell Sage Foundation, 2006).

Min Zhou is professor of Sociology and the founding chair of the Department of Asian American Studies at the University of California, Los Angeles. Her main areas of research are international migration and immigrant adaptation, education and the new second generation, race and ethnicity, Asian America, and urban sociology. She has published numerous articles and chapters in academic journals and edited volumes. She is the author of *Chinatown: The Socioeconomic Potential of an Urban Enclave* (Temple University Press, 1992), coauthor of *Growing up American: How Vietnamese Children Adapt to Life in the United States* (Russell Sage Foundation Press, 1998), coeditor of *Contemporary Asian America* (New York University Press, 2007), and coeditor of *Asian American Youth: Culture, Identity and Ethnicity* (Routledge, 2004). She is currently writing a book examining how local social structures and patterned interpersonal relations facilitate the formation of ethnic resources conducive to education in Los Angeles' Chinese and Korean immigrant communities.

Index

confidentiality, 325
oversight by data contributors, 324-325
safety in data use, 206, 284
trust, 325
Data-Driven Decision Making (DDDM), 273-276, 279-280, 281-284, 287-288
Data-driven instruction and practice. *See also* Data-Driven Decision Making, 11, 30-31, 199-208, 275-276, 298-300, 355-358
assistance in using data, 30, 282-284, 285
Datnow, A., 6, 9, 11, 14, 90, 154, 161, 272, 271, 355, 356, 358, 362
Davies, P. G., 264
Davis, H. R., 9
Decision makers. *See* Contexts of organizations and of change efforts
Deficit approach. *See* Strengths approach
Desimone, L. M., 5, 6, 8, 15, 84, 151, 153-157, 159, 161-163, 198, 352, 354
Development. *See* Achievement; Civic engagement; Socioemotional development; Strengths approach
Developmentally focused interventions and programs, 24-26, 63-64, 193, 196, 317
Deyhle, D., 110
Diamond, J. B., 103, 109
Diffusion of innovation. *See* Theories of change
Discrimination, 135-136
Disparities, racial. *See* Achievement gap
Diversity. *See also* Inclusive excellence, 116-117, 126, 358-360
Dodge, K. A., 65
Dornbush, S. M., 22
Doyle, D. P., 274
Dweck, C. S., 86

Earl, L., 274
Early College High School Initiative, 97
Eccles, J., 3, 16, 22, 25, 136, 314, 315, 350
Ecology, social. *See also* Contexts of organizations and of change efforts; Multilevel interventions, 23, 63, 69, 72, 88-90, 97, 129
Eden, D., 87
Education as route to success, 233, 242, 244
Education Management Organizations (EMOs), 274
Ellickson, P., 305
Elliott, D. S., 293, 305
Elmore, R., 271
Elmore, R. E., 272
Elmore, R. F., 156

Ely, R. J., 104
Embedded contexts. *See* Contexts of organizations and of change efforts
Embry, D. D., 41
Emmer, E. T., 65
Emotional support. *See* Support
Empowering settings. *See also* empowering leadership *under* Leadership; inspirational belief systems *under* Beliefs and values; Opportunity structures, 120-123
Empowerment, 120, 180, 183, 184, 188, 214
Engagement, youth, 21-27, 63-64, 66
Entwisle, D., 66
Equity, 84, 97, 103-105
Erickson, F., 103n
Eslea, M., 134
Ethnic groups. *See* Immigrant groups; Racial/ethnic minorities; Specific groups
Ethnic social environment. *See also* community forces *under* Contexts of organizations and of change efforts, 230-234, 239, 240, 244
Ethnic system of supplementary education, 232, 238-240, 244
benefits for parents, 238, 240-241
benefits for social capital and community, 238, 240-241, 244-245
benefits for youth, 235, 241-243, 245
costs, 235-236, 242-243, 245
relationship to mainstream institutions, 234, 238, 239, 242
Ethnography. *See also* ethnographic audits *under* Assessment, 102
Evaluation. *See also* Accountability; Assessment of settings; Experiments and experimental design; Quasi-experimental design; Student evaluation, 61-63, 179, 185, 333-334, 361-362
Evidence-based programs and practices, 165 192-193, 293, 301-302
Expectations. *See also* expectancy beliefs *under* Beliefs and values, 81, 88-90, 97-98, 122, 199
communication of, 82
differential expectations and treatment, 83-86
expectancy effects. *See also* Self-fulfilling prophesies, 81, 87
expectancy interventions, 90-96
Experiments and experimental design, 61, 69, 72, 207, 334, 361